Business Studies

Susan Hammond

Longman

London and New York

Longman Group UK Limited,
Longman House, Burnt Mill, Harlow,
Essex CM20 2JE, England
and Associated Companies throughout the world

Published in the United States of America
by Longman Inc., New York.

© Longman Group UK Limited 1988
All rights reserved; no part of this publication
may be reproduced, stored in a retrieval system,
or transmitted in any form or by any means, electronic,
mechanical, photocopying, recording, or otherwise,
without the prior written permission of the Publishers.

First published 1988
Third impression 1989

Set in 10/11 point Linotron Plantin
Produced by Longman Group (FE) Ltd
Printed in Hong Kong

ISBN 0 582 35572 9

British Library Cataloguing in Publication Data
Hammond, Susan
  Business Studies.
  1. Business education
  I. Title
658   HF1106

ISBN 0-582-35572-9

Library of Congress Cataloging in Publication Data
Hammond Susan
  Business studies.

  Bibliography: p.
  Includes index.
  1. Business. 2 Industrial management. I. Title.
HF5351.H2525 1988   650   87-3725
ISBN 0-582-35572-9 (U.S.)

Acknowledgements

We are indebted to the following for permission to reproduce copyright material:
the Associated Examining Board and the University of Cambridge Local
Examinations Syndicate for questions from past examination papers; The Economist
Publications Ltd for an adapted extract from 'Business Brief' in *The Economist*
29/10/83; W.H. Freeman and Company for an adapted extract from the article 'Laser
Applications in Manufacturing' by Aldo V. Rocca in *Scientific American* March 1982
Copyright © 1982 by Scientific American Inc. All rights reserved.

Contents

Part I   The business environment

Introduction

Teachers do not find it easy to write textbooks. They may have knowledge relating to the subject – and what knowledge they do not have they can research. They will have experience of the examinations the students may face. They may even have the ability to write clear, accessible prose!

All teachers will acknowledge that their approach to the subject will differ from that of colleagues. Their approach will also differ from group to group depending on the interests, experience and ability of the group being taught. That is where a textbook differs. Once the words have been written and the type set the textbook is fixed until it finally falls to pieces in the hands of a student. The book needs to cater for a wide variety of abilities and interests simultaneously.

The way in which you use this book will depend on the type of person you are, the situation in which you are learning and your previous experience. The following sections are only suggestions as to the ways in which you might proceed.

The lone student

If you have already taken a course in business studies or in a related subject such as economics or commerce, you should read chapters 1, 2 and 3 to refresh your memory.

If you have never studied these subjects before, you should read these chapters carefully. They introduce ideas and terms frequently used in writing about business, and unless you have some knowledge of them you will find your further reading hampered.

In a class

Your approach to the subject will be decided by your class teacher. This loss of freedom is compensated by the fact that you will have the support of a person who can explain unfamiliar terms and direct your studies according to your progress.

1   Begin with one of the suggested activities at the end of each chapter. You do not need any knowledge of business to investigate the marketing or production of a company. You pose the questions why? where? when? how? at what cost? and to whom? The answers will give you the first insight into the behaviour of businesses. You can then use the chapters of the book to put your new-found knowledge into context.

2   Study the chapters in turn and test your knowledge before you begin to

experience the wide range of practice prevalent in the world of business. The discoveries you make may shake your confidence in this book. They should not do so. Business, like the world in which it exists, is changing all the time. A textbook can only provide you with the tools to observe and then interpret what you see.

3   One step further: personal investigation into the circumstances and/or problems of a business provides valuable experience, not least in developing the ability to collect original data through observation and interview, organise the information into a coherent report, draw conclusions from the evidence and present recommendations with confidence.

Lack of time does not always permit this approach. Secondary material, the result of other people's research, published in specialist books and articles, is a relatively quick and easy way of acquiring knowledge. Like all skills there are accepted methods that can make this process easier. If you are new to studying you might find the structured approach outlined in such books as *Strategies for Studying* by M. Coles and C. White, published by Collins Educational (ISBN 0–00–197284–7) useful.

Specialist textbooks will obviously treat different aspects of business in more depth than is possible in this book. There is a selection at the end of the book. The shelves of a good library will produce a great many more.

The financial pages of national newspapers such as the *Guardian, The Times, The Independent,* the *Daily Telegraph,* the *Financial Times,* the *Sunday Times* and the *Observer* will give many examples of the way in which changes in society affect business and the way in which individual businesses respond to them. *Management Today,* published by the British Institute of Management, contains excellent articles on individual businesses and industries, while publications such as *Marketing,* designed for the professional practitioner, give revealing insights into the problems associated with different business functions. Trade-union journals offer a different, but none the less valid, perspective to the business world, as do political articles.

Conclusion

If the last section has made you despair of Business Studies you may be consoled by the thought that every experience in your life will give you useful material to help you understand business. After all, it is people who make the business, and people are all around you. Very few of the examples and quotations given in this book are pure invention. They all have a solid grounding in the experience of a local community concerned with earning a living. That knowledge is available to you.

This book can help you make sense of this world by offering a body of knowledge in what is hoped to be a coherent and logical order. But, of course, that knowledge is always changing.

Chapter 1 **What is business studies?**

The human body requires a minimum of food, drink and protection from the extremes of climate in order to survive. People co-operate in order to satisfy these basic needs, with the family as the most basic economic group. In some societies the amount produced is just enough to keep people alive. These are known as **subsistence economies**. Other people are more fortunate and are able to produce a surplus in some goods. This surplus may be stored as an insurance against future hardship or traded for goods and services which the society cannot produce for itself.

Very early in human history it was realised that individuals possess different talents and that, if they concentrate their efforts on the activities in which they excel, the standard of living of the whole community will improve. This **specialisation** also implied that trade would have to take place. The weaver might have had a higher standard of living by concentrating all his efforts on making cloth. He also needed food and shelter, which would be provided by other individuals or groups of individuals. The activities in which people engaged were no longer directed towards the satisfaction of all their own needs – and luxuries, if they were fortunate – but were concentrated on a relatively narrow range of goods and services which they would exchange with other people. People began to be described by the work they did, a development which is reflected in some English surnames.

The word 'busy' is used to describe a person who is engaged in action – that is, occupied. We tend to be selective in the way in which we use it. You seldom hear people describe themselves as being busy if they are engaged in a hobby. The word is used to describe activities people regard as being important to their survival or comfort. Look at the following list of activities. Imagine that you are engaged in each of them in turn and somebody asks for your help. In which of these situations are you more likely to make the response 'I'm busy'?

- Cooking the evening meal for the family.
- Watching television.
- Writing an essay which has to be handed in the next day.
- Writing a letter.
- Getting ready to go out.
- Cleaning the tools of your trade so they will be ready for use the next day.

A reasonable response might be that it would depend on the request for help. If you thought it was trivial you might make the response 'I'm busy' in all of the above situations. If the request was urgent enough you might not make that response at all. Most people would make the response 'I'm busy' in the first, third and last situations described. In the fourth situation the type of letter being written would help decide your answer. The purpose of this discussion is to emphasise the fact that we use the word 'busy' to describe actions that we consider important.

In developed economies very few people attempt to satisfy the full range of their needs and wants by their own direct work. Most people sell their skills as carpenter, teacher, plumber, manager, accountant or lawyer to other people, and use the money they get in return to buy the goods and services they need to live. The activities necessary to keep us alive are carried out in a place of business where a group of people with different skills can co-operate to produce goods and services for sale to other people.

Some people, of course, continue to work from home for a variety of reasons. It may be cheaper or more convenient, or the amount of work undertaken may not justify a separate workshop/office. A business may be defined simply as a person or group of people producing goods and services for sale.

This definition leaves a problem. What about the people employed in state education, the health services, defence and other central and local government activities? The word 'business' is generally used to describe organisations that sell a product. However, central and local government organisations share many of the same problems and use the same techniques as commercial enterprises. You will find examples drawn from these areas in a number of chapters in this book.

> **SELF-ASSESSMENT**
> 1 Define (a) a business and (b) specialisation.
> 2 What is the main purpose of all business activity?

The diverse nature of business

In a wealthy society business is not just concerned with the satisfaction of basic needs. From our definition we can see that the existence of a business community in a society means that surpluses have been generated. The wealthier the society, the more advanced the technology, the wider the range of goods and services there are available. Take an author as an example. He works in a small room.

1 The shelves were erected by a local joiner. The joiner employs one man and takes on another if he has sufficient orders.

2 The desk was purchased from a shop specialising in the sale of second-hand office furniture. It was made by a business specialising in the manufacture of office furniture.

3 The carpet and curtains were manufactured by companies with a **turnover** (that is, the total amount of money the business has received from sales) of several million pounds a year.

4 A computer manufactured by a British business employing fewer than a thousand people.

5 A monitor manufactured by a Japanese business with several very large factories in a number of countries.

6 A telephone service supplied by British Telecom which has a virtual **monopoly** (that is, it is the only producer of that good or service) on telecommunications in the United Kingdom.

7 Electricity for light and power supplied by the Central Electricity Generating Board, a business which is owned by the state.

Then there are the publishers responsible for the books, the manufacturers of filing cabinets, paper clips, paper, waste paper baskets and so on.

This long – and incomplete – list of the business activity needed to satisfy the author's wants in just one part of his life could be discouraging for a potential student. To acquire knowledge, analyse it, form opinions and make judgements on such a wide range of activities must seem an impossible task in the comparatively short period of time available.

It would be an impossible task if we attempted to take each separate business activity and study it in detail. Instead, our aim is to develop a broad understanding of the way in which all businesses work. We shall do this by:

- concentrating on the activities and experiences they have in common;
- grouping businesses according to characteristics they share when this will add to our understanding of their behaviour. This process is called **classification**.

There are four main elements that are common to all business activity:

- objectives;
- the resources used by the business;
- the functions undertaken by the business;
- the constraints on achieving their objectives.

The objectives of business

A company is required by law to state the type of business activity it intends to undertake before it can begin trading. In addition to these stated aims the managers of a business will have a number of long-term objectives that it will attempt to achieve.

Profitability

The word 'profit' should be approached with caution. It has a number of meanings which vary according to the context in which it is used.

- To an economist profit is the reward for risk-taking. The person who takes the risk of organising resources to produce a new product is sometimes referred to as an **entrepreneur**. A man mortgages his house in order to raise money to start a business. He is risking everything he owns in this enterprise and is putting more into it than his own labour. Profit is seen as the reward for this extra commitment.

- An accountant would define profit as the difference between revenue and expenditure – that is, the difference between the money received as a result of the activities of the business (the **revenue**) and the costs associated with those activities. If it costs £100000 to produce a certain number of goods which, when sold, bring in a revenue of £125000, a profit of £25000 has been made.

- In political terms a profit can be elevated to the most important drive in the economy of a country, encouraging people to work hard and take risks which will lead to greater wealth for all. Other people see profit as the result of employers using their power to take an unfair advantage of the people they employ; profit, in this case, is believed to exist because wages and salaries have been unfairly depressed (**exploitation**).

Again, economists in stating the objectives of a business assume that each business will attempt to **maximise** its profit – that is, to continue to expand production until it has made the greatest amount of profit of which it is capable. In practice it is more likely that a business will **satisfice**. This unpleasant word simply means that the business will decide on a profit level it considers to be satisfactory, taking into account the amount of capital employed, the general profit level of the industry in which it is operating, the profits it has achieved in previous years, the personal ambitions of its owners and managers and the overall objectives of the business.

The following examples will give you some insight into the way in which the importance of profitability can vary according to the circumstances in which a business finds itself.

The owner of a small business deliberately decides against acquiring more assets because he wants his business to stay small. Expansion might bring higher profits but the additional responsibility would interfere with his private life.

A very large business with factories in a number of countries (**multi-national**) deliberately selects a very low price for a new product in a particular market. In the short term it sacrifices profits. In the long term it drives its competitors out of business and is therefore in a position to make higher profits.

A business is running at a loss. It can remain in operation for two years. There is reason to believe that within the next twelve months more people will buy the goods it sells and within eighteen months it will make a profit once more. A decision is made that it should accept the present losses and stay in operation rather than sell the business and re-invest the proceeds of the sale in a more profitable venture.

The examples given above were designed to show that the profit motive, although essential for the survival of a business, can be superseded in the short term if other objectives are seen to be more desirable. The small businessman in the first example was satisficing. He was making enough profit to finance his lifestyle and had no wish to sacrifice his personal objectives to make more money.

Profit defined as a **surplus of revenue over expenditure** is the most important objective of any business.

1   It provides money to buy raw materials, employ labour and pay for the services needed to keep the business in operation.

2   It provides a reserve for future investment. The small businessman who refused to expand in order to achieve greater profit might find his valued lifestyle threatened if a change in technology lowers the price of his competitors' goods when he has insufficient reserves generated by profits to buy the new machines.

3   It can make it easier for a business to raise capital from outside sources. People are more willing to buy a share of a business that is making a good profit than one that is making a low profit compared with the rest of the business community.

4   Profit can act as a measure of the success of a business. We will examine this more closely in chapter 6. Here it is sufficient to say that everybody tends to judge their success or failure compared with that of other people. It is, for example, one of the problems of a teacher or lecturer's job that if the whole class achieves low grades on an exercise students are more likely to blame the marking rather than their individual achievement and still see themselves as top if they manage 19 marks out of 100. In other words, they are judging themselves by the achievements of their fellow students rather than by the standard which they might expect to achieve.

5   Profit can act as an incentive to greater effort. In chapters 10 and 11 we will examine the role of money in persuading people to work harder. For some people money is a **motivator** – something which has a powerful effect on the way in which people behave – whereas for others money is relatively unimportant.

Because profit allows a business to continue in existence and is essential for future investment, it is regarded as the prime objective of all businesses owned by private individuals as opposed to those owned by the state.

Survival

This must be as important an objective for a business as it is for individuals. We saw in the third example given under profitability how the need to survive can override the profit motive in the short term. The **divorce of ownership and control** – the situation in which the business is owned by one group of people and managed/controlled by another group – can lead to a conflict of objectives. The management might be more interested in survival strategies to secure their jobs.

Survival can be a short-term objective to achieve future profits or it can be seen as a subversive, unrecognised objective arising out of the personal experience and objectives of the people employed. When it is the latter it can be described as **sabotage**, an action designed to hinder the achievement of a stated objective.

Prestige

The desire for prestige – that is, to be held in high regard by other people whose opinion you value – does not seem to contribute a great deal to either the profit motive or survival. It can contribute to both, and some businesses actively seek to enhance their prestige in order to increase sales. A business might seek prestige for high-quality products, care for the environment, the use of the latest technology or care for its employees. Essentially it is attempting to build up an image for excellence in one area of its operations that will attract potential customers or present a more favourable impression of its operations to the world. If customers believe that the activities of a business undertaken to acquire profit are in some way dishonourable, they may withdraw their own custom from that business.

The pursuit of prestige could lead to lower profits in the short term when money might be spent on advertising, improving quality control or the provision of better employee services. In the long term a company with prestige can expect to find a better quality of applicants for any jobs they advertise, an increase in sales and, potentially, an increase in profits.

Growth

The objective of growth might be rationally based on the fact that if the business grows larger the cost of each item it produces will fall (**economies of scale**); it might be the result of a personal desire on the part of the owner for more power; or it might be a desire to take over and eliminate competitors so that there will be more scope for greater profit. In the first and last case the profit motive dominates. In the second case it is an example of personal motives subordinating purely business motives.

Society

A business can be defined as a person or group of people who offer goods and services to the rest of the community in return for payment. From our analysis of business objectives we could add 'for a profit' to this definition. Profit can be seen as an advantage derived from an action, not necessarily expressed in monetary terms. The social benefits, such as cheap transport services or lower fuel costs, derived from nationalised industry can be interpreted as a 'profit' to the community. In the latter case the industry may run at a loss for some years and receive payments from the Treasury to cover the losses (**subsidies**). The extent to which this occurs is a political decision.

SELF-ASSESSMENT

1 Give two arguments to support the view that profit is the most important long-term objective of a business enterprise.
2 Give two circumstances in which other objectives might be more important than profit.

The resources of business

For ease of reference it is usual to divide the resources used by business into **land**, **labour** and **capital** known collectively as **factors of production**.

- Land is used to describe all natural resources, including those obtained from the sea, such as minerals, wood, water and the land itself.

- Labour describes the physical and mental skills of the population who are able to work.

- Capital is used to describe all man-made things which are used to produce other goods and services. This implies that at some time in the past people have sacrificed the opportunity to use some goods immediately (consume them) in return for a higher standard of living in the future.

- Some economists would add **enterprise** (the ability and willingness to take risks) to this list.

Of course, not all businesses will require the same type of resource in the same quantities and at the same time. Some businesses need a small number of highly skilled people while others need large numbers of unskilled people. The generation of electricity on the scale demanded by modern society requires a great deal of capital – for example, a hydro-electric scheme could require a capital investment of £450m. The joiner mentioned in the list of businesses at the beginning of the chapter runs his business on a very small amount of capital. Electricity generation uses large quantities of oil and coal; the joiner uses small quantities of wood. Despite these differences all the businesses mentioned need the factors of production. This they have in common.

The functions of business

All businesses, irrespective of size, product or the technology used, have the following functions in common.

Production

The production function relates to all activities concerned with the creation or making of the goods and services the business intends to sell. This will include the purchase of raw materials, the location of the business, the organisation of the work process and the control of quality. Methods of production will vary according to the product of the business, its size, the size of the market and the technology available to it.

Marketing

The marketing function includes researching the market, product planning, packaging, pricing, advertising, sales promotion and the distribution of the product to the final consumer. These activities are known collectively as the **marketing mix**. They are the ingredients in any marketing plan, but their relative importance will vary according to the type of product, their customers (either consumers or other firms) and the objectives of the business.

Finance

Every business needs money to start and to remain in operation. The management of money is, therefore, essential for business survival.

Control

A business has its objectives, and all its activities should be directed towards achieving those objectives. It needs to establish ways of testing whether or not this is happening. To do this it will use a variety of methods, many based on statistical and accounting techniques.

People

All businesses need to manage people. Even the smallest business in which the owner is the only person concerned has this function. The owner has to manage him/herself! If you do not believe this think about how often your own ability to achieve your objectives depends on such apparently trivial things as getting out of bed early enough in the morning, organising a study programme or simply remembering to make a list of the things you need to do. Managing yourself is probably the most difficult task in man or woman management!

Constraints

A constraint is a restriction placed on an individual or a group of individuals which prevents them achieving their objectives. Constraints can be **internal** (availability of finance, available skills in the workforce, existing plant) and **external** (the state of the economy, legal requirements, the behaviour of competitors and customers, social and political attitudes).

SELF-ASSESSMENT

1 From the information given in the text explain why the design of a new product is the concern of all the business functions.
2 Distinguish between internal and external constraints.

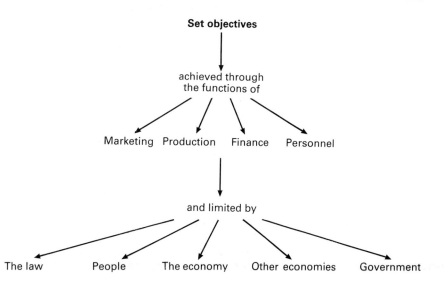

Figure 1.1   What all businesses do

Describing the difference

The first part of this chapter has been concerned with the **common experience** of all business enterprise, which is summarised in Figure 1.1. Even a superficial reading of the section should have made you realise that, at any one time, no business has precisely the same 'mix' of objectives, resources, functions or constraints. Products differ and resource requirements will vary both in size and type.

Businesses which appear very different may have certain characteristics in common that have a significant effect on their behaviour in certain situations. For example, the size of a business will determine the financial resources it has at its disposal. When studying business it can be useful to group together all businesses that share a particular characteristic in order to gain an insight into the problems they face or the advantages they enjoy as a result. This grouping is known as **classification**.

You should remember that grouping disparate items into classes for ease of reference is normal practice. Classes in schools and colleges are good examples. 'The business studies group' is a convenient term of reference for staff in some situations.

Classification by size

Businesses are generally classified as being small, medium-sized or large – a simple statement that disguises a number of problems of definition. The terms of reference of the Bolton Committee (1971) defined small firms as those with not more than 200 employees. This proved to be inadequate. How would you classify a business with fewer than 100 employees but with a high-value product and a turnover of £1m per annum? There are of course some businesses that clearly fall into one category or another. Nobody would dispute that Ford (UK), ICI and Unilever are very large businesses. Equally, the one-man corner shop is a very small business. The classification of businesses by size can be done according to the following criteria.

1 *The size of its market share*   The market share of a business is its total sales expressed as a percentage of the total sales of the industry in which it operates. We will examine the importance of this in chapter 3. In this chapter it is sufficient to point out that if a business employs fewer than 100 people but has a 90 per cent share of the market in which it operates, the influence it exerts on that market will be greater than the influence that, say, Austin Rover can exert on the domestic market for family cars.

2 *Annual sales* (**turnover**)   A high-cost product can generate more turnover per employee than a low-cost product.

3 *The amount of capital employed*   A business which uses advanced technology is likely to have relatively few employees. Automation will intensify this trend.

4 *The way in which it is organised*   The Bolton Committee argued that personal management by the owners of a business was a characteristic of a small firm. As businesses increase in size the workload becomes too great for a small group of people, managers are employed and the control exercised by the owners decreases. We shall look at this in the next section of this chapter when we discuss classification by ownership.

Classification by size is an introduction to the importance of scale in business. The word 'scale' indicates the way in which you should think of the size of a business. It is not the *absolute* size which is important but the size of a business *in relation to* the size of other businesses. Throughout this book the theme of scale will constantly recur.

Classification by ownership

The major distinction is between businesses owned by central or local government – that is, the **public sector** of the economy – and businesses owned by individuals or groups of individuals, the **private sector** of the economy. This classification is useful when speaking in general terms.

> The Government has set a limit of 3 per cent on all wage increases for public sector employees.

> It is difficult to estimate the effect of the cutback in Government spending on the private sector.

Neither the public nor the private sectors are homogeneous (that is, of identical structure) in terms of ownership, and when discussing the problems associated with different types of ownership it is important that we specify which type we are talking about.

Forms of private ownership

1   *The sole trader*   This term is used to describe a business wholly owned by *one* person although there may be a number of people employed in running the business. Businesses owned by one person are often, but not necessarily, small. Their growth is limited by the amount of capital available, and this in turn is limited by the personal resources of the founder and his or her success in trading.

The sole trader is accountable only to him/herself, and this can make this form of business ownership very attractive to people who have strong ideas on the way in which they want their business to be run. Added to this there are very few legal restrictions on the formation of a one-man business, which increases its flexibility. The owner of the business does not have to consult other people before making decisions which can improve the speed with which the business responds to changing conditions.

The lack of specific business skills on the part of the owner is often considered a drawback, but this can be overcome by employing people with these skills or by using the professional services offered by other businesses – for example, accountants, solicitors, marketing and advertising agencies.

The sole trader is entirely responsible for the debts of the business. Should it fail and there is insufficient money to pay the debts of the business the owner can be declared **bankrupt** through legal process. All the property of the business and the personal property of the owner will then be sold to pay the debts and, should the money realised by the sale prove to be insufficient for this purpose, the court will have a claim on the income of the bankrupt until all the debts have been paid. The sole trader is thus said to have **unlimited liability** for the debts/conduct of the business.

2   *Partnerships*   Partnerships are groups of people who contribute capital and management expertise to the same business enterprise and accept joint responsibility for the operation of the business. The minimum number of partners is, of course, two. The maximum number in most cases is twenty. Because several people share responsibility and the actions of one partner could have serious consequences for the rest (like the sole trader, partners are liable for all the debts/conduct of their business) there are legal restrictions on the responsibilities of the partners to each other. These are defined by the Partnership Act 1890. Among other things this Act states that partners

should receive an equal share of the profits. When partners have contributed varying amounts of capital this is unreasonable. To deal with this and similar situations, partners can vary the conditions of the Act by drawing up a legal document, a **deed of partnership**, which sets out the conditions under which they agree to do business together.

Partnerships can benefit from having more capital and expertise than the sole trader. A solicitor with experience in conveyancing (the transfer of property rights) might seek partners with experience of the legal problems of business and divorce. These are not automatic benefits of a partnership. The man setting up business as a sole trader with £40000 in capital will have a stronger financial base than three men contributing £5000 each to a partnership. Again, a man with a wide and varied experience as an industrial manager will have more expertise at his disposal as a sole trader than two friends setting up as partners in their first business venture.

3   *Limited companies*   As the size of business enterprises increased in the nineteenth century, the amount of capital required increased and the ability of sole traders and partners to accumulate the necessary finance declined. Many people were willing to lend small amounts of money to a business, but they had no control over the way it was used. They were at the mercy of the owners of the business. The solution to this problem was sought in law.

● Companies – that is, groups of people who collectively own a business under certain legal conditions – were established as **separate legal entities** from the people who owned them. This meant that the company would be treated as a separate person in law from its owners. The company could sue and be sued, own property and survive the death of its owners.

● The company was granted **limited liability**. This can be seen as a logical extension of the fact that the company is a separate legal entity. The company is responsible for its own debts and conduct of business. If the company cannot pay its debts it may be forced to sell all its assets. This is **involuntary liquidation**. However, the personal property of the owners cannot be touched.

● Legal restrictions were placed on the formation of companies to ensure that the privileges given above were not abused.

The first instance of the granting of limited liability to a restricted range of businesses was in 1662. General limited liability was extended to all **registered** companies by the Limited Liability Act 1855. The conditions under which a company can register with the **Registrar of Companies** (a Civil Service function) are defined by the Companies Acts. The first of these Acts was passed in 1844, but the formation of modern companies is regulated by the Acts of 1948, 1967, 1976 and 1980.

Public enterprise

The public sector of the economy offers many goods and services to the consumer, some of which are financed entirely by money the government obtains from taxes or by borrowing and which are offered to the consumer free of direct charge. Other goods and services are offered for payment.

SELF-ASSESSMENT

1   Define the term 'unlimited liability' and state two types of business organisations to which it applies.
2   Give two advantages of the company as opposed to the sole trader as a form of business ownership.

Classification by activity

Another way of describing the types of business in an economy is by grouping all businesses according to the type of product, whether goods or services, that they produce. The broadest definition is in terms of the **primary**, **secondary** and **tertiary** sectors.

- The primary sector refers to all businesses engaged in mining, quarrying, farming and fishing. These are sometimes referred to as the **extractive** industries.

- The secondary sector includes manufacturing, assembly, construction and the nationalised industries/public utilities such as gas, electricity and water.

- The tertiary sector includes public and private service industries: banking, insurance, retailing, health services and education are some examples.

These main divisions of business activity can be broken down into subdivisions. An article discussing the effects of government policy on agriculture might distinguish between its impact on arable as opposed to livestock farming and further subdivide those two categories into cereal/non-cereal producers and dairy/beef cattle farmers.

SELF-ASSESSMENT

1 Distinguish between the primary, secondary and tertiary sectors of the economy.
2 Give two advantages of classifying business activity in this way.

Conclusion

We began this chapter by stressing the diversity of business activity and developed the idea that it was possible to study very different organisations by concentrating on the characteristics they have in common and also by grouping similar businesses together.

In the next chapter we will treat all businesses as if they are identical and examine the role of business in society.

Review

1 Read each of the following statements and decide to which of the possible objectives of the business concerned they refer.
  (a) 'We need to increase sales by 50 per cent if we are to remain comparable with our nearest rivals.'
  (b) 'Taking over Baxen Ltd will double our production.'
  (c) 'The potential profits might be excellent but we cannot afford the risk.'

2 Classify the following business activities into primary, secondary and tertiary sectors. State also whether or not you would consider them to belong to the public or private sector.
  (a) An independent transport business, organised as a private limited company and employed mainly in carrying agricultural produce.
  (b) Two people who jointly own a small pottery.
  (c) A bottle reclamation plant owned by a local authority.
  (d) A football club whose first team plays in the first division in England and Wales.
  (e) A multi-national company which manufactures cars.

(f) A small independently owned fishing boat engaged in taking tourists on fishing trips.

(g) Britoil before privatisation.

Activities

1 Conduct a survey of (a) a local high-street shopping centre, (b) a transept of a city centre, and (c) an industrial estate. In each case:
(a) classify the type of business you find;
(b) explain the logic of their location in that area.

2 Interview several small businessmen. You are interested in
(a) their motives in setting up a business;
(b) the satisfactions they gain from running their own business;
(c) their ambitions for the future.
As a group compare the anwers you were given, noting any similarities and differences.

3 Visit several business organisations, preferably one from each of the primary, secondary and tertiary sectors. You should find out the answers to the questions given below and any other questions that interest you:
(a) What is the name of the business?
(b) When was it formed?
(c) What is the legal organisation of the business?
(d) Is this its only location? If not, how many other factories does it have (i) in the United Kingdom? (ii) in the world?
(e) Where is its headquarters?
(f) Is the business organised into departments? If so, what are they?
(g) What is the product of the business?
(h) What goods and services does it buy in?
(i) To whom does it sell its products?
The purpose of these visits is to familiarise you with the diversity of business enterprise. If you have studied business before you may already be aware of this. Those of you who have not should write a formal report in a suitable format drawing attention to the points of similarity you have noticed and the extent to which the businesses differ.

Suggested projects

1 Should a business register as a limited company?

2 Make a critical comparison of the business objectives and strategies of two businesses.

Essay questions

1 Comment on the factors a business should take into account when assessing the advisability of becoming a public limited company.

2 Analyse the possible effects on the private sector of an increase in state control of business.

3 Evaluate the contribution made by the small business sector to the economy of the United Kingdom.

4 The practice of classifying business enterprises is a useful analytical tool provided that the limitations of a particular classification are recognised. Discuss this statement, illustrating your answer with reference to the business community.

Chapter 2 Business and the economic system

In chapter 1 we accepted the fact that each business was unique, and looked at the different ways in which we could group businesses together for ease of study. In this chapter we will assume that all business enterprises are identical – whether we are talking about multi-national giants like Unilever or the corner shop – and examine the relationship between the business community and the rest of society. To do this we will use the general framework of the systems approach but in a descriptive rather than an analytical form.

What is a system?

A system can be defined as an assembly of parts that are connected together in such a way as to achieve a particular objective. Each part of a system affects and is affected by the other parts, and the removal or change of a part will affect the way in which the system operates.

This is a very general definition and can be applied to the physical structure of the universe, to biology as in the respiratory and circulatory systems of a mammal, to technology, to the functions of a business and to a collection of businesses, each with a different role but with a working relationship.

The following definitions will prove useful, not only in understanding the systems approach to problems but also in understanding the relationship between businesses and in bringing order into the diverse and complex world of modern business.

1 *Environment* Anything outside a system which has an effect on the way in which it operates. In chapter 1 we discussed external constraints on business behaviour. These constraints can also be seen as the effect on a business of the environment in which it operates.

2 *A sub-system* A system which is an integral part of another system. A bank is a system, it is also a sub-system of the banking system which, in turn, can be seen as a sub-system of the economic system of the country.

3 *An open system* All systems are open in their operation – that is, they are affected by the behaviour of other systems and the environment. An economist discussing international trade will refer to an **open economy** – one which is affected by the behaviour of other economic systems. The area over which this interaction takes place is known as the **interface**.

In chapter 1 we outlined the major functions of a business enterprise. Each of these can be seen as parts of a system. They are interdependent, and the way in which one department operates will affect the operation of other departments. A dynamic and efficient marketing team will place demands upon the production department. It may be necessary for it to change the way in which it is organised to meet the increased demand for its product. A change in senior management (another part of the system) may lead to an increased emphasis on profitability. This implies changes in each of the departments to meet new targets (for example, in productivity).

The individual business is also a part of the overall economic system of the country. It is a sub-system. A healthy economy depends on the performance of the businesses that comprise it. The state of the economy affects the businesses. The business is therefore an open system.

Each department within a business can be seen as a system. The effectiveness of the sales force will depend on the support provided by advertising and sales promotion.

SELF-ASSESSMENT

1 What is a system?
2 Distinguish between an open and closed system.

The economic system

The economic system of a country describes the relationship that exists between customers, producers and the state.

We saw in chapter 1 that all resources needed to satisfy the wants and needs in a society can be grouped under the headings of land, labour and capital. These resources are insufficient at any one moment in time to satisfy all the desires of people – which can be regarded, for all practical purposes, as insatiable. There is therefore the need to choose between the various uses of resources, and this choice implies a sacrifice. The true cost of anything is the sacrifice made to obtain it. This sacrifice is known as the **opportunity cost**.

The basic economic concepts of **scarcity**, **choice** and **opportunity cost** mean that resources have to be shared out (**allocated**) by society to various uses, a fact that is summarised in the phrase '**allocation of resources**'.

A simplified model of the economic system has three parts:

1 *Businesses of various types*   Businesses use resources to produce goods and services.

2 *Consumers*.

3 *The state*.

The relationship between these parts of the system will, of course, determine the way in which the system works. How much control does the government exercise over the conduct of business? What proportion of the resources of a country are in the control of the government? What standards of behaviour are acceptable in a society? What importance do the people in that society place on certain types of goods and services?

The economic system is a sub-system of the political and social systems of a country which will have been determined by historical and cultural factors.

Types of economic system

The two extreme forms of an economic system for the allocation of resources are: the **free** or **market** economy and the **planned** economy. Both types of system have fervent supporters whose judgements are often based on political rather than economic criteria. No economy is totally planned or totally free. Most possess elements of each, in which case they are called **mixed economies**.

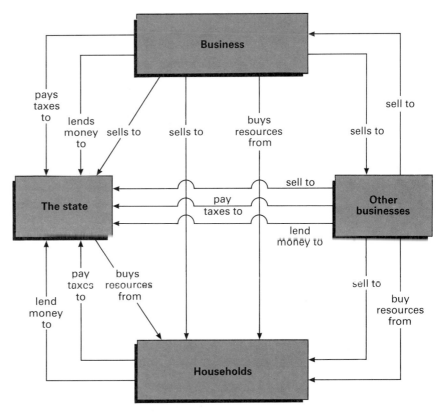

Figure 2.1 Some interrelationships among business, the state and households

The free or market economy

Price is the determining factor in a free market economy. Consumers decide how they will spend the money they have at their disposal. The producers of the favoured goods will receive a larger revenue than the producers of less favoured goods. They will therefore be in a better position to buy the resources they need. Some producers will go out of business, and the resources freed will be employed in making the goods and services people want to buy.

The idea of a free market economy is very attractive. It appears that it is the consumers who decide on the allocation of resources by an accumulation of millions of personal decisions. This idea is known as **consumer sovereignty**. A free market economy also responds well to changes in consumers' wishes; that is, it is flexible.

Because the decisions are taken in response to changes in the market there is no need to use additional resources to make decisions, record them and check on whether or not they are being carried out. The size of the civil service is reduced.

It is also argued that competition between producers in a free economy is an incentive to efficiency: the lower the cost compared with the quality of the product and the price that can be charged for it, the more efficient the use of resources.

Free economies do have serious disadvantages, particularly when viewed in relation to the political and social objectives of a society.

Disadvantages of a free economy

1   In many societies it is considered socially and politically desirable that each person should be allocated the minimum amount of resources needed to

provide for the basic survival needs of food, warmth and shelter. There is no guarantee that a free economy would achieve this objective. A person with a high level of skill that was in great demand could receive a larger portion of the wealth of that society than a person whose talents, although considerable, were unwanted at that time.

There is also no guarantee that individuals would use the resources at their disposal in ways that might be desirable for the collective good of the community; for example, by making a decision not to buy educational services.

2   The nature of some goods and services makes it difficult to exclude people who are not willing to pay. Law and order and defence fall into this category. Those who are unwilling to spend more on law and order or who wish to reduce the amount spent on defence are forced to accept the level of service provided by the government.

3   Although the advantages of the price system includes the speed with which it reacts to changes in demand, in certain circumstances its response might be unacceptably slow in political and social terms. A rapid change in technology might lead to a high level of unemployment and threaten the political security of the government in power. Cynical observers of the political scene hold that the more unacceptable aspects of a market economy are minimised in the months before a general election.

4   Consumer sovereignty can be seen as the ideal rather than the reality of a modern economy. Many businesses produce in advance of consumer demand and then use advertising to persuade people to buy the goods they have made.

5   Competition between businesses can lead to a duplication of products and a waste of resources. Prior to the nationalisation of the railway system many large towns and cities had several railway stations and tracks each belonging to a different company and, in some cases, duplicating services between towns.

6   The operation of a free market economy depends upon producers having confidence that they will be able to sell what they produce. If they see the risk as being too great they will not employ resources and the general standard of living in a country will fall.

Planned economies

These are sometimes known as **command** economies because the major decisions about the allocation of resources are made by the state. The economic system in planned economies is more responsive to changes in political objectives.

The planning system varies from country to country, but in general we can say that it will include the following activities:

- the collection of statistical information relating to the resources available;
- the setting of overall objectives – for example, that agricultural output will increase by 5 per cent – for a period of time, usually five years;
- the establishment of objectives at regional level to achieve the overall objectives; and
- the establishment of targets for each production unit (factory or farm) to support regional and national objectives.

Later in the book you will examine the importance of planning and the planning process in a business enterprise. This will help you understand some of the problems inherent in a planned economy, bearing in mind that economies are larger and more complex than most businesses and that this fact will increase the problems facing a government.

Advantages of a planned economy

1 Resources can be distributed more equitably according to the values of the society. This does not mean that everybody will necessarily receive the same income. Political objectives might regard some parts of the economy as more valuable than others and reward them accordingly.

2 Duplication of resources can be avoided.

3 The state can use its economic power to achieve its own social and political objectives, which may be taken to reflect the collective will of the majority of the people.

Disadvantages of a planned economy

1 The collection of data, the planning process itself and control of planning will use resources.

2 The lack of scope for individual incentives may lead to a lack of initiative. It is argued that in the market system the desire for profit acts as a stimulus to individuals to undertake risks.

3 The lack of profit motive, it is argued, means that opportunities for improvements which could lead to a more efficient use of resources are missed. In a command economy the incentive offered by the profit motive might be replaced by personal ambition or a political ideal. Some observers of command economies argue that the profit motive does not disappear but is driven underground. Personal profit is sought in gifts and bribery.

4 A serious problem in command economies, as in market economies, is the anticipation of the wants of the consumer. Once basic needs have been met people may abstain from consumption rather than buy goods which they find unattractive or of poor quality. Production usually takes place ahead of demand, and, in this situation, command economies can suffer from the same problems of resource waste as market economies. Command economies often try to avoid this problem by making sure that demand exists before production commences. This leads to waiting lists.

The precise proportions of 'free' and 'planned' parts in an economic system and the relationship they have with each other will vary from country to country depending on the interaction of the political, social and economic systems and the cultural history of society.

SELF-ASSESSMENT

1 Distinguish between a market economy and a planned economy in terms of ownership and control.
2 Give two arguments in favour of a mixed economy.

Business in market and planned economies

In general terms the word 'business' is only used in relation to a free market economy or the private sector of a mixed economy. If you read the definition of 'business' given in chapter 1, you will see that a privately owned business producing shoes in the United Kingdom has a great deal in common with a similar, but state-owned, business in the USSR.

1 They both use the same resources.

2   Both aim to generate a surplus; that is, they aim to increase wealth as a result of their activities. The surplus of the UK business will be appropriated by the owners of the business, who will make individual decisions about the way in which they intend to use it. In the USSR the surplus will be distributed by the central authorities or their agents.

3   Both businesses will have constraints when involved in decision making. The constraints will vary in magnitude but will still fall into the same categories given in chapter 1.

4   Both businesses will undertake the same productive processes.

How can the type of economic system affect a business?

- The business in a free economy appears to carry a higher degree of risk than that in a planned economy. Sustained losses may cause the failure of the business, whereas it is often assumed that in a planned economy uneconomic businesses are subsidised in order to maintain employment. In practice the business in a planned economy may be dependent on the political objectives of the government rather than market forces. In a planned economy if a business is failing to meet targets it might face closure so that its resources can be redeployed.

- In a free economy the business has to find its own resources and pay the price asked. In a planned economy resources are allocated to the business. This can mean that the business does not receive resources of the right quality or specification, particularly if the allocation is made by civil servants with little understanding of business requirements.

- In a free economy businesses are affected by a large number of constantly changing factors. The planning process of the command economy might give an appearance of stability. It should be remembered that the command economy will interact with market systems and is not, therefore, totally protected.

> **SELF-ASSESSMENT**
> 1 Explain briefly the way in which a command economy can be defined as an open system.
> 2 State three ways in which a business in a planned economy (a) is similar to and (b) differs from a business in a market economy.

The monetary system

Throughout this book money values will be used frequently to refer to wages, the value of machinery and anything else when we want to allocate a value or compare it with other goods. It will be useful therefore to take a brief look at money and the monetary system in the United Kingdom. The monetary system is a sub-system of the economic system.

What is money?

Societies with a low level of specialisation or which generate little or no surplus with which to trade have little need for money. They may trade their surplus goods by **barter** – that is, the direct exchange of one good or service for another. The system works well provided that the range of goods and services to be exchanged is limited and the number of transactions undertaken is relatively small. The main problem with barter is finding somebody who has what you want and is willing to accept what you have to offer in exchange for it. This is known as the **double coincidence of wants**. Barter is not unknown in modern, Western economies. Neighbours exchange services and goods without using money. One man may take care of another's garden while he is on holiday and be paid in vegetables. A cabinet maker who wants his son tutored in mathematics may pay the tutor by renovating his furniture.

Complex societies use money for most of their commercial transactions. This is because a more flexible and convenient method of exchange is needed to make a larger number of exchanges feasible. If you cannot understand this, imagine the time and effort needed to find the partner in an exchange using barter. Money – that is, any good that fulfils the following functions – is the solution to this problem. Money is:

- A **medium of exchange**   Money will be accepted in exchange for any good or service, so eliminating the need for a double coincidence of wants.

- A **store of value**   Under the barter system it is necessary to make purchasing decisions within a short period of time, particularly if the goods concerned are perishable. A man offering perishable goods for barter will have to take what is on offer before his goods deteriorate.

- A **unit of account**   When the value of goods and services are expressed in monetary terms it is possible to compare the value of very different goods. How many cows equal one barrel of oil? Using money values it is possible to say. Chapters 4 and 6 will explore some of the anomalies contained in this oversimplification, but it is still a useful attribute of money.

Money as a **standard of deferred payment** follows from its function as a unit of account. If the value of goods and services can be measured in money, then the amount owing can be agreed upon and a future date for payment can be fixed. It is this function of money that makes the purchase of goods and services on credit possible.

Types of money

In theory anything can be used as money provided people trust it. In practice it was early discovered that precious metals were an ideal form of money. They were of high value in their own right, they were durable and, because their value was high in relation to their quantity, they were portable. Early traders in Europe used bars of iron from which pieces could be flaked and weighed in payment. The use of the term 'precious' is relative to the society and technology in which the metals are used. Very early in the history of Western civilisation it was realised that if the metal was cast into units of standard weight and value (**coins**), many problems in trading would be solved. The guarantee that a coin was of the correct weight was invested in the head of the king or emperor. This placed a significant degree of economic power in the ruler. It also carried with it a responsibility to maintain the value of the currency.

Metals are heavy. Over the centuries the amount of goods and services a given quantity of metal would buy became less. In order to finance their normal business transactions people were having to carry a great weight of coins with them and thus risked being robbed. It began to make sense to leave the gold with a businessman who had the facilities for safeguarding it and to accept a piece of paper from him promising to pay that amount of coinage when the note was presented to him. These **promissory notes** were a legal contract and the forerunners of our modern bank notes. The legal form is still in use.

The history of money is fascinating, but to go into too much detail is irrelevant in this book. The detail given so far is intended to take the magic out of the idea of money. We have progressed so far from the societies that used metal as a scale against which they judged value that today much of our money has no existence other than as figures in a bank account with notes and coins being used as a convenient way of servicing minor transactions. The notes and coins are worth less intrinsically than the transactions they finance.

This process has occurred because money is a unit of account. Provided records are kept about the value of a person's transactions there is no need for a physical record of the transactions. It has also come about because of abuses to the systems in operation. Criminals like cash because it cannot be traced. Nineteenth-century bank managers were greedy for profit. They realised that they could lend more than they held. The Bank Charter Act 1844 set in motion a chain of events that concentrated the power of issuing bank notes with the Bank of England and the Bank of Scotland.

In the United Kingdom, at the time of writing, the total supply of money, known as sterling (the word used to describe British money), can be defined as:

- *M0*   Notes and coins.

- *M1*   Notes and coins plus **sight deposits**, which are deposits with financial institutions that can be withdrawn without notice.

- *Sterling M3*   This consists of M1 plus **time deposits** held in sterling. Time deposits are those deposits which require notice before money can be withdrawn from them.

- *M3*   This is Sterling M3 plus deposits of people resident in the United Kingdom which are held in the currencies of other countries.

This is the **nominal** money supply of the United Kingdom – that is, the total amount of money expressed in terms of pounds and pence. The **real** money supply is the term used to describe the purchasing power of the nominal money supply.

The neutrality of money

The real economy is the goods and services which are produced and the efficiency with which this process takes place. Money can therefore be seen as no more than a symbol for these events, a convenient way of representing them and making it easier for transactions to take place. Money is also a good in its own right. People may prefer to hold their wealth in money rather than in real goods or to buy services.

The value of money can **rise**. *Less* money will then be needed to buy goods and the general price level will **fall**. This situation is called **deflation**. The opposite situation, **inflation**, is characterised by a *fall* in the value of money and a *rise* in the price level. Inflation has been the most prevalent situation in the world in recent economic history.

SELF-ASSESSMENT
1 State two ways in which money can improve the efficiency of an economic system.
2 Explain why it is important to distinguish between the nominal and real money supply of an economy.

The monetary sector

The monetary sector in the British economy includes all businesses whose activities are concerned with taking deposits, borrowing and lending money and which are under the control of the Bank of England according to the terms of the Banking Act 1979. It also includes the banking department of the Bank of England. A brief review of the businesses in the monetary sector and other **financial institutions** will provide you with background information which will prove useful when you study chapters 7 (Finance) and 13 (Business and the economy).

- The Bank of England is the central bank and, together with the Treasury (a government department), is responsible for the monetary policy of the government, which can influence the supply of money in the economy, the rate of interest and the foreign exchange rate. Later in this chapter we will discuss the relationship which exists between the business community and the political system. You should note at this level the relationship is very close. The Bank of England translates government policy into practice by its dealings in the monetary system.

- The Bank of England lends money to the **discount houses**. These institutions are defined as banks under the 1979 Act. Discount houses make their profits by borrowing money from other banks and buying **bills** (evidence of a debt) before the debt is due to be paid. The bills are bought for less than their face value, the price paid being arrived at by discounting from the amount due when they **mature**. The date of maturity is the day on which the debt needs to be paid. Discount houses invest in treasury bills (short-term government debt) and commercial bills.

  Discount houses borrow from banks **at call**, that is, the banks can ask for repayment at any time. When banks recall their loans or do not make them available, the discount houses can borrow money from the Bank of England or the Bank of England will rediscount bills. The decision lies with the Bank of England, not the discount houses. The rate of interest charged or the discount rate for this service is usually 1 per cent or 2 per cent higher than the market rate. In this way the Bank of England can influence interest rates in the economy as a whole. The Bank of England is acting as **lender of last resort**. The extent to which it is prepared to do this will depend on government policy.

- The clearing banks are the banks with which most people are familiar. They have a large number of branches, which has earned them the title of **high street banks**.

- Accepting houses are banks which specialise in guaranteeing **bills of exchange**. Bills of exchange are used to finance international trade – although the extent to which they are used varies – and were precisely defined by the Bills of Exchange Act 1882. For the purposes of this chapter it is sufficient to say that they resemble a post-dated cheque where the amount appearing on the cheque is the original amount lent (the **principal**) together with the interest payable. A bill of exchange guaranteed by an accepting house is known as a **first class bill of exchange**.

- There are other financial institutions which are licensed to take deposits from the public.

- The National Girobank is part of the public sector and provides a range of payment and banking services.

SELF-ASSESSMENT

1 List the parts of the monetary system of the United Kingdom as given in this chapter.
2 List the major institutions which form the monetary sector of the economy. Using information from chapter 1, explain briefly why it is called 'the monetary sector'.

Business and the political system

It is not the role of business studies to describe the political system in detail. It is important to remember that politics is about government and that those who govern a country have power over the setting of objectives for the overall management of the country. This implies rules of conduct which will be embodied in law and which will affect business as a part of the society which is being governed.

Politics is also about the relationship between a country and other countries. In the extreme case of war this can mean that a business will be required to produce goods needed by the armed forces rather than the goods and services that people want. It might also mean that they are forbidden to trade with countries whose political philosophy is considered undesirable by their own government, a policy known as the imposition of **economic sanctions**.

Politics is also about ideas. A government with an ideological commitment to the free market economy rather than a command economy will put into practice policies that will influence business ownership and control. It is also likely to reduce grants to business enterprises and so increase the proportion of costs of production that they have to bear for themselves. The reverse is also true. Political commitment to planning might increase grants but put constraints on the decision-making activities of the business.

The parts of the political system of a country include obvious organisations such as political parties. Conservative, Labour, the Liberal/SDP Alliance (the order is alphabetical!) have a high profile in political activity. Their declared policies are influenced by the behaviour of **pressure groups**, organisations with an interest in having particular policies implemented and which use a variety of methods to persuade the government and individual members of Parliament to adopt the policies they advocate. The business community, working through organisations such as the Confederation of British Industry (CBI) can be seen as part of the political system. The CBI, acting as a pressure group, might attempt to persuade the government to follow policies leading to lower interest rates, lower wage increases, reduced taxation if it sees these to be in the interest of its members. Trade unions, acting as a political pressure group on behalf of their members, might advocate similar policies but are unlikely to agree on the subject of low wages.

The success or failure of pressure groups will depend on the political objectives of a government, which in turn will depend on the political ideology of the party. In a democracy it can also depend on the degree of popular support a policy appears to enjoy. Governments are supposed to reflect the will of the people. The more cynical would argue that governments adopt the policies that give them the highest chance of remaining in power.

Business and the ecological system

The ecological system is concerned with the relationship between living organisms and their physical environment. The building of a factory changes the environment of plants and animals. The existence of a pool of hot water, a by-product of a factory cooling system, creates a new environment for plants and animals. The farming methods employed will create or destroy existing environments and can affect the structure of the soil.

Business has always been part of the ecological system. Adverse effects have always received more publicity than beneficial effects. When the activities of business are also seen to have political impact in this area the matter becomes one of public debate and a constraint upon the decisions made by business.

Business and the social system

The social system is the relationship which exists between all parts of society. It is the system of which all other systems we have briefly described are parts. Theoretically it is possible to assume a simple social system. In reality any social system is an extremely complicated amalgam of ideas, attitudes, patterns of behaviour and organisations that have their roots in the economic, religious, ideological, political and social history of the society concerned. Consider the problem of Sunday trading in the United Kingdom.

Sunday trading

In the United Kingdom a number of services, such as health and transport, are offered legally on a Sunday. Factories which rely on the operation of continuous processes also continue to function. Some goods and services, which are considered essential, can be sold on a Sunday while other, apparently similar goods, cannot. The law relating to the buying and selling of goods and services is complicated and open to abuse. In fact, it is known that the law is flouted by small shops and circumvented by national organisations. In 1985 the British government introduced a Bill designed to rationalise the law relating to Sunday trading, the most important effect of which was to extend the legality of shops opening on a Sunday. In support of the Bill was evidence of illegal opening, changing social habits (for example, the increase in the number of working wives, the growth of shopping as a leisure activity, particularly for items in the do-it-yourself trade, consumer durables and gardening requirements). The government's proposals stated in the Bill met opposition from a wide variety of sources. The Union of Shop, Distributive and Allied Workers (USDAW) opposed the Bill on the grounds that it would lead to more unsocial working conditions for its members. Employees in the retail trade are, for a variety of reasons, difficult to organise into trade unions and tend, as a result, to have less power in negotiations concerning pay and conditions than employees in other industries. The Lord's Day Observance Society resisted on the evidence of the Old Testament of the Christian Bible, 'Six days shalt thou labour, and do all thy work: But the Seventh day is the sabbath of the Lord thy God: in it thou shalt not do any work' (Exodus 20: 9–10).

The issue cut across party political lines, the decision of individual members of Parliament being influenced by the reaction of the voters in their constituencies and their conscience rather than the requirements of their political allegiance in Parliament. Although many political commentators agreed that the proposed Act of Parliament was a necessary and belated tidying-up process and despite the lobbying of business interests in support of the Bill, it was defeated. Religion and the social history of shop workers was triumphant.

The above example is an over-simplification, and the fact that it has to be so is in itself significant. Relatively small groups within the population appeared to have protected their interests to the inconvenience of other people. Perhaps their vocal opposition to the Bill carried silent support from the rest of the voters. The desire to open on a Sunday might have been a desire on the part of big business to increase their profits. The matter is open to interpretation and that will depend on each individual and his or her view of the world in which he or she lives!

Conclusion

Business is an integral part of the society in which it operates. Every action of business will be influenced by the state and values of that society and will influence that society. This chapter has outlined business as a part in a limited number of systems. This theme will be developed in Part III of this book. It is important that you appreciate the external constraints on business activity, because without such an appreciation you will not understand the internal behaviour of a business organisation which is described in Part II.

Chapter 3   **Markets**

The market is part of the environment within which a business operates. In this chapter we shall outline the different types of market, examine the ways in which markets operate and consider some of the implications of market operation both for an individual business enterprise and for society as a whole.

What is a market?

The word 'market' is used in a variety of contexts which, at first sight, seem to have little in common. Read the following passages carefully. You will see that the word 'market' is used in a number of different ways. Can you find anything in common?

A farmer talks of taking his produce to market. This market has a physical existence either in the local town or city. It is an open space or a building where farmers and their customers meet for the purpose of buying and selling farm produce. In a town the existence of the market also attracts other traders who erect their stalls on the designated market day. The town is called a **market town** and draws its custom from the surrounding countryside. Its sphere of influence (that is, the area from which the town will draw consumers and producers) will depend on the number of people living in the area and the ease with which goods can be transported. Market towns not only provide a place for the buying and selling of produce and other goods, in the past they were also the places in which labour was hired and the centres for the provision of services such as banking. This is still the case in some rural areas of the United Kingdom. In a rural economy with a relatively sparse population, most business transactions can be fitted into a couple of days in each month and permanent shops may well be a waste of money. Produce is sold from temporary stalls or directly from the cart or baskets in which it arrived. The word 'market', in this context, is used to describe a building or open space, in which livestock and goods are bought and sold.

A businessman, in seeking his market, wants the answers to the following questions: What am I selling? Who are my potential customers? What other businesses are selling a similar product? Where am I selling? When he has answered these questions to his own satisfaction he will be able to say, 'The market for my good is . . .'

At first sight the word 'market' may seem to be used in two entirely different ways. In fact, the uses of the word 'market' have common elements: the product, buyers, sellers, price and place. We can say that the market for any one product is defined by these parameters. The distinction is in the point of view. An economist would bring these elements together in a single succinct definition: a market can be defined as a geographical area over which the price of a good or service is the same.

Determining the market price

The final market price for a particular product will depend upon the interaction of the results of individual decisions made by the purchasers of the good or service, the producers and, possibly, the government.

The purchasers

Individuals decide whether to spend their money or save it. Spending decisions lead to the purchase of consumer goods (food, clothes and so on), durable consumer goods (for example, washing machines, cars or refrigerators), and services (such as hair-dressing or transport). They may also make investment decisions (house purchase or unit trusts). Saving decisions include building society accounts, savings certificates and deposit accounts.

A business organisation buys labour, raw materials and capital equipment such as machinery, to carry out production. Businesses also buy commercial services – for example, banking, advertising and insurance. Governments buy labour, the services of business organisations to build roads, airports and bridges; and they buy weapons and consumables (such as paper) to help them to carry out their work. Each group has a particular set of constraints which influence its buying behaviour.

Consumer buying behaviour

The consumers who choose to buy one product in preference to other products constitute the **demand** for that product. Total demand for a particular type of product (for example, the total demand for motorcars in a particular economy) is determined by the following:

1 *The price of the good or service*　It is obvious that the lower the price of a particular good or service the more of that good or service will be bought.

2 *The price of substitute goods and services*　If the price of potatoes rises sharply, rice and pasta products will become relatively cheaper and some consumers will stop buying potatoes and switch to buying rice and/or pasta.

3 *The price of complementary products*　To use a car you need to buy oil and petrol, pay tax and buy insurance. The cost of running a car should be taken into account when deciding to purchase it. When the purchase of one product implies that you must purchase another product, then the demand for each will be dependent on the demand for the other. A rise in the price of one such product is likely to lead to a decrease in the demand for both products.

4 *The taste and preference of the consumer*　In chapter 2 we discussed the working of a free market economy and the idea of consumer sovereignty. In a market economy each person makes a separate and distinct decision to buy based on their own perception of their life and what is needed to give them satisfaction. Taste and preference is a by-product of an individual's personality. It is for the marketing man to exploit the 'grey areas' (the areas where there is no strong taste and the buyer can be influenced to change his choice).

5 *The income of the consumer*　In general, the higher the income of the consumer the more goods and services he or she will consume and, therefore, the higher the demand for a particular good or service. This statement must be qualified and a distinction made between *money* income and *real* income.

Money income is income without relation to purchasing power. Real income is what you can buy with the money you have. It relates income to the average price level of goods and services – in other words, the purchasing power of money. We have mentioned this problem in chapter 2 and we will consider the implications of the value of money in chapters 6 and 12. In chapter 14 we will examine some of the influences on changes in the value of money. To put the situation simply: a high money income and a relatively low price level is likely to lead to an increase in demand. People can buy more goods and services with a given quantity of money because the price level is low. They have a high *real* income. Should the price level rise *real* income will *fall*.

As a general guide to the way in which the purchaser's individual choices influence the demand for a good the above analysis is adequate so far as it goes, but it does not answer all the questions a businessman might want to ask.

Read the following passage and then try to answer the question after it.

Mrs Sherratt is an old-age pensioner with an adequate pension from her late husband's firm. She owns her home, has a comfortable lifestyle and is very fond of drinking tea. For the past five years Mrs Sherratt has been a devoted consumer of Brand X tea. Her only concession to change in that time has been to buy tea-bags in place of packets of loose tea and it took two years for Mrs Sherratt to make that change. In June 1985 Mrs Sherratt received a legacy of £15 000 on the death of a relative. In the same month she was given, as a gift, a quantity of high-quality and extremely expensive loose tea; she appreciated the taste.

Will Mrs Sherratt stop buying Brand X tea and buy the more expensive tea?

There is, of course, no way in which we can even attempt to answer that question unless we know Mrs Sherratt very well and could judge how willing to change she might be. Mrs Sherratt might prefer the taste of Brand X tea. She might be conditioned by years of careful spending to select the cheaper of two products. She might simply forget to buy the more expensive tea and buy the cheaper brand out of habit. She might be worried in case people realise she has inherited money if her habits change. She might be concerned that her friends would think she was merely trying to impress them. She might . . .

In fact, Mrs Sherratt's buying decision would be extremely complex. She may not herself be aware of some of the reasons behind her final decision.

When you remember that Mrs Sherratt is only one of millions of people who buy tea every day, you can appreciate the fact that the analysis of buying behaviour is extremely important. It is, of course, of great interest in marketing and a considerable amount of research has been undertaken in this field of human behaviour. This research tends to confirm the complexity of understanding the buying behaviour of individuals.

Traditional economic theory assumes that all purchasing decisions are made on a rational basis with the objective of maximising the individual's satisfaction. It does not require a great deal of thought to realise that if this were so in all cases, the family shopping would be a mammoth task involving a large number of small decisions. The outcome of each decision would then have to be weighed against the outcome of other decisions to check that the final 'basket' of choices was the combination that would give maximum satisfaction to the family. We can isolate certain groups of factors that influence buying decisions. The particular influence of a given decision, however, will depend on the personality, perceptions, prejudices and education of the individual. It is this that makes the research into human buying behaviour so fascinating.

1 *Internal stimuli* The individual has basic physical needs which must be met merely for survival. These are food, warmth and shelter. There are also security needs (protection, safety), social needs (love, group support), status needs from which the individual gets a feeling of self-respect and prestige, and self-actualising needs (the needs which arise for an individual out of their own personal goals). It is usual to see the lower order needs as being those satisfied by straightforward economic buying decisions. Social and status needs may, however, require reinforcing by material possessions and the satisfaction of self-actualising needs might demand the sacrifice of material possessions.

2 *External stimuli* These can include the impact of marketing on the buying decision – the customer's response to advertising and sales promotion.

3 *Cultural norms* Each person is a member of society and throughout life learns to conform to the demands made by society. Patterns of child-rearing and the formal education system introduce children to the social rules they will be expected to obey, and, through reward and punishment, adults enforce obedience to these rules. Although there is a general consensus in society as a whole, sub-groups will have their own rules and children brought up within a group will be expected to conform to the rules of that group. This is a very generalised statement and one which ignores the vast academic research that has gone into the subject. It is adequate for our present purposes. The expectations of a group will affect the buying behaviour of members of that group. If status is measured in terms of a house, car and a number of consumer durables, then this is likely to influence buying behaviour. If success is measured in terms of professional achievement or becoming a successful businessman, then this could be the way in which group members measure their success rather than by the possession of certain goods. Cultural norms are not fixed although they do tend to change slowly. Recent research has indicated that women's attitudes have changed to the point where appeals to their prowess as housewives common to many advertisements for family consumer goods were producing a negative rather than positive response – a matter of some concern to the producers!

A typical buying decision would include the weighing up of the advantages of one choice compared with others, the rational element, together with the influence of the less obvious factors listed above. The customer might respond through habit or loyalty. There may be an imperceptible shift in cultural norms. We will examine the ways in which a marketing team responds to these constraints in chapter 8. For the moment we are only concerned with defining them.

So far we have established that the demand for a product is likely to increase as price falls; that there are a number of general influences on the demand for a product; and that consumer buying behaviour is complex, and although we can isolate the influences on an individual's decisions they are so much a product of that person's uniqueness that no outsider could predict the response to a given situation. In chapter 5 we will show how the use of statistical techniques can go some way to helping business with this problem of market analysis.

SELF-ASSESSMENT

1 Make a list of all the factors that would influence your personal decision to take a particular continental holiday. Classify the list according to the main influences on the demand for a product.

2 Give two reasons why consumer buying behaviour is complex.

The demand for a product is shown graphically in Figure 3.1. Reading from the graph, we can see that when the price is 4p per kg, the demand for potatoes in Coxton will be 14 tonnes. A rise in price to 12p per kg reduces the demand to 6 tonnes. It is possible to read off the potential demand for potatoes at each price from 1p to 18p per kg. A closer inspection of the information reveals that the demand for potatoes in Coxton does not respond in the same way to each change in price.

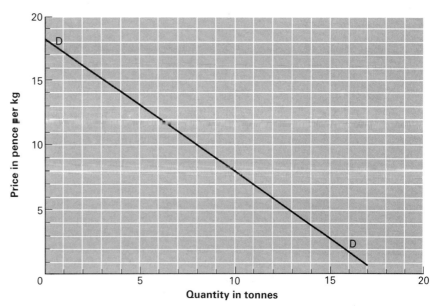

Figure 3.1 The market demand for potatoes in Coxton, March 1985

The degree of responsiveness of demand to a change in price is of obvious interest to a businessman. A measure of this responsiveness is obtained by comparing the percentage change in demand to the percentage change in price. This measurement is called the **price elasticity of demand**, or PED for short.

The calculation of this measure for a change in price from 2p to 4p is as follows:

$$\text{PED} = \frac{\text{Percentage change in quantity}}{\text{Percentage change in price}}$$

$$= \frac{\text{Change in quantity/average quantity}}{\text{Change in price/average price}}$$

$$= \frac{(15.75 - 13.75)/14.75}{(4-2)/3}$$

$$= \frac{2/14.75}{2/3}$$

$$= 0.203$$

When potatoes are sold at 4p per kg, the revenue (that is, price × quantity sold) is £560. A price increase to 6p leads to a revenue of £720. The higher price leads to a higher revenue. A similar calculation for a price change from 14p to 16p results in a fall in revenue from £525 to £280.

In general, if an increase in price leads to an increase in revenue or a decrease in price leads to a decrease in revenue then demand is said to be **price inelastic**. In this case the numerical measurement will be less than 1. If the reverse is true – that is, if an increase in price leads to a fall in revenue or a decrease in price leads to a rise in revenue – then price is said to be **elastic**. The numerical measurement is greater than 1. This information is useful to a businessman in the following circumstances:

- If he hopes to capture a larger share of the market by lowering his price. If the market is not responsive to a change in price he will find himself with a lower revenue and no increase in his market share.

- Faced with an increase in costs (for example, a pay rise for labour), the businessman might be tempted to pass on the extra costs to consumers as a price increase. Inelastic demand would make this possible. If demand is elastic it may leave him worse off.

- Similar to the above case is an increase in tax on a product. The producer has to decide whether to absorb the tax increase, or part of it, or pass it on to the consumer. Again, in an inelastic market it is likely to be the consumer who shoulders most of the tax burden. In chapter 14 we shall examine the implications of this for government policy formation in more detail.

- A change in the exchange rate can also have implications for a business which exports its goods, imports raw materials/components, or faces competition from foreign firms in the home market. If the domestic currency appreciates (becomes more valuable in terms of the amount of foreign currency it can buy), then imports will become cheaper and exports more expensive to foreign customers. If the market is elastic, then this could result in a fall in demand for the business's goods abroad but it would minimise the impact of foreign competitors in the home market.

Demand is not only responsive to changes in price. We have seen that the price of complementary and substitute products can also influence demand. **Cross elasticity** (the responsiveness of demand to the changes in the price of other products) and **income elasticity** (the responsiveness of demand to changes in income) are also useful concepts. A businessman would also be interested in how the demand for his product responded to an increase in his expenditure on advertising or sales promotion. This is sometimes called **promotional elasticity** or **advertising elasticity**. In each case the variable can be seen as a *force* acting on the demand for a product. The relevant measure of elasticity is calculated by dividing the percentage change in quantity demanded by the percentage change in the variable.

As a general rule, the following factors will tend to encourage consumer habits that will be translated into elastic demand:

- the availability of good substitute;
- a luxury product, although, if it is habit-forming, people might continue to buy it;
- a market that has shown itself to be responsive to new ideas;
- a feeling of insecurity in the society leading to an unwillingness to take risks;
- a low level of national income;
- expensive products, which encourage careful consumer buying behaviour; or
- products which are bought frequently and in small units.

SELF-ASSESSMENT

1 Calculate the price elasticity of demand for a good when a 10 per cent increase in price leads to a 5 per cent fall in the quantity demanded.

2 Give two circumstances in which you would expect the income elasticity of demand for a good to be inelastic.

The supply of goods to a market

The total supply of a good to a market is determined by the willingness of businesses to supply the product and their ability to do so. Each business will have its own set of priorities when deciding whether or not to supply, and the extent to which a business feels it can satisfy the customers in a particular market will be determined by its own unique set of constraints. However, it is possible to summarise the general influences on the supply of a product to a market as follows:

1 *The cost of producing the good compared with the price it is possible to obtain when the good is sold* Because the higher the price of the product the greater will be the number of businesses willing and able to produce that product, therefore the total supply of the product to the market will increase.

2 *The price/cost structure in other markets* A small general store, for example, offering a range of food, tobacco products, newspapers and a video library service finds that, as a result of competition from a near-by supermarket, the profits from the sale of the food lines are declining. By limiting the number of food lines it carries to those which are most profitable and increasing the shelf space devoted to the video library the total profits of the shop are increased. The supply of goods and services to the food market has declined.

    Not all businesses would find it so easy to switch from one product to another. Changing the use of agricultural land from one use to another, for instance, could mean a break in production ranging from months to years, and a farmer might want reassurance that the high profits that are attracting him at the moment will continue for some time before he is prepared to risk his capital and livelihood in the change.

3 *The technology available to a society will also influence total supply* Improvements in technology may increase the number of goods that can be supplied from a given amount of raw material and/or labour. It can, as in the case of home computers, give a product the opportunity to exploit a new market previously denied to it because of high production costs.

4 *The objectives of business will also influence supply in a market* Profit is important to a business, but other factors, not necessarily financial, may sway the final choice of individual decision makers. In the example of the general store given above, the owner of the store might well have decided to accept lower profits if the majority of customers for food were old people who could not easily make the journey to the supermarket. Whether or not the business would survive such a decision and the service continue to be supplied to that market would depend on how much profit the store was making originally. If the switch to the video library was a matter of survival the owner might well have no choice.

The supply of a product to a market is also subject to varying degrees of responsiveness to changes in price (**elasticity of supply**). This can be calculated in a similar manner to price elasticity of demand.

The general supply position of markets can be shown by a supply curve (see Figure 3.2). If you compare this sketch of a supply curve with the demand curve illustrated in Figure 3.1 you can see that it is possible to sketch them using the same axes. The intersection between the two curves is the point at which the amount that can be supplied coincides with the ability and willingness of the buyers to purchase that good.

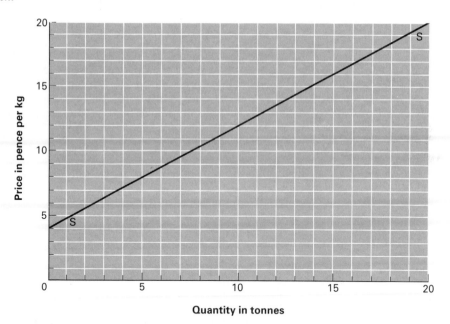

*Figure 3.2   The market
supply of potatoes in
Coxton, March 1985*

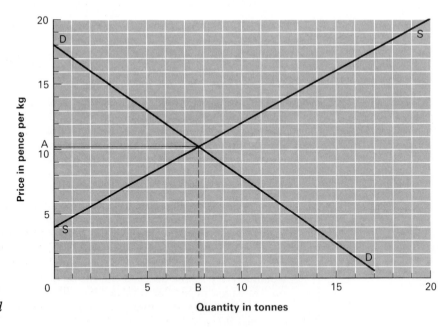

*Figure 3.3   Demand and
supply curves superimposed*

In Figure 3.3 the market price is designated by OA and the quantity
supplied to the market by OB. The total revenue from sales in that market is
market price × total quantity demanded and supplied. In this example what
would that be?

An increase in demand for a product – apart from a decrease in price – can
be caused by an increase in population, an increase in real national income, a
decrease in the price of a complementary product and an increase in the price
of a substitute product. This can be illustrated by a shift in the demand curve
to the right (see Figure 3.4).

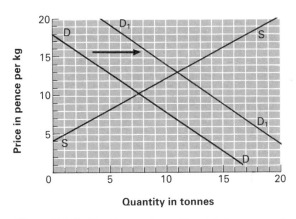

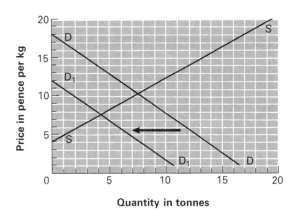

Figure 3.4 (left) Demand curve shifted to the right

Figure 3.5 (right) Demand curve shifted to the left

Provided the supply stayed the same, the price of the product would rise. A decrease in population (or even part of the population, such as the number of children), a fall in real national income, a rise in the price of a complementary product or a fall in the price of a substitute would shift the demand curve to the left, and the price of the product would fall, as shown in Figure 3.5.

Changes in such variables as technology and the costs of raw materials can have similar effects on the supply curves of a product. Figures 3.6 and 3.7 illustrate the effects of shifts in the supply curve on the price of a product.

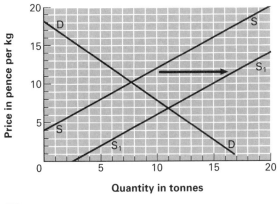

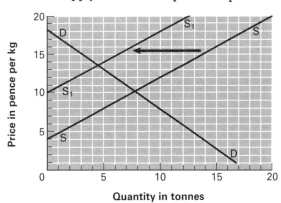

Figure 3.6 (left) Supply curve shifted to the right

Figure 3.7 (right) Supply curve shifted to the left

You may have noticed that in the analysis given above we have assumed that demand and supply are independent of each other. This makes it relatively easy to study the results of a change in demand or supply. In the real world a businessman, noting that the demand for one of his products was falling, would be likely to lower production levels and, if possible, switch his resources to a more profitable product. A shift to the left in the demand curve would be followed by a shift to the left in the supply curve. There would be a time lag and, depending on how rapidly producers reacted to the new situation, the price would fall. Figure 3.8 shows the influences on price.

SELF-ASSESSMENT

1 Explain how the objectives of firms can influence the supply of a product.
2 Improvements in technology lower the manufacturing costs of a product. Show, with the aid of diagrams, the effect of this on market price (a) if demand is elastic and (b) if demand is inelastic.

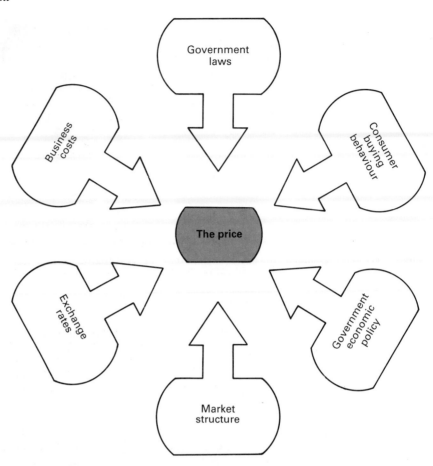

Figure 3.8   The influences on price

Classification of markets

The analysis of market behaviour given so far is general enough to apply to all cases and to provide an outline guide to the way in which you would expect the demand and supply for a product to respond to a number of influences. It is important to remember that this provides a general guide and that the market for every good and service offered in an economy has its own unique combination of influences.

In chapter 1 we saw how the wide range of activities in which people were involved could be classified for ease of reference. The same principle can be applied to markets. One way to do this is to divide markets by their geographical size. Other ways include the type of product and the degree of power a single producer is able to exercise over the market. This is known as **market structure**.

The geographical definition of a market

Markets may be described as local, regional, national, continental and world. Companies producing crude oil operate in a world market. This simply means that the users of crude oil, whether in the United Kingdom, Malaysia or Japan, will tend to pay the same price for crude oil, and if any difference exists in price the buyers and the sellers will react quickly enough to iron this out. The currency market (the buying and selling of foreign currencies by recognised dealers) is also a world market, and dealings in foreign currency in

Hong Kong will have an immediate effect on the London Exchange Market. On the other hand, the market for a product such as soap powder is likely to be a national market. The marketing team responsible for a brand of soap powder might be able to perceive regional differences in the way in which people respond to their product, but whether or not this influences their marketing decisions will depend on the magnitude of these differences and their effects on profits. If the differences were so great that the price had to be markedly different in one region of the country compared with another, then they would no longer be operating in a national market.

Classification by product

We have already touched upon this distinction when we talked about consumer goods and consumer durables. The distinction is a useful one in analysing market behaviour because the influences upon the buying decisions vary between these categories of goods. Consumer durables, for example, are often bought on credit. As a result of this practice an increase in the cost of borrowing money (the **interest rate**) can be seen as a complementary cost to the buying decision for these goods.

Another major grouping of goods is **industrial goods**. This category includes a wide range of products. The major car manufacturers sell a significant proportion of their output to businesses who need cars to carry on their own production role. Cars might, therefore, be called an industrial good. However, they are also a consumer durable, because they are bought for the pleasure and convenience of owning them by individuals who do not use them directly as part of their work. The car manufacturer is operating in two markets. This example illustrates the difficulty of making a clear definition of consumer goods.

Possibly the most simple distinction that we can make rests on the idea of **derived demand**. This simply means that the demand for a good will depend on the consumer demand for the final product that particular good will help to make. The following example might clarify the distinction between different categories of goods. A product that can be bought for both personal and industrial use can be defined as belonging to an industrial market when demand for it depends on the demand for another product to whose production it contributes.

In his Budget of April 1985 the Chancellor imposed value added tax (VAT) on a number of building operations which had previously been exempt from tax. These included the installation of domestic central heating. By August 1985 the Chairman of the Heating, Ventilation, Air-conditioning and Refrigeration Equipment economic development committee stated, in a submission to the Chancellor, that the tax had resulted in a 25 per cent drop in sales immediately after the imposition and demand was still, after recovery, only 90 per cent of the previous year's trading. This was in a market which had been growing at a steady 10 per cent per annum. The situation was causing problems for companies engaged in the manufacture of parts, for example, central heating boilers and radiators, and businesses which were engaged in the installation of systems. Approximately 4000 jobs had been lost as a result.

The imposition of VAT had effectively increased the cost of installation of central heating systems. We must assume that this increase in cost had been passed on to the customer in increased prices and, as a result, the demand for these systems had fallen. There would therefore be a fall in the demand of contractors for parts and a fall in the demand for labour by both contractors and manufacturers. The demand for labour and the demand for parts can therefore be seen to derive from the demand for central heating systems. More succinctly, it is a derived demand.

Classification by competitive structure

A Cumbrian sheep farmer takes a dozen lambs to market and returns grumbling about the price he has had to take for them. His only choice has been in whether to sell at that time or wait until a future date, by which time the price might have improved. On the other hand, it may have fallen still further. The sheep farmer has no control over his market. He lacks power.

A company such as British Telecom has a far greater degree of control over its market. British Telecom is virtually the only supplier of a telephone service in the United Kingdom. A decision to increase the price of a telephone call is likely, the management will know, to lead to a reduction in the number of calls made. This reduction in sales for the company will not be as great as it would be if another supplier existed. British Telecom can therefore select the combination of price and projected sales that is most satisfactory to it. The company has some power over its market.

The examples given above are oversimplified, but they illustrate the fact that the control a producer has over the market in which he operates varies according to the number of buyers, the number of sellers, the type of product, the ease of entry into that industry and the total market share (that is, the percentage of total sales for a product accounted for by a business) attributable to a stated number of the largest producers. This latter concept is called a **concentration ratio**.

Some of the major distinctions in market structure can be classified as follows:

1 *The perfect market*   For this to exist there must be a large number of buyers, a large number of sellers, relative ease of entry into the market and good communications so that people can make informed choices and switch rapidly from one product to another if the price rises. This implies that there is no difference between the different products. Because there are a large number of buyers and sellers no single individual or business can affect the way in which the market behaves and a business is a **price taker** – that is, it must accept the price offered on the market or not sell the product. It also implies that the demand curve for the firm, although not necessarily for the industry, is highly elastic. Examples of perfect, or near perfect markets, include those for agricultural products, industrial raw materials and stocks and shares.

2 *Monopoly*   This is a market in which there is only one producer of a given product – for example, the supply of electricity in the United Kingdom. If an individual wishes to buy the good or service then they can only purchase it from the monopolist. The power of a monopolist is not absolute. Too high a price may bring government intervention and the threat of increased legal control; there may be substitute products that are available to the consumer. If we develop the example of electrical supply and consider the implications of the domestic heating market we can see that electricity is in fact in competition with piped gas, coal (both of which are monopolies), oil and bottled gas in this market.

3 *Oligopoly*   A market of this type has relatively few producers and a large number of consumers. For practical purposes oligopolistic industries are usually defined by a study of concentration ratios. There may be a large number of businesses producing a particular good, but if the five largest firms account for 75 per cent of sales in a particular market then it is reasonable to

suppose that the behaviour of that market will be oligopolistic rather than approaching the perfect model. Each business has some control over the market, but any change in the behaviour of one business is likely to cause changes in the behaviour of its competitors. An oligopolist, for example, may hesitate to lower the price of his product for fear of instigating a potentially destructive price war in which victory would go not necessarily to the business with the best product but to the one with the greatest financial resources. An oligopolist is more likely to compete by emphasising the ways in which his product is superior to those of his competitors and to use advertising, branding and packaging to achieve this aim.

SELF-ASSESSMENT

1 Explain why the smaller the number of producers there are in a market the greater the market power of individual producers.
2 Give one reason why an oligopolist might avoid lowering the price of his product to gain more custom if it has a number of close substitutes.

Market constraints on business decisions

We began this chapter with the statement that the market is the environment in which a business operates and, so far, we have given a brief description of the way in which markets operate and a general classification of markets. We shall now look at some of the markets in which a business operates and the ways in which they can act as a constraint on the decision-making process within the organisation.

The labour market

In a time of high unemployment there is a tendency to refer to 'labour' as if each person produces an identical type of labour and therefore belongs to the same labour market. Common sense and experience reveal the fallacy of this approach. Each individual has a unique set of personal abilities and acquired skills which we group together (classification again!) according to our purposes. In general terms we can talk about skilled and unskilled labour, but a business is not talking in general terms. A particular business enterprise will have a very specific shopping list for the type of skills it needs in its labour force. If this type of labour is readily available then it will have no problems. It may even be able to pay lower wages and impose stricter conditions of service than had proved possible a few years previously. If the type of labour required is scarce, then the business is faced with a variety of questions to be answered: Is it possible to redesign the job so that it can be performed by people with a lower skill level? Can we use machinery instead of labour? If we decide to use machinery, what will be the financial implications of this decision? Can we afford to offer higher wages to attract the sort of labour we want? The organisation of the market for a particular type of labour can also have implications for a business. A powerful trade union can make the supply of a particular skill a virtual monopoly. A lack of union organisation can make it easier to pay low wages.

The market for raw materials

In this market the businessman may not be competing only with firms producing the same goods as himself. Raw materials have a wide variety of uses and the business may find itself competing with other more prosperous producers of different and more popular products who are able to buy at higher prices. Is it possible to use a substitute product? Can research devise a substitute product?

The financial markets

A business both borrows and lends money. Even if it were possible for it to exist in complete financial independence it would still be necessary for the business to be aware of the price of money on the various financial markets, so that it was aware of the opportunity cost of using its own finance for a project. Changes in the cost of borrowing money can cause a business problems in terms of paying debts, investment decisions and, depending on the product, the demand for its own goods. An increase in the interest rate means an increase in the overall cost of living as, for example, the cost of mortgages increases. This can lead to a decline in the demand for certain types of goods, particularly luxury goods.

In chapter 2 we looked at the financial institutions that comprise the market for money – that is, those institutions which buy and sell short-term bills that finance government expenditure and trade. This market affects and is affected by the capital market (the market for medium- and long-term debt). A rise in interest rate in one of these markets will attract funds from the other market.

The market for the firm's product

We have dealt with this aspect of marketing at some length in the first part of the chapter. It is necessary to emphasise that the market in which a firm sells its products will affect marketing policy (pricing, advertising, packaging, promotion, distribution and transport), the production policy (quality and quality control, purchasing, research and development, location, production method and organisation) and the financial, organisational and personnel policy of the business. This is true whether or not the business is production- or market-oriented. The distinction might be that the market-oriented firm appreciates the effect the market has on it while the production-oriented firm is either blind to that effect or has such a position of market power that it can afford to ignore it.

Each time a business purchases the smallest good or service it is operating in a market. Each time it sells it is operating in a market, and a change in any one market creates ripples of cause and effect that spread through inter-related markets.

Government and markets

We have already seen that the workings of a free market economy do not always result in a fair or desirable distribution of resources. A business which has a large share of the market can exert pressure on customers and suppliers to prevent new firms (which may have a better product and be more efficient) from entering that market. Collusion between businesses operating in an oligopolistic market can keep prices high either by agreeing a price between themselves or by limiting the quantity produced or by limiting the level of investment. These agreements are generally illegal but can exist informally. When legal and accompanied by legal agreements they are known as **cartels**. The word is often applied to all such practices whether legal or not.

Collusion can only exist in an oligopolistic market. The logistics of enforcing the agreement in markets with a large number of producers make it impossible. It therefore seems reasonable to suppose that if more competition could be introduced into a market the businesses involved would become more efficient. Working against this simple solution is the fact that some businesses operate at lower costs if they are large in size. We will discuss the reasons for this in chapter 9. In these circumstances a greater number of firms in the same market would lead to a duplication of effort and a waste of resources. This was recognised in the 1960s when an Act of Parliament established the Industrial Reorganisation Corporation (IRC) in 1966. The purpose of this was to encourage businesses to combine to make better use of resources and so make them more competitive on international markets. The IRC was abolished in 1971.

The opposite trend is represented by the anti-monopoly legislation. In 1948 the Monopolies and Restrictive Practices Act was passed, which established the Monopolies Commission with powers to investigate any accusations of unfair dealing such as price and quota fixing. Collectively these are known as **restrictive practices.** Where there was evidence of such dealings the commission's report was submitted to the minister and the practice could be declared illegal.

By 1956 there was a general feeling that the Monopolies Commission lacked sufficient power. The burden of proof lay with the commission rather than the businesses accused. As a result the Restrictive Trades Practices Act, passed in 1956, established a register for all agreements together with a Restrictive Practices Court. The burden of proof passed to business. A restrictive practice was illegal unless the business could justify it on one of the following criteria:

1 that the removal of the restriction would lead to a substantial increase in unemployment;

2 that the removal of the restriction would deny the public certain advantages – for example, abnormally high prices were needed as an incentive to research;

3 that the agreement was necessary to counteract the existing market power of other businesses which were either suppliers or customers;

4 that the restriction was necessary to protect the consumer from injury;

5 that the restrictions made the industry more competitive in the export market; and

6 that the restriction was necessary to support another restriction which had been ruled in the interests of the public – for example, the imposition of production quotas in support of a price-fixing agreement.

In 1965 the Monopolies and Mergers Act was passed. '**Merger**' is a general term to describe the amalgamation of two businesses, whereas '**takeover**' is the term used to describe the acquisition of one business by another as the result of the purchase of a majority of the shareholding. The 1956 Act had forbidden collusion between businesses. As a result, many businesses began to undertake mergers in order to protect their outlets (**forward integration**), their supplies (**backward integration**) or to control their competitors (**horizontal integration**). Again this was a cause for concern, and the 1965 Act empowered the government to stop and break up a merger or to impose conditions under which it could proceed.

The Fair Trading Act 1973 established the role of the Director General of Fair Trading with the power to investigate trading activities and refer suspect cases to the expanded Monopolies and Mergers Commission. The Act also reduced the level of market share at which a monopoly situation is said to exist, from the one third laid down in 1948 to 25 per cent. Nationalised industries also became liable for trading practices defined as unfair, and restrictive labour practices (for example, an attempt by a trade union to take advantage of a monopoly situation in a labour market) could also be referred to the commission.

The powers of the Office of Fair Trading were extended by the Competition Act 1980 to include local authorities and was empowered to investigate any trading activity it felt was unfair. The Monopolies and Mergers Commission is still the final judge.

Conclusion

Markets are the environment in which a business operates. It buys in markets and sells to markets. Survival depends on the ability of a business to understand these markets, appreciate the relationship between them and exploit that relationship to achieve its objectives. Chapter 4 will offer an overall view of the situation. Part II will examine the functions of a business in more detail. Market behaviour was one of the earliest areas of consumer protection, and this is an area we will consider in more detail in Part III.

A case study: the oil market, 1950–86

The international oil market has received so much attention from governments, economists and the media over the past fifteen years that to introduce it as a case study is to run the risk of becoming boring. However, the advantages of using it do outweigh this.

1 It is a clear demonstration of the operation of a cartel.

2 The importance of oil as a raw material and a fuel means that changes in its price have a traceable impact on a wide variety of markets.

3 The extraction and refining of oil is the work of governments and very large multi-national businesses. Many of the issues fall into the realm of diplomacy and politics. A study of the oil market provides material on the interaction between political and economic systems.

4 The price of oil is not an historic issue. For the student this has the advantage of providing continuing material for a case study with the possibility of unforeseen developments.

Background

The most easily accessible oil deposits were found in the United States and in developing countries of the Middle and Far East and Africa. For many of these countries oil was the only resource they possessed which was easily marketable and which could earn them foreign currency to invest in development programmes. In order to buy the technology and expertise of the developed countries a developing country must rely on aid or what it could earn by its own exports. The importance of oil to the developed countries gave the oil-producing countries a valuable resource.

From 1950 to 1970 the price of crude oil (oil before refining has taken place) fell from approximately $1.70 a barrel to $1.30 a barrel. Market power lay with the users of oil rather than the producers, whose income fell.

In 1960 a group of oil-exporting countries formed the Organisation of Petroleum Exporting Countries (OPEC). Representatives of each country meet regularly to agree, among other things, the price of crude oil exports.

Present members include Algeria, Ecuador, Gabon, Indonesia, Iran, Iraq, Kuwait, Libya, Nigeria, Qatar, Saudi Arabia, the United Arab Emirates and Venezuela. These countries account for approximately 90 per cent of world oil exports and 60 per cent of world oil production. Potentially they have a position of considerable market power if they act together.

Demand for oil is relatively inelastic. On the simplest level a householder who has invested in oil-fired central heating is faced with capital expenditure if he or she converts to another fuel. The same is true of power stations. Figure 3.9 gives hypothetical demand and supply curves for oil in 1970. Notice that the supply of oil is elastic relative to the demand for it.

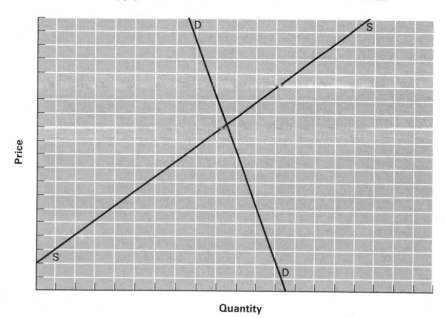

Figure 3.9 Hypothetical demand and supply curves for oil, 1970

In the early 1970s political tensions in the Middle East (notice how many of the OPEC countries are in that geographical area) led to fears of oil shortages. Demand for oil rose as the oil companies and consumers increased their stocks of oil in anticipation of shortages. The world price of crude oil began to rise. Using the terminology we developed in chapter 2, we can see this as the interaction between political and economic systems. In other words, it is an example of how the environment in which it operates can affect the business community.

The member countries of OPEC took advantage of the movement of the market in their favour. In 1973 they agreed on production quotas which led to a sharp reduction in supply. The supply of oil, in the short term, was no longer responsive to price changes. It became perfectly inelastic. This is illustrated in Figure 3.10.

By 1980 oil cost $28 a barrel. The control of the market by OPEC was by no means perfect, and the history of the organisation in the 1970s illustrates some of the problems associated with the management of cartels.

- There was a constant temptation for poorer members to break ranks and over-produce. In this way they could benefit from the higher prices induced by the cartel and increase their own revenue.

- Although the demand for oil is relatively inelastic in the short term, the effect of high oil prices was a lowering of economic activity throughout the world

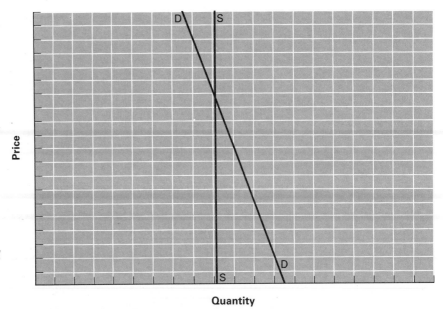

Figure 3.10   Hypothetical demand and supply curves for oil after 1973 OPEC agreement

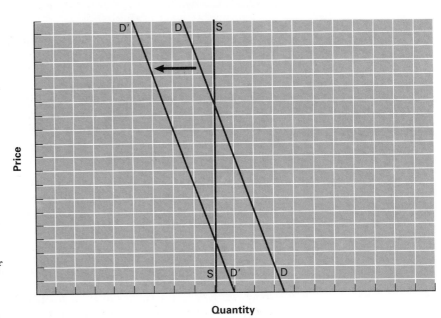

Figure 3.11   Change in demand for oil as a result of a lower level of economic activity throughout the world

which, in turn, resulted in a fall in the demand for oil. The demand curve shifted to the left.

Internal pressures in the cartel resulted in a split in policy in 1976. A dual-pricing system was introduced. Saudi Arabia and the United Arab Emirates decided to keep price rises to the minimum in response to changes in the market demand for oil. In 1980 oil prices rose sharply again as the Iran/Iraq conflict led to a reduction in supplies.

Oil and the world economy

Crude oil is a raw material for a wide variety of products that underpin the economies of the developed countries.

1 As a fuel it is used to generate electricity, fire boilers, smelt metals and supply commercial transport services.

2 As a raw material it is used in the manufacture of plastics and man-made fibres.

3 It is used by households for heating and domestic transport.

The developed economies had become accustomed to cheap and plentiful supplies of oil. The sudden rise in price had an immediate and telling impact. The explanation given in this chapter is deliberately oversimplified. We will return to this problem at the end of chapter 13 when you will have a clearer understanding of the working of the economic system. You should remember that the consequences given below were spread over a number of years.

The oil-importing countries were immediately faced with an increase in the cost of oil. As a result, the total value of the goods they imported exceeded the total value of the goods they exported. The classic response to this situation is to reduce the ability of people to spend money, which would then reduce the demand for imported raw materials (derived demand) and so reduce the overall bill for imported goods. Unfortunately, the relative price inelasticity of oil meant that it was other oil-importing countries which suffered as a result. Movements in the economy generally are the result of millions of decisions made by individuals and organisations independently. Look at the following example.

Between 1968 and 1972 a married couple made a number of employment and investment decisions. They took jobs in separate towns and bought a house equidistant between the two towns. Public transport was infrequent, so they ran two cars. They invested in oil central heating because it was the cheapest option available. The sudden rise in oil prices in 1973 reduced the income they had to spend on other goods and services. To some extent this was offset by a sharp rise in their salaries (1974 saw settlements which gave wage and salary increases of 25 and 30 per cent), but this was soon eroded by government policies. Wages did not keep pace with the increase in the price of goods.

This pattern, repeated on a less dramatic scale throughout the country, meant that people cut back on their spending. Demand for home-produced goods and services fell. Employers began to reduce their workforce and the rising level of unemployment contributed to the decrease in demand. Demand for imported goods and services fell and, as the same policies were being followed throughout the developed world, demand for exports fell too.

To some extent these policies have worked for the industrial countries whose imports and exports are again in balance, but this has been at the expense of high levels of unemployment. Unemployment has also been exported to non-industrial oil-importing countries. The fall in the demand for industrial goods caused a fall in demand for raw materials other than oil – some of which are imported from developing and relatively poor countries.

By 1985 the changes in the world economy as a result of the initial rise in the price of oil had begun to affect the demand for and the price of oil. Energy conservation had only a marginal effect in industrial countries, but in oil-importing developing countries rationing was introduced. Households and businesses began to use alternative fuels where this was possible. Oilfields (for example, the North Sea) which would have been uneconomic when oil prices were low began to be developed. Not all the new oil-producing countries joined OPEC, which weakened its cartel. In 1986, partly as a consequence of market movements and partly as a result of deliberate decisions on the part of OPEC, oil prices fell to $6 a barrel.

The future development of this case study is now the responsibility of you, the student. You may find it difficult to follow all the arguments used at this stage in your course. A collection of newspaper cuttings will provide you with valuable and up-to-date material for analysis when you are studying Part III of this book. You should not limit your collection to the workings of OPEC and the problems of governments. Remember that changes in the price of oil will have their effects on individuals and businesses.

Review

1   You are the economist of Landun Cars, a medium-sized company producing luxury cars in the £45000 to £70000 price range Your department has isolated the following trends:

   - a sharp fall in the price of petrol;
   - an aggressive marketing campaign by a rival manufacturer;
   - a change in the structure of income tax which favours the higher income groups;
   - sustained growth in the economy generally;
   - a rapid increase in house prices;
   - the stockpiling of raw materials by governments;
   - increased emphasis by businesses on the reduction of costs.

   (a) Prepare a report explaining how these trends may, or may not, affect the demand for your company's products.
   (b) Would a manufacturer of a small family car selling at £4500 experience the same impact on his market?
   (c) To what extent do the manufacturers of luxury cars operate in the same market as the manufacturer of the small family car?

2   Fine Fastenings Ltd produces pre-packaged nails and screws for the do-it-yourself market. The prices of its five most popular lines are given below:

   Product A   £0.25
   Product B   £0.40
   Product C   £1.00
   Product D   £1.50
   Product E   £2.00

   The quantities sold are respectively 100000, 70000, 20000, 150000 and 50000. The price elasticities of demand are estimated at 0.1, 0.5, 0.4, 1.2 and 0.3 respectively.
   (a) Calculate the total sales revenue of Fine Fastenings Ltd.
   (b) What effect would a 10 per cent increase on the price of all the products listed above have on the sales revenue of the company?
   (c) Fine Fastenings Ltd wishes to increase its sales revenue by £100000 in order to cover an increase in costs and maintain its existing profit margins. Which products should bear the brunt of the price increases? Explain your answer.

3   Read the case study on oil given at the end of the chapter before attempting to answer the following questions. You should illustrate your arguments with clear sketches of demand and supply curves where these are appropriate.
   (a) In 1986 OPEC limited production of oil in order to stimulate an increase in the price. Explain the reasoning behind this strategy and comment upon its possible effectiveness.
   (b) One reason given for the fall in the price of oil has been the world

recession. Explain how lower oil prices could lead to a future demand for oil.

(c) During the years of high oil prices there was considerable interest in energy-efficient technology. Electronic control systems, for example, use less energy than electrical systems. What are the implications of this trend for the arguments you have obtained in your answer to (b)?

(d) In spite of the fall in the price of oil the search for new oilfields has continued. The table below gives the number of years that existing oilfields are expected to last according to geographical area.

Area	Years
Africa	30
Asia	16
Central/South America	19
Middle East	100+
Soviet Union	14
United States	10
Western Europe	18

Given the above information, together with the fact that Japan, the United States and Western Europe are among the world's heaviest users of energy, explain why, in spite of low oil prices, exploration for new fields is continuing.

Activities

The investigation of a local market: the market for private housing.

1 Identify a range of houses prevalent in your area – for example, 2-bedroomed/3-bedroomed terraced houses, 3-bedroomed semi-detached, etc.

2 Divide the area into neighbourhoods. If you live in a city this stage may be based on old villages that have been swallowed by the city. In London you may compare Camden Town with Hampstead; in Liverpool, Calderstones with Knotty Ash. In both examples the pairings are random.

3 You will need a sample of house prices covering the range of houses and the areas you have chosen over a period of three weeks. The property guide in the local newspaper will give you a starting point. When you have studied chapter 5 you will realise that this may not be a representative sample.

4 Interview several people who are considering buying a house on the qualities they look for when viewing a house.

5 What are the economic factors involved? Income, the policy of building societies, the role of insurance companies and banks are all important. Visit and invite speakers from these institutions. Your main purpose is to investigate their role in the housing market, but you should remember that they are also part of the capital and monetary systems of the economy.

6 Interview the owners of property. Do they think they have any control over the price they could ask if they wanted to sell? What reasons do they give to support their answers?

7 New houses in the lower and middle price ranges are usually built in anticipation of demand. You need to:
(a) compare and contrast these products;
(b) discover the percentage of the total market for new houses they command;

(c) assemble examples of their advertising, noting any special offers/price reductions that might appear;

(d) discover any special problems – for example, the availability of sites, the cost of materials, the cost of labour, the attitudes of local government that may influence their decisions.

8 Investigate the economy of the area, in particular the level of unemployment.

9 Investigate the availability of alternative forms of housing, including local authority housing and co-operatives. What is the policy/attitude of the local authority to private housing? What effect does this have on the market for private housing?

You can explore this market for a long time and still make discoveries. The approach is that of the economist, an overall view. However, this investigation will provide you with valuable data that will give an insight into the behaviour of markets and the impact of market structure on the pricing and promotion of products.

Suggested projects

1 A critical appreciation of a local market.

2 The importance of a company's market position on its pricing policy.

Essay questions

1 The market in which it operates determines the strategies of a business. Discuss this statement with reference to the policies of a business concerning:
(a) pricing;
(b) production;
(c) recruitment;
(d) investment.

2 Outline and discuss the effects of a minimum wage policy on the part of a government on
(a) a labour-intensive business;
(b) a capital-intensive business.

3 Comment on the factors which might affect the demand for continental holidays
(a) in the short term;
(b) in the long term.

4 A business has a market share of 23 per cent. Its three largest competitors have a combined market share of 40 per cent. Assess the implications of this situation for the first business.

Chapter 4   **Starting and running your own business**

The first three chapters of this book have taken a very general look at the world in which a business must operate. After studying these chapters you should realise:

- that business activity exists to satisfy the needs and wants of people;
- that although each business is unique, by classifying businesses we can study the characteristics they have in common;
- that businesses operate in markets; and
- that all businesses carry out the functions of production, marketing, finance, control and personnel.

It is on this last point that we will concentrate in this chapter. By taking the process, and the problems associated with it, of starting and running your own business we will examine the interdependence of business functions.

Why start a business?

There are probably as many reasons and combinations of reasons for starting a business as there are people who make the attempt.

- An inventor or a person with an original idea for a service might decide to go into business to exploit the idea himself rather than try to find somebody prepared to adopt it.
- Some people go into business because they hope for a higher standard of living as an owner of a business rather than as an employee.
- The desire for independence can also inspire people who are already employed.
- Redundancy and the fear of never finding another job may persuade a man to take on the risks of a business. The experience of redundancy can also bring on a feeling of revulsion against being dependent on the decisions of other people and a determination to have more control over life.

Whatever the reason for starting a business there are feelings of conviction, determination and optimism on the part of the entrepreneur (that is, a person who accepts the risks of business and organises resources to produce a good or a service). He must be careful to find the answers to the following questions if the business is to live.

1   *Have I the skills, experience and determination to run a business?*   The owner of a business is a resource of that business. He will be offering production and management skills to the small business. We can say that the answer to this question lies within the function of *personnel*. The success or failure of all the other functions will depend on the skills of the people engaged in them. Yet even the most skilful workforce cannot succeed if it lacks the support of finance, materials, market and organisation.

2   *What product will I make or what service will I provide?*   The answer to this question must go further than a statement of the good or service. Among other things it must concern itself with design and quality. The decision will depend upon who will be likely to buy and the ability of the business to produce the good or service. This lies within both the *marketing* and *production* functions.

3   *Will people buy my product? Who will buy it? Where will it be bought and at what price?*   Before an answer can be found to these questions the entrepreneur will have to research his market. This activity is part of the *marketing* function.

4   *Can I supply the product at the right time, in the required quantities, at the desired quality and at the right price?*   These questions relate to the *production* activities of the firm.

5   *Can I get the product to my customers at the right time, in the right quantities and at the right price?*   *Marketing* has the responsibility for answering this question too, together with the problem of informing and persuading people to buy.

6   *Have I the money to buy the necessary premises, materials and machinery? Can I afford to employ labour? Which machines will give me the greatest profit? Which product will give me the greatest profit?*   The answers to these questions lie in the function of *finance*.

7   *How am I to combine the different functions listed above so that they will work together and give the maximum reward for the minimum input?*   The term used to describe this concept is 'efficiency'. The answers lie in the area of *organisation* and *control*.

The first step

Mrs Jones decides to take her three children for a day at the seaside during their summer holidays. She chooses the resort, finds out about train and bus times, discovers the cheapest way of travelling there and books the tickets. The night before she packs a complete change of clothes for the youngest child because experience has told her it is likely to be needed. She makes sandwiches because she cannot afford to buy all the food that will be necessary. In short, Mrs Jones plans her day out carefully.

If you think about your life you will realise that you are planning all the time. A decision to go to a disco will involve other decisions – such as who to go with, where the money is coming from, if your parents will allow you to go, what transport to use and so on. Starting or buying a business also needs planning. In this section we will look at:

• a definition of planning;
• the need for business planning; and
• the contents of a business plan.

What is planning?

A plan is a detailed statement of the way in which a person or a group of people intends to reach long-term objectives or short-term targets. The difference between the planning of individuals and the planning in business lies in the objectives and targets set and in the activities needed to achieve them.

The principles of planning

1 *Information* Plans should be based on accurate and factual information. When detailed information is not available the planner will have to rely on experience and judgement. This should not be dismissed as mere guesswork.

2 *Time* The environment in which a business operates is constantly changing. The plan drawn up for a business will therefore vary according to the period of time for which it is intended. A short time scale demands a detailed business plan. For a longer period the plan will be less detailed.

3 *Flexibility* A plan should be changed as circumstances change and as more information becomes available.

4 *Control* The existence of a plan does not ensure success. The progress must be constantly checked if it is to be implemented properly. Control relies on accurate information.

The business plan

It may be months or even years between the birth of an idea and the starting of a business. During this time the would-be entrepreneur should be developing and refining the business plan. There are three reasons for this:

1 A thorough investigation into the costs, markets and available finance, clearly presented, will identify the areas of weakness in the original idea and allow them to be eradicated before they cost money or lead to failure.

2 A good business plan will impress such people as bank managers, both for its information and for the businesslike qualities of the person who has drawn it up.

3 The discipline of drawing up a business plan can draw your attention to the areas in which you lack experience.

Contents of a business plan

- A brief description of the business will include the goods it intends to offer to its customers, an indication of its market and sources of supply. How brief this introduction is will depend upon the business. For a small, one-man start-up business 100 words might suffice. A more complex organisation will need a more detailed and, therefore, a longer description. This part of the business plan is important if it is to be used to support a request for external investment. Many organisations offering capital to new businesses specialise in certain types of business activity. If they are going to reject a plan it is in the interests of the businessman that they do so quickly. Then he can seek more sympathetic organisations without too great a loss of time.

- Information relating to the personal experience of the entrepreneur will indicate the chances of success to the bank manager or anyone else he is approaching for capital. It can also draw the businessman's attention to his own lack of specialised knowledge and suggest the need for a course in, perhaps, business management before he starts trading.

- A detailed description of the product would include production costs and the proposed selling price. It should also try to isolate what sets this product apart from all similar products on the market. Is the technology more advanced? Is the idea innovative? The closer a product is in type to an existing product the harder it will be to attract customers – and the more difficult it will be to persuade people to lend money to the business.

- The business plan should also include a description of the market at which the product is directed. This will include the geographical area over which it is to be sold, the number of competitors and the special points which will set this business apart from its competitors. It should also indicate the potential for growth in the area.

- The location chosen for the business should be stated and explained. The explanation might include details of premises and the site chosen in terms of costs and in relation to the market.

- Methods of production and marketing selected should also be explained and justified. Again, this justification should be related clearly to costs, including labour costs.

- The business plan should also include the amount of funding that will be required. If the plan is intended to persuade people to invest in the business it should also state the return the investors can expect. For an existing business this statement should be accompanied by the financial statements of the business over several years. A new business might include *projected* financial statements. A **projection** states what is expected to happen rather than what has happened.

SELF-ASSESSMENT

1 Give three reasons why a business plan is important to the success of an enterprise.
2 List the major headings that should be included in a business plan.

Getting help

The business plan is likely to highlight problem areas in a proposed business. Where can the businessman get help in solving these problems? If the business is small he will not be able to employ specialists on a full-time basis. He may not be able to afford the services of specialist agencies – for example, in areas such as advertising. Where can he get help?

1 *Business courses* Polytechnics, colleges of further education and other educational institutions offer courses designed to help people judge whether their idea for a new business has the qualities needed for success and to help them through the difficulties of establishing a business. Other courses, such as Accounting for the Small Businessman, Computers in Business, attempt to improve specific skills.

2 *The Small Firms Service* This is provided by the Department of Industry and operates small firm centres in London and the major provincial towns. The centres offer advice on marketing, finance, training, exporting and the introduction of new technology.

3 *The Council for Small Industries in Rural Areas (CoSIRA)* Help from CoSIRA is limited to businesses in rural areas with central populations of fewer than 10 000 people. CoSIRA offers training courses and a range of consultancy services which give advice on accounting, marketing and finance.

4 *Other organisations* These can range from government departments to the British Institute of Management whose Small Firms Information Service provides pamphlets and leaflets of help to the small businessman.

5   *Solicitors, accountants and bank managers*   These can also provide expert help.

We can summarise what we have learnt so far as follows:

1   A business must perform a number of functions in order to survive.

2   Although the individual functions of a business can be studied separately, the profitability and ultimate survival of a business depend upon the way in which they interact. It is useless for a production department to make 5 000 items if it is only possible to sell 2 000, for example.

3   Planning is vital if problems are to be foreseen and overcome.

4   Planning must be based on accurate information if it is to be successful.

5   It is important for the manager of a business or part of a business to know the extent to which the business plan is 'on course'. In other words, they need to be able to *control* the business.

Acquiring a business

1   *Buy a business that already exists*   An existing business will have records of sales and profits, which will remove some of the uncertainty from your enterprise. You should, of course, insist on seeing these records before you buy and have them examined by an accountant. The amount of capital needed to buy an existing business can vary enormously. A small shop, bought as a going concern, might be bought for £5 000. At the other end of the scale a **management buy-out** can require capital in excess of £10m. Management buy-outs are not new but they have received publicity recently. They occur when a large company decides to stop making a particular product and close the factory. If the management of that factory has faith in the future profitability of the product it may decide to buy the right to manufacture the product and the plant and machinery needed to make it.

2   *Invest in a franchise*   Under this system a successful business idea is shared by the person who developed it (the franchisor), *who sells or 'rents' the use of the idea to other people (the* franchisees*). Under a franchise agreement the franchisee might be required to pay royalties to the franchisor for the use of the idea. He may have to agree to decorate his premises in a particular way or conduct his business according to a certain code of behaviour. These regulations are usually linked to the reasons why the original business was a success. In return the franchisor might provide:*
    * *loans to help in the start-up of the business;*
    * *training in the conduct of the business;*
    * *any special products that are needed; or he might*
    * *undertake to finance a national advertising campaign; or*
    * *guarantee a geographical area as the sole market for each franchisee.*
    Franchising offers the advantages of belonging to a large business organisation combined with the satisfaction and greater control that can be found in a small business. The capital required for buying a franchise can vary from £3 000 to £200 000.

3   *Start a new business*   This option carries with it the greatest degree of risk. The business has no history to help you and you will lack the support offered by franchising. On the other hand, it may be possible to begin on a very small scale without risking too much capital. You will also have greater freedom of action. You will not be limited by decisions other people have taken in the past (buying a business) or the limitations placed on you by a franchise.

Finding the money

The new businessman has, by now, investigated his idea and decided whether or not it is viable. In this the business plan has helped point out any weaknesses and he has sought help in eliminating them. He has decided whether or not to purchase an existing business. The question now remains as to where he will get the money to start this business.

There are three ways in which a business acquires money:

- by investment of money in the business by the owner or owners, including any profit which they decide to reinvest;
- by borrowing money from private individuals or from another organisation;
- by buying goods and services on credit – that is, having the use of the goods and services before they are paid for.

The basic principles of acquiring capital may be simple but the reality is far more complex. Each business will have its own particular requirements based upon such factors as:

- The size of the business.

- The stage of development it has reached. Two businesses, for example, with a similar number of employees and making a similar profit may have totally different capital requirements. One business might be able to fund future investment from profits already made. What is more, its future investment potential might be limited. The other business may need a large injection of capital if it is to take advantage of the market.

- The owner of the business may wish to retain control, and that will mean loans to expand the capital rather than sharing the ownership with other people.

- The organisations that make money available to business have their own preferences. Some opt for lending to a business with growth potential where there is a large element of risk. Financial organisations such as these will be looking for a business that can give them a return on their capital as high as 45 per cent and will be looking closely at the record of the business in the past, together with the skills of the management team. Another organisation might be prepared to accept lower returns but will demand a stake in the business as a condition of making money available.

Basically this is a matter of products and markets. The organisations lending are offering the product 'capital' in the way in which it will give them the profits they want with an acceptable level of risk. The businesses taking the money are buying 'capital'. They will want to buy a product that suits their needs and circumstances.

The end result is a number of markets with what appears to be the same service – namely, capital – but with a variety of additional services that make separate products. You should refer back to chapter 3 if you do not understand this argument.

In this chapter we are not going to concern ourselves with the complications of the markets for money and capital, nor with the factors a business will take into account when deciding on how to finance its particular requirements. This will be dealt with in the chapter on finance. Instead we will look at some basic definitions and the ways in which a very small business just starting up might find its capital in the first years of its life.

1   The money the owner of the business invests in it. This can come from savings or the sale of his possessions. It may be a redundancy payment or a legacy, or he may have won it in the football pools. The important thing to remember is that it is his money and he can do with it as he wishes. If he loses the money it is his loss.

2   Money can be borrowed using possessions as a security. This statement means simply that if a man cannot repay the money then the person or organisation which lent that money can claim or sell that possession in order to recover the money lent. An insurance policy which guarantees a payment of £5000 in three years' time may be used as a security for a loan of £2000. The lender of the money will hold all the documents and claim the money due to the borrower if the loan is not repaid. Mortgages are a specialised form of a loan on security. The security in this case is always property. Loans are usually made for a fixed period of time, for a fixed amount and at a fixed rate of interest.

3   Hire purchase and credit sales for equipment have a great deal in common. The difference lies in the ownership of the item. If a retailer buys a display refrigeration unit on hire purchase he does not own it until the last payment has been made, although the law does give him some protection against arbitrary repossession by the owner. On the other hand, if it is a credit sale, he will own the refrigeration unit as soon as he has made an initial payment.

4   Trade credit is a system whereby a business receives the ownership of goods or services and does not have to pay for them immediately. The time involved can vary. It may be as little as a few days or a week or as long as three months. In some businesses the goods or services bought in can be used and have brought in income before they have to be paid for. This is a death trap for the businessman who is too optimistic.

Businesses can also lease equipment. If the equipment is only needed for a short period of time then this can be paralleled to hiring in a domestic situation. A householder wishes to dig over his garden. He needs the mechanical cultivator that will make the work easy only once in the year. It is sensible to hire it for two days at a cost of £30 rather than pay £400 to buy it. If the equipment is going to be used continuously then it is better to compare leasing equipment with renting a house. There may be an initial down-payment followed by regular payments. This does not increase the capital of a business, but by leasing rather than buying equipment it can mean that there is more capital to be used elsewhere.

SELF-ASSESSMENT

1 Classify the sources of capital according to the three major ways in which a business acquires finance.
2 List three factors that will affect the capital requirements of a business.

Running a business

A business, like the people who run it and the society in which it exists, is constantly changing. The way in which it develops and its ultimate success or failure depend upon:

1   *People*   The person who starts a business might be prepared to work long hours to make it a success. As it becomes more secure he might prefer more leisure time to increased profits. The way in which the business develops can be helped or hindered by the available skills in the labour force.

2   *Technology*   Changes in technology can make a product or a production method obsolete (that is, old-fashioned or out of date). New products will have to be found, new machinery bought and the labour force retrained.

3   *The economy*   A high level of unemployment in an economy can mean a reduction in labour costs. It can also mean less demand for the product and a more competitive market. This will have implications for the costing, pricing and marketing of a product. It can also lead to changes in production methods and will certainly affect profitability.

4   *The government*   Governments make laws. A change in the laws governing health and safety in the workplace can lead to increased production costs. Other laws might increase the clerical work required of a business. The Data Protection Act 1984, for example, requires businesses to register if they hold information about an identifiable, living person on a computer. Businesses are responsible for making sure the registration is accurate and up to date.

   Governments can also affect the general level of demand in an economy by the way in which it raises money and the way in which it spends it. If the government decides to increase the tax on a particular type of good then it is likely that the demand for that good will fall. As we saw in chapter 3, the extent to which the demand falls will depend on its price elasticity.

5   *Other organisations*   The attitudes and power of trade unions and the activities of pressure groups can also affect the development of a business. A powerful trade union can influence working practices and raise the labour costs of a business. A political pressure group might mount a campaign to stop people buying certain types of goods.

6   *The market*   The markets in which a business operates will also affect its development. This was dealt with in detail in chapter 3.

   The impact of these forces will vary from business to business and will depend, among other things, upon the size of the business, the quality of its management, the finance available to it and the way in which it has developed in the past. Whatever the effect on a business, the business plan must be constantly reassessed and modified to take changing circumstances into account. The managers of even the smallest business need information from both internal sources and external sources.

Internal sources of information

Information from internal sources is found in the records a business keeps. It is tempting in a small business for owners or managers to believe that they can keep all the necessary information in their head. That way lies disaster. It is too easy to convince yourself that a project is possible and will be profitable, whereas five minutes' examination of the records will convince you that it is impracticable. Records may be a simple filing system of all documents or a more elaborate system involving a computer. Whichever is chosen, the records must be kept.

Chapters 5 and 6 are subtitled 'An aid to decision making and control'. Both chapters are concerned with the techniques that can be used to help the businessman pinpoint the problem areas of his business and decide what steps he can take to make them less of a problem. The techniques are useless unless they have accurate and detailed information to work with. A very small business will find the discipline of keeping records sufficient to point up the problems. A larger business must use the techniques outlined in chapters 5 and 6.

Some of these records are for the use of the business alone. Others are needed to enable the businesses to meet the requirements of the law.

Legal obligations

1   *Tax*   People employed by a business have their income tax deducted from their wages before they receive them. This system is known as Pay As You Earn (PAYE). Once the Department of Inland Revenue has decided on the tax code of an individual, the responsibility for ensuring that each person pays the correct amount of tax lies with the employer. Businesses with a large number of employees have found it profitable to computerise their payroll either by contracting out to a computer agency or by installing their own computer system. Tax on business profits is levied on an annual basis using the accounts of the business. It makes sense for a businessman to make sure his records of payments and receipts are accurate in order to avoid paying excess tax.

1   *Value Added Tax*   VAT was introduced in 1973. At the moment it is charged at a rate of 15 per cent on the sale of virtually all goods and services. Necessities such as food for human consumption are zero rated – that is, the tax is 0 per cent. A business charges VAT on all sales to customers and pays this money to Her Majesty's Customs and Excise at the end of each quarter. Any VAT the business has paid to its suppliers is deducted from this total. The business, therefore, pays VAT only on the value it has added to the goods and services it has bought, hence the name of the tax. A business is liable to prosecution if it pays too little tax. Conversely, it makes no sense to pay too much tax. VAT records are therefore important.

3   *The Department of Health and Social Security* (DHSS)   Everyone in full-time employment has to pay National Insurance contributions to contribute to the provision of the health service and social security payments including unemployment benefit. Again, it is the responsibility of the employer to collect these contributions and forward them to the DHSS.

Other records

A business should also keep records of all the activities in which it is engaged. These include:

1   The quantity and money value of raw material, semi-finished and finished goods it is holding as part of its business activity. Collectively these items are referred to as **stock**. Too great a quantity of stock may mean that there is too much money tied up and not enough money to finance other parts of the business. The amount of stock held will depend upon the following:
(a)   The costs of holding stock. If the goods held in stock require constant attention to maintain their usefulness, then this will cost in terms of labour. A stock of coal will cost less to maintain than goods that need refrigeration and checking to make sure they are still saleable.
(b)   The time between reordering and receiving the order is known as the **lead time**. If this is three months for a firm, then that firm will obviously carry more stock than a firm which has a lead time of one week.

(c) A business that has a **seasonal demand** – that is, demand is greater in some parts of the year (such as at Christmas) than at others – will carry a greater stock of finished goods just before the Christmas season than it would at other times of the year. In other words, a business must carry sufficient stock to allow it to meet the demands of its market.

(d) A business might find that if it orders in large quantities it can buy at a lower price. Of course, this must be compared with the costs of storing the goods.

2   The amount of money owed to the business as a result of credit sales (that is, payment to be made in the future rather than when the sale took place). Customers who receive credit sales are known as the **debtors** of the business. Customers who do not pay their bills are receiving an interest-free loan and the business is deprived of cash. Those two reasons alone should convince a businessman that a careful scrutiny of debtors is sensible.

3   The amount of money the business owes to its suppliers. The businesses to which the money is owed are known as the **creditors** of the business. If a business does not pay its debts it gets a bad reputation. People do not lend money or give credit to businesses with bad reputations.

4   A record of sales according to the season of the year, the customer, geographical area, quantity and value can also provide useful information for future planning. This can mean a lower stock level, planned recruitment of staff, meeting customer demand with ease rather than panic measures that cost money in overtime payments to workers.

5   In a small business employing fewer than ten people the owner/manager is probably aware of the strengths and weaknesses of his workforce. In larger businesses and those with the potential to grow larger it is important that personnel records should be kept. A high absentee rate may alert the businessman to other problems.

6   Costs change, and any business must be constantly aware of the changes. An increase in costs will affect profits. The problem is whether or not the increase in costs is temporary. If it is temporary, the business may be able to ignore the increase and endure a lower profit. If it is permanent, then production methods may have to change and prices rise. In turn this may mean redundancies and changes in the attitude of people buying the product. A businessman needs warning of these trends so that he can formulate a plan to deal with them.

7   A cash book should also be kept recording all payments and receipts. At the very least, a cash book tells you how much money you have available.

The larger a business grows the more records it needs to keep so as to provide the managers with the information they need to control the business and make decisions. This increases the amount of form-filling that has to take place and, therefore, increases the work-load on the employees. More people may need to be employed and the costs of the business rise. Computers are useful aids to storing, analysing and reproducing records. Where the burden of filling in forms and providing information becomes too great we describe the situation as a **bureaucracy**. This is derived from the French word for office, *bureau*. It means, in simple terms, an organisation ruled by the needs of the office.

By now you should have realised that starting and running your own business is both more difficult and more complex than simply making a product and trying to sell it.

Conclusion

This chapter has given you some insight into the various activities a business must undertake if it is to function and be successful. In Part II you will study each function in greater depth, but if you are to understand the business world you must remember that a business is a living organism. It is born; it will, eventually, die. The time of its death will depend on the health of the original idea, the care lavished upon it and the world into which it was born.

Case study A: the Baines nursery

Joseph Baines trained as an engineer. When he was in his late twenties his father, who ran a bookmaking business, wanted to retire, and Joseph took over the business. This was located in a suburb of a large city and close to a small group of shops, including a post office and a pub. There was a large general hospital within five minutes' walk. The betting shop was sited in a side road, 20 yards from a major trunk road. The whole cluster of buildings was the remnant of a village that had been swallowed up by ribbon development from the town. When Joseph took the business over it consisted of one shop in a semi-detached cottage. The other cottage was his home.

Within five years Joseph was becoming bored. He was not interested in racing and regarded the management of the shop as an exercise in decision making and administration. On two separate occasions Joseph acquired additional shops, but for a variety of reasons did not regard the ventures as successful and sold both. Opening the second shop had involved him in considerable legal expense as his application for planning permission had been opposed by local residents. This experience had made him wary of legal complications.

In 1986 Joseph Baines was in his mid-forties. His children were independent and were living in other parts of the country. He was unwilling to continue in his present occupation for the rest of his working life. As he saw it there were two alternatives open to him. He could sell his existing business and use the capital to start another business or he could close the business and look for employment. Both alternatives had problems associated with them.

1 He could not think of another field of business enterprise to which his knowledge and experience suited him. His training as an engineer was out of date and his capital was too small to equip an engineering workshop.

2 The interdependence of the house and betting shop proved a handicap in selling the property. Nobody wanted to buy a 4-bedroomed house next door to a betting shop, and a separate purchaser for the betting shop would have had to invest money in providing staff facilities.

3 The area was one of high unemployment and there were few opportunities for a man in his mid-forties.

It was Joseph's wife who suggested a partial solution to the problem. Mary Baines had been working as a voluntary helper in the nursery class of the local school for fifteen years. She had a wide range of friends and acquaintances based on family, work and social contacts. With her family grown up Mary was anxious to work and had already started to take temporary jobs in local shops. Her preference was to work with children, and she suggested to her husband that they should close the shop and open a nursery for two- to five-year-olds.

At first Joseph did not take the idea seriously. It would not solve his employment problem. His involvement with the business would be on a management/administrative level, and he knew that once the business was running satisfactorily he would be under-employed. He did, however, have a great deal of respect for his wife's abilities. He saw her as a shrewd judge of character, a firm but kind manager of children and a hard worker. The nursery had very clear advantages.

1 In the short term it would provide him with employment while he looked for another job.

2 It would provide his wife with long-term employment.

3 It would contribute significantly to the family income, particularly when he was earning.

4 It would use their existing resources productively.

Early in 1986 Mr and Mrs Baines decided to go ahead with their plans to open a nursery.

Market research

The Baineses approached the Social Services Department of their local authority. Officials confirmed that there was a shortage of nursery facilities in the area, the authority itself having only two nurseries some 5 miles from the proposed Baines nursery. Informal canvassing in the district produced an enthusiastic response from parents. Mr Baines also phoned a number of nurseries outside the area, posing as a prospective customer, to find out their charges. These ranged from £30 to £40 per week. The nurseries were open from 8 a.m. to 6 p.m. Further investigation into the legal requirements concerning staffing ratios revealed the fact that there was a high staffing ratio for the under-two age range. On the basis of this research the Baineses designed their product. They did not feel that the accommodation was suitable for this age group.

The product

Nursery services for two- to five-year-olds from 8 a.m. to 6 p.m. inclusive of meals and at a charge of £40 per week for a six-day week. Parents booking their children into the nursery for a limited number of days would be charged a rate of £10 per day. This higher charge was to compensate for potential loss of custom.

The Social Services Department

The social workers and officials of this department were both enthusiastic and helpful. They approved the accommodation for twenty-five subject to agreed alterations at an approximate cost of £10000. The business would need to employ four full-time staff, at least one of whom would be a full-time nursery worker.

Financial projections

The Baineses drew up the financial projection for their first year of trading; this is illustrated in Table 4.1 on the basis of twenty-five children at £40 per week for forty-nine weeks, giving a total annual income of £49 000.

	£	£
Revenue from sales:		49 000
Less: Materials	2 000	
Wages	40 000	
Ins./heating, etc.	1 000	43 000
Gross profit:		6 000
Less: Interest on loan	600	
Tax	1 800	2 400
Net profit after tax:		3 600

Table 4.1 Projected financial statement, first year of trading, Baines nursery

Funding

The Baineses estimated that they would need £15 000 to complete alterations and equip the nursery. They intended to introduce £5 000 from their own resources and borrow £10 000 from their bank. Their bank manager indicated his willingness to make the advance on their financial projections, taking into account their experience and reputation in business.

Marketing

At this stage the Baineses were sufficiently confident of the success of their venture to invest in some publicity. They had three dozen black and white posters printed announcing a proposed nursery which they distributed to libraries and clinics in the area. The response from prospective customers was gratifying. There were sixty enquirers, approximately 75 per cent of whom were prepared to book for the full week and commit themselves to paying for the forty-nine weeks in the year.

Planning permission

The Baineses applied to the local authority for planning permission to change the use of their premises. An inspector from the Highways Department brought their only major setback in the enterprise. He informed them verbally that he would not support their application. He gave the following reasons:

1 proximity to a major road;
2 lack of car-parking facilities for staff;
3 lack of car-parking facilities for parents, which would mean that they would have to park in a narrow road while delivering or collecting their children.

What the Baineses did

- They made contact with the brewery which owned the public house. The entrance to the car park of the pub was directly opposite the proposed nursery and was largely unused during the day. The brewery gave verbal permission for parents and staff to use the car park but refused written permission, citing possible legal complications. The tenant of the pub, however, was prepared to give written permission to use the car park.

- They got in touch with their local councillor and arranged for the hearing of their application before the Planning Sub-committee to be deferred on the grounds that they had been given insufficient time to prepare their case.

Some points to note

1   The mix of motives that went into the decision to start the nursery.

2   The level of the market research. The costs, in time and phone calls, were kept to a minimum until the Baineses were reasonably sure of the viability of their project.

3   The importance of location. The suburban location provided a nucleus of business and professional families who were prepared and able to pay for the services of the nursery. The proximity of two large hospitals increased this catchment area.
    The siting of the buildings was a disadvantage when it came to obtaining planning permission.

4   The importance of experience and reputation when it came to floating a loan. In chapter 6 we will investigate the significance of their personal investment in the enterprise compared with the size of the loan.

5   The external constraints on the Baineses' decisions. These included legal constraints on the number of children they could take, the number of staff to be employed and the minimum facilities which had to be provided. The interpretation that the highways inspector placed on his instructions was also important. This might be classified as an external personnel constraint.

6   The interaction between the economic and political systems is also clearly illustrated. It is the political system which has the power to approve or disapprove the use of resources. It was through the political system (the councillor) that the Baineses gained time to prepare their case.

7   The comparative flexibility in the use of capital as opposed to labour resources. An estimated £15 000 would convert the premises from a bookmaker's shop to a nursery. The time involved would be approximately one month. For Joseph Baines to retrain he would need a minimum of one year, and his fees plus living expenses for his family would require an investment of £10 000.

It would be pleasant to report that the Baines nursery is now in operation. Unfortunately this is a real situation but in chapter 6 we will assume that the Baineses have been given planning permission and use their experiences in setting up the business as an on-going case study.

Case study B: how not to start and run a business

I was a laboratory technician with a multi-national pharmaceutical company. In 1978 they began a rationalisation programme in response to the world recession and the introduction of advanced technology. They needed to shed 500 of the 2 500 employees at the plant where I was employed. The area was one of high unemployment and, mindful of their public image, they offered voluntary redundancy to their employees on very favourable terms. I took it.
    It was a spur-of-the-moment decision – not thought out at all. I was twenty-nine, hated the discipline of arriving for work at a given time – flexi-

time was still a thing of the future – hated taking orders, and thought that running my own business would give me freedom to do just what I liked. I knew it was going to be hard work – how hard I did not appreciate.

My redundancy payment was £10 000. I bought a car for cash which left me with just over £5 000. I decided I would buy a shop. This would provide me with living accommodation as well as a business. The classified advertisements in the local paper gave me several possibilities in what I thought was my price range. I decided on a very busy shop in a small, well-frequented shopping precinct. The price of the business was £19 000. Stock was at valuation (s.a.v.). The business market was not booming at the time, the owners were anxious to sell (they wanted to retire) and I was anxious to buy. It seemed ideal.

I went to my own bank for a loan. The manager was unenthusiastic. He pointed out that the shop was on a comparatively short lease and the bank preferred freehold property as a security for loans. As the stock was valued at £10 000, I would need a loan for £25 000 at least. I could not understand this. I had the audited accounts of the existing business. It would bring me enough money to live on. He asked me if existing suppliers were willing to continue to supply on credit. I was new to business, he said; they might be cautious. The interest on the loan would be a massive burden on the business.

Four banks later I found my funding. A friend helped me draw up an impressive business plan. The maximum the bank would offer was £15 000. I took it and went back to the vendors with a proposition. Would they run down their stock until it was at a level I could afford? They agreed. This was my first big mistake. One of the major attractions of the shop was its wide range of stock and its accessibility. The takings plummeted but the vendors were glad to get rid of the place and I was brimming with confidence that I could build the business up again. I moved in.

I can catalogue my mistakes:

1   I thought that being your own boss meant freedom. I was a slave to that business. I was there from 6 in the morning until 10 at night. If I was not serving I was doing the books. My social life disappeared. I was sleeping and working.

2   I found I did not like people. Dealing with customers is a different matter from meeting people socially. Some dither, some complain and some are downright rude. The shopkeeper has to keep smiling. If you are rude to them they won't come back.

3   I did not keep my records. Customers bought on credit and did not pay promptly. I did not chase them up. That involved writing letters, and at the end of the day I just could not be bothered. The wholesalers were more efficient. I began to find myself with no cash, a bill from a wholesaler for, say, £200, and outstanding customer debts of £300. People don't mind gentle reminders, but a distraught shopkeeper knocking on their door demanding payment can be embarrassing. The customer did not come back.

4   I was not really aware of profit margins. I did not shop around for the cheapest supplier. There were four good cash-and-carry wholesalers in the neighbourhood but I took the easy way out. I dealt with wholesalers who would deliver. Their delivery margins eroded my profit.

5   It took longer to build up the stock the vendors had run down than I had appreciated. For six months I had £10 a week to feed myself and buy other essentials. There were times when I had to choose between food and a visit to the local launderette. Even then I tried new lines rather than relying on the old tried and tested items. Some new lines sold, too many did not.

6   I had not had a structural survey done on the shop. The lease said I was responsible for repairs. The building was old, incorporated into a modern precinct to add character. It needed a great deal of money spent on it. In my naivety I employed a solicitor to argue the case. More money!

The problems built up. I tried to ignore them but my creditors were not so generous. They began bankruptcy proceedings. The court officials served the papers in March 1985. I was glad to be rid of the place.

Case study C: how to start and run your own business

My family are farmers and small businessmen. When I left school I went to agricultural college, then worked in Canada for a couple of years before settling in England. Marriage, two children and the low pay in agriculture set me looking for another job. I went into retail furnishing and, by the time I was thirty, was managing a large furnishing store for a national company. Then the recession hit. People started to find it difficult to make ends meet and the first luxury they cut back on was new furniture. I was made redundant three times in five years. The third time was the last straw. I was unemployed for six months and I made a conscious decision that I would never again be dependent on anybody. I began to think about my own business. I had very clear objectives:

- to be independent;
- to have the time and money to pursue my own interests;
- to work; and
- to give my children a good start in life.

I also made a list of my advantages/disadvantages:

1   I had no money;
2   I had considerable experience and contacts in the furnishing business.

It took me another six months to come up with a viable business idea: carpets. I worked hard on my business plan, though at the time I did not realise that that was what I was doing. I was just determined not to fail. I came up with the following:

1   *Product*   Buying and fitting carpets to order. I rented a small shop in the high street of the local town. I created a display of carpets by using the central cardboard roll and covering them with the scraps of carpet I could buy cheaply from wholesalers as remnants. This gave the illusion of a well-stocked shop. A chair, desk, printed stationery and a number of pattern books were the only additional equipment. I took orders from the pattern books, measured the rooms in the evening and, only then, ordered the carpet. I sold on service.

2   *Market potential*   Small private houses and the occasional business contract. Potential for development into a large-scale business was limited. I did envisage opening several similar shops.

3   *Competitors*   Competition was high. There were two branches of large furnishing businesses in the town. Their delivery times were longer than mine and their service less efficient. For example, if I found the carpet ordered was not in stock at the wholesalers I would call at the house with my samples, give a delivery time and ask if they wanted to re-order. Most

customers chose another pattern and I would have it fitted within the week.

4 *Staff* I was the only employee. After six months I used a self-employed carpet fitter. He was excellent at his job.

5 *Funding* It cost £500 to pay six months' lease on the shop and equip it. I had bought my house for £4 000 and at that time its market value was £17 500. The bank advanced me £2 000 on the security of the house. I was able to pay the loan off in twelve months and negotiate overdraft facilities of £3 000 to finance the Christmas trade. My trade tended to be seasonal. Everybody wanted their new carpet for Christmas. After Christmas they were saving up for their holidays! The overdraft was cleared by the end of February.

6 *Future expansion* I tried expanding twice. The first time I opened a shop organised on the same lines in a very similar area about 12 miles away. It lost money. The second time I bought the paint and wallpaper shop next door. That, too, lost money. I decided to stay with the trade I knew.

Review

1 Read the case studies at the end of the chapter before attempting the following questions:
   (a) Compare and contrast the stated motives of each of the entrepreneurs for starting their own business.
   (b) Using the information given in the chapter analyse the mistakes made by entrepreneur B.
   (c) Explain the reasons for the comparative success of entrepreneur C.

2 When the Albert Dock was built in the nineteenth century it was the world's largest enclosed dock basin and a symbol of Liverpool's dominance as a port. Changes in shipping technology and the decline of the Port of Liverpool left it a derelict monument to past glories. In the early 1980s the Merseyside Development Corporation began an ambitious scheme which converted the existing buildings to provide private apartments, shops, offices and restaurants. The complex also houses television studios and has been awarded a contract for the Tate Gallery. The area now attracts over 1.5 million people each year.
   In the summer of 1986 the visitors included a Chester businessman and his family. For some time he had been considering opening a specialist shop but without any clear idea of the type of goods he would sell. His experience lay in small-scale manufacturing. Until his visit to the Albert Dock he had intended to open the shop in Chester when suitable premises became available. He made some preliminary enquiries and discovered the following information:
   (a) The trading pattern was seasonal. Easter to October was the most profitable period, with a further rise in sales just before Christmas. January to March was relatively quiet.
   (b) Takings varied in one shop from £50 per day in the off season to £1 200 per day in the peak season.
   (c) A twelve-month lease for the size of retail unit in which he was interested was £10 000.
   (d) There were a number of specialist shops already trading, apparently with success.
   The businessman estimated that he had approximately £30 000 to invest in this enterprise and, with his successful record of trading, envisaged no difficulty in obtaining additional capital from his bank.

(i) What additional information would he need before deciding on the type of shop to open?

(ii) From the information given in the passage, outline the advantages of opening a shop in the development rather than in the nearby city centre.

(iii) What risks are associated with this enterprise?

3   Study the extract from the advertisement by Computerland and answer the questions which follow:

Between 1979 and 1981 sales of personal computers rose from £500 million to £2.5 billion. By 1985 they are expected to reach £18.6 billion. As a ComputerLand® franchise owner you would be a member of the world's largest chain of franchised computer retail stores.

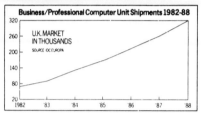

Business/Professional Computer Unit Shipments 1982-88

U.K. MARKET IN THOUSANDS
SOURCE OC EUROPA

Yet you would still manage your own independent business. The huge advantage of franchising is that it allows you to combine your own entrepreneurial spirit with the unparalleled buying power of a major chain.

How do you begin?

A ComputerLand franchise needs a $35,000 franchise fee, plus a minimum investment of £150,000 – £200,000 (depending upon location), of which 50 per cent must be in liquid assets. For this, ComputerLand will set you up as the independent boss of your own ComputerLand store. This includes stock, working capital, professional help with the complete store design, and intensive training. As a ComputerLand owner you will have access to the very best names in computers, software and peripherals, at the very best prices.

* Trademark of the ComputerLand Corporation USA

You will also benefit from our national advertising support and marketing expertise.

How safe is it?

That really depends on you. No ComputerLand owner needs to be a total computer boffin – but you should have a considerable degree of sales or marketing experience and natural business acumen.

One thing is for sure – the ComputerLand franchising formula does work: in 1976 there was only one ComputerLand store. Today there are over 600 successful franchise stores worldwide.

If you are interested in owning your share of the fastest-growing business in the world, just fill in the coupon below. We'll send you a complete portfolio of everything you need to know about becoming a ComputerLand franchise owner.

CONFIDENTIAL COMPUTERLAND PORTFOLIO REQUEST

Send to: Hendrik Vergauwen, Development Manager, ComputerLand Europe S.A.R.L., Dept. 1 ECO 01. Rte de Trèves, L-2632 Findel, Grand Duchy of Luxembourg. Tel: Luxembourg 437751.

YES ☐ I'm interested in finding out more about the opportunities ComputerLand offers its franchisees. Please send my confidential portfolio today. Of course, there's no obligation.

Name_____

Address_____

Phone_____

ComputerLand®
OVER 600 ■ STORES WORLDWIDE
Make friends with the future.

Source: *The Economist*, 28 July 1984

(a) Explain the term franchise in this context.   (2)

(b) Give *three* reasons for buying a franchise.   (3)

(c) What reasons might there be for the company selling franchises instead of opening the shops themselves?   (6)

(d) Examine the graph and identify *three* ways in which it may be misleading.   (9)   1986 (AEB)

Activities

1   Draw up a plan for a small business. The type of business you choose will depend upon your local area. A small shop, a craft workshop or a mini-company based in your school/college are only examples of a wide range of possibilities. To make the exercise worthwhile you will need to discover the full range of costs you are likely to incur: cost of premises, length of lease, heating, lighting and insurance, equipment and its fitting, material supplies and stocks. Research should be undertaken into the market and the suitability of the location, together with possible sources of finance.

2 Invite a bank manager to examine your completed business plan and discuss it with you.

Suggested projects

1 A comparative study of the effect of location on the success of a business.

2 A critical evaluation of a mini-company over a period of twelve months.

Essays

1 The personality of the owner is the most important single factor contributing to the success of a new business. Discuss.

2 Outline the control systems required by a small business and comment on their importance.

Part II

The functions of business

Chapter 5

Statistics: an aid to decision making and control

The problem

Mr Felton, a small manufacturer, felt the need to diversify. He identified a local market for a new product and confirmed its existence by research. The new product was attractive to him because, except for one component, he already had the machinery and expertise available for its manufacture. The component in question was, however, something of a problem. No local firm manufactured it, and firms that did make it used most if not all of their production themselves. They appeared reluctant to increase production to accommodate him.

This doubt about continuity of supply, together with transport costs should he find a willing producer, led Mr Felton to consider manufacturing it himself. He calculated as best he could the additional costs involved: extra labour and/or overtime, training/retraining, energy, the price of the machine, depreciation on the machine, plus the opportunity cost of all the above, minus a possible resale value. He concluded that the project was viable.

The largest immediate outlay concerned the machine necessary to produce the component. There were two machines available, one made by Arundel & Co (which we shall call Machine A) and the other by Butterworth & Sons (Machine B).

There was little difference in the price, Machine A being slightly more expensive. Mr Felton considered leasing, but dismissed the idea as being less potentially profitable than buying.

Raw data

Despite their reluctance to produce for him, Mr Felton found that other manufacturers were willing to help him to the extent of providing production figures. He obtained figures for five machines of each type, all over a period of twelve working weeks – that is, sixty weeks' production figures for each machine. These figures are shown in tables 5.1A and 5.1B.

49	50	51	53	54	56
58	63	40	45	47	48
49	50	52	53	55	56
59	64	41	45	47	49
49	51	52	53	55	57
59	67	42	46	47	50
50	51	52	54	55	57
60	42	44	46	48	33
50	51	52	54	56	58
61	38	45	46	48	43

28	55	47	39	61	52
70	48	42	60	54	47
38	58	51	44	35	56
72	52	46	37	57	50
43	30	55	48	41	60
32	56	49	42	62	54
47	39	59	41	44	66
40	57	52	46	37	58
51	44	33	55	48	65
45	32	56	50	43	64

Table 5.1A (left)
Machine A: the raw data
Table 5.1B (right)
Machine B: the raw data

Mr Felton estimated that he would need to produce at least forty-five components per week, so do these figures help him to decide which machine to purchase?

At first sight the answer must be, 'Not much!' They ought to contain relevant information, but it is far from being immediately obvious. We are in the all too common position of not being able to see the wood for the trees!

The figures, as presented, are what are known as **raw data**. The objective is to compare the performances of two machines, A and B, but there is little hope of any direct help from the raw data

Determining the range

A start can be made on establishing some discipline out of the chaos by rearranging both sets of figures in numerical order. This is done in tables 5.2A and 5.2B.

33	38	40	41	42	42
43	44	45	45	45	46
46	46	47	47	47	48
48	48	49	49	49	49
50	50	50	50	50	51
51	51	51	52	52	52
52	53	53	53	54	54
54	55	55	55	56	56
56	57	57	58	58	59
59	60	61	63	64	67

28	30	32	32	33	35
37	37	38	39	39	40
41	41	42	42	43	43
44	44	44	45	46	46
47	47	47	48	48	48
49	50	50	51	51	52
52	52	54	54	55	55
55	56	56	56	57	57
58	58	59	60	60	61
62	64	65	66	70	72

Table 5.2A (left)
Machine A: sorted data
Table 5.2B (right)
Machine B: sorted data

We can now see at a glance the highest and lowest production figures for each machine. The difference between these extreme values is called the **range**.

Range for A = 67 − 33 = 34
Range for B = 72 − 28 = 44

This points up a difference between the recorded performances of the two machines.

A distribution

Each set of figures is called a **distribution**. What is wanted is a concise set of measures that will describe a distribution without discarding anything essential. We do not want to throw the baby away with the bath-water!

Statistic(s)

Before we go any further we will take a closer look at the differing ways in which we use the word 'statistic(s)'. Each item of raw data is referred to as a statistic (singular). Each measure we develop to describe a distribution is also referred to as a statistic. Collections of items of raw data have been made, mainly by the state for tax purposes, from the earliest recorded times, and include those in our 'Domesday Book'.

The mathematical processes that are employed to develop the 'measures' from the raw data are known, collectively, as 'statistics' (plural). We shall be using statistics to determine two types of 'measure' (each a statistic). The first type, a **measure of the middle**, or **of central tendency**, will be dealt with immediately. The second type, a measure of how the raw data are scattered, or **measure of dispersion**, will be dealt with later in the chapter.

Measures of central tendency

The mid-range
The **mid-range** of a distribution is, as the name implies, a value that lies midway between the extreme values of the distribution.

The constituent of a distribution – in our case, a weekly production figure – is called the **variate**, and the figures themselves are called 'values of the variate'. Hence the mid-range is the number that lies mid-way between the greatest and least values of the variate. It is the **arithmetic mean** of the extreme values of the variate. From Table 5.2 we can see that:

the mid-range for A $= (67 + 33)/2 = 50$
the mid-range for B $= (72 + 28)/2 = 50$

The mode
The individual items of data are the values of the variate, usually designated x. The number of times each value occurs is called the **frequency** of that value, usually designated f. For example, from Table 5.2A, for Machine A, when $x = 50$, $f = 5$ (count them!). The sum of all the frequencies is called the **total frequency**, and is, of course, the total number of individual items, in our case(s) 60.

The value of variate that has the highest frequency is called the **modal value**, or just simply the **mode**. It is quite possible for more than one value of variate to have the same frequency, and for this frequency to be more than all the others. Such a distribution is said to be **multi-modal**.

In order to determine the mode or modes of a distribution, it is necessary to count the number of times each individual value of variate occurs. This is easily done from Table 5.2. The results are shown in tables 5.3A and 5.3B.

We can now see immediately that the modal value for Machine A's distribution is 50. The distribution for Machine B is multi-modal. What are the modal values for Machine B's distribution?

The median
The **cumulative frequency**, designated $c.f.$, of the value of a variate is the frequency of that value plus the frequencies of all values less than it. For example, the $c.f.$ for $x = 42$ is 6, and when $x = 46$, $c.f. = 14$. It is convenient to express the $c.f.$ as a percentage of the total frequency; that is:

$$\frac{c.f.}{\text{Total frequency}} \times 100\%$$

Thus when $x = 46$, $c.f. = 14$ or $1400/60 = 23.33\%$

A full table of cumulative frequencies for Machine A's distribution is given in Table 5.4.

x	f
33	1
38	1
40	1
41	1
42	2
43	1
44	1
45	3
46	3
47	3
48	3
49	4
50	5
51	4
52	4
53	3
54	3
55	3
56	3
57	2
58	2
59	2
60	1
61	1
63	1
64	1
67	1

Table 5.3A (left) Data classified by frequency, Machine A

x	f
28	1
30	1
32	2
33	1
35	1
37	2
38	1
39	2
40	1
41	2
42	2
43	2
44	3
45	1
46	2
47	3
48	3
49	1
50	2
51	2
52	3
54	2
55	3
56	3
57	2
58	2
59	1
60	2
61	1
62	1
64	1
65	1
66	1
70	1
72	1

Table 5.3B (right) Data classified by frequency, Machine B

x	f	c.f.	%
33	1	1	1.67
38	1	2	3.33
40	1	3	5.00
41	1	4	6.67
42	2	6	10.00
43	1	7	11.67
44	1	8	13.33
45	3	11	18.33
46	3	14	23.33
47	3	17	28.33
48	3	20	33.33
49	4	24	40.00
50	5	29	48.33
51	4	33	55.00
52	4	37	61.67
53	3	40	66.67
54	3	43	71.67
55	3	46	76.67
56	3	49	81.67
57	2	51	85.00
58	2	53	88.33
59	2	55	91.67
60	1	56	93.33
61	1	57	95.00
63	1	58	96.67
64	1	59	98.33
67	1	60	100.00

Table 5.4 Cumulative frequencies for Machine A's distribution

The **median** of a distribution is that value which has as many values of variate less than it as it has greater than it. It is the value corresponding to a *c.f.* of 50 per cent. Looking down the column of percentages, we can see that because 50 per cent lies between 48.33 per cent and 55 per cent the median lies between 50 and 51.

A more precise value is obtained by straight (linear) proportion, or interpolation.

$$\frac{Median-50}{51-50} = \frac{50-48.33}{55-48.33}$$

$$= \frac{1.67}{6.67}$$

$$= \ 0.25 \text{ (to two decimal places)}$$

so Median$-50 = \ 0.25$

Median $= 50.25$

SELF-ASSESSMENT

1 Determine the median of Machine B's distribution. (The answers to self-assessment questions in this chapter are on page 84.

The mean

We defined 'mid-range' as the arithmetic mean of the extreme values of variate. The **mean** of a distribution is the arithmetic mean of the whole distribution. It is the **average** value of the variate.

The mean, usually designated *m*, is probably the most important of the measures of central tendency. It certainly crops up very frequently in statistics (plural!).

It can be calculated by adding up all the individual values of *x* and dividing the sum by the total frequency. However, suppose we had a distribution containing 1 000 items and 73 of them were 22, it would surely be rather naïve to add 22 to itself 73 times! Far better to multiply 22 by 73 and so obtain a part total with much less effort.

The mean is calculated by multiplying each value of the variate (*x*) by its corresponding frequency (*f*), adding up these part totals (*fx*), and dividing this sum by the total frequency. This is just an extension of Table 5.3 and is shown in full for Machine A in Table 5.5 on page 72.

SELF-ASSESSMENT

2 Construct a table for Machine B's distribution similar to Table 5.5 and determine its mean.

Grouped data

The mean can be calculated more concisely, and ultimately, more usefully, with a negligible loss of accuracy, by dealing with the values of variate in groups rather than as individuals.

The raw data are split into **classes** of a predetermined size. The chosen size dictates the upper and lower bounds of the classes – that is, the **class limits**. All values of the variate that fall between the same class limits are grouped together in the same class.

x	f	fx
33	1	33
38	1	38
40	1	40
41	1	41
42	2	84
43	1	43
44	1	44
45	3	135
46	3	138
47	3	141
48	3	144
49	4	196
50	5	250
51	4	204
52	4	208
53	3	159
54	3	162
55	3	165
56	3	168
57	2	114
58	2	116
59	2	118
60	1	60
61	1	61
63	1	63
64	1	64
67	1	67
Totals 60		3056

Mean = 50.93

Table 5.5   The mean, Machine A

x	f	fx
35	1	35
40	5	200
45	11	495
50	20	1000
55	14	770
60	6	360
65	3	195
Totals 60		3055

Mean = 50.91

Class width 5

Table 5.7   Calculation of the mean

In what follows a class width of 5 has been choosen. This means that variate values 33, 34, 35, 36 and 37 are grouped in the same class. Variate values 38, 39, 40, 41 and 42 are in the next class and so on, until all the data are exhausted.

The class limits are 32.5, 37.5, 42.5 and so on. These limits reflect the class width, as the difference between successive limits is 5. Note that no value of variate can fall into more than one class.

The grouping is achieved by means of a 'tally sheet'. A tally sheet for Machine A's distribution is shown in Table 5.6. It is **a** tally sheet rather than **the** tally sheet because a different selection of class width would need a different tally sheet. Note the conventional way of ticking off the count in groups of five with every fifth tick used to cross out the previous four.

Range	Tally	Total
33 to 37		1
38 to 42	ⵌ	5
43 to 47	ⵌ ⵌ	11
48 to 52	ⵌ ⵌ ⵌ ⵌ	20
53 to 57	ⵌ ⵌ ||||	14
58 to 62	ⵌ |	6
63 to 67	|||	3

Table 5.6   A tally sheet

SELF-ASSESSMENT

3 Draw up a tally sheet, class width 5, similar to Table 5.6, for Machine B's distribution.

The mid-point of each class is taken to represent all the values in that class, and this is used as the value of x. The total number of individuals in each class is called the 'class frequency', and is again designated f. These values of x and f are now used to find the mean of the distribution. The method, which is shown in Table 5.7 for Machine A, is similar to our previous calculation (Table 5.5) but much more concise.

Compare the value obtained in 5.7 with that of 5.5. Remembering that in this problem we are dealing with components, and therefore whole numbers, is the difference significant? A different choice of class width will produce a different value for the mean. The larger the class width the more values of variate the midpoint is being called upon to represent. The smaller the class width the nearer the calculated mean will come to the value found by Table 5.5. In fact, Table 5.5 can be thought of as a calculation of grouped data, with a class width of one!

SELF-ASSESSMENT

4 Use your tally sheet of self-assessment question 3 to find the mean of Machine B's distribution using grouped data.

Illustrating the data

Consider two plane triangles.

Triangle 1 has sides 22 cm by 34 cm by 51 cm.
Triangle 2 has sides 18 cm by 40 cm by 49 cm.

Compare the two triangles. What can be said about them? They both have three sides! Their perimeters are identical. But they are not the same triangle, are they? In what way are they different?

A very simple way of showing up their differences, or at least some of them is to *draw them to scale*. It has been said that one good political cartoon is worth a thousand words of polemic. The same is true about the presentation of statistics.

We have two distributions. Each contains 60 values of variate. Their means are quite close. But they are from different makes of machine, so in what way or ways are they different? We can adopt the same stratagem, and draw them to scale.

The bar chart

In the bar chart each class is represented by a thick horizontal line. (Some bar charts are shown by means of vertical lines, but this is to be avoided, at least at first, as it can lead to confusion. We will return to this point later.)

The *length* of the line for each class is proportional to the frequency of that class. It is conventional, though by no means universal, to leave a blank space between adjacent lines. A tally sheet is used as before to determine class frequencies. This has been done to help construct a bar chart for Machine A's distribution, shown in Figure 5.1.

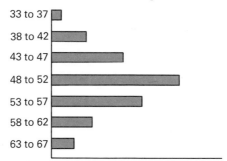

Figure 5.1 The bar chart for Machine A's distribution

SELF-ASSESSMENT

5 Use your tally sheet to construct a bar chart for Machine B's distribution.

By looking at the two bar charts we can see that the two distributions are indeed different.

A word of caution. It would be foolish at this stage to start thinking about which machine is the 'better'. It is very easy indeed to misinterpret a diagram, unless you keep firmly in mind what the various parts of the diagram represent.

The pie chart

In the bar chart the frequencies were represented by lengths of lines. In the pie chart, or pie diagram, the frequencies are represented by areas of slices of a circular pie – that is, by sectors of a circle. The areas of different sectors of the same circle are proportional to the angles of the sectors, so the angles of the different slices are proportional to the class frequencies. The complete angle at the centre of a circle is 360°, so a frequency of, say, 30 in a distribution of total frequency 200 would be represented by a sector of angle

$$\frac{30 \times 360°}{200} = 54°$$

The pie chart for Machine A's distribution is shown in Figure 5.2.

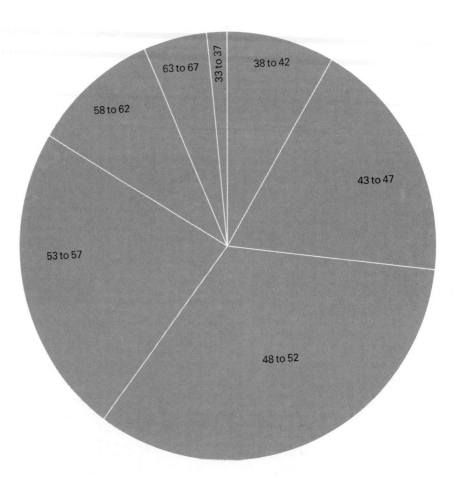

Figure 5.2   The pie chart for Machine A's distribution

The ogive

The ogive is the name given to the graph of cumulative frequency against value of the variate. The graph (shown in Figure 5.3 for Machine A's distribution) is a series of straight line segments. It is common practice to 'smooth out' the graph by drawing a continuous curve through the points.

The histogram

The distribution is illustrated in a histogram by a series of vertical rectangles. The *widths* of the rectangles are proportional to the class widths, and the *areas* of the rectangles are proportional to the class frequencies.

If the class widths are all the same, the areas are proportional to the heights of the rectangles and hence the heights are proportional to the class frequencies.

It must be stressed that this only occurs if the class widths are all equal. If the class widths differ, then the heights have to be adjusted so that the areas represent the class frequencies.

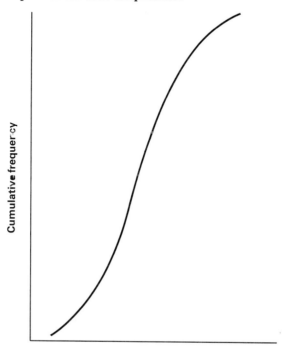

Figure 5.3   The ogive for Machine A's distribution

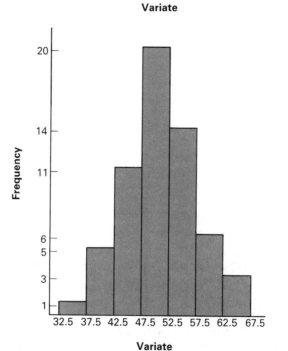

Figure 5.4   The histogram for Machine A's distribution

Figure 5.4 is the histogram for Machine A's distribution with equal class widths of 5. Since the left-hand rectangle represents a frequency of only 1, it would in some circumstances be reasonable to combine the first two rectangles. The frequency represented by the first rectangle would then be 6, and the class width 10 (twice the class width of all the others) and so the height of the rectangle would be 3.

A histogram is *not* a bar chart. If all the class widths are equal they look very similar. It is essential to remember that in the histogram it is the areas that represent the frequencies. To avoid possible confusion, it is advisable to construct horizontal bar charts, with a space between the bars.

The frequency polygon

The frequency polygon is formed by joining the mid-points of the tops of the rectangles by straight lines. It is conventional to imagine an extra class with frequency zero, at either end, thus completing the polygon. The frequency polygon for Machine A is shown in Figure 5.5.

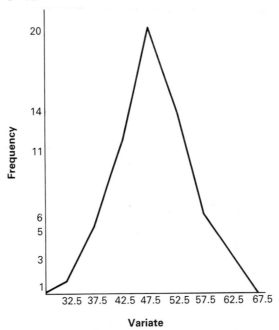

Figure 5.5   The frequency polygon for Machine A's distribution

Figure 5.6 shows the polygon superimposed upon the histogram. Elementary geometry can be used to show that

area of triangle a = area of triangle b
area of triangle c = area of triangle d
area of triangle e = area of triangle f
area of triangle g = area of triangle h
area of triangle i = area of triangle j
area of triangle k = area of triangle l
area of triangle m = area of triangle n
area of triangle o = area of triangle p

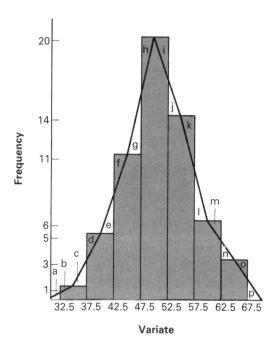

Figure 5.6 The polygon superimposed upon the histogram

Subtracting from the histogram triangles b,d,f,h,i,k,m, and o and adding on triangles a,c,e,g,j,l,n, and p turns the histogram into the polygon. It follows that the area of the polygon is equal to the area of the histogram and represents the total frequency of the distribution. This is an important point to which we will return later.

Measures of dispersion

We have dealt with finding the middle of the distribution – the measures of central tendency – but these do not tell us how the values are distributed about the middle.

Look at the following two distributions of numbers:

X   5,5,6,6,7,8,8,9,9

Y   1,1,2,3,4,4,5,6,7,8,9,10,11,12,13,13

Both have a mean of 7, but the numbers in Y are much more scattered or dispersed than those in X. Such scattering is referred to as variation or dispersion.

We have already met one measure of dispersion, the range, from which it is easy to determine the more usual statistic, the half-range. It is rather crude, and does not tell us very much.

Quartiles, deciles, percentiles

The median, you will recall, is that value which has as many values less than it as it has greater than it. More succinctly, it is the 50 per cent value. The **quartiles** are the 25 per cent (lower quartile) and the 75 per cent (upper quartile) values. The median is the middle quartile. Upper quartile minus lower quartile is called the **inter-quartile range**.

As their name implies, the **deciles** are the 10, 20, 30 per cent values (and so on), while the **percentiles** are the 1, 2, 3, 4 per cent values (and so on).

Deviation

The **deviation** of a variate is defined as the value of the variate minus the mean. It is, strictly, the deviation from the mean, but is rarely given the longer title. Each value of variate will have its associated deviation, so there are as many deviations as there are values of variate. Just as we wanted a single measure of central tendency, we would also like a single measure of dispersion.

The mean deviation

The average or arithmetical mean of the deviations seems the obvious measure to go for. However, a word of caution: if we simply multiply each deviation by its frequency, add up the products and divide by the total frequency, we must of necessity get an arithmetic mean of zero!

A little thought will reveal why this must be so. If we reduce every value of the variate by, say, 5, then the value of the mean must reduce by 5. If we increase every value by 10, we will increase the mean value by 10. It follows then that if we decrease every value of the variate (x) by the value of the mean (m), which is what is done to find the deviation, it follows that we reduce the mean value by m, and hence get zero as a result.

To avoid this obviously useless measure of dispersion, the *absolute* values of the deviations are taken. The absolute value of $x - m$ is $x - m$ if x is greater than m, and $m - x$ if x is less than m. Either can be taken when $x = m$. Another way of expressing this is to say we take the difference between x and m. The word 'difference' implies that we take the smaller from the larger.

The standard deviation

It turns out that the mean deviation is not a very useful measure of dispersion. It does not lend itself very happily to manipulation. There is, however, another method of avoiding the negative values of deviation thrown up by $x - m$, and that is to square them, since the square of any number cannot be negative.

The mean of these squares is called the **variance**, and the positive square root of the variance is called the **standard deviation**.

We take each deviation, $x - m$, and square it. Then we multiply the result by its frequency, and total up these products. Dividing the sum of the products by the total frequency gives the variance, and taking the positive square root of this gives the standard deviation.

Students of mechanics, or applied mathematics, may recognise that, just as finding the mean of a distribution is like finding the position of the centre of gravity of a system of weights, the standard deviation of a distribution is analogous to the radius of gyration of a system.

On the other hand, students of electricity, who have studied AC theory, may realise that we have taken the mean of the squares of the deviations, and then taken the square root of this mean of squares; that is, we have the root mean square or RMS value of the deviations.

The standard deviation is designated s, and its calculation for Machine A's distribution is shown in Table 5.8. The table repeats the evaluation of the mean from Table 5.7, of which it is an extension, so as to bring the whole calculation together.

Populations and samples

We started out with a set of production figures for each of two machines. These machines have, presumably, been producing in the past, and are

x	f	fx	$(x-m)$	$(x-m)^2$	$f(x-m)^2$
35	1	35	-15.92	253.34	253.34
40	5	200	-10.92	119.17	595.86
45	11	495	-5.92	35.00	385.07
50	20	1000	-0.92	0.84	16.80
55	14	770	4.08	16.67	233.43
60	6	360	9.08	82.50	495.04
65	3	195	14.08	198.34	595.02
Totals	60	3055			2574.58

Table 5.8   Standard deviation of Machine A's distribution

Mean = 50.91
Variance = 42.9
St. deviation = 6.55
Class width 5

continuing to produce now, and will do so into the future. The raw data we started with are a **sample** of the production figures. The complete production figures constitute what is called the **population**. You may be familiar with these terms from such things as opinion polls. A sample of those people eligible to vote is taken and this sample represents the population of those eligible to vote. It is very rare indeed to be able to deal with a complete population. It is often far too big, and may even be endless – that is, an **infinite population**. All that can be done realistically is to take a sample of manageable size, find some things out about the sample, and assume that these things hold good for the whole population. There are various techniques to assist in getting a representative sample, and of assessing the likelihood that it is representative, but they are beyond the scope of our present task. All that will be said is that they work pretty well when dealing with things (production figures, for example), but not when people are involved.

Mr Felton has obtained a sample for each of two machines. He has no way of knowing whether the samples are truly representative or whether, in the jargon of statistics, they are proper **random** samples. They are all he has, and he must make do with them in deciding which of the two machines to purchase.

The normal distribution

It was said earlier, when dealing with the ogive, that it is usual to draw a smooth curve through the points. This is usually a reasonably easy operation. Doing the same thing with a frequency polygon is by no means as simple. The best way of solving an awkward problem is not to have the problem in the first place. There is no real need to draw an accurate smooth curve through the points (vertices) of the polygon.

It is not necessary to draw the curve to realise that it will have a 'bell-like' shape. The larger the sample – that is, the more data that are obtained – the more the shape will tend to be bell-like. Experience has shown the validity of this last statement. A distribution of measurements becomes more and more bell-like as the amount of data increases – that is, as more measurements are taken.

The mathematician Karl Fredrich Gauss discovered a curve that has this distinctive bell-like shape. Its formula, which he developed from a consideration of probabilities and their attendant histograms, is

$$y = \frac{1}{\sqrt{2\pi}} \, \mathrm{Exp} - (0.5 \, x^2)$$

Figure 5.7 shows the curve we are talking about.

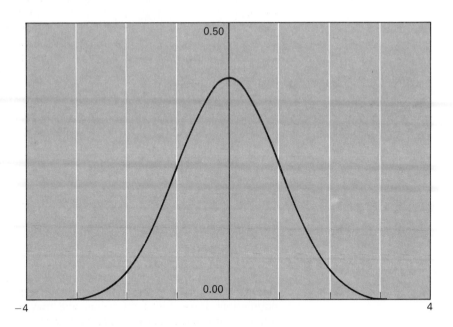

Figure 5.7   The normal curve

This curve is the 'smoothed' polygon of a distribution that has a mean of zero and a standard deviation of 1 – that is, unity. Incidentally, its mode and median are also zero. The total area under the curve is 1, unity. It dies away very rapidly at its extremes, so that despite the fact that it goes on forever in either direction, the whole area can be considered to be confined between x = − 4 and x = 4. For $x = 4$, $y = 0.00005339$, so you can see that there cannot be much area lying to the right of $x = 4$!

The curve is symmetrical about $x = 0$, so we can say that for $x > 0$ the area is 0.5, and for $x < 0$ the area is 0.5.

Also we can say that the area contained between say $x = − 2$ and $x = 0$ is the same as the area contained between $x = 0$ and $x = 2$. We shall find the last two statements very useful in what follows.

Because experience has shown that a distribution involving measurement tends towards this shape for its 'smoothed' polygon, as the amount of data increases, it has become known as the **normal** shape of the population distribution, and is referred to as the curve of the **normal distribution**.

However, the distributions we have do not have (a) total area of 1; (b) mean of zero; or (c) standard deviation of 1.

These are quite minor hiccups because they are easily dealt with by means of some simple algebraic manipulations which do not alter the shape of the frequency polygon, and hence of the curve.

(a)   The area under the polygon equals the area under the histogram. This area represents the total frequency, hence to reduce the area to unity all that is needed is to divide each frequency by the total frequency, and consequently the total frequency, by the total frequency. A variate's frequency divided by the total frequency is called the **relative frequency** of the variate. It measures how likely the variate is to occur in the distribution. It amounts to the *probability* that the value of variate occurs. So far as the curve is concerned, all it does is to change the scale of the vertical (the *f*) axis.

(b) In considering the mean deviation it was pointed out that reducing every value of variate by the same amount resulted in reducing the mean by exactly the same amount. It is easy, therefore, to obtain a zero mean for any distribution. All that is necessary is to reduce every value of the variate by the value of the mean. In symbols x is replaced by $x - m$. So far as the curve is concerned, all this does is to shift the origin from the value of the mean of the distribution to zero, the new mean. Usually, and for distributions involving measurements certainly, the curve shifts to the left.

(c) $x - m$ is, of course, the deviation of x from the mean. Dividing each deviation by the same amount will divide the standard deviation by the same amount. (Think about it!) It follows then that dividing each deviation by the standard deviation will automatically create a standard deviation of unity. So far as the curve is concerned all this does is to change the scale of the horizontal (the x) axis.

The variate has been changed from x to $(x - m)/s$. This is usually designated as z, that is:

$$z = \frac{x - m}{s}$$

Any smoothed polygon will conform approximately to the normal curve provided the value of each variate (x) is replaced by its corresponding z value. The z values are called the **normalised** or **standardised** values. In some contexts they are called standardised scores.

In (a) above, it was remarked that areas under the curve now represent probabilities. The area between two z values represents the probability that z lies between the two values. It also, consequently, represents the probability that x lies between the corresponding two x values. Table 5.9 is a table of areas under the normal curve. The shaded area in the diagram above it indicates the area that is obtained from the table; z is entered to two decimal places, the integral part and first decimal from the left-hand column, and the second decimal from the top row. For example, to find the area corresponding to $z = 1.45$ look down the left-hand column to 1.4 and then along the row under 5. The number .4265 is the area under the curve between $z = 0$ and $z = 1.45$. It is the probability that z lies between 0 and 1.45.

The area between any two z values can be found by exploiting the symmetry of the curve about zero, and the fact that the total area is unity.

Examples

1 Given that a certain distribution has a mean of 57 and standard deviation 4, find the probability that a value of the variate is less than or equal to 62.

We have $x = 62$, $m = 57$, and $s = 4$ so the corresponding value is given by

$$z = \frac{62 - 57}{4} = \frac{5}{4} = 1.25$$

From Table 5.9 we obtain the number, .3944. A rough sketch (left) is useful in answering a question like this.

The area marked (a) in the sketch is .3944, whereas we want (a) + (b), that is, z less than or equal to 1.25. Area (b) is half the area under the curve – that is, 0.5 – so the required area and hence the probability that x is less than or equal to 62 is $0.3944 + 0.5 = 0.8944$.

This means that between 89 per cent and 90 per cent (89.44 per cent) of the values of the variate are less than or equal to 62.

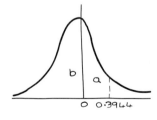

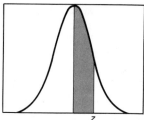

z	0	1	2	3	4	5	6	7	8	9
0.0	.0000	.0040	.0080	.0120	.0160	.0199	.0239	.0279	.0319	.0359
0.1	.0398	.0438	.0478	.0517	.0557	.0596	.0636	.0675	.0714	.0754
0.2	.0793	.0832	.0871	.0910	.0948	.0987	.1026	.1064	.1103	.1141
0.3	.1179	.1217	.1255	.1293	.1331	.1368	.1406	.1443	.1480	.1517
0.4	.1554	.1591	.1628	.1664	.1700	.1736	.1772	.1808	.1844	.1879
0.5	.1915	.1950	.1985	.2019	.2054	.2088	.2123	.2157	.2190	.2224
0.6	.2258	.2291	.2324	.2357	.2389	.2422	.2454	.2486	.2518	.2549
0.7	.2580	.2612	.2642	.2673	.2704	.2734	.2764	.2794	.2823	.2852
0.8	.2881	.2910	.2939	.2967	.2996	.3023	.3051	.3078	.3106	.3133
0.9	.3159	.3186	.3212	.3238	.3264	.3289	.3315	.3340	.3365	.3389
1.0	.3413	.3438	.3461	.3485	.3508	.3531	.3554	.3577	.3599	.3621
1.1	.3643	.3665	.3686	.3708	.3729	.3749	.3770	.3790	.3810	.3830
1.2	.3849	.3869	.3888	.3907	.3925	.3944	.3962	.3980	.3997	.4015
1.3	.4032	.4049	.4066	.4082	.4099	.4115	.4131	.4147	.4162	.4177
1.4	.4192	.4207	.4222	.4236	.4251	.4265	.4279	.4292	.4306	.4319
1.5	.4332	.4345	.4357	.4370	.4382	.4394	.4406	.4418	.4429	.4441
1.6	.4452	.4463	.4474	.4484	.4495	.4505	.4515	.4525	.4535	.4545
1.7	.4554	.4564	.4573	.4582	.4591	.4599	.4608	.4616	.4625	.4633
1.8	.4641	.4649	.4656	.4664	.4671	.4678	.4686	.4693	.4699	.4706
1.9	.4713	.4719	.4726	.4732	.4738	.4744	.4750	.4756	.4761	.4767
2.0	.4772	.4778	.4783	.4788	.4793	.4798	.4803	.4808	.4812	.4817
2.1	.4821	.4826	.4830	.4834	.4838	.4842	.4846	.4850	.4854	.4857
2.2	.4861	.4864	.4868	.4871	.4875	.4878	.4881	.4884	.4887	.4890
2.3	.4893	.4896	.4898	.4901	.4904	.4906	.4909	.4911	.4913	.4916
2.4	.4918	.4920	.4922	.4925	.4927	.4929	.4931	.4932	.4934	.4936
2.5	.4938	.4940	.4941	.4943	.4945	.4946	.4948	.4949	.4951	.4952
2.6	.4953	.4955	.4956	.4957	.4959	.4960	.4961	.4962	.4963	.4964
2.7	.4965	.4966	.4967	.4968	.4969	.4970	.4971	.4972	.4973	.4974
2.8	.4974	.4975	.4976	.4977	.4977	.4978	.4979	.4979	.4980	.4981
2.9	.4981	.4982	.4982	.4983	.4984	.4984	.4985	.4985	.4986	.4986
3.0	.4987	.4987	.4987	.4988	.4988	.4989	.4989	.4989	.4990	.4990
3.1	.4990	.4991	.4991	.4991	.4992	.4992	.4992	.4992	.4993	.4993
3.2	.4993	.4993	.4994	.4994	.4994	.4994	.4994	.4995	.4995	.4995
3.3	.4995	.4995	.4995	.4996	.4996	.4996	.4996	.4996	.4996	.4997
3.4	.4997	.4997	.4997	.4997	.4997	.4997	.4997	.4997	.4997	.4998
3.5	.4998	.4998	.4998	.4998	.4998	.4998	.4998	.4998	.4998	.4998
3.6	.4998	.4998	.4999	.4999	.4999	.4999	.4999	.4999	.4999	.4999
3.7	.4999	.4999	.4999	.4999	.4999	.4999	.4999	.4999	.4999	.4999
3.8	.4999	.4999	.4999	.4999	.4999	.4999	.4999	.4999	.4999	.4999
3.9	.5000	.5000	.5000	.5000	.5000	.5000	.5000	.5000	.5000	.5000

Table 5.9   The normal distribution

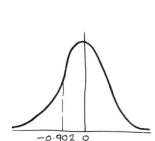

2   For the same distribution, what is the probability that x is less than or equal to 49?

$$z = \frac{49 - 57}{4} = \frac{-8}{4} = -2$$

Again a rough sketch (left) will help.

Again the required area is the left-hand tail, this time from $z = -2$ downwards, area (a) in the sketch. Negative values do not appear in the table, but we can again exploit the curve's symmetry about zero. The area from $z = -2$ to $z = 0$ (area (b)) is the same as the area between $z = 0$ and $z = +2$ (area (c)).

From the table:

$$\text{Area (c)} = 0.4772$$
$$\text{therefore area (b)} = 0.4772$$
$$\text{but area (a) + area (b)} = 0.5$$
$$\text{therefore area (a)} = 0.5 - 0.4772 = 0.1227$$

Let us now return to Mr Felton's problem, recalling that he had estimated that he would require at least forty-five components a week.

For Machine A we have $x = 45$, $m = 50.91$, and $s = 6.55$, so

$$z = \frac{45 - 50.91}{6.55} = \frac{-5.91}{6.55} = -0.902$$

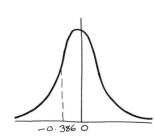

From the table:

with $z = 0.90$ we get 0.3159
with $z = 0.91$ we get 0.3186
so with $z = 0.902$ we get 0.3164 by interpolation.

The area for z greater than or equal to -0.902 (x greater than or equal to 45) is $0.3164 + 0.5 = 0.8164$.

For Machine B we have $x = 45$, $m = 48.83$, and $s = 9.93$, so

$$z = \frac{45 - 48.83}{9.93} = \frac{-3.83}{9.93} = -0.386$$

From the table:

with $z = 0.38$ we get 0.1480
with $z = 0.39$ we get 0.1517
so with $z = 0.386$ we get 0.1502 by interpolation.

The area for z greater than or equal to -0.386 (x greater than or equal to 45) is $0.1502 + 0.5 = 0.6502$.

This means that on this evidence, and it is all Mr Felton has got, Machine A would be expected to attain or exceed the required production of components 81.64 per cent of the time, while Machine B would be expected to do it 65.02 per cent of the time.

Now it is up to Mr Felton. There are further tests he could do if he is still undecided. There is a test of whether or not there is any difference between the machines. This could be done by hypothesising that both distributions are from the same population. The test, which is beyond the scope of this chapter, would give the probability that they are from the same population. There is then a technique for assessing how likely it is that an error has occurred.

The mathematics cannot make his decision for him. Both machines average above his projected requirements. Machine B is slightly cheaper than Machine A. Are they equally reliable? Would exceeding forty-five components per week, so as to build up a stock to cover underproductive weeks, involve him in overtime payments? What about storage costs? Items in stock are an asset, but are in effect dead money.

It is his money and it is his decision.

Solutions to self-assessment questions

Self-assessment question 1   48

Solution to self-assessment question 2

x	f	fx
28	1	28
30	1	30
32	2	64
33	1	33
35	1	35
37	2	74
38	1	38
39	2	78
40	1	40
41	2	82
42	2	84
43	2	86
44	3	132
45	1	45
46	2	92
47	3	141
48	3	144
49	1	49
50	2	100
51	2	102
52	3	156
54	2	108
55	3	165
56	3	168
57	2	114
58	2	116
59	1	59
60	2	120
61	1	61
62	1	62
64	1	64
65	1	65
66	1	66
70	1	70
72	1	72
	60	2943

Mean = 49.05

Solution to self-assessment question 3

Range	Tally	Total
28 to 32	IIII	4
33 to 37	IIII	4
38 to 42	HHT III	8
43 to 47	HHT HHT I	11
48 to 52	HHT HHT I	11
53 to 57	HHT HHT	10
58 to 62	HHT II	7
63 to 67	III	3
68 to 72	II	2

Solution to self-assessment question 4

x	f	fx
30	4	120
35	4	140
40	8	320
45	11	495
50	11	550
55	10	550
60	7	420
65	3	195
70	2	140
Totals	60	2930

Mean = 48.83

Class width 5

Solution to self-assessment question 5

28 to 32
33 to 37
38 to 42
43 to 47
48 to 52
53 to 57
58 to 62
63 to 67
68 to 72

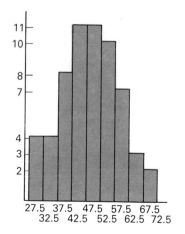 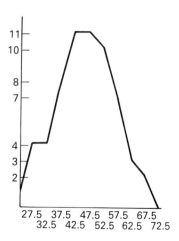

27.5 37.5 47.5 57.5 67.5
   32.5 42.5 52.5 62.5 72.5

Solution to self-assessment question 6

Review

1 Calculate the mean and standard deviation of Machine B's distribution using a class width of 5, and hence confirm the figure of 65.02 per cent given in the text.

2 A company produces cylindrical iron bars by a continuous extrusion and cropping process. One machine is set to produce bars 10 metres in length with a tolerance of 25 mm – that is, the length required is within the range 10 ± 0.025 metres.

   The output is monitored by taking a random sample of 100 bars every week and measuring them individually. The results from one week's sample is shown in the table below (measurements in mm).

9955	9962	9966	9967	9971	9975	9978	9980	9983	9983
9985	9985	9987	9987	9988	9988	9988	9991	9991	9992
9993	9994	9995	9995	9995	9996	9996	9996	9997	9997
9997	9997	9998	9998	9998	9998	9998	9998	9999	9999
10001	10002	10003	10003	10003	10003	10004	10004	10004	10004
10005	10005	10005	10005	10005	10006	10006	10006	10006	10006
10007	10007	10007	10008	10008	10009	10009	10009	10009	10011
10011	10011	10012	10012	10013	10014	10015	10015	10016	10016
10017	10017	10017	10019	10019	10022	10023	10023	10026	10027
10029	10030	10030	10032	10034	10036	10040	10043	10047	10054

Use these figures to determine:
(a) what percentage of output can be expected to be acceptable;
(b) what percentage can be made acceptable by grinding because they are too big.
   (*Hint*: Use a class width of 10.)

3 Undersized bars are recycled. It is considered that not more than 10 per cent recycling is acceptable.

   In the subsequent four weeks the following results were obtained:

	mean	*st.dev.*
Week 2	10004.73	17.80
Week 3	10004.85	18.48
Week 4	10004.68	18.96
Week 5	10004.54	19.49

Assuming that this trend continues determine, graphically or otherwise, how long it will be before the machine requires resetting?

4   The local librarian wishes to discover what the local population thinks of the service the library provides. He decides to set a questionnaire.
(a) What factors need to be kept in mind when compiling any questionnaire?   (6)
(b) The replies to the question 'Which of the following do you consider should be given top priority?' are given below.

Alternative answers	Men	Women	Children
Increase the number of library staff	2	6	4
Extend hours of opening	22	10	6
Buy more fiction books	20	32	25
Buy more non-fiction books	16	27	10

   (i) Draw a bar chart to illustrate the above data.   (5)
   (ii) Comment on how well you think your bar chart presents this information.   (2)
   (iii) How does a histogram differ from a bar chart?   (2)
(c) 60% of those surveyed said that they were satisfied with the service provided by the library. Can the librarian be confident that the majority of the local population would agree with this view if the sample size was:
   (i) 100;   (2)
   (ii) 200?   (2)
   (iii) What assumptions have you made in your answers to the above?   (1)
(d) Discuss the advantages and disadvantages of the various ways the librarian could distribute the questionnaire. How could the method of distribution affect the results obtained?   (5)   1986 (CLES)

5   (a) Explain the differences between the following types of sample:
   (i) random,
   (ii) stratified,
   (iii) quota.   (6)
(b) A firm wishes to fix a piece work rate for its employees and to do this it needs to know the average number of operations per person per day. Rather than make this calculation for all its staff, the firm decides to take a sample.
   (i) Describe how the firm might decide on the kind and size of sample it would need.   (4)
   (ii) Discuss which of the measures of central tendency would be the most appropriate to use and explain why you think this is the case.   (4)
(c) Suppose that workmen had previously been paid a flat rate of £25 per day, on the basis of an arithmetic average of 100 operations per day. Suggest why, and at what levels of operations, you might introduce bonus payments, if the results of the sample showed that the arithmetic mean was 100 operations, with a standard deviation of 30. (You may use the table below if you think this is appropriate.)   (5)

Proportionate parts of the area under the normal curve

Distances from Mean in terms of standard deviation in one direction	0–1	1–2	2–3	over 3
Proportion of area in above range	34%	14%	2%	Negligible

(d) Suppose a workman performed the following set of operations over a 10 day period:

180   180   150   130   190   200   150   160   170   180

What would you conclude about the workman and/or the sample results? Explain your reasons. (You may assume that the standard deviation remains at 30.)   (6)   1985 (CLES)

6   The data given below refer to a manufacturing company, XYZ Ltd. In 1970 the company employed a workforce of 2000, but by 1983 this number had dropped to 1000.

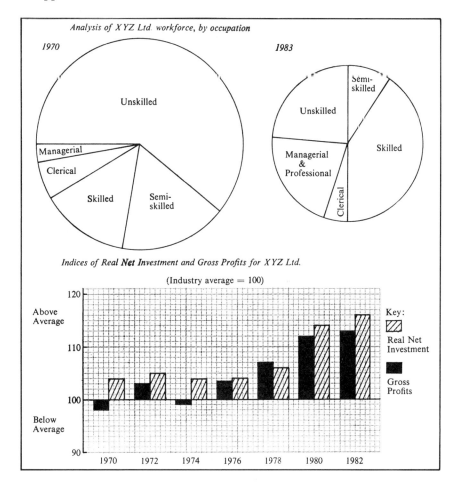

Analysis of XYZ Ltd. workforce, by occupation

Indices of Real *Net* Investment and Gross Profits for XYZ Ltd.

(a) State *one* advantage and *one* disadvantage of presenting data in the form of a pie chart.   (4)
(b) Give *one* reason why the pie charts above are of different sizes.   (3)
(c) Describe briefly the changes that have taken place in Company XYZ between 1970 and 1983.   (5)
(d) Using the data given above, state and explain *one* possible reason for the decline in the number of people employed by XYZ Ltd.   (4)
(e) Outline *three* problems the company might have faced as a result of the changing occupational structure of the workforce.   (9)   1985 (AEB)

Activity

Visit a local supermarket and, with the manager's permission, record:
(a) the number of customers who approach the checkout in at least twelve five-minute periods;
(b) how long the cashier takes to deal with each customer; and
(c) the length of the queue.

From (a) calculate the *mean* (m) number of customers in a five-minute period.

The **Poisson distribution**, named after a French mathematician, can be used to calculate the probability that a chosen number of customers will arrive at the checkout in a five-minute period.

The formula is:

Probability that r customers arrive, $p(r) = EXP(-m) \times m^r/r!$
where m is the mean and r! is r factorial (that is, r multiplied by every positive whole number less than r).
For example, $5! = 5 \times 4 \times 3 \times 2 \times 1$

You do not need statistical tables to calculate these probabilities. The exponential function (Exp) is given in most sets of four-figure tables and on many hand-held calculators, though it usually appears in the form e^x or Inverse Ln(x). Remember that e^{-x} is the reciprocal of e^x.

Calculate $p(0)$, $p(1)$, $p(2)$, $p(3)$ and so on until the number obtained is less than 0.01.

This task is not as horrendous as it first appears. We have

$$p(r) = e^{-m} \times m^r/r!$$
and $\quad p(r+1) = e^{-m} \times m^{(r+1)}/(r+1)!$

Now $m^{r+1)} = m^r \times m$ (law of indices) and $(r+1)! = (r+1) \times r!$ so
$$p(r+1) = p(r) \times m/(r+1)$$
For example: $p(5) = p(4) \times m/5$

This is an example of what a mathematician calls a recurrence relation.

Factorial zero is defined as unity, i.e. $0! = 1$ and $m^o = 1$ so $p(0)$ is very simple:

$$p(0) = e^{-m}$$
then $p(1) = p(0) \times m$
$\quad p(2) = p(1) \times m/2$
$\quad p(3) = p(2) \times m/3$ etc ... etc.

carry on until $p(r) < 0.01$ and then reduce the probabilities to two decimal places.

Next calculate the probabilities of the times the cashier takes to deal with a customer. This is simply:

$$p(\text{a customers takes } x \text{ minutes}) = \frac{\text{Number of customers taking } x \text{ minutes}}{\text{Total number of customers}}$$

We now have two sets of probabilities. The situation can be simulated by means of a table of random numbers. Many books on statistics contain such a table, as do books of statistical tables, and again many hand-held calculators have a random number facility. Assign the 100 pairs of numbers from 00 to 99 first to the probabilities of customer arrival and then to the probabilities of times, in proportion to the size of the probabilities.
For example: If $p(0) = 0.04$, $p(0)$ is assigned the numbers 00, 01, 02 and 03 and if $p(1) = 0.07$, $p(1)$ is assigned the numbers 04, 05, 06, 07, 08, 09, 10 and so on. You should find that you use up all 100 pairs.

Start anywhere in the table of random numbers and, going in any direction, pick a pair of digits. This pair will give the number of customers in a five-minute period. The subsequent pairs of numbers give the length of time each customer in turn takes at the checkout. From these numbers see how a queue builds up and compare its length with the lengths recorded in (c) above.

The five-minute period is by no means sacrosanct. If a sufficient number of recorders are available and the supermarket is busy enough, a one-minute period may be more appropriate.

It does not have to be a supermarket. The same exercise could be used on the cars calling at a petrol station, especially if it is a self-service station.

Essays

1   State and discuss the criteria on which a statistical report should be based. Comment on the extent to which the presentation of data is as important as accuracy.   1984 (AEB)

2   'The collection of statistics is expensive in time and consequently in money. It is not really cost effective.' Discuss.

3   It is very easy to deceive people with the illustration of statistics by means of graphs, bar charts, pie charts and histograms. Detail the methods of deception and how they may be detected and guarded against.

4   (a) Outline two distinct types of problem where the use of probability techniques might be of help in business, and illustrate, using numerical information, how the analysis might proceed.   (15)
    (b) What non-numerical factors or criteria would also be relevant to the problems?   (10)   1986 (CLES)

Chapter 6	# Accounting: an aid to decision making and control

Since men and women have owned property they have devised methods of keeping a record of what they possessed and its value. They wished to keep an account of what they had and, when responsible for other people's property, they needed to render an account of how they had used it. This chapter is concerned with some of the techniques that have developed, sometimes over centuries, to satisfy this need for knowledge.

In general we will be concerned with the use of accounting information in the following areas:

- To determine, as accurately as possible, the profit or loss a business has made over a period of time and to provide a statement of the assets and liabilities of a business at a given moment of time. For the moment we will define **assets** as the properties, machinery, investments and cash owned by a business and which are used to achieve its objectives. **Liabilities** are the moneys owed by a business.

- To provide information to assist owners/managers in achieving their objectives by improving decision making and control.

- To provide information to assist people who wish to invest or lend money to a business to make judgements concerning the potential profitability and safety of their investment.

Traditionally the accounting profession has been divided into **financial accountants**, whose professional association is the Institute of Chartered Accountants, and **management accountants**, who are members of the Institute of Cost and Management Accountants.

Financial accountants are primarily concerned with making sure that the accounts of a business are a *true and fair* record of the financial transactions of the business. They may do this by drawing up the accounts of a business from the records kept by the various departments, or, acting on behalf of another business, they may examine existing accounts and declare them to be a true and fair record. This process is known as **auditing**.

Management accountants are more interested in the information they can derive from financial accounts. It is this aspect of accounting which is most important in this chapter, although to begin with we will examine some concepts and techniques which are the province of the financial accountant.

Definitions

We have already given brief definitions of the assets and liabilities of a business. Now we need to be more precise.

Assets

These are the resources owned by a business. They are classified as **fixed** assets and **current** assets.

Fixed assets

Fixed assets are normally those which the business intends to hold for more than one year and are not intended for resale. They are the resources the business needs to function, but may also include investments in other firms.

The conventional order for fixed assets begins with the most **illiquid** – that is, the asset which is most difficult to turn into cash without loss of value – and ends with the most **liquid** asset – the one most easily turned into cash without loss of value. This order also tends to reflect the life of an asset within a business. In normal circumstances land and buildings would be the last assets to be sold if the business went bankrupt or into liquidation. It is therefore classified as the most fixed asset. Cash is changing all the time.

An outline listing of fixed assets can be given as:

1 *Freehold land*   The word 'freehold' means that the owner has absolute rights over the land and does not have to pay rent for it.

2 *Freehold buildings.*

3 *Leasehold land/buildings*   A **lease** is a legal agreement between the owner of a property and another person that the lessee shall have the use of that property for a specified period of time. The time clause means that a leasehold is both less fixed in terms of ownership than freehold property and also more difficult to sell without loss of value. You should note that in Case study B in chapter 4 the fact that the business property was leasehold made it more difficult for the prospective businessman to obtain a loan.

4 *Plant, machinery and equipment*   After buildings you need the physical equipment to produce the good or service. Without them the business could not function, so they are only marginally less fixed than the buildings. This category also tends to be specialised. For example, Austria possesses a nuclear power station which has never functioned; a national referendum (a vote on a proposal by all the citizens in a country) went against its opening. Estimates based on media reports suggest that it cost £400m to build and that the sale of parts for re-use or scrap might bring in £30m. That is a fixed asset.

5 *Vehicles*   A van or car is both more flexible in use and has a shorter working life than a piece of machinery or a factory. It therefore ranks as less fixed than both.

6 *Goodwill, patents and trademarks*   are easy to define but more difficult to value.

- Goodwill is the favour and prestige a business enjoys which adds value to it beyond the value of its physical assets. It is sometimes defined as the difference between the audited value of a business and the market price it could command on the expectation that existing customers would repeat their orders. Unfortunately, there is no way of knowing the value of goodwill until the business is sold. To ignore it totally would be to deny an asset of the business. Estimates of goodwill should be conservative.

- Patents are legal documents securing to an inventor the exclusive right to make or sell an invention. Once an inventor (an individual or a company which has the right to claim an invention) has secured the **letters patent** to an invention they may license other people to use the invention. Again this is a legal agreement and the inventor will receive **royalties** in payment for his licence. Patents usually refer to the invention of machinery. In the media (books, films, records, videos) and the world of computer software the equivalent protection is **copyright**. Both patents and copyright attempt to protect the originator of an idea from exploitation by other people, and, by allowing a period of years in which they have a monopoly over their idea, encourage further invention.

- Trademarks identify a product and help build up consumer loyalty. If you bought a factory manufacturing the well-known Megamints you would want to be able to continue using that name. A successful trademark is the end result of good marketing and quality control. It ensures continuing sales.

7   *Investments*   which are not expected to be held beyond the present accounting period. An accounting period usually lasts for one year. A business that starts trading on 1 August 1986 would end its first accounting period on 31 July 1987.

Current assets

Current assets are those which are 'used up' in the day-to-day operations of a business and which can be converted into cash faster than others and without potential loss of value. Their listing follows the same convention as fixed assets: the most permanent and illiquid are placed first, while cash is last. Current assets include stock, debtors and prepayments, cash at bank and cash in hand. Debtors are those businesses which have taken delivery of goods but which have not yet paid for them – in other words, firms to which the business has granted trade credit.

Liabilities

Strictly speaking a liability is a contribution of resources to a business for the use of which a business has to render an account. As we have already seen, the formation of a company gives the business a separate legal identity, and those who run the business must, by law, account for the way in which they have used the money entrusted to them. This will include money lent to the business and also money invested in the business by the owners – that is, **shareholders' funds**. Sole traders and partnerships are not subject to the same legal constraints as companies, but the accounts of these businesses, although not separated by law from the owners, are treated as if the business is a separate entity from the owner. This has the practical advantage of allowing the owners of the business to keep a clear record of how much money they have invested and therefore of being able to judge the profit/loss situation of the business more accurately. In the case of the sole trader, the owner's capital would be presented as **proprietor's funds**. The usual practice is to start with owner's funds, follow this with loans which will not have to be repaid in the current accounting year, then with current liabilities.

Current liabilities

Payments which will have to be made in the current financial year include provision for repayments of debts expected to mature and other expenses such as tax, bank overdrafts and creditors. There is no conventional order for the presentation of current liabilities.

SELF-ASSESSMENT

1 Define the word 'liquid' and explain why cash is the most liquid of assets.
2 Distinguish between shareholders' funds and proprietor's funds. Justify including them in the liabilities of a business.

Double entry bookkeeping

Double entry bookkeeping is based on common sense. If you go into a shop and buy a sweater for £15 your cash assets have declined by that amount but your physical assets have increased by £15. Isaac Newton's Third Law of Motion, which attempted to explain the behaviour of objects in the physical world, states that for every action there is an equal and opposite reaction. Double entry bookkeeping applies the same principle to the activity of recording transactions.

1 Action: stock purchased for £4000 in cash.
   Reaction: cash balances reduced by £4000.

2 Action: stock purchased for £4000 on credit.
   Reaction: creditors increased by £4000.

3 Action: business borrows £4000 from bank to pay off £4000 of credit.
   Reaction: medium-term debt increases by £4000.

4 Action: business pays off £4000 of debt using cash.
   Reaction: cash balance reduced by £4000

We can summarise the above statements in terms of changes in the assets and liabilities of a business.

Assets + indicates that as a result of a transaction the total value of assets has increased.

Assets − indicates that as a result of a transaction the total value of assets has decreased.

The same notation can also be applied to liabilities.

1 Action: assets +.
   Reaction: assets −.

2 Action: assets +.
   Reaction: liabilities +.

3 Action: liabilities +.
   Reaction: liabilities −.

4 Action: assets −.
   Reaction: liabilities −.

We can use double entry bookkeeping to record the transactions of Joseph Baines in setting up his nursery. Let us assume that the present value of the building in which he intends to site the nursery is £30000. He 'gives' the property to the business. Remember that Joseph is a sole trader. The property remains his, but to make his accounting accurate it must be counted as an asset being used by the business. The assets of the business have increased by £30000 plus the £5000 he intends to introduce from his own resources (savings).

Should Joseph Baines decide to close the business he will want this money back. As far as the business is concerned the property and cash invested in it by the Baines family are liabilities. The business has now received assets of £35000 and, at the same time incurred liabilities of £35000. In the terminology of double entry bookkeeping we can say:

- Assets: + £35000

- Liabilities: + £35000

Assets and liabilities are balanced. If you think about the idea of accounting – giving a true and fair record of the way in which resources (liabilities) have been employed (assets), you can see that this must always be the case.

Balance sheets

A **balance sheet** provides a summary of the way in which a business has used the resources available to it over a period of time. In Table 6.1 you can see the balance sheet of the Baines Nursery at the start of trading.

Table 6.1   Balance sheet, Baines Nursery at start of trading

Balance sheet: Baines Nursery as at 30 September 1986

Freehold land/buildings	£30 000	Proprietor's capital	£35 000
Cash at bank	£ 5 000		

Between 1 October and 14 November the Baineses employ a builder to undertake the necessary alterations. For the purposes of this case study we will assume that the cost of the alterations was exactly the same as his estimate, £10 000. He funded the alterations by borrowing £10 000 from his bank. This gives the following action:

- Assets (freehold property)   + £10 000

combined with a reaction:

- Liabilities (bank loan)   + £10 000

Table 6.2   Balance sheet, Baines Nursery, after alterations to premises

Balance sheet: Baines Nursery as at 30 November 1986

Freehold land/buildings	£40 000	Proprietor's capital	£35 000
Cash at bank	£ 5 000	Bank loan	£10 000

The Baineses buy fixtures and fittings together with equipment to the value of £5 000. Again this is an assets +/assets − transaction.

Table 6.3   Balance sheet, Baines Nursery, after purchase of fixtures, fittings and equipment and grant of bank loan

Balance sheet: Baines Nursery as at 31 December 1986

Freehold land/buildings	£40 000	Proprietor's capital	£35 000
Fixtures & fittings	£ 5 000	Bank loan	£10 000
Cash at bank	£———		

The last transaction was not sensible, but it does give us the opportunity to examine two other actions/reactions involved in double entry accounting. The Baineses are now short of money. They negotiate an overdraft for £1 000. This increases both their liabilities and their assets.

Balance sheet: Baines Nursery as at 31 January 1987

Table 6.4   Balance sheet, Baines Nursery, after negotiation of overdraft

Freehold land/buildings	40 000	Proprietor's capital	£35 000
Fixtures & fittings	£ 5 000	Bank loan	£10 000
Cash at bank	£ 1 000	Overdraft	£ 1 000

After six months in operation, the Baineses have accumulated enough cash to pay off their overdraft with £500 to spare. Their cash figure will fall (assets −) but so will the overdraft disappear (liabilities −) and the proprietor's capital will be increased by the amount of their own money now in the bank.

Balance sheet: Baines Nursery as at 31 July 1987

Freehold land/buildings	£40 000	Proprietor's capital	£35 500
Fixtures & fittings	£ 5 000	Bank loan	£10 000
Cash at bank	£ 500		

This is, of course, a very simple form of balance sheet but it does illustrate the principles contained in all balance sheets. On the right are the liabilities or the *sources* of funds used by a business. On the left the listed assets show *how* these funds have been used.

The way in which this balance sheet is presented is called the 'T form'. It is still in use but most large businesses now use the **columnar** form. This has the major advantage of distinguishing clearly between the sources and use of funds and it is generally accepted as an easier form to interpret.

Balance sheet as at ....

	£000	£000	£000
ASSETS EMPLOYED			
FIXED ASSETS	Cost	Deprec.	Net
Freehold premises	4 000	1 000	3 000
Leasehold premises	1 000	370	630
Plant and machinery	5 000	2 355	2 645
Motor vehicles	970	200	770
	10 970	3 925	7 045
Investments			795
CURRENT ASSETS			
Stock (inventories)		5 500	
Debtors and prepayments		1 500	
Marketable (liquid) securities		500	
Bank balance and cash		100	
		7 600	
Deduct			
CURRENT LIABILITIES			
Creditors	1 754		
Tax and prepayments in coming year	500		
Bank overdraft	451		
Proposed dividends	335		
		3 040	
NET CURRENT ASSETS			4 560
NET ASSETS EMPLOYED			12 400
FINANCED BY:			
SHARE CAPITAL			
Ordinary shares			5 300
Preference shares			2 100
			7 400
RESERVES			2 500
			9 900
LOAN CAPITAL			
Debentures			2 500
			12 400

The balance sheet shows the position of a business at a given moment but it does not tell us how the business reached that position, the level of its sales and how the profit made had been divided between the various parties with a claim to it. For this information we need two other financial statements: the profit and loss account and the funds flow statement.

The profit and loss account

The profit and loss account is a statement of the amount of profit or loss a business has made in a period of time. For convenience and ease of interpretation the information is contained in three sections.

1   *The trading account*   This includes the revenue from sales and the costs associated with producing those sales.

Revenue − Cost of sales = Gross profit

2   *The profit and loss account*   Payments such as interest and directors' fees are deducted from the gross profit to give **net profit before tax**. Tax is then deducted to give **net profit after tax**.

3   *The appropriation account*   'To appropriate' means to set aside for a purpose or to make something the private property of an individual or an organisation. The appropriation account tells interested parties how the business has used the net profit after tax. A company's appropriation account would include the amount distributed to shareholders, the amount transferred to general reserve and the retained profit.

The presentation of a profit and loss account is shown in Table 6.7.

Profit and loss account for year ending 30/6/87

	£000	£000	£000
SALES			10795
Cost of sales			8650
GROSS PROFIT			2145
Less OVERHEADS			
Administration:			
Wages and salaries	235		
Stationery	95		
Heat and light	50		
Rates, rent, insurance	75		
Depreciation	10	465	
Finance:			
Interest	100		
Bad debts	95	195	
Selling:			
Salaries	100		
Distribution	50		
Advertising	150	250	910
Net profit			1235
Corporation tax			375
Net profit after tax			860
Ordinary share dividend			400
Reserves			460

Table 6.7   A profit and loss account

SELF-ASSESSMENT

Compare the net profit of Baines Nursery after tax with the amount of money they invested in the business. Assuming banks are paying 10 per cent interest on deposit accounts should the Baineses be pleased with the results of their first year's trading? Explain your answer.

The funds flow statement

A funds flow statement shows the sources and uses of funds employed by a business over a period of time.

If you look at the information given in a funds flow statement and compare it with the information given in the balance sheet you will see many apparent similarities in the information. The difference lies in the period of *time* summarised by each statement. The balance sheet gives the sources and uses of funds from the *beginning* of the life of a business. The funds flow statement usually relates to a shorter period of time.

Value added statement

The value added statement indicates the difference between the cost of bought-in goods and services and the sales revenue of the business. It is the value added to these things by the effort of the particular business.

Timing of financial accounts

Companies are required by law to publish their accounts once a year. Managers may want more frequent statements to provide them with information for decision making and control. The increased use of computers in business has made this easier. Information can be fed into the computer on a routine basis and the existing programs (**software**) will organise it in a suitable form. As a result of this technological advance, accounting information can be produced with a relatively low cost in terms of time and labour on a monthly, quarterly or even weekly basis when it is felt that it is needed.

Companies are required to have their annual accounts **audited**. This means that an independent and suitably qualified accountant known as an **auditor** inspects the accounts and agrees that they are a true and fair record of the financial position of the company.

Sole traders and partnerships are not required by law to have their accounts audited, but to do so can place them at an advantage when seeking more capital from banks.

Interpreting company accounts

Valuation of assets

Strictly speaking, the valuation of assets is part of the role of the accountant rather than a matter for interpretation. As we shall see, the way in which assets are valued can be of interest to potential investors and for that reason has been included in this section rather than in the description of accounts. The only sure way of knowing what an asset is worth to a business is by offering it for sale – hardly a practical proposition when it is still needed. We will limit ourselves to a brief outline of the ways in which assets can be valued, concentrating on the valuation of fixed assets and stock.

Valuation of fixed assets

Fixed assets such as machinery and vehicles have a limited life span, although at times it can run into decades. Throughout their life their value is falling. If this change in value is ignored, the profit declared by a business can appear low compared with the amount of capital employed. It is usual, therefore, to write off some of the value of a machine each year. This appears as a charge on the profit and loss account *before* tax is paid. This charge is called **depreciation**.

By depreciating its fixed assets a business saves on tax and increases profit. However, depreciation itself is not a method of saving up for replacement machinery. That is a decision taken separately by the business when deciding how to use its profit. Depreciation reduces the book value of an asset; that is, its value after depreciation has been charged. The book value does not reflect the market value of the asset and in itself depends on the method of depreciation used.

The two most common methods of depreciation are (1) straight line depreciation and (2) declining balance depreciation.

1   The straight line method of depreciating assets reduces the book value of the asset by the same amount for each year of its life. An asset which cost £12 000 with an expected life of ten years and a **residual value** (that is, the amount for which the business expects to sell the machine at the end of its working life) of £2 000 would be depreciated by £1 000 per year:

$$\frac{\text{Cost of asset} - \text{Residual value}}{\text{Life of asset}}$$

Straight line depreciation is a simple and straightforward calculation. It gives a higher level of profit to the business in the first years of life of the machine and is particularly useful when the business is expecting constant returns over the life of the asset. An example of straight line depreciation is given in Figure 6.1.

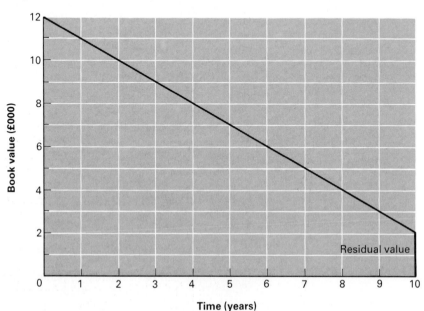

Figure 6.1   Straight line depreciation

2   The declining balance method of depreciation reduces the book value of the asset by a fixed percentage calculated to apportion the value of the machine

after residual value has been subtracted from initial cost over the expected life of the machine. This means that depreciation is highest in the early years of the life of the machine. The use of the declining balance method takes into account that, as the machine grows older, its running and maintenance costs are likely to increase and its earning power will decrease. As a machine gets older it is more susceptible to obsolescence and may be more difficult to sell. Figure 6.2 shows declining balance depreciation.

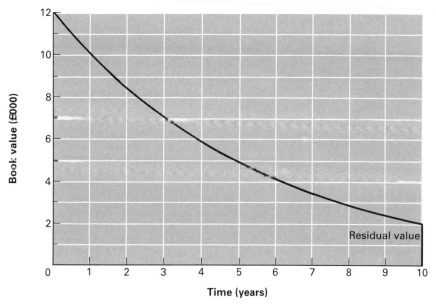

Figure 6.2 Declining balance depreciation

Valuation of stock

All businesses hold supplies of raw materials, components and goods which they require to carry out their production processes. Some types of business will also hold stocks of semi-finished and finished goods. The quantity of stock held by a business will depend on the type of business, its size, the amount of capital it has available and the supply of stock. We will look at the importance of stock levels in more detail in chapter 9. In this chapter we are only concerned with the way in which a business allocates value to existing stock for accounting purposes.

In January 1986 a builder was offered a quantity of timber sufficient to supply his normal requirements for twelve months. He decided to take advantage of this bargain. In June 1986 he was preparing an estimate for the renovation of a house, his business insurance was due to be renewed and he was hoping to float a bank loan to extend his business. He was faced with the problem of placing a value on his remaining stock of timber for each of these reasons. Should he value the timber at the price he paid for it, that is its **historic cost**, or the cost of replacing it which was 20 per cent greater?

There are three basic methods the builder might use to solve his problem.

1   **Valuation using a weighted average**   This is the simplest method and can be used successfully when the cost of buying stocks does not vary greatly over time. Look at the following example.

Value of stock bought on 1 January	£2 000 (200 × £10)
Value of stock bought on 1 February	£3 000 (200 × £15)
Value of stock bought on 1 March	£1 800 (150 × £12)

The total quantity of stock held on 1 March is 550 at a historic cost of £6 800. The value of each unit of stock held can therefore be calculated as:

$$\frac{£6\,800}{550}$$

$$= £12.36$$

2   **Last In First Out** (LIFO)   Using this method all stocks of a similar nature are valued at the last price paid for those stocks. This is a useful method when prices are rising as it takes into account the fact that the stocks used must be replaced at the current market price. Failure to do this might give an inflated profit in the accounts of a business and the payment of too much tax.

3   **First In First Out** (FIFO)   FIFO values all stock at the purchase price of the oldest unit used. In the example given above all stock would be valued at £10 per unit until the supplies bought on 1 January were used up, then at £15 per unit until the supplies bought on 1 February were exhausted and so on.

SELF-ASSESSMENT

1 Give two factors which will help determine the level of stock held by a business.
2 Distinguish between LIFO and FIFO as methods of stock valuation.

The life of an asset

So far we have referred to the 'life' of a machine as if this spanned a fixed period of time. The life span of a machine can vary according to the situation in which the business finds itself. Museums contain many examples of working machines that are obviously still in existence but whose usefulness is finished.

- *The market life of a machine*   A machine is only useful as long as the product it makes sells. As soon as that product becomes obsolete either through technical advance or because tastes have changed the machine loses its usefulness, although it may still be in perfect physical condition.

- *The technical life of a machine*   This will depend upon speed of innovation – in other words, how quickly a new model will appear that will make the machine obsolete. The importance of this life will depend upon the degree of innovation. A new model which cuts costs by half will have a greater impact on the business than one which cuts costs by 5 per cent. In the first case it may mean replacing the machine at once to maintain competitiveness in the market. In the second case it may be possible to keep the machine in operation until one of its other 'lives' comes to an end.

The two lives given above are beyond the control of the business. To be safe a business will calculate the *economic* life of the machine on the basis of the shortest of these lives.

The span of time chosen to depreciate a machine can be seen as another life. It should be remembered that as depreciation has an effect on profits, the period of time over which an asset is depreciated is often chosen in order to minimise tax.

Ratio analysis

Managers, shareholders, investors and potential investors want information on the performance of a business so that they can make decisions in their own interest and further the objectives of the business. The information in which a group is most interested varies slightly according to the group but, in general, we can say that they are all concerned with liquidity, return on investment and the ratio of equity capital to borrowed funds. Ratio analysis is used to isolate the required information.

Ratio analysis compares one piece of accounting information with another. Ratios, once calculated, must be *compared* with other ratios if they are to be of value in the process of decision making and control. It is usual to compare a given ratio with:

1 the same ratio of the business in previous years, for example, the current ratio for 1987 compared with the current ratios of that business in the years 1980–1986;

2 the same ratio of other businesses for both the current period and over a period of time; and

3 an accepted standard based on the cumulative experience of business. We shall see that the accepted standard for the liquidity ratio is 2:1. Too great a degree of variation from that standard might give cause for concern.

Ratios may be presented in the conventional form – for example, 3:1, as a percentage or as a fraction. The form chosen will depend on convenience and clarity of interpretation.

Liquidity ratios

A business must be able to pay its debts if it is to survive. It therefore needs to hold cash. On the other hand, if it holds too great a proportion of its assets in cash it may be sacrificing opportunities for greater profit. There are two ways of measuring the liquidity position of a business:

1 *the current ratio*
Current assets:Current liabilities

2 *the acid test ratio*
Liquid assets:Current liabilities

The current ratio includes all current assets and all liabilities which will have to be paid in the current accounting period. It is often suggested that an ideal current ratio is 2:1, the higher proportion of assets being necessary because some assets (for example, stock) are less liquid than others. In an emergency, therefore, the business cannot be certain that it would be able to dispose of these assets at their book value. A business which carries little stock might be satisfied with a current ratio of 1.5:1 or even lower.

The acid test ratio is an attempt to judge whether a business will be able to meet all its short-term liabilities without the sale or run-down of its stocks. It takes only the liquid assets (debtors and cash) and compares them with current liabilities. An acceptable ratio is 1:1. In this case the business has sufficient liquid assets to cover its immediate liabilities but is not sacrificing additional income.

The analysis of the liquidity position of a business is useful to managers in the management of cash and working capital. We will look at this more closely in the next chapter.

Investment ratios

Ratios which measure the profitability of a business are of interest to investors and managers. In general, investment ratios may be described as providing information on profitability and growth of a company. The different ratios give different insights into the performance of a business.

1   *Return on equity ratio* 'Equity' is a term used to describe the capital contributed by ordinary shareholders. Each ordinary share carries the same investment and the same rights and responsibilities. Each share is equal to all others. The return on equity ratio is usually expressed as a percentage. This gives a single figure which is more easily compared with other information; for example, if you had a sum of money which you intended to invest in ordinary shares you might compare the return on equity ratio of several companies before you made your investment decision.

Net profit after tax
Shareholders' funds

2   *Dividend yield ratio*   If you refer back to the profit and loss account on page 96 you will see that net profit after tax is not necessarily distributed to the shareholders. The directors of a company may decide to retain profits in order to finance further growth. This policy will appeal to an investor who wants his investment to grow in value over time, but it will be less attractive to a person whose primary objective is a high income.

Dividend per share
Share price

3   *Price earnings ratio*   A practical method of estimating the degree of risk involved in a particular investment is to calculate the length of time over which earnings from the investment accumulate sufficiently to cover the initial cost of the investment. You should compare this with the payback method of assessing physical investment decisions in chapter 7.

Market price of share
Earnings per share

Place yourself in the position of a person considering buying shares in a company when the current market price is £8 and the expected annual earnings per share are £2. It will take you four years to recover your initial investment. Before making the final decision you should ask yourself a number of questions:

(a) Will the company survive that long? An examination of its liquidity ratios may make you more confident.
(b) You should also look at the product. Will people tire of it in the next four years or is this only the first stage of its life? After all, the product might sweep the market before it and establish itself in a dominant position.
(c) You should look at the economy in general. If the product is a luxury and a rise in unemployment is expected, you may be less than happy about its prospects in future.
(d) How else can I use my money? There may be other investments that will pay you back in a shorter period of time. The risk may appear greater but the payback time is less.
(e) How important is the existing management team to the company's success? Are they likely to stay with the company for the next four years?

Potentially the list of questions is endless. It can include querying future labour relations, the likelihood of new technology emerging, a change in existing laws and so on. The ultimate question for the investor is: How long will this state of affairs continue and will I get my money back before it changes?

4   *Gearing ratio*   When you look at the balance sheet of a business you can see that the assets purchased are financed partly by the money the owners have put into the business and partly by borrowed funds in a variety of forms. The

relationship between equity capital and borrowed funds is expressed by the gearing ratio.

Long-term borrowing
Net assets employed

Borrowed money has to be paid for in terms of a fixed rate of interest. When the profits of the business are rising this can be seen in terms of a fixed cost that becomes relatively smaller compared with the volume of business generated. In these circumstances borrowed funds are an advantage to the business. When revenue falls the fixed cost of interest payments can be a problem. It can, for example, affect the liquidity position of a business.

There are many more ratios that can be applied both to the accounts and the statistics of a business to help in decision making and control. They will be introduced as appropriate in other chapters. Ratios should not be seen as the solution to all problems. Like any form of analysis, their value is affected by the quality of the data used and the expertise of the people using it. Below is a summary of some of the problems associated with ratio analysis.

Criticisms of ratio analysis

1 Ratio analysis is an attempt to use information relating to an existing situation so as to predict the future. The accuracy with which this can be done will depend upon the accuracy of the figures used.

2 Ratio analysis is just one of a number of techniques designed to help in the control of a business and in decision making. The results of ratio analysis must be judged in the context of other information available. A business might have an excellent financial history but, if the product it makes is about to be made obsolete, it would be inadvisable to invest.

3 Ratios used by interested parties external to the business – for example, trade unions and potential shareholders – are based on published accounts. These reflect the state of the business at the time they are drawn up and are not necessarily a good guide to that business. In the period before the accounts were published a business might have had an unusually high proportion of liquid assets. This may have been because it was expecting a need for them. It might also have been a deliberate move on the part of management to make the accounts more acceptable to shareholders!

4 When ratios are used to compare the performance of one business with another it must be remembered that they are seldom completely comparable. Businesses have different ways of recording information and different ways of valuing their assets. This diversity of approach is not always obvious in the accounts but it may invalidate the conclusions drawn from an inter-firm comparison. On the other hand, ratios can provide a general comparison between businesses of a similar size, operating in the same market and using similar production processes.

> **SELF-ASSESSMENT**
>
> A business has issued £1m worth of £1 shares the market value of which is now £3. It has also borrowed £400 000. The last dividend declared was 49p per share. Calculate the relevant ratios.

Budgetary control

A budget can be defined as a statement of the financial position of a person, business or other organisation for a future period of time based on estimates of expenditure and proposals for financing them. Budgeting is a process with which most people are familiar, if only at the simplest level. A household will plan its expenditure in advance on the basis of expected income. The time period over which a family prepares budgets will often depend on the frequency with which the major wage-earner in the family is paid. This may be weekly or monthly. In addition, households will include some longer-term planning in these short-term budgets. Provision will be made for bills that have to be paid on a quarterly or yearly basis. Unforeseen circumstances may mean that the budget has to be revised if the family is to achieve its objectives.

Budgeting in business has the same characteristics as domestic budgeting:

1 *Planning*   The objectives must be set. This is the responsibility of the owner of the business (the Board of Directors in a company), who will state expected profit levels and proposed expansion to be financed by profit.

2 *Information*   In order to forecast expenditure and estimate the amount of money required to fund it, a business will need detailed information on production capacity, cost of materials, labour available, degree of re-training required (if any), the availability and cost of capital and expected sales. In a large business the provision of this information will be the responsibility of the marketing, production, finance and personnel departments in the form of departmental budgets. In a small business it may be the responsibility of the owner.

3 *Co-ordination*   In a small business the process of co-ordination is inseparable from the activity of collecting information. The fewer the people involved in the budgetary process the more likely it is that people concerned have an understanding of the interaction between the different variables. In larger businesses the co-ordination of departmental needs may be the responsibility of the finance department or possibly a committee of departmental heads. The precise form will depend on the way in which the business is organised.

4 *Review*   Once the co-ordination process is finished the summary is presented to the policy makers. This summary of departmental budgets is known as the **master budget**. The policy makers are then in a position to judge the extent to which their original objectives are feasible. They may need to adjust their objectives as a result of the budgeting exercise.

5 *Control*   As the budget is put into operation the managers are able to measure their actual performance against projected performance. The techniques used to analyse the difference between the two are contained in **variance analysis** (see the next section). The information they obtain as a result of this exercise will help in the preparation of future budgets.

A budget period

A budget period can cover a week, month, year or several years. The time chosen will depend upon the needs of the business. In a fast-changing market budgets may need to be drawn up more frequently.

Rather than draw up budgets too frequently, with all the work involved, a business might draw up several budgets at the same time, each one based on a different set of expectations about the behaviour of the market and/or output. Once it becomes apparent which budget approximates most closely to reality, that budget can be adopted. This is known as **flexible budgeting**.

Variance analysis

Look at the following example:

A business has a production budget for 50000 items over a given period of time. Its actual production is 40000 items, a variance of 10000 items or 20 per cent. Should the production manager be concerned about this variance?

The probable answer is Yes. A variance of 20 per cent is something to be concerned about. A larger business with the same absolute variance of 10000 might only have a relative variance of 1 per cent.

Although analysing the variances appears simple, the reality will be more complex. It is even more difficult to isolate the factors that caused the variance. In effect, the production manager will have to analyse a number of subordinate variances within his own department relating to stocks, personnel, finance, organisation and available machinery.

Cash flow budgets

The cash budget is used here as an example of a departmental budget which contributes to the master budget. It is important for a business to identify the timing of inflows and outflows of cash if it is to meet its payments (see Table 6.8).

	June	July	August	Sept.	Oct.	Nov.
Cash at beginning of month	50	60	75	95	130	145
Add: Receipts from sales	150	160	170	150	100	50
A Total cash	200	220	245	245	230	195
Subtract:						
Wages	70	70	70	50	30	20
Materials	40	45	50	35	20	15
Expenses	30	30	30	30	35	35
B Total outflow	140	145	150	115	85	70
Cash at end of month	60	75	95	130	145	130

Table 6.8 Example of a cash-flow budget (£000s)

The role of the budgetary system

Some of the advantages of the budgetary system are shown below:

- A budget based on full and accurate information can act as a check on senior management and prevent the setting of unrealistic objectives.

- Managers who have been actively involved in the budgetary process are more likely to be motivated towards the success of the business.

- By comparing expected results with achieved results managers can discover the weak areas in the business and take steps to strengthen them.

- When all departments are involved in the budgetary process they are more likely to become aware of the problems and constraints faced by other departments. Activity is more likely to be co-ordinated in this situation than if managers had budgets imposed upon them from above.

Costs and costing

Costs are incurred by all the activities a business undertakes. Every decision, no matter how small, involves a corresponding cost. The importance which should be attached to cost in any business enterprise cannot be surprising when it is remembered that

Profit = Revenue − Costs.

Some basic cost definitions are given in this section.

Fixed costs

Fixed costs are those costs which, over a given period of time, tend to be unaffected by changes in output. For example, a factory capable of producing 100 000 engineering parts in a certain period of time might have fixed costs in terms of rent, heating, lighting and cost of machinery of £100 000 in that time. If the factory produces only 80 000 units, it will still have to meet the costs associated with 100 000 units.

The total number of goods and services a business is capable of producing is known as its **capacity**. You should realise that a business offering services will also have a limit to the total amount it can provide for its customers. A hairdressing salon has a given number of seats, sinks, driers and stylists. A restaurant is limited in the number of meals it can supply by its kitchen capacity, by seating accommodation, the number of staff and the number of meals they can serve. The TV repairman is limited by his level of skill and time on the number of repairs he can undertake in one day.

When a business produces less than the amount of which it is capable, we say it is *operating at less than full capacity*. This is usually expressed as a percentage of full capacity.

$$\frac{\text{Number of units produced} \times 100}{\text{Capacity of business}}$$

In the example given above this would be

$$\frac{80\,000 \times 100}{100\,000}$$

= 80 per cent

Figure 6.3 shows the position of a business with a capacity of 100 000 at a fixed cost of £100 000 in a given period of time.

Average fixed cost is the proportion of total fixed costs carried by each item produced, and is calculated by dividing total fixed cost by output. When the business described above is producing at full capacity, then the average fixed cost will be £1. When it is operating at 80 per cent capacity, the average fixed cost will be £1.20.

Try the same calculation for different levels of output for the above business. You should find that the lower the level of output the higher the average fixed cost. This fact has a significance for businesses when setting prices and deciding whether or not to accept a particular order. Figure 6.4 shows average fixed costs declining as output increases.

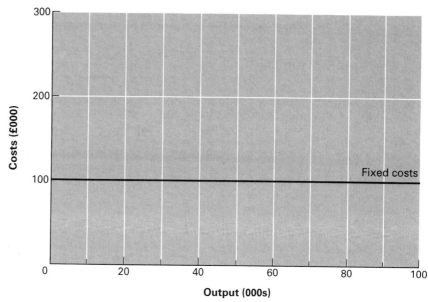

Figure 6.3   Fixed costs

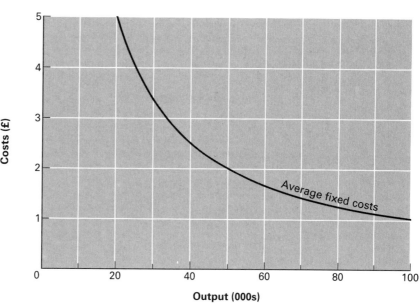

Figure 6.4   Average fixed costs declining as output increases

Variable costs

An increase in output will tend to lead to an increase in the amount of raw materials being used, an increase in the power consumed and an increase in certain types of labour. These costs are known as **variable costs** because they vary with output.

The simplest example of variable costs assumes that the cost of raw material, labour and power will be the same for each unit produced regardless of the level of output. This simplifying assumption is made to illustrate the concept of variable costs. A business might find that raw material costs decline as output increases, because suppliers are willing to reduce the price of orders above a certain size (a **bulk discount**).

Variable costs of £2 per unit produced (the **average variable cost**) would result in *total* variable costs of £20 000 at an output of 10 000 units, £40 000 at an output of 20 000 units and so on, until the maximum capacity of the plant was reached. This would give a straight line graph, as illustrated in Figure 6.5.

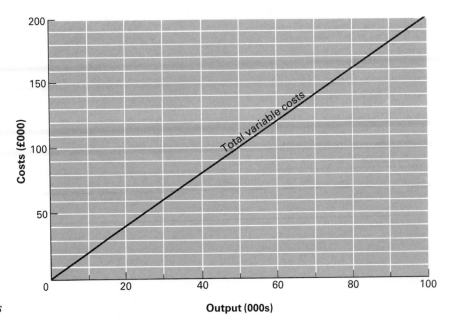

Figure 6.5   Variable costs

Semi-variable costs

The rent of a hired car is a fixed cost, the petrol to keep it running is a variable cost. This marriage of fixed and variable cost is common in business.

Direct cost

Direct cost is a cost that can be clearly allocated to a particular product. The labour and materials will be referred to individually as **direct labour** and **direct materials**.

Indirect costs

Indirect materials will cover stores that are used for all departments – for example, lubricants for machines. Indirect labour will include the cost of supervision and maintenance among other things.

Overheads

A business performs a number of other functions in addition to production: for example, marketing, managing personnel, research and development and finance. Costs which are clearly attributable to one of these functions are termed **overheads**. They include labour, materials and expenses.

Marginal costs

In economic theory **marginal cost** is defined as the cost of producing one extra unit of output. It is calculated by subtracting the total cost (total fixed costs + total variable costs) of the first level of output from the total costs of the second level of output. The level of output of a business can be defined as the number of goods and services it produces in a given period of time.

Accountants use the same basic definition of marginal cost but use only direct costs in its calculation. They may be interested in variations in output as low as one – for example, in the production of a piece of equipment to order – but will also apply the definition to larger variations in output. We shall explore this idea further when we examine marginal costing later in this chapter.

Imputed costs

This is the cost of using something the business already owns. It can be seen as a method of giving a monetary value to the opportunity cost of using a resource.

Classification of costs

The classification of a cost varies according to the use of the resource and the purposes for which the classification is being undertaken. Labour, for example, can be classified in a variety of ways:

1   Labour employed in the production of a good or service is a *direct cost*.

2   Labour employed in selling a product is an *overhead* – unless, of course, that labour is employed in retailing, when it may be classified as a *direct cost*.

3   Labour which can be laid off when output falls can be classified as a *variable cost*. A man working on a production line might be classified as both direct labour and as part of variable costs.

4   When union agreements make it impossible to lay off labour, then labour costs must be regarded as fixed for the period of time covered by the agreement. This situation might also arise if management has a policy of continuous employment.

SELF-ASSESSMENT

1 Distinguish between fixed costs and variable costs.
2 Given that a business can produce 150 000 items in a month, that its fixed costs per month are £10 000, that the average variable cost is £5 per unit and that it is operating at full capacity, what is the cost per unit? Calculate the total production costs.
3 The owner of a business described in question 2 wishes to make a profit equivalent to 25 per cent of his production costs. At what price should he sell his output?

The break-even point

What is the lowest possible output at which a business can operate without losing money? The answer is called the **break-even point**. At this level the costs of production are exactly the same as the revenue received from sales, assuming the whole output is sold.

We can illustrate the break-even point graphically by merging information on Figures 6.3 and 6.4, in Figure 6.6.

1   Fixed costs stay the same irrespective of output.

2   Total costs = total fixed costs + total variable costs. As we saw in Figure 6.4, the total variable cost curve passes through the origin. By introducing fixed costs we have added a constant to the equation which defines the curve. The total cost curve always cuts the vertical axis at the level of fixed costs.

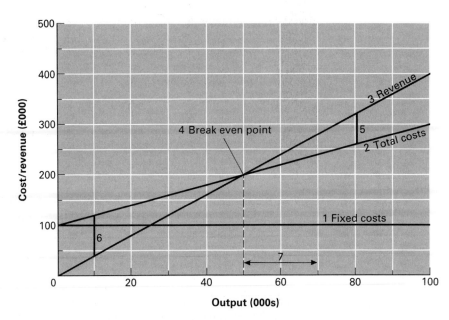

Figure 6.6   Break-even chart

3   The revenue line is found by multiplying the selling price of each unit by the level of output. In this instance the selling price is £4.

4   The point at which the revenue curve and the cost curve intersect is the break-even point.

5   To the right of the break-even point revenue is greater than total cost. The vertical difference between the two curves at any given point will give the total profit.

6   To the left of the break-even point, a similar calculation to that described in 5 will give the total losses of the business at any given level of output.

7   If the business is operating at 70 per cent capacity, it will still make a profit. The difference between the output at which a business is operating and the break-even output is known as the **margin of error**.

Criticisms of break-even analysis

Break-even analysis is a relatively simple and cheap technique which shows the relationship between fixed costs, variable costs and revenue. It can highlight problem areas that management can then examine in more detail. However, the advantages of break-even analysis will be lost if its limitations are not recognised:

1   A break-even analysis is only as good as the information on which it is based. You should remember that the gathering and storing of information generates costs. The greater the degree of accuracy required the more it will cost to gather the information. Too much money spent on accumulating information will reduce the advantages of speed and cheapness associated with the technique.

2   The information on which the break-even analysis is based may have been accumulated for other purposes. Assumptions may have been made when classifying costs that were valid for that purpose but which invalidate the break-even analysis. Direct labour may, for example, be classified as a fixed cost for periods of up to a month. This information may have been used in the drawing up of projected profit and loss accounts to aid in management

decision making. Used uncritically for a break-even analysis covering three months, it will present a distorted picture. This is a very simple example, but it is important to remember that information should not be accepted at face value. Unrecognised assumptions may be built in to its collection and processing.

3   Both simple and complex models are *forecasting* models. A sudden increase in the market price of a commodity, a union agreement on pay or the unilateral decision of an international producers' cartel will make the analysis out of date.

4   Break-even analysis assumes that all production will be sold. In some ways this is a reasonable assumption if the business is confident in the results of its market research. Break-even analysis translates production into immediate profits. A business might be producing in expectation of future demand, perhaps building up stock in anticipation of the Christmas buying boom. Some of the profits shown by break-even analysis may not be realised in the period covered by it because part of output will be stored as finished goods.

SELF-ASSESSMENT

1 Reading from the information given in Figure 6.6, state whether or not the business will be making a profit or loss at each of the following levels of capacity: 20000, 35000, 55000, 70000, 90000.
2 What is the margin of error when output is 80000 units?
3 State two disadvantages of break-even analysis.

Costing

A business produces 15000 units per year. The total costs of running the factory, advertising and selling the goods is calculated at £90000. The cost per unit is, therefore, £6.

This is the simplest form of costing. Unfortunately it does not help with many of the problems which confront a business and in which cost information is essential if the final decision is to help in achieving the objectives of the business.

Costing and decision making

The following are some examples of decisions in which an analysis of costs is essential:

1   *Make or buy?*   A business uses a large quantity of a certain component in assembling its product. The component is not difficult to make, and it is suggested that it would be both more convenient and cheaper if the business was to make it itself. Can it be produced more cheaply than the market price?

2   *Entering a market*   All businesses have a level of profit which they consider acceptable. On entering a new market with a given market price a business will need an accurate assessment of costs to estimate whether or not it will be able to achieve this profit level. We saw a practical example of this in the case of the Baines nursery in chapter 4.

3   *To cease production or to continue?*   Although a business may be losing money on a product, it may be profitable for it to continue manufacture while the costs of production are fixed. In economic terms this would be known as the **short run**, defined more precisely as the period of time in which at least one

factor of production is fixed in supply. A business can continue to produce in the short run providing it can cover its variable costs.

4   *Accept or reject an order?*   A business may be offered a contract at a price that does not cover the full cost of producing the goods. If the business is operating at less than full capacity it may still be advantageous for it to accept the order.

Each of the situations outlined above will require a different cost analysis and a different method of costing. We will examine costing methods in the next section.

Methods of costing

Costing would be relatively simple in the following circumstances:

- if all costs could be clearly allocated to one product or area of production. This is known as a **cost centre**. If you look again at the definitions of costs you will see that overheads and indirect costs may be used by several cost centres. The marketing department may be responsible for several products. How much time does any one person in that department spend on any one product? It may vary with the time of year, if a product is having unusual problems, and it may also vary according to the role of the person. A product may be of minimal importance to the departmental manager but require a great deal of time from a clerical assistant.

- if all decisions were of the same type. All make and buy decisions require the same type of costing definitions, and the records to be kept could be standardised.

- if the situation did not change. Unless a business has a very dominant position in the market it will have to take note of its competitors' pricing/promotion policies. Government decisions will also change the environment in which the business operates by increasing taxation or reducing its spending. We can also mention trade unions, changes in consumer buying behaviour, changes in social attitudes and decisions by foreign governments as some of the variables that might cause a business to analyse its costs.

In practice the complexity of the situations faced by a business enterprise and the wide variety of decisions that management is called upon to make has led to the development of a number of costing techniques each of which isolates the relevant information required by a decision and/or control problem. In this chapter we will examine just two of these costing methods: absorption costing, and marginal costing (sometimes called contribution costing).

1   *Absorption costing* absorbs the fixed costs and overheads into the production of a good. In a single-product business, absorption costing would produce the same result as the total cost approach. In many businesses the same machine can be used for a number of jobs.

A tea packaging plant makes tea-bags, and boxes them for a number of different brands all produced by the same company. There is no difference in the size of the tea-bag or box used and the same machinery copes with all brands. (*It would be useful if you remember this when we outline the advantages of standardisation – making every one of a type identical – in chapter 9.*) The blends of tea used differ, the number of perforations in the tea-bag differ between blends, and the design of the packaging is distinctive according to the market at which it is aimed. How should the costs of acquiring and running the machines be allocated to each brand?

The costs can be allocated according to the length of time the machinery is used for a particular tea. Thus, if the total costs for the running of the machinery over a period of time is £20000, Brand A might have used the machines for 40 per cent of the time and will be allocated costs of £8000. Brand B is allocated £5000 and Brand C £7000.

Absorption costing is useful in giving a general cost of production and in the valuation of stocks of finished and semi-finished goods and the allocation of fixed costs between goods when there are reliable production statistics for guidance. It is less useful in the allocation of overheads. When overheads involve services to a product they are difficult to cost subjectively and expensive to cost objectively.

2 *Marginal costing* This method is useful if a business has to make decisions on whether or not to accept an order or whether or not to continue in business. Marginal costing accepts that, in the short run, certain costs are fixed and must be paid by the business whether or not it continues in operation/is operating at full or less than full capacity.

In the definition of marginal costs a distinction was made between an economist's definition and that of an accountant. We will use the accountant's definition in the discussion of marginal costing. *direct costs of production subtracted from revenue*. This ignores fixed costs. They have to be paid, so any *contribution* towards them minimises the losses of the business in the short run.

A loss-making shop has six months to run on its lease, the cost of which is £5000 per year. The owner of the shop is annoyed with himself for renewing the lease – business had already begun to decline at that point – and wishes to discontinue trading. His accountant is less positive. The accountant suggests a closer look at the trading figures. The owner of the shop is legally liable for £2500. If he continues trading the cost of bought-in stock, heating, lighting, staff and other expenses that would cease if he stopped trading would be £31000. The revenue generated by this would be £33000.

The owner of the shop will be *worse* off if he stops trading than if he continues. If he stops trading with six months to run on his lease he will have debts of £2500. If he continues trading his debts will be reduced to £500 – assuming he has taken into account his own living expenses!

Mr Arkwright mass-produces pressed steel gates. The cost of a single gate to fit a 3-foot opening is £30, of which £10 can be classified as indirect cost. A leading mail-order company approaches him and asks him to supply 500 gates at £28 per gate. Mr Arkwright's first inclination is to refuse. He then looks at the order more closely. His busiest time is in the summer, when he operates at 100 per cent capacity. This order is for the period September to December when he operates, on average, at 200 under capacity. The mail-order company will include his product in their spring catalogue which is sent to agents in February. Mr Arkwright does some rapid calculations.

1 The indirect costs are £10.
2 His direct costs are £20.
3 He would receive £28 in revenue.
4 £20 would cover his direct costs of production, and he would have £8 to *contribute* to a lowering of his indirect costs.

Mr Arkwright accepted the order.

> **SELF-ASSESSMENT**
>
> 1 The sales of a business are falling but it can still cover direct costs. At what point should it cease trading?
> 2 Define a cost centre as the term is used in this chapter.
> 3 State two problems associated with allocating costs to a product.

Conclusion

In this chapter it has only been possible to give an outline of the accounting techniques used in business. It is important to remember that these techniques *summarise* the activities of a business. Giving a monetary value to the opportunity cost inherent in decision making provides information which is open to analysis, the result of which can be used in decision making and control.

Unfortunately, the use of money/numerical values can lead to a false sense of security. Figures are often based on human judgement, a fact we shall explore in more detail in chapter 12. As a conclusion to both chapters 5 and 6 you are recommended to bear in mind that numerical information is only as good as the care that has gone into compiling it. That compiling information will depend on decisions about what is/is not important. That compiling information *costs* money!

Review

1 Read each of the following statements and decide whether or not they are *true* or *false*. Give a brief explanation of your answer.
   (a) A change in the assets of a business must be accompanied by a corresponding change in its liabilities.
   (b) The acid test ratio of a business must be 1:1.
   (c) If a company has made a profit over an accounting period its reserves will increase by that amount.
   (d) The business accounts of a sole trader are treated as separate from his private accounts in order to facilitate an accurate assessment of the profitability of the business.
   (e) The purpose of depreciation is to allow businesses to accumulate funds for replacement investment.
   (f) Fixed costs never change.
   (g) A business should only accept an order if the price offered will cover all production costs.
   (h) If the time period is short enough, all costs may be regarded as fixed.

2 The information given below is a summary of the transactions of a small business during its first year of trading.

	£		£
Cash received		Cash paid	
Proprietor's funds	15 000	For stock	25 000
Loan from bank	5 000	For rent of premises	3 000
Sales revenue	40 000	For fixtures and fittings	15 000
		For rates	1 500
		For administration expenses	500
		Owner's drawings	5 000
		Heating/lighting	1 000

The following information is also available at the end of the accounting period:

(i) The business is owed £2000 by its customers.
(ii) There is a stock of goods worth £5000.
(iii) Cash and bank balances total £1000.
(iv) The business owes suppliers £4000.
(v) Cost of lease £10000.

(a) Draw up the profit and loss account for the business at the end of the first year of trading.
(b) Draw up the balance sheet of the business at the end of the first year of trading.
(c) Comment on the comparative success or failure of the business with the help of the appropriate ratios.
(d) What other information would you need in order to estimate the business's chances of survival?

3   A businessman purchases a machine at the beginning of an accounting period for £50000. It is expected to have a useful life of ten years and a scrap value at the end of that period of £5000.
(a) Compare the book value of the machine at the end of five years using both straight line and declining balance methods of depreciation at 21 per cent (actual percentage 20.567 to three decimal places).
(b) In what circumstances might the declining balance method of depreciation be preferable to the straight line method?
(c) The machine was sold for scrap after eight years. Assuming that the business is still operating profitably, give *three* reasons why it might have taken this course of action.

4   Reston's Ltd is a small, single-product company selling to the industrial market. In 1984 it owned a single factory capable of producing 250000 units per year with a selling price of £25 per unit. All the output was sold at this price. The managing director of Reston's was eager to expand production. The Board of Directors were less convinced of the advisability of the strategy. As a result, the company accountant was asked to draw up projections evaluating the different courses of action open to the business. These were:

(A) Production and selling price to remain unchanged at 250000 units at £25 per unit.
(B) Use existing plant capacity more intensively. The production manager estimated that he could increase output by 10 per cent but this would mean overtime payments. The selling price would remain the same.
(C) Expand production capacity to 400000 units. If this option was selected the marketing manager recommended a reduction in price of £3 to ensure the sale of all units produced.

The following information was also available:

(i) At the present production levels fixed costs were £2m per annum. The increase in overheads arising from the adoption of Projection B would increase these by £275000, while Projection C would mean fixed costs rising to £4.5m.
(ii) Current variable costs per unit are £12. These would rise to £14 for Projection B, but the improved factory layout, discounts for the bulk purchase of materials and a reduction in the amount of direct labour required as a result of improved machinery were expected to reduce variable costs to £8 per unit if Projection C were to be adopted.

(a) Draw up a report, using diagrams where appropriate, to evaluate each of the three possible courses of action outlined above.

(b) Assuming the reduction in price was necessary to sell the additional output, comment on the price elasticity of demand for the product and the implications of this for the business.

(c) Projection C is adopted. In the first twelve months of operation sales are 350 000 instead of the expected 400 000. Reston's are approached by a large company which offers to buy 40 000 units at £21 per unit. Should the firm accept the order? Explain your answer.

5   Brady Boating is wholly owned by Andrew Brady. The business specialises in the repair of dinghies and day boats for the leisure sailor. Brady had inherited the workshop from his father together with a pride in the fact that it was a family business. By 1985 it was becoming obvious that essential equipment was reaching the end of its useful life. Replacement of equipment together with an extension to the boat workshop was estimated to cost £50 000. The bank was prepared to make a loan of £20 000. Andrew Brady had £20 000 for investment in the business but was unsure how he could raise the additional money required by 31 March 1986.

At this time a local businessman, Peter Doyle, approached Brady with the following suggestions:

(i) Brady Boating should be registered as a limited company.

(ii) An injection of £250 000 capital would be made by the businessman and other interested persons.

(iii) The additional capital would be used to update the workshop equipment, open a retail shop selling sailing accessories and clothes and a catering establishment.

(iv) Andrew Brady would be the managing director of the new company.

After careful consideration Brady decided that he did not want to accept this offer. He preferred to expand more slowly and, as a first step towards this objective, he collected the following budget information:

	Sales (£s)	Cost of sales (£s)
Sept.	15 000	10 000
Oct.	12 000	8 000
Nov.	10 000	6 700
Dec.	9 000	6 000
Jan.	9 500	6 300
Feb.	11 000	7 400
Mar.	16 000	10 700

Monthly expenses include: wages and salaries – £1 500; rates – £60; heating/lighting/power – £200; transport – £100; miscellaneous – £250. Telephone charges average £150 per quarter payable in November. The business insurance is due for renewal in March. Mr Brady expects the premium to be £1 000.

(i) On 1 November Brady expects to have a cash balance of £5 000.

(ii) He allows customers two months in which to pay their debts but pays his suppliers cash.

(a) Assuming that the business proposition put forward by Peter Doyle satisfies financial criteria, give two reasons why Andrew Brady might have decided against it.

(b) Prepare a cash flow budget for Brady Boating. Will Andrew Brady be able to finance his own expansion?

6   The cost accounts for the Suntrap Hotel for the period 1 January 1985 to 31 December 1985 are shown below:

	Total number of room/nights let	Revenue per room per night (£)	Variable Cost per room/per night (£)
April	160	8	6
May	180	10	6
June	220	12	7
July	280	15	8
August	340	15	8
September	170	10	6

Total annual semi-variable and fixed costs are: £1 440.

In the past the hotel has had a season of six months per annum from 1 April to 30 September. In an effort to increase profits, the proprietor is considering extending his 1987 season to cover the period from 1 March to 31 October. Market research suggests that in each of March and October he can expect to sell 100 room nights at £7. Variable costs are estimated to be £6 per night, and annual semi-variable and fixed costs are expected to rise by £100.

(a) What is the difference between a fixed cost and a variable cost?   (4)
(b) Calculate the profits for 1985.   (10)
(c) What effect would the plan have on his overall profits?   (2)
(d) If he were to have opened during March and October in 1985, what is the minimum that he would have had to charge during March and October per room per night, if he were to break even *during those months*?   (6)
(e) Give *four* examples of alternative ways for the proprietor to increase profits.   (8)   1986 (AEB)

7   (a) What is the significance of fixed costs and variable costs in determining the break-even point for a product? Illustrate your answer by calculating the break-even point for the following figures:
Sales volume 120 000 units
Fixed costs £6 000
Variable costs per unit £5
Selling price per unit £8   (3)
(b) A certain product sells at £5 per unit. The company plans to manufacture 100 000 units at a variable cost of £2.50 per unit and a fixed cost of £200 000.
    (i) Draw a break-even chart to represent these figures.
    (ii) Define the terms 'planned profit' and 'margin of safety',
    (iii) Show these on your graph.   (7)
(c) PT Ltd produces three products (X, Y and Z). The relevant data is shown below:

	per unit		
	X	Y	Z
Sales price	£2.00	£2.50	£3.25
Direct materials used (at 10p per kg)	£0.30	£0.40	£0.50
Direct labour used	£0.90	£1.00	£1.00
Variable overheads	£0.40	£0.60	£0.85

The company's fixed costs amount to £10 000. The raw material used in these products is in short supply and may limit the output of PT Ltd.

(i) State which product the company should concentrate on, assuming that there are no marketing constraints on the products. Support your answer with appropriate figures. (7)

(ii) It is anticipated that 200 000 kg of raw material will be obtained in each month. Showing your calculations, calculate the most profitable product mix and expected profit if the projected monthly demand for X, Y and Z is 5 000, 16 000 and 30 000 units respectively. (8)   1985 (CLES)

8   OP Ltd produces one product for which a standard costing system was introduced at the beginning of this year. The following standards were calculated for one unit of the company's products:

(i) standard price of direct material   £0.45 per kilo;
(ii) standard quantity of direct material   12 kilos per unit;
(iii) standard direct labour   £2 per hour;
(iv) standard number of direct labour hours   10 per unit.

(a) Explain the meaning of each of the above terms (i–iv). (4)

(b) Discuss the ways in which the standards may have been set. (4)

(c) The company budgeted to produce 10 000 units during May 1985 but, in fact, produced 8 000 units, with the following results:
Direct material bought and used (94 000 kilos) £48 880
Direct labour used (84 000 hours) £189 000
From the given figures calculate:
(i) the standard cost per unit of output,
(ii) the actual cost for May 1985,
(iii) the total cost variances. (6)

(d) Define the following terms, and calculate from the given figures:
(i) the material usage variance,
(ii) the material price variance. (6)

(e) Explain why the use of 'standard costs' is considered to have advantages over the comparison of actual costs with past costs. (5)   1985 (CLES)

9   (a) David Woodman is a sole trader manufacturing furniture who is considering forming a company to avoid the problems of personal liability. He is concerned about how to draw up accounts and has asked for your help.
      Explain the following accounting conventions as they would apply to David Woodman:
      Separate Entity
      Realisation
      Historic Cost
      Double Entry   (4)

   (b) David Woodman's records show that from 1 June 1985 to 31 May 1986, the following transactions have been made:

	£
Wages to self	7 500
Wages to apprentice	3 100
New work bench and electric saw	1 200
(bought on 30 November 1985	
with an expected life of 10 years)	
Lease of premises for a year	2 100
Cost of electricity, telephone	
and other sundries	420

Value of goods sold	19 500
Interest paid on bank loan	400
Repayment of part of loan	500
Sale of old work bench	100
(book value £0)	
Cost of materials	4 800

Draw up a profit and loss account for David Woodman for the year ending 31 May 1986, giving as much detail as possible.

You may find the following information useful:

(i) Stock in hand (materials and finished goods) on 1 June 1985 £2 200
on 30 May 1986 £3 000

(ii) David Woodman estimates that he spends one-tenth of his time on administration and marketing work, which should be included as an overhead cost;

(iii) Value of capital equipment on 1 June 1985 was £2 500, and it had an average expected life of five years;

(iv) Tax is payable at the rate of 40 per cent on profits;

(v) Amount owing to suppliers is £500.   (13)

(c) On further examination of David Woodman's records you discover the following:

(i) A table was sold in June 1985 for £250 but the cheque was not honoured and no progress has been made in recovering the money;

(ii) A kitchen dresser which cost £800 had been in stock now for three years. An offer of £600 has just been received for it;

Discuss in each case what amendment, if any, you would make to the profit and loss account to allow for these factors, and why.   (6)

(d) Briefly explain how the profit and loss account would need to be altered to make it suitable for publication, if David Woodman decides to form a company.   (2)   1986 (CLES)

Activities

1 Analyse the published accounts of a company, noting any explanations the accountant considered necessary.

2 Using the information you collected as the result of activity 1 in chapter 4, prepare a cash flow forecast for the business.

3 From the financial pages of a newspaper select ten quoted companies. You should choose well-known companies whose activities are likely to be reported in the press. Keep a record over a period of time of changes in the price of shares, the yield and the price earnings ratio. Over the same period of time find out as much as you can about the activities of these companies and note any changes in the economy or society as a whole that might affect them. Are these changes reflected by changes in the data you are collecting? Attempt to explain any correlations you may observe.

Essays

1 Comment on the usefulness of ratio analysis as a tool for decision making and control.

2 Accounting techniques are designed to present a true and fair picture of the activities of a business. Why is this essential (a) for a sole trader and (b) for a public limited company?

3   Discuss the view that budgetary control is an essential part of the co-ordination processes of a business.

4   Outline and comment on the circumstances in which a contribution approach to costing would be more useful than absorption costing.

5   Comment on the value of break-even analysis in the decision-making process. What additional constraints should a manager bear in mind when using information provided by break-even analysis?

6   To what extent would ratio analysis enable you to draw meaningful conclusions about the performance of different public companies?

7   (a) How might inflation distort the annual accounts of a company?   (10)
    (b) Briefly propose a way for overcoming these problems.   (5)
    (c) How might your suggestion affect the convention, that 'consistency of treatment' and a 'true and fair view' should always characterise the published accounts of a company?   (10)   1985 (CLES)

8   (a) In what ways would accounting information, when prepared for internal management, differ from that compiled for the use of other interested parties?   (15)
    (b) What kind of information would a supplier require of a new customer ordering £1m worth of raw material on a regular basis?   (10)   1986 (CLES)

Chapter 7   Finance

A study of the finance of a business is concerned with three areas:

- the monetary resources of a business;
- the acquisition of monetary resources by a business; and
- the effective management of monetary resources.

Money and its markets

The common denominator of each of the three areas described above is the word 'monetary'. In chapter 2 we examined the nature of money and the role it plays in our society. To summarise that argument, we can say that money, in whatever form a society uses it, represents the claim of an individual, a business, an organisation or the state on the collective wealth of the society. In other words, how much money you hold is your slice of the cake of national wealth. Whether or not the cake is shared fairly is a problem for politicians and will be decided by the culture of a society. We are concerned with how accumulated wealth – that is, wealth that has been *saved* rather than *consumed*, is shared among the people who want it.

In simple terms, money is a resource and it obeys market forces. Unlike other goods money is not bought or sold. It is borrowed and lent. The documents which record the transaction of borrowing and lending (referred to as **bills** and **stocks**) are bought and sold. The price of using money is the **interest rate.** If there is a comparatively large amount of money available compared with the demand for it, then the interest rate will tend to be low. Should demand rise or the supply of money be restricted, then the interest rate will rise. However, the situation is not quite as simple as that. Market power operates in the money market just as it does in other markets. The government, for example, is a major borrower and, as a result, is in a position to influence the interest rate. When the banks change their interest rate there is pressure on the building societies to follow suit. Both are hoping to attract funds from a similar group of savers.

The use of funds

In chapter 6 we looked at the balance sheet of a business and emphasised the fact that the balance sheet showed the sources of funds used in a business and how these funds had been used. In this chapter we will look at the sources of funds in more detail and examine some of the techniques a business will use in making decisions about the use and management of the funds available.

In the simplest terms, a business spends money on acquiring factories and equipment, on buying in stock with which to carry on the business and in paying labour and other expenses necessary to the business. Reality is, of course, more complex. Look at the following example:

A husband and wife own and jointly run a small general store in an inner city area. They live in a flat over the shop. Property prices in the area are not high and they were able to buy the leasehold of the shop and flat for £20 000. Stocking the shop required another £20 000, and they required another £5 000 each year to meet expenses. In common with many other small businesses the owners did not pay themselves a set wage. Instead, they drew enough money from the business each week to meet their immediate expenses and reserved large items of personal expenditure for times when the cash balance of the business was sufficiently high, in their judgement, to cover foreseeable business outgoings and still leave a surplus. At 31 December 1985 the cash balances of the business stood at £15 000.

At 31 December 1985 this business employed a total capital of £55 000. Of this approximately 36 per cent was invested in **fixed assets** (buildings, fixtures and fittings), a further 36 per cent in stock, and approximately 27 per cent in liquid assets (cash). The flat in which the couple live has been regarded as part of the business because it would be impracticable for it to be let or sold separately from the business.

Now look at the next example:

A multi-national company decided to sell one of its subsidiaries. Three members of the existing management team decided to buy the business. (This is known as a **management buy-out**.) The price was £10m. For this money the new owners got the factory, machinery, existing stock, existing orders and the right to use the trade name under which the products were already being sold. They also raised an additional £1m.

A breakdown of the asset structure of this business gave fixed assets 60 per cent of the total, stock 23 per cent and liquid assets 17 per cent. Which of the two businesses had made the right decisions in deciding how they would use the money they had available to them? The answer is, from the evidence given here, we don't know! Both may have been right. Equally, one or both could be very wrong. The decision about how a business should use its funds and what proportion it should devote to any particular use depends on a number of factors. Some are quantifiable; others depend upon skill and judgement. The following list must only be seen as an indication of the way in which a business might be influenced in the final decision.

1 *The technology used*   A business which uses advanced technology is likely to employ a larger proportion of its total assets as fixed assets. Advanced technology is usually expensive but it can offer savings on labour and materials. If it is easier to use, it can reduce training costs and the need to employ expensive skilled labour.

2 *The nature of the business*   An engineering firm will need the premises and machinery to carry out its work. Stock levels may be kept quite low. A retailer, on the other hand, could have relatively low fixed costs but needs to hold a higher level of stock.

3 *The size of the business*   Even within the same industry a small business might show a different asset structure from a large business. It could be that, although classified as being in the same industry, they are making different products or that the smaller business cannot afford the technology available to a larger business. It could be a matter of scale. Small firms might have to buy stocks in larger quantities than their situation demands whereas a larger business with greater market power could regulate its stocks according to its needs.

4 *The stage of development*   A new or expanding business is likely to have a distorted asset structure compared with a business in the same industry that is in a more settled phase of its life.

5   *The size of the market*   A business with a large, constant market for its product will be more likely to use production methods that require the use of large amounts of capital equipment.

6   *The skill of the management* may also affect the asset structure. Bad management can produce a bad asset structure.

7   *The government*   Tax concessions can affect the asset structure of a business, as can grants. The effect may be marginal but it still exists.

8   *The state of the economy and business confidence*   This factor can be seen as part of the stage in the development of a business. A flourishing economy is likely to encourage expansion. An economy in recession could result in investment in labour-saving machinery.

Influences on the asset structure of a business are illustrated in Figure 7.1.

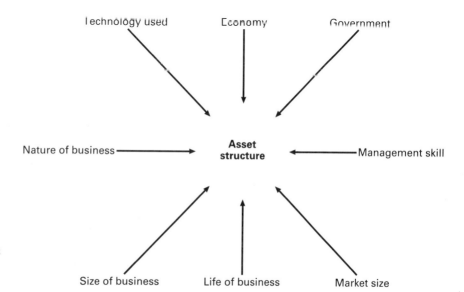

Figure 7.1   Influences on the asset structure of a business

Sources of finance

In chapter 6 we pointed out that there are three main sources of finance for any business: (1) owners' capital; (2) borrowing from other people or organisations; and (3) obtaining goods on credit.

Owners' capital

In a small business or partnership this is limited to the personal wealth the owners put into the business at the beginning and any profits subsequently reinvested.

Methods of increasing owners' capital are listed below:

1   Sole traders and partners may use some of their private wealth to give an injection of capital to a business.

2   Sole traders may take a partner, and partnerships may increase the number of partners.

3   Sole traders or partners might decide to float their business as a company.

4   Existing companies may issue more shares.

5   Profits may be left in the business and used to finance further investment. These profits are sometimes referred to as **ploughed-back** profits.

Advantages of owners' capital

1   Interest has to be paid on borrowed funds. When the interest is not paid the debtors can start legal proceedings that can result in bankruptcy or involuntary liquidation. Shareholders have no right to demand a dividend. Sole traders and partners are not required to make a profit from their business. A high proportion of owner capital can give stability to a business during its initial development and in periods of economic recession when demand might be falling.

2   Owner capital does not carry with it any fixed costs. The interest on loans must be paid and a business might find this difficult in a recession.

3   Shareholders who do not receive the level of dividend they had hoped for can challenge the directors at the Annual General Meeting of the company. Theoretically, shareholders can vote the directors out of office. This seldom happens in practice. A high proportion of share capital, therefore can give the directors greater power in deciding to finance growth from retained profits.

Disadvantages of owners' capital

1   The capital is tied up in the business throughout its life. A sole trader can overcome this problem by taking a partner; partnerships may expand in size by taking additional partners; both may decide to convert to companies. The owner of shares in a company can only convert his holding in the company into cash by selling his share to somebody prepared to buy it. This is relatively easy if the company in which he holds the share is **listed** on the Stock Exchange. The body that runs the Stock Exchange (**the Stock Exchange Council**) will only accept a company for listing – and therefore for its shares to be bought and sold by members – if it meets stringent financial requirements. People holding shares in unlisted companies find it more difficult to sell them. Aware of this problem, the Stock Exchange opened another market for shares in 1980. This is known as the Unlisted Securities Market (USM). The financial requirements needed to enter this market are less stringent than those required for listed securities but they still provide safeguards for people buying and selling shares on the Stock Exchange.

2   A high proportion of owner capital increases the owners' risk. They may be shareholders in a listed company, but if they wish to dispose of their shares at any time they may have to sell for a lower price than they paid – particularly if the dividends of the company have been low compared with the prevailing rate of interest or the dividends paid by other companies.

3   Raising money by issuing more shares is expensive in administrative costs. A **rights issue**, where shares are offered to existing shareholders, is the cheapest method. It is also difficult for a company to estimate the market price of its shares and, if they are under-priced, there is an additional cost to the company. Issuing shares by **tender** attempts to overcome this problem by stating the minimum price the company will accept for its shares and inviting the public to state how much they are prepared to pay for them.

Apart from the administrative costs of floating a share issue, owner capital appears the cheapest method of acquiring funds. The opportunity cost of using owner capital – that is, the earning potential of alternative investment – should not be forgotten.

Preference shares

Between owner capital and loans there is a less well-defined area of **preference shares**. The holder of a preference share

1 is not an owner of the company;
2 receives a fixed rate of return but has no legal right to it;
3 has priority over ordinary shareholders when a dividend is declared;
4 has priority over ordinary shareholders when the company goes into liquidation.

Apart from these four points the rights of preference shareholders will vary from company to company. Companies design their preference shares to attract investors who do not want to take the risk of holding ordinary shares and who either do not have sufficient capital to lend to the company or wish to spread the risks of lending money. **Cumulative preference** shares have the right to claim arrears of dividends if the company does not pay a dividend in one year. **Redeemable preference** shares can be bought back by the company after a stated number of years. Some preference shares carry voting rights, others do not. The rights of the preference shareholders are laid down in the Articles of Association of the company.

Borrowing

Borrowing money places an obligation on a business to repay specified amounts of the money borrowed when they are due and to meet regular interest payments of an agreed amount. This obligation remains, irrespective of the size of the company. Apart from these basic principles, the terms of loans negotiated between businesses and people or organisations prepared to lend money vary according to the needs of the business and the conditions the lenders feel are required to safeguard their money. The following list of definitions will give some indication of the variety of agreements that can be made between those who borrow and those who lend:

- *Secured loans* In return for granting the loan, the lender insists on some asset of the business being tied to the repayment of the loan. In the event of bankruptcy or liquidation that lender will then have priority on the money from the sale of that asset for the repayment of that loan. A specialised form of secured loan is a **mortgage**. In this case the asset is always land or property. These securities are known as **collateral** for the loan – properties pledged by the borrower to provide security for the lender. Unsecured loans are repaid from the fund generated by the sale of all other assets if the firm goes bankrupt or into liquidation. Lenders are less certain that they will be repaid.

- *Syndicated loans* A syndicate is a group of people who join together to carry out a certain transaction. Where a great deal of money is borrowed, no one person or organisation may be able or willing to provide the total sum. In these circumstances a syndicate may be formed to provide the money, each member of the syndicate stating how much he is prepared to lend.

- *Personal guarantee* Limited liability protects the owners of a business from the need to repay debts above the amount they have directly invested in a business. A bank lending to a small limited company may demand a personal guarantee that the debt will be repaid. Effectively, this removes the advantages of limited liability for the principal shareholders in that they will have to use personal assets to repay the loan if the assets of the business are inadequate.

- *Debentures* These are known collectively as **stock**. A debenture is a long-term loan which does not have to be repaid until an agreed date (**maturity**). Debenture holders are entitled to a fixed rate of return each year and have priority over all shareholders. Unlike other forms of debt, debentures can be bought and sold on the Stock Exchange. The company will continue to pay the agreed rate of return to the new owner.

  Because the rate of return is fixed when the loan is negotiated the price of a debenture will fluctuate according to the rate of interest. A fixed rate of interest of 10 per cent means that for every £100 the company gains from a particular debenture they will pay each year £10 to whoever owns that debenture. Let us assume that the rate of interest paid by a commercial bank on deposit accounts rises to 12.5 per cent. In practical terms it means that if a 10 per cent debenture stock is purchased at the price at which it was first issued, the buyer would be sacrificing £2.50 for each £100 of stock bought. The *maximum* price he would be prepared to pay would be one which gave him a return of 12.5 per cent. The maximum price the purchaser would be prepared to pay would be £80. You should try the same calculation assuming a general interest rate of 8 per cent. The value of stock varies inversely with the rate of interest.

- *Loans by organisations* It was pointed out in chapter 4 that CoSIRA was prepared to give loans to businesses intending to trade in rural areas. A number of other organisations – for example, local authorities wishing to attract industry – offer loans to businesses. Sometimes the organisation offering loans comprises central and/or local government interests as well as private business. A Development Agency for a region might negotiate a loan for a project that calls on a syndicate of these three interest groups. Finance for Industry (FFI), established in 1973, provides loans through two subsidiaries: the Industrial and Commercial Finance Corporation (ICFC) and the Finance Corporation for Industry (FCI).

- *Bank loans* These are possibly the simplest forms of loans available to business. The average bank manager dealing with a small to medium-sized firm and responsible to his superiors for the performance of his branch uses a set of well-defined criteria when making a loan. Like other loans, a bank loan is for a fixed amount at a fixed rate of interest. There is likely to be a demand for regular repayments.

> **SELF-ASSESSMENT**
>
> 1 What is the minimum opportunity cost to a small businessman who invests £10 000 in his own business when the rate of interest paid on bank deposit accounts is 9.5 per cent? What other sacrifices might be involved in his decision?
> 2 Draw a graph showing the changes in the value of stock with a nominal value of £100 when the interest rate changes as follows: 8 per cent, 10 per cent, 12 per cent, 14 per cent, 11.5 per cent.

In practical terms a business may simply see its loans as those which will need to be repaid in the next accounting period (**current**) and those which have more than a year to run.

Shares or borrowing?

We have already pointed out that the interest on a loan is a fixed charge on the business; that is, it *must* be paid irrespective of the amount of money the business has generated in a year. The higher the level of debt capital in relation to equity capital, therefore, the greater the risk to the holders of equity capital. In addition to the need to service the loans, the dates for repayment may fall at times when the business finds it difficult to meet them. An otherwise healthy business may have a period of poor trading. If it needs to borrow more money it will be at a disadvantage and may have to pay a higher rate of interest and/or accept more stringent terms than it would otherwise have had to do.

The holders of a debt are likely to watch closely the progress of a business to which they have lent money. In a small business, for example, a condition of being granted a bank loan might be the careful monitoring of the business by a bank. This can inhibit business decision making.

Financing by borrowing can also have its advantages:

1   In periods of inflation the *real* rate of return on fixed interest loans falls. This simply means that the interest payments will purchase fewer goods and services as inflation progresses. The same is true of the repayment of the principal. It will be worth less in real terms than it was when the loan was floated.

2   The cost of borrowing money is a stated cost which can be useful in assessing the costs of production.

3   There are tax advantages in that tax is paid after interest has been paid. This means that a business has to earn more money if it is to give the owners the same rate of return that it pays to subscribers of loan capital.

SELF-ASSESSMENT

1 State two disadvantages to a business of borrowing money.
2 A business is expected to grow rapidly over a period of three years. State two possible advantages to the business of funding this growth by borrowing.

Other sources of funds

Medium-term funds

It is usually accepted that medium-term finance is for a period of one to five years.

1   *Hire purchase*   Under a hire purchase agreement goods are hired to the user who has the option to purchase them at the end of the hiring period. The ownership of the good remains with the hirer. The funds for hire purchase are provided by specialised financial companies known as **finance houses**. The usual practice is for the finance company to give the full purchase price to the *seller* of the good and negotiate repayment terms with the *buyer*. Both the seller and the buyer benefit: the seller because he gains the purchase price immediately and because the availability of hire purchase can attract buyers; the buyer because he does not have to wait until he has accumulated the necessary capital to have the use of the good.

2   *Leasing and hiring*   At first sight leasing and hiring appear to be different terms used to describe the same situation – namely, that a business does not own an item of capital equipment but pays to use it for a limited period of time. This definition describes **hiring**.

A business will **lease** equipment that it needs for a longer period of time. Under a leasing agreement a finance company will purchase a specific item of equipment for use by a business. The equipment remains the property of the finance company but the business has the sole use of it for which it pays an agreed rent. The agreement may be for a given period of time or for the life of the equipment. The terms of each agreement will vary. Specialised equipment might have a maintenance clause. The company leasing it will provide maintenance to avoid problems arising from inexpert handling. Where the technology to maintain a piece of equipment is generally available maintenance is more likely to be the responsibility of the lessee – that is, the business leasing the equipment.

Advantages of leasing are listed below:

(a) Leasing can help preserve the liquidity of a business. Where the purchase of a piece of equipment will affect current and liquidity ratios leasing can be a more attractive alternative.
(b) A time lease can give the business the opportunity of keeping abreast with a changing technology. In fields where technology is changing rapidly it may be more sensible to lease a piece of equipment than to tie up capital in machinery which will be obsolescent within a few years.
(c) Like fixed interest loans the leasing payments are constant, and are charged against the income of the business before tax is calculated. This reduces the cost of leasing to the business and gives it some protection against fluctuations in interest rates.
(d) A servicing agreement may be both an advantage and a disadvantage to the business. A lease might state that servicing must be done by nominated firms or their own engineers. The cost of such servicing can be high in that the leasing agreement creates a monopoly. To be offset against this are clauses that guarantee substitute equipment during the repair period.
(e) Like all fixed financial obligations, the burden becomes less in real terms during a time of inflation.

The disadvantages of leasing are as follows:

(a) It is a fixed obligation on the business which may be too great in a recession.
(b) Should the equipment become obsolete before the expiry of the lease it may affect the profitability and competitiveness of the business.
(c) The business has to forgo the advantages of owning the equipment.

In psychological terms, ownership may convey prestige and an impression of stability. In financial terms, assets bought during a profitable time of trading can be a security for loans in less profitable times.

The final decision as to whether or not to lease will depend upon the situation in which a business finds itself and the terms of the lease offered. It will take into account such factors as the growth potential of the business, the rate of technological change, the value of the asset to be purchased and the expertise of management in making investment decisions.

Short-term funds (less than one year)

A **bank overdraft** is an arrangement between the business and its bank to draw more money from the current account, to an agreed limit, than is deposited in it. An overdraft has the advantage of being flexible and, as the amount of money on which interest is paid is reduced with each deposit, can prove a cheap form of finance. Against this is the ease with which the bank can withhold overdraft facilities. This could cause serious cash-flow problems for a business which had come to rely on its overdraft.

The owner of a small shop selling consumer durables holds a limited amount of stock, chiefly for display purposes, and buys only when there is a firm order from a customer. The customer does not pay until the purchase is delivered. The capital available to the owner is adequate to cover these transactions for most of the year. Christmas brings a sharp increase in orders. The owner of the shop finances his Christmas trade with an overdraft. The maximum length of time for which it is needed is two months, and during that period there is a steady inflow of payments, thus reducing the overdraft.

Trade credit can also be viewed as a short-term loan. The purchaser does not have to pay for the goods immediately, and during that time he has the use of the money. No formal interest is paid but the sacrifice of **cash discount** has the same effect.

SELF-ASSESSMENT

1 Explain why an overdraft can be a cheap form of finance for a business.
2 Servicing a loan is a fixed charge on the business. In what way can that be an advantage in times of inflation?

The internal management of finance

Once a business has assembled its capital what does it do with it? We have already seen, at the beginning of the chapter, that the asset structure, as it appears on the balance sheet, will depend on the individual circumstances of the business. It is now time to look more closely at some of the problems facing a business when it is deciding how to use its available capital.

How much cash should the business hold? Economic theory states that **liquidity preference** – that is, the desire to hold resources in cash rather than other forms, is governed by three motives:

- the **transactions** motive, which is concerned with the need to have sufficient money to undertake necessary buying;

- the **precautionary** motive, which can be summarised as 'just in case' – the money is held to provide security for the business; and

- the **speculative** motive, which is governed by the desire to have sufficient liquid capital to take advantage of future opportunities for profit.

The definitions of the motives for holding money given here are superficial rather than precise in economic terms. However, they can give some indication of the way in which a business might respond to different situations.

1 In a period of inflation a business will need to hold a higher cash level than in a period of price stability. When prices are high more money will be needed to finance transactions and more money will need to be held to give security against an unexpected decline in trade. This will not necessarily affect the asset structure of the business. If all assets are valued at current cost, the proportion of the total held in cash could remain the same. On the other hand, if fixed assets are valued at historic cost this situation will give a distorted view of the business's position.

2 When interest rates are high the business is sacrificing more income by holding funds in cash than when they are low. In these circumstances there is a temptation to hold minimum cash balances and invest the rest.

The final decision about how much cash a business will hold will depend upon a mixture of these motives and will be influenced by the circumstance of a business and the judgement of its managers. Even in times of high inflation some businesses are affected less than others.

Working capital

Working capital is defined as the excess of current assets over current liabilities, otherwise known as **net current assets**. In chapter 6 we defined the current ratio as

Current assets:Current liabilities

and stated that a frequently quoted ideal ratio was 2:1. It is this excess of current assets over current liabilities that provides the business with the capital it needs to carry on its day-to-day activities. The management of working capital can be crucial to the survival of a business.

Management of working capital

The main objectives in the management of working capital can be summarised as follows:

1   To keep the time lag between the *input* of resources into production and the *payment* for goods and services produced as short as possible. This will reduce the amount of current assets (stocks, debtors and cash) the business needs to invest in at any one time. The same amount of investment is working harder.

2   The financing should be kept as efficient as possible to ensure the greatest possible return on capital employed.

The management of working capital is the application of common sense. They are the principles used by any person managing his or her income:

•   Do not borrow too much money when the ability to repay depends upon uncertain income. If you are relying on people who owe you money to be able to meet your own liabilities the failure of one person to pay will cause problems.

•   Do not borrow on a short-term basis to finance medium- or long-term purchases: the short-term loans might dry up. The technical term for this is **overtrading**.

•   Do take into account the opportunity cost. This service/course of action might appear expensive but what are the hidden advantages (i.e. cost reductions) for my business?

•   Ultimately, for a business or an individual, the question is: Will I be able to meet my debts?

The effective management of working capital depends upon the co-operation of all the departments in a business. We can use the control of stock level as an example of this.

The valuation of stocks is usually based on the cost of stocks or their **net realisable value** (that is, what the business would receive if it sold them on the open market), whichever is lower. However, the *level* of stocks held will also depend on a number of other factors, for example:

•   The ability of the purchasing department to maintain a flow of necessary supplies at a rate linked to their usage. If purchasing is erratic, the business may have to hold higher stocks than is strictly necessary.

- The expertise of the marketing department in estimating future demand and the ability of the production department to maintain a steady flow of production to meet that demand. Over-estimating demand can lead to a build-up in stocks of finished and semi-finished goods and, if production is laid off, the build-up of raw materials and components.

Methods of increasing working capital

Working capital can be increased in a number of ways, but it is important to remember that each method will carry with it its own disadvantages.

1   By minimising the **cash operating cycle** – that is, by reducing the time between the buying of resources and the income generated by the use of resources. This is the best way of improving efficiency in the use of working capital provided it does not lead to such things as poor quality control because the emphasis on throughput is too great.

2   Businesses can also increase their working capital by selling assets and leasing them back. This liberates funds but also commits them to regular payments of leasing fees which could become a burden on the business if its income falls for any reason. It also reduces the fixed assets of the business and may limit its opportunities to raise loans.

3   A business may use the services of a debt-factoring company. This is a service in management accounting. The book debts of the business are sold to a specialist firm who will then keep a check on the sales ledger of the company concerned and collect bad debts. In the services it offers debt-factoring differs from **invoice discounting**. The latter can be simplistically described as the sale of debts for an amount below their book value to a business which will collect. The difference between book value and the sale value of the debt provides the income of the invoice discounting company. Debt factoring is expensive; it does, however, provide accounting services which can be of great value, particularly to a small business. Both debt factoring and invoice discounting release finance, allow more accurate cash-flow projections and save administrative costs.

    Increasing the amount of cash available to the business should not be confused with increasing the working capital of a business. In the short term, a business which is short of working capital might wish to increase the cash available to it.

4   A bank overdraft is cheap, easy and quick to negotiate and renew, and offers flexibility. The value of using an overdraft depends on the use to which it is put. A business that uses an overdraft to provide finance because its debtors are late in paying is paying twice for the same money. If the overdraft is used to increase sales then there is the potential of greater profit. Whether or not an overdraft should be used in these circumstances depends on the judgement of the businessman concerned. Potential profit must be greater than the cost of the overdraft.

5   Trade credit can be tempting, but creditors increase the risk of bankruptcy or liquidation. Too many small businesses have failed, particularly in the retail sector, because they have ignored the basic principles of control of creditors. Discounts for prompt payment should not be ignored. They will improve the ability of a business to meet unexpected debts. In other words, they are part of the cash management of a business.

6   Tax and rate payments can often be delayed but, unfortunately, local authorities and government departments are frequently the most aggressive of creditors if the payment cannot be met on time.

If you do not understand the distinction between increasing working capital and increasing the cash available for a business to use, re-read the definition of working capital and refer back to the T form balance sheet in chapter 6 (page 95). If a business is granted an overdraft for £1 000 this will increase cash at the bank by the same amount – but will it change the relationship between current assets and current liabilities?

SELF-ASSESSMENT

1 Define the term 'working capital'.
2 How can an analysis of the accounts of a business help a potential investor judge the efficiency with which working capital is managed by a business?

Investment decisions

The word 'investment' is one of the many words in the English language that appear to have a number of different usages. An investment can be a siege or blockade in military terms, it can be the purchase of stocks and shares, the decision as to whether to buy another business (which is in the area of mergers and takeover bids) or it can be the decision whether to buy a particular piece of machinery. All the possible definitions of investment have one thing in common: resources are risked in a venture that might, but not necessarily will, bring future advantage.

- A town is besieged. The men, guns, food, ammunition and the rest of the army are committed to reducing that town. The advantages of a siege are difficult to express in monetary terms. It can only be judged by cost/benefit analysis: if we besiege this town it will cost us £x; if we do not besiege this town its garrison may attack us from the rear.

- Buying this business will cost a certain amount of money. On the other hand, it will allow us to operate more effectively in the market. What is the cost? What are the potential gains?

- Buying this machine will increase our productive capacity/reduce costs/ improve our image. What are the costs? What are the potential gains?

The techniques of decision making are all concerned with attempts to measure cost and potential gain. The method chosen will depend on the circumstances of the business.

The payback method

The payback method calculates the period of time it takes for an investment to pay for itself out of the profit it generates (see example on p. 133).

A short payback period can be useful in the following circumstances:

1 When technology is changing rapidly. A business does not want to purchase an expensive piece of equipment and find that it is obsolete before it has been paid for. Of course, this may not be very important. A machine does not have to employ the latest technology to do the job it was designed for effectively. In certain circumstances, however, innovations can carry with them cost and efficiency advantages that put the users of older machines at a disadvantage in the market. The payback method allows a businessman to estimate whether or not he will 'break even' on the purchase of the machine before he needs to replace it.

2   When machines or products become obsolete. (It is not only machines that become obsolete; products, too, can go out of favour with customers before they have brought in sufficient revenue to repay the costs of investment. This is particularly true of high-fashion products whose life may be only a few months before another product takes their place. It can also be true of technical products when innovation is moving rapidly.)

3   The payback method, like all methods of investment appraisal, can be used to compare the advantages of machines with similar performance but with different costs.

A machine is bought for £10 000. The purchaser makes an estimate of the additional revenue per year that will be generated as a result of using the machine and the annual direct and maintenance costs required to support this revenue.

	£
Sales	20 000
Direct labour	5 000
Direct materials	6 000
Indirect labour	700
Maintenance	300
Total cost	£12 000

The machine will give the business an extra income of £8 000 per year and will pay for itself in 1.25 years.

SELF-ASSESSMENT

1 Explain why the payback method is a useful technique in a high-fashion market.
2 If the original cost of a machine was £20 000 and it is expected to increase profits by £4 000 per year, what is the payback period?

Return on investment

The income generated by a machine, over and above the costs attributable to that machine, can be regarded as the 'profit' made by possessing that machine. Of course, this figure will still be subject to overheads, tax and other charges before it makes its contribution to net profit. This 'profit' can be expressed as a return on investment in precisely the same way as a potential investor might express the expected dividend on a share as a percentage of the purchase price in order to compare its income yield with alternative investment opportunities.

To compare the income generated by the use of a machine with its total purchase cost would not give a true picture of the return on investment. It is more usual to spread the cost of the machine, minus its value at the end of that time (**residual value**) evenly over the life of the machine.

A machine costs £12 000 and is expected to have a life of ten years. At the end of that time the business expects to sell it for £2 000. The cost of the machine to the business is, therefore, £12 000 − £2 000 = £10 000. Spread over the ten years of the life of the machine we can say that it is costing the firm £1 000 per year.

If we assume that the machine generates a profit of £100 each year, then the rate of return on this investment can be given as 10 per cent.

This method of judging an investment provides a useful comparison with the return on other uses to which the available capital could be put. It contains elements of the payback method, in that the expected life of the machine and its residual value will be based on the rate of technical innovation and the length of time the market for the products is expected to last.

Neither the payback method nor the rate of return make allowances for the fact that future money is worth less than present money. Both methods become more precise if the concept of present value is incorporated into the calculations.

Net present value (NPV)

The idea of **present value** is founded in the concept of opportunity cost. If you have £500 to invest at this moment, and place it in a bank account where it will earn 10 per cent interest, at the end of twelve months you will have £550. It can therefore be said that the present value of £550 in twelve months' time is £500. Re-invested for another twelve months at 10 per cent interest, the original £500 would be worth £605, and so on.

How can this information help a businessman in his investment decisions? Let us assume a businessman has £5000 and two courses of action open to him. He can either leave the money in his bank account, in which case he will earn 10 per cent interest, or he can buy a piece of equipment for his business. He makes some calculations, and estimates that the annual income generated by owning the piece of equipment will be as follows:

Year 1	£2000
Year 2	£2500
Year 3	£4000
Year 3	£5000
Year 4	£4500
Year 5	£4000

Before he can judge whether or not this investment is worthwhile he needs to know the present value of the income flows. He can calculate this by **discounting**. The simplest way of viewing discounting is to see it as the reverse process of calculating compound interest. Instead of starting with a sum of money and calculating how much it will earn if it is invested for a period of years and if all interest earned is re-invested, we begin with the future sum of money and reduce it by an agreed percentage for each year it has been invested. At the end of this process we have the **principal** – that is, the sum of money which, when invested, would have resulted in the future sum of money.

In the example given above, the businessman expected the equipment to earn £2000 by the end of the first year of its use. £1 discounted at 10 per cent would have a present value of £0.909. The £2000 would therefore have a present value of £2000 × 0.909 = £1818. The money earned in Year 2 would be discounted at 10 per cent, but over two years instead of one. The present value of each £1 would therefore be lower at £0.826, giving a total present value for the £2500 of £2065.

To save people the trouble of making individual calculations, present value tables have been drawn up which give the present value of £1 over a range of time and at different discount rates. An example of such a table is given in

Table 7.1. Many calculators have a discounting function, and computers can, of course, be programmed to perform the operation.

Years

%	1	2	3	4	5	6	7	8	9	10
1	0.9901	0.9803	0.9706	0.9610	0.9515	0.9420	0.9327	0.9235	0.9143	0.9053
2	0.9804	0.9612	0.9423	0.9238	0.9057	0.8880	0.8706	0.8535	0.8368	0.8203
3	0.9709	0.9426	0.9151	0.8885	0.8626	0.8375	0.8131	0.7894	0.7664	0.7441
4	0.9615	0.9246	0.8890	0.8548	0.8219	0.7903	0.7599	0.7307	0.7026	0.6756
5	0.9524	0.9070	0.8638	0.8227	0.7835	0.7462	0.7107	0.6768	0.6446	0.6139
6	0.9434	0.8900	0.8396	0.7921	0.7473	0.7050	0.6651	0.6274	0.5919	0.5584
7	0.9346	0.8734	0.8163	0.7629	0.7130	0.6663	0.6227	0.5820	0.5439	0.5083
8	0.9259	0.8573	0.7938	0.7350	0.6806	0.6302	0.5835	0.5403	0.5002	0.4632
9	0.9174	0.8417	0.7722	0.7084	0.6499	0.5963	0.5470	0.5019	0.4604	0.4224
10	0.9091	0.8264	0.7513	0.6830	0.6209	0.5645	0.5132	0.4665	0.4241	0.3855

Table 7.1   Net present value of £1.00

So far we have talked about the income generated by the investment as if there were no expenses involved. In fact, the businessman would need to deduct operating expenses and the production costs associated with the machine before he could judge the 'profit' it would bring him. In other words, he would draw up a projected cash flow as generated by the machine. This appraisal technique is usually known as **discounted cash flow** (DCF).

For an investment to show the possibility of profit the total of all discounted cash flows for the life of the machine should be *greater* than the proposed investment. If the discounted cash flows for a proposed investment of £5 000 total £7 000, it means that the businessman would have had to invest £7 000 at 10 per cent in order to earn that money. The investment is earning a higher rate of return than 10 per cent.

Conclusion

The decisions that face businesses in the raising of capital, the management of cash and working capital and investment decisions have been reduced in this chapter to a few simple principles explained in terms of relatively uncomplicated examples. In reality, decision makers are faced with a number of options each of which will offer advantages and disadvantages which will vary according to the situation of the firm. Changes in technology, the law, availability and the cost of finance may be experiences shared by a number of businesses, but the response of individual firms to these external influences will depend upon the leadership and skill of the management, the power of trade unions, the past profitability of the business and the confidence the management has in its future. In short, financial decisions translate the needs of the various functions of a business into monetary terms just as management accounting provides summaries of the working of the business in monetary terms.

Review

1 Banks Ltd produces glass-reinforced plastic products for the industrial market. The production manager wants to invest in a machine for one of the processes. The machine design is based on advanced technology of which the employees of Banks Ltd have little personal experience. The production

manager has seen the machine at a trade exhibition and is impressed with its specifications and the claims made concerning its importance. He argues strongly for its purchase.

Other members of the management team are less convinced. They point out that the new machine will cost £150000, whereas the existing machine still has a useful life of five years and replacement with conventional technology would cost just £50000. The existing machine generates an income of £10000 per annum after running costs and depreciation (calculated on the straight line method) of £5000 per annum have been deducted. They also point out that alterations to the factory to accommodate the new machine would cost an additional £20000 and that this sum would have to be paid out again if, in future, they decided to revert to the more traditional technology.

The production manager counteracted with the information that the new machine would generate income of £60000 per annum after the deduction of running expenses and depreciation (also calculated on a straight line basis) of £30000.

Banks Ltd normally requires a minimum of 15 per cent return on any of its investment projects.

(a) Assuming that the income figures have remained the same throughout the life of the original machine and that depreciation is based on the working life of the machines with minimal residual value, evaluate the options open to Banks Ltd using the investment appraisal techniques outlined in this chapter.

(b) Which method of investment appraisal might be most appropriate for the new machine? Give reasons for your answer.

(c) What other information would you require before making the final decision?

2   Doyle's Electronics Ltd intends to invest £500000 in an extension to the factory. It is estimated that the increase in income generated by this investment and available to service the capital requirements will be:

Year	Income (£000s)
1	50.0
2	62.5
3	75.0
4	87.5
5	100.0

(a) Assuming that 80 per cent of the capital required is provided by the company from its own resources and the rest of the money is raised by secured loans at 15 per cent, calculate the annual earnings of the company as a percentage of capital invested.

(b) Assuming that 80 per cent of the capital required is raised by secured loans at 15 per cent interest, calculate the annual return to the company as a percentage of capital invested.

(c) What is the significance of the information you have derived from (a) and (b) in assisting the company in making the investment decision? What other factors should it take into account?

3   Freshfields DIY Emporium is a large shop situated in the suburb of a city. It carries a wide range of materials and tools designed to appeal to the home owner and gardener. The emphasis of the range is on decorative and luxury items rather than on the purely utilitarian. As many of his customers are commuters, the owner of the shop, a sole trader, offers credit to his

customers, many of whom have developed the habit of phoning their orders into the shop during the week. The goods are then delivered on the Friday evening and payment is made at the customer's convenience in the following weeks. All supplies are paid for in cash. There are very few bad debts.

Overall the business made a satisfactory profit, but several times in 1986 the owner found it necessary to use overdraft facilities to finance his purchases. This trend caused him some concern and he examined his annual accounts for 1985 and 1986 with more than usual care. These are shown in Table 7.2.

Freshfields DIY Emporium

Balance sheet as at 31 December 1986

	1985		1986	
	£	£	£	£
Fixed assets		60 000		65 000
Current assets				
Stock	10 500		21 250	
Debtors	25 150		37 630	
Cash	5 000		1 000	
	40 650		59 880	
Deduct				
Current liabilities				
Bank overdraft	1 000		12 000	
Creditors	—		—	
	1 000		12 000	
Net current assets		39 650		47 880
Total assets		99 650		112 880
Financed by				
Proprietor's funds		50 000		55 000
Retained profit		49 650		57 880
		99 650		112 880

Profit and loss account

	1985		1986	
	£	£	£	£
Revenue from sales		240 000		265 000
Cost of sales		160 000		176 000
Gross profit		80 000		89 000
Expenses				
Sales	25 000		36 250	
Admin.	10 000		10 000	
Heating, lighting	5 000	40 000	6 000	52 250
		40 000		36 750
Interest		100		1 200
Net profit before tax		39 900		35 550
Tax due on profit		11 970		10 650
Net profit after tax		27 930		24 900

Table 7.2   Freshfields DIY Emporium, annual accounts, 1985 and 1986

(a) Assuming that all sales are on credit, comment on the average number of days when any particular debt is outstanding in both years using the following ratio:

$$\frac{\text{Debtors at the end of the year}}{\text{Sales}} \times 365$$

(b) Calculate (i) the rate of interest paid on the overdraft.
(ii) the rate of tax paid on net profit.
(iii) the real rate of interest paid on the overdraft by the Freshfields DIY Emporium.

comparing 1985 with 1986.

(c) From the figures available to you explain why the position of the business was worse in 1986 than in 1985.

(d) The average length of time goods remain in stock can be calculated by:

$$\frac{\text{Finished goods stock}}{\text{Cost of sales}} \times 365$$

What is the average length of time of stock holding by the Freshfields DIY Emporium?

(e) Outline the ways in which the owner of the Freshfields DIY Emporium might improve his management of his working capital. What other factors might he need to take into account before making his final decisions?

(f) Comment on the liquidity position of the business, using appropriate ratios.

4 Micro Ltd is a small private electronics company run by Anne Little, who owns 60 per cent of the equity. It is a fast-growing profitable business with sales of £800 000 over the last year ending 30 April 1986, giving a post-tax profit of £60 000. The company is anxious to expand, as the market demand for its product is growing fast. It needs finance, however, to do this.

(a) (i) What are the main external sources of finance available to Micro Ltd?
(ii) What factors should Anne Little consider in choosing which to use? (8)

(b) Over the next two years, Micro is planning rapid expansion and it expects sales and profits to increase each year by 25 per cent of the present level. It also aims for:

stocks = 3 months' sales
debtors = 2 months' sales
creditors = 1 month's sales.

As no new capital equipment has been bought during the last year, Micro plans to spend £100 000 on replacing existing machines during the next two years, and the same again on new machinery.

The present situation of the company is shown on the balance sheet below.

Balance sheet for Micro Ltd year ending 30 April 1986

1985 (£000s)		1986 (£000s)	1985 (£000s)		1986 (£000s)
410	Shareholder funds	430	150	Land and buildings	150
120	Long-term loan	120	220	Machinery	200
110	Creditors	120	245	Stock	250
170	Bank overdraft	130	195	Debtors	200
810		800	810		800

Stating clearly any assumptions made, calculate the following:
(i) the cash required to support this expansion; (4)
(ii) the extent to which internal funds will contribute. (5)
(c) Using the information given in the balance sheet above calculate the following ratios: (i) Current, (ii) Acid test and (iii) Gearing. On the basis of these ratios, make recommendations as to how the company should raise any external finance necessary for its expansion? (5)
(d) If it cannot raise the necessary cash, what alternatives are open to the company? (3) 1986 (CLES)

5 (a) Describe the main options open to British companies if they wish to raise long-term capital. (5)
(b) A small engineering firm (Blacklock Ltd) consists of four departments, three of which are production departments (P_1, P_2 and P_3), whilst the fourth (D) deals with the administration of the whole business. Data for the four departments are given below:

	P_1	P_2	P_3	D
Number of Employees	10	8	8	5
Average wages per employee per week	£225	£200	£150	£100
Fixed costs per week	£2500	£1000	£1500	£1000
Other variable costs – average per employee per hour	£40	£20	£40	None
Capital used, at cost ('000)	£150	£100	£50	£10
Working hours per week	30	30	30	30

(i) Which of the methods described in answer to part (a) above would you recommend if Blacklock wished to raise a modest amount of capital and obtain a quotation on the Stock Exchange for the first time. Explain the reasons for your recommendation. (5)
(ii) From the data above, prepare a weekly budget of costs for the total business and for each of the four departments. You should assume that each department is to be charged with interest at 10 per cent per annum (assume a 50-week year) and that since D does not earn revenue, its costs are to be aggregated and then allocated to P_1, P_2 and P_3 in the proportions of 40:40:20 respectively. (10)
(c) What other sources of finance are available to Blacklock Ltd, if they finally decide not to get a quotation from the Stock Exchange, and what might be their advantages and disadvantages from Blacklock's point of view? (5) June 1985 (CLES)

Activities

1 Investigate the working of the Stock Exchange. Collect as much information as you can about the deregulation of the financial markets in October 1986, and comment on any insights that this information may give you into the working of a market.

2 Interview a retailer and a small manufacturer/craftsman concerning their management of their working capital. Pay particular attention to any practices that may seem less than ideal and the reasons given for following them.

3 Compare the capital structure of a number of companies from their published accounts. Attempt to explain any differences you might observe.

Essays

1   In what circumstances might a businessman decide to lease rather than buy a piece of capital equipment?

2   The directors of a company are considering floating it on the Unlisted Securities Market. Comment on the factors which might influence their decision.

3   Discuss the factors which will determine the capital structure of a business.

4   Outline and discuss the methods of investment appraisal that a business might use.

5   The management of both cash and working capital is essential to the survival of a business enterprise. Discuss.

6   A business that relies too heavily on borrowing in order to finance capital expenditure is too vulnerable. Discuss.

7   The following is an extract from the balance sheet of a public limited company:

Ordinary shares	£
Authorised 800 000 at £1 each	800 000
Issued and fully paid 700 000 at £1 each	700 000
General reserve	50 000
Long-term borrowing	
Debentures 10% (2010)	250 000
Capital employed	£1 000 000

The company now wishes to raise an additional £500 000 to finance the development of a new product. Assess the implications of the relevant alternative sources of finance.   1986 (AEB)

8   (a) What is the role of the average rate of return when evaluating investment projects?   (5)
   (b) When might the payback period be a better technique?   (5)
   (c) What advantages and disadvantages would the discounted cash-flow technique have over other methods when evaluating investment decisions?   (15)   1986 (CLES)

9   Your firm has decided to make a take-over bid for a firm supplying you with raw materials. The question arises as to whether you should offer equity capital or cash.
   (a) What factors should be taken into account when making the decision whether to offer equity capital or cash?   (15)
   (b) What might be the financial consequences for shareholders of the company being taken over?   (10)   1986 (CLES)

Chapter 8　Marketing

Which comes first, marketing or production? Goods must be made before they can be sold, and services must be available before the customer can buy them. In the logical sequence of events production comes first. Before goods are made and services are provided it would seem sensible to make sure that there is a demand for the products of the business at a price the business can meet. This is a function of marketing.

The functions of production and marketing are interdependent. In a **market-oriented** business the demands of the market will form part of the constraints of the production function. The design of the product, the methods of production used, packaging and investment decisions are just a few examples of decisions to be made by the production department which will be affected by the market.

Agriculture would, at first sight, appear to be one industry that enjoyed relatively stable demand in terms of the product. People have to eat and, apart from the luxury end of the market (for example, the more exotic fruit and vegetables), the diet of the majority of the population tends to be relatively conservative. It is reasonable to suppose that farmers producing for this market can grow food in advance of sales with confidence. There is, however, a growing concern with the production methods used by farmers. Publicity relating to the use of hormones to induce rapid growth in livestock, the conditions under which battery hens are reared and the effect on fruit and vegetables of the continued use of fertilisers and insecticides are just some of the production practices of modern farming which are causing concern. It would be overstating the case to say that this publicity is affecting the majority of farmers. The trend in consumer thought exists and there is a section of the agricultural industry which is responding to it. The word 'organic' is an important part of the marketing vocabulary of some parts of the farming community and of the industries which supply the domestic gardener.

The interdependence of production and marketing is almost an article of faith to writers on and students of management and business studies. The Department of Trade and Industry offers a Design Advisory Service for business. This offers free initial advice with a sliding scale of charges according to the requirements of the business concerned. It was found that many of the businesses that approached the service had only the most rudimentary marketing policy, and many of them had not undertaken market research. In chapter 4 it was pointed out that the owners and managers of small and medium-sized businesses often lack a specific area of expertise. When the businesses have been built on the technical and practical skills of the founder it is likely that marketing expertise will be the one in short supply. In recognition of this the Department of Trade and Industry offers an advice scheme in marketing similar to that offered in design.

Marketing strategy

Marketing strategy is the organisation of all the resources available to the marketing function to achieve given objectives. The term may also be used to describe the plan drawn up by the marketing function in order to achieve those objectives.

The objectives of marketing

Marketing objectives do not exist in isolation from the rest of the business. They are subordinate to, and should support, the overall objectives of the business. In large businesses this can cause problems of co-ordination, communication and control. The marketing manager who sees his rivals launching a major advertising campaign may argue powerfully that his own business should do the same. Unless his counterparts in production and finance can counter with equally powerful arguments it is likely that he will have his way. There is no guarantee that this course of action would support the overall objectives of the business in terms of profitability and survival.

A business may have a stated objective to increase profitability within a given period of time. This may involve decisions to increase production capacity by an extensive investment programme and enter new markets. In support of this the marketing department may set objectives in the following areas:

1 *Sales volume*   This is the total number of sales made by a business in a given period of time. If profitability is to increase but the profit margin on each unit sold is to remain the same, then the number sold must increase.

2 *Market share*   We have already encountered this term in chapter 3. A business that wishes to achieve a greater degree of market power will want to increase its sales until they account for a larger percentage of the total number of sales of that product and similar products over a period of time.

3 *Product development*   No product has an unlimited life on the market. We shall look at this in more detail later in the chapter when we discuss the product life cycle. One of the objectives of the marketing function is to have products ready to replace those whose sales are falling.

4 *Sales revenue*   The amount of money the business expects to receive from sales will have to take into account production costs, the price the market will bear and the profit margins required by the business.

You should not forget that, although the mareting objectives should support the overall objectives of the business, marketing information has been taken into account when formulating these overall objectives. Marketing information is part of the business plan – the formal statement of business strategy – and will contribute to the budgetary process.

Once the marketing objectives have been formulated there are two broad areas in which the business needs to take action:

- The setting of targets to be achieved in terms of time, geographical area and product. The precise nature of these targets will vary from business to business. A six-months' sales target might be set for Product X in Region Y. Monitoring these targets will enable the business to judge whether or not they are likely to reach their final objective.

- The way in which they will achieve the objectives is also important. Will an intensive marketing campaign increase sales, or would a price reduction be more effective? A review of the way in which the product reaches the final consumer might lead to greater sales, or perhaps a new design might give the product greater appeal to the customer. Any marketing campaign will involve a mixture of these approaches. Collectively they are known as the **marketing mix** and are summarised in the four words '*product*', '*price*', '*promotion*' and '*place*'. A detailed study of the elements of the marketing mix will be given in the second part of this chapter.

SELF-ASSESSMENT

1 Define the market-oriented business.
2 List the major marketing objectives of a business.
3 Distinguish between marketing objectives and targets.
4 What are the major elements of the marketing mix?

Market information

The activities concerned with collecting information on which to base marketing decisions are known collectively as **market research**. It is customary to divide this into two areas:

1 Desk research, which is the collection, analysis and evaluation of information from such sources as government statistics, specialist journals and business accounts.

2 Field research, which involves the collection of data directly from a sample of potential consumers.

Although desk and field research are given as two separate activities, you should remember that the field research of one business can provide the material for desk research in another business. The person who visits your home with a detailed questionnaire on the type of durable consumer goods you possess, the purchases you have made in the last two years and the ones you intend to make in the near future, is unlikely to be working for one manufacturer. The data will be used to compile a report on the market for consumer durables in general, which will then be sold to interested companies.

The cost of field research is high, and requires specialist personnel if it is to be accurate; for those reasons alone it makes sense for many businesses to use the services of agencies rather than to maintain their own departments.

Methods of field research

1 *Questionnaires*   These are the basis of all field research and carry with them a number of problems. It is difficult, for example, to design questions which elicit the information required without ambiguity or without influencing the answer of the person being interviewed. If the questions asked are too narrow, important information may be lost. If they allow the person being interviewed to make too free a response, the information may be difficult to analyse and compare with other questions.

2 *The use of interviewers* to ask prepared questions has the twin disadvantages of being expensive and carries the risk that the interviewer might, consciously or unconsciously, lead the person being interviewed to give a 'desirable' answer. This is known as **interviewer bias**. An experienced interviewer can adapt the question to suit the person being interviewed (the **interviewee**). Unfamiliar words can be explained, the purpose of the question made clear. If you look at the disadvantages of the personal interview and compare them with the disadvantages of the questionnaire you will see a close connection between them. Rephrasing questions takes time and is therefore expensive. It also increases the risk of bias.

3   *Postal questionnaires* rely on precise, unambiguous questions and the willingness of people to return them. In a busy life the answering of questionnaires may receive a very low priority. Even the provision of a reply-paid envelope will not ensure that the questionnaire will be answered and posted. Postal questionnaires depend upon an up-to-date mailing list of the type of people who are likely to be interested in the product. There is the risk that the people receiving the questionnaire will see it as part of their 'junk mail'. This can lead to resentment, suspicion of the way in which the name and address has been acquired (a suspicion which can be transferred to the business undertaking the market research) or the throwing away of the questionnaire into the waste paper basket.

4   *Telephone questionnaires* appear to combine the advantage of the cheapness of postal questionnaires with the one-to-one contact of an interview. They have their own built-in bias: only people with telephones can be contacted. Protection of privacy can cause people to react adversely to this type of market research. Good practice usually begins with a letter to the person about to be interviewed explaining the purpose of the telephone call he or she will receive and asking for co-operation.

>   Mrs Chadwick received a letter from magazine publishers apologising for their invasion of her privacy but hoping she would co-operate in a telephone interview relating to her response to their new title. She was willing to co-operate. The magazine fulfilled many of her needs, but she wanted to make the case for the inclusion of a certain type of article. The phone call was duly made. It was unproductive. The questions to be asked related specifically to the March 1986 issue. This had not been made clear in the letter and Mrs Chadwick had lost the issue. Apologies were made on both sides.

>   Both postal and telephone questionnaires reduce the cost of the research but share the risk of bias with personal interviews.

5   *Panels* are groups of people who agree to keep a record of all their actions as a consumer. The record might be specific, relating to one type of product, or general, relating to a 'basket' of decisions. Again, there is the danger of bias arising from the selection of individuals, but the data are objective.

SELF-ASSESSMENT

1 Explain why questionnaires administered during a personal interview are likely to be more expensive than postal questionnaires.
2 Give **one** reason why panels might be preferred to other methods of field research.

Sampling and bias

We saw in chapter 5 that the total number of people (or things) from which information could be collected is known as the **population**. With a UK total demographic population of 56 million it is unrealistic for a survey to include every person. It would also be uneconomic. A child of five years of age is unlikely to be either interested in or able to pay for a washing machine. Market research data are based on a **sample** of the total population – that is, a part of the whole population whose characteristics are studied in order to reveal the characteristics of the population as a whole.

At first sight this may appear a simple exercise. You have a product. You think it will appeal to the 18–30 age group. It would be a waste of money to sample people outside that age range. But are you right? If the product is new you may have misjudged your market. Even the manufacturers of established products cannot afford to be complacent about the **market segment** to which they are directing their marketing strategy. They may think their market segment is clearly defined in terms of age, income, sex, occupation and geographical distribution, but changes in society as a whole could change the composition of their markets. An increase in home ownership in the 20–25 age group could increase the interests of this group in domestic appliances and domestic consumer goods such as cleaners. Their priorities in buying decisions may be very different from those of other age groups.

The decision about the sample to be taken can introduce a tendency on the part of the sample to deviate from the true result which would have been obtained if the whole population had been questioned. This is known as **statistical bias**. A decision to aim at a particular market segment when investigating the market will introduce bias.

In chapter 5 you were introduced to the idea of the normal distribution. A sample which approximates to this can provide a statistician with information concerning the **probability of error** in the information (**raw data**) he has at his disposal. If the sample is small he might use techniques known as the 't distribution' and the 'chi-square distribution'. There is also the Poisson distribution. The important thing about each of these techniques is that they rely upon *known* properties of a certain distribution in terms of mean, median, mode and standard deviations. Consequently, they can be used to make an approximation to the result that would have been achieved if the *whole* population had been questioned.

The two main methods of sampling are as follows:

- *Random* Using this method every element of the population has the same probability of being questioned. In certain circumstances this may be *simulated* by generating random numbers using a computer.

- *Quota* A specified number of people may be interviewed by any of the methods outlined above. The questionnaires or interviews may include a certain number of people in a particular age or income group.

The sample may be based on selecting every tenth person on the electoral role, or by selecting a suitable town or district that includes a representative sample of the whole population.

The reasons for market research

A business needs information on all aspects of the market in which it operates. It also needs to evaluate the effect of its own policies on sales. Five main reasons are given below for market research:

1   The population can be classified according to age, sex, occupation and income. The business needs to know if the main demand for its product lies with a particular age, income or geographical grouping in order to adopt effective pricing, promotion and distribution strategies (the market segment). If you read marketing magazines you will often see advertisements by other publications, such as newspapers, which give a breakdown of their readership in terms of occupation, income and age. They are using their own market research to target a market segment and are using that to sell advertising space in their newspapers to businesses which have identified this segment as being their market.

2   The product itself is tested. Research in this area may be concerned with monitoring the progress of existing products and people's reaction to them or it may be concerned with testing reaction to a new market. In the latter case

the product may be marketed in a region before being put on the national market. This allows the business to test reaction to the product and to monitor other elements in the marketing mix at a lower cost. This is known as a **test market**.

3   The price at which potential competitors are selling their products is important. For a new product the business has to discover the price which will enable them to achieve the marketing objectives and, through them, the overall objectives of the business.

4   Packaging has the utilitarian function of protecting the product against damage and deterioration with a view to prolonging its **shelf life** (the period of time for which it can be stored before it must be discarded). For some goods it can also add to the convenience of the retailer. Pre-packaged tea and sugar is easier for the retailer to store and sell. Packaging may also be part of the promotion policy of the business by creating an image in the mind of the consumer which, allied to advertising, can encourage **brand loyalty** (a tendency on the part of a consumer to continue to use the same brand).

5   Advertising is expensive, and a business wants to make sure it is getting value for money. It will be interested in the reaction of the market to its advertising campaign. In chapter 3 we introduced the idea of demand elasticity. The same concept can be used to analyse the impact of advertising on the market.

$$\frac{\text{Percentage change in quantity demanded}}{\text{Percentage change in advertising expenditure}}$$

If the market is responsive to advertising, the numerical measurement will be greater than 1 and revenue will increase by a larger amount than the additional expenditure on advertising. An inelastic market means that an increase in advertising would add to the costs of the business without a corresponding increase in revenue.

The information required by a business covers all the elements of the marketing mix.

SELF-ASSESSMENT

1   Give two ways in which bias may be introduced into a sample.
2   List three reasons why a business needs to establish the market segment for its product.

Elements of the marketing mix

We have already defined the elements of the marketing mix – product, price, promotion and place – on page 142. It is now time to look at each one in more detail and examine some of the problems associated with them.

Product

The description of a product includes the technical specifications, appearance and quality. It may also include the services associated with it (after-sales service in the case of technical goods). The customer is not only buying the good or service but also the associated services and the status the product is thought to confer upon them. We shall look at the design process more closely in chapter 9; in this chapter we will limit our study to the product in relation to its market.

The product can be defined in terms of its final use. Industrial goods are those sold to other businesses for use in their production processes. Industrial goods can vary in price from several million pounds to a few pence. Consumer goods are sold to the consumer to satisfy their immediate and personal needs and wants. In both markets the elements of the marketing mix are the same but the emphasis varies. When products are sold in both markets a business may lose sales if it fails to identify and exploit the overlap. There is also a danger that in adapting a product to move from one market to another the appealing features might be lost. Products that sell in both markets include cars, office furniture and equipment, and computers. The appeal of industrial products to the consumer might lie in their durability and versatility. A similar range adapted for the consumer market which lacks one of these characteristics but has gained visual impact could very well be a failure.

The product range

Businesses which produce more than one good or service are known as **multi-product** firms. The products may be related to one another – for example, by using the same raw materials, using the same technology or the same production processes – or they may be totally unrelated. In the latter case they are known as **conglomerates**. The process of increasing the number of products supplied by the business is called **diversification**. In order to diversify, a business might merge with another business with complementary or different product lines, introduce a new line very similar to those already produced which could be serviced by existing technical and marketing expertise, or move into a totally different product area on the basis of its own research and development.

The introduction of a new product always carries with it a certain amount of risk. There may be a lack of expertise in marketing. The product may be technically excellent, but a failure to define the target segment of the market on the part of the marketing personnel could lead to failure. Alternatively, patent protection might be inadequate. The success of the product could lead to potential competitors seeking to satisfy the same need with a product that is technically different but has the same use. The battle for market supremacy in video-recording systems and the attempts of camera producers to satisfy consumer demand for rapid results are examples of this.

Diversification is a strategy adopted by a business in order to achieve its overall objectives: that is, to achieve its desired level of profitability and ensure survival. Reasons for diversification may relate to the product life cycle, the market in which a business is operating and its marketing strategies.

1   The product life cycle   No product has an unlimited life. Consumer tastes will change or the product may become obsolete as the result of changes in technology. In Figure 8.1 you can see a formalised statement of the life cycle of a product.

   (a) *Introduction/development*   This is the most expensive stage in the history of the product. The costs of research, both technical and marketing, have to be borne, the product is not yet contributing revenue to the business and there is the risk of failure.

   (b) *Growth*   The product is establishing itself in the market and sales are increasing over time.

   (c) *Maturity*   The market has been fully exploited (although it may not have reached the sales levels originally hoped for). It is said to be **saturated**. At this stage competition increases as rival firms fight for a bigger share of the market.

   (d) *Decline*   Total sales are falling.

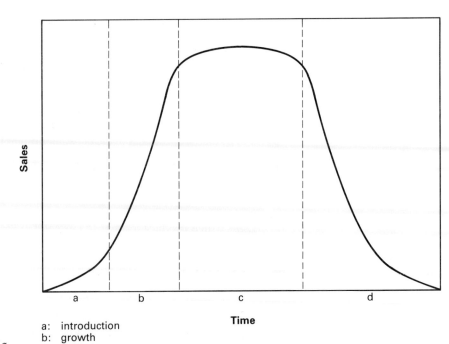

Figure 8.1   Life cycle of a product

a: introduction
b: growth
c: maturity
d: decline

Businesses may attempt to extend the maturity phase of a product's life by **extension strategies**. These may include finding new markets and new uses for the product, persuading people to use it more frequently, changing the physical appearance/packaging of the product to appeal to new tastes and developing a new range of associated accessories.

Figure 8.2 shows the relationship between the life cycle of a product and the cash flow generated by it.

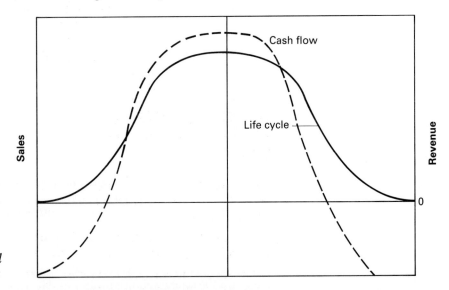

Figure 8.2   Life cycle and cash flow

If you study this figure you can see that for part of its life a product is taking money from the business and making no contribution to the profit of the business. An ideal pattern of product management is given in Figure 8.3.

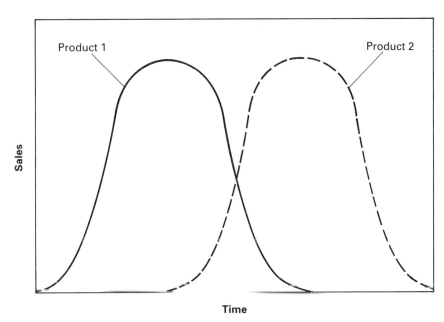

Figure 8.3 An ideal pattern of product management

At any one time the cash flow generated by mature products is helping to nurture the immature products through the early stages of their life cycle. A multi-product business may have a contribution pattern as illustrated in Figure 8.4.

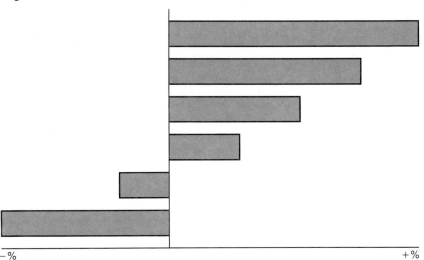

Figure 8.4 Contribution to profit in a multi-product business

2 In markets where sales are seasonal or which are subject to fluctuations the same principle of diversifying the product range in order to provide income is put into practice.

3 A wider range of products may also increase the selling power of a business and benefit from previous marketing strategies.

Not all the advantages of product diversification are in the area of marketing. A business may want to use its production capacity more fully and make use of by-products of existing production processes. We shall examine these reasons more closely when we look at economies of scale in chapter 9.

Pricing

In chapter 3 we saw how the interaction of demand and supply established the market price for a product. That is an overall view. From the perspective of a business the situation is not so simple. The marketing team has to decide where its product fits into this overall picture. If the product is new it may not be sure which market segment it is targeting.

The price chosen will, of course, be in line with the marketing objectives of the business which in turn will be established so as to support the overall objectives of the business. A pricing strategy must be decided upon before the method of pricing is established.

Pricing strategies

The overall pricing strategy chosen will depend upon the following factors:

1 The type of product and the market at which it is aimed. A high-quality product aimed at a high-income group might suffer a reduction in demand if its price is low compared with that of its competitors. A great deal will depend upon the consumers' attitude towards the product. Are they buying it for its intrinsic qualities, or are they buying it to confer status?

2 The type of market in which the business is operating. In a perfect market the business is a price taker. It can only react to the existing market price and decide, on the basis of its own costs of production, whether or not it can afford to compete. Some products can be *differentiated* from their rivals. The actual differences may be small, but the use of branding and advertising can persuade people that one product is considerably better than another.

3 Innovatory products have a monopoly position in the market. The success of pricing policy in this case will depend on the skill of the marketing team in analysing and evaluating the results of their market research – and also on the accuracy with which they describe the product to potential consumers.

4 The expected life span of the product. As a general rule, the shorter the life span the higher the price, in order to make sure the business covers the costs of development and initial production.

5 The degree of interdependence within the product range. It might make sense to sell a product at little more than cost if the possession of that product will encourage people to buy accessories to go with it.

Different pricing strategies may be used to suit individual market conditions, as shown below.

• The main objective of **market penetration** is to capture a large share of the market as quickly as possible. In the short term this may lead to lower profits, but if the business can establish itself in the market the long-run profits might be high. A great deal will depend on the expected product life and the power of businesses already operating in the market together with the financial resources of the business adopting this strategy. A short product life cycle will not give the business time to recover development costs if the price is too low. Powerful market leaders with larger financial resources than the emerging product could follow a policy of price-cutting.

- **Market skimming** might be likened to skimming the cream off the top of the milk. A high price resulting from high profit margins means a quick recovery of development costs. A business might follow this strategy if its product was technically innovative but if it had reason to believe that its competitors were likely to launch imitative products in a short period of time. Fashion products – not only in the garment world but also in games, gimmicks, toys and so forth – might also follow this policy. It is a viable option for businesses that expect their product to have a long life span but are in a position to charge a relatively high price in the short term, perhaps with the intention of reducing the price as an extension strategy in the medium to long term.

- When there are a number of suppliers of a good or service offering it to the same group of people each business will have to match the price of its competitors unless it can persuade consumers that its product is, in some way, more desirable than those of its competitors. The more similar (homogeneous) the goods and services are the more the business is dominated by its competitors. Two hairdressing salons may offer identical skills in the cutting and dressing of hair, but one might set out to provide a more 'up-market' image. This might justify an increase in the price of its services. It is also likely to mean an increase in the costs of production.

- **Tendering** is a pricing strategy that is imposed on businesses by market conditions. Governments and local authorities will require businesses to submit a price for a particular job and give a detailed breakdown of costs. Householders engaging builders ask for estimates of the work to be undertaken. The supplier is working without detailed knowledge of his competitors' prices. The customer has the task of ensuring that the prices tendered are comparable for the work to be done.

- The use of **price discrimination** can be seen intuitively as a combination of the strategies of market penetration and skimming. It can be employed when the same product can be offered at different prices to different groups of consumers without the possibility of resale from one group to another.

Methods of pricing

Having established the strategy it intends to follow, the business now needs to work out the price it will charge. This will depend on the costing method it decides to use, which in turn will be dependent on the market in which it is operating and its target profit.

1 **Absorption** or **full cost pricing**   Total production costs are added together, the required profit added to this and the result is divided by the output. At first sight this method of pricing appears to take little account of the market. In a variation of total cost pricing a business might decide what the market will bear, subtract the desired profit from it and then decide whether or not the good can be made for that price. If the answer is in the negative there may be an investigation into the way in which costs could be reduced – perhaps by changing the quality of the item. This carries with it the danger of accidentally eliminating just those qualities which appeal most to the customer.

2 When a business has excess capacity or when it produces a number of products it may decide upon the price for a product by **contribution pricing**. Provided the price covers the direct costs of production and makes a

contribution to fixed costs, then it will be accepted. In the short term a business with excess capacity might accept orders at below full cost provided the price offered makes a contribution to fixed costs. A business which sees the opportunity of exploiting an additional market through price discrimination may be prepared to price at less than full cost.

Promotion

The word 'promotion' can be used in a general sense to describe collectively the activities of advertising, competitions, money-off offers, in-store display, the visual impact of packaging, and any other device that an advertising team can think of to draw attention to their product. In a more specific sense advertising is usually treated separately, and the other techniques are described as **sales promotion**.

The importance of sales promotion in a market will depend on a number of factors, such as the type of market in which the business operates. In a market dominated by a few powerful producers all manufacturing similar products price competition carries with it the dangers of a price war and reduced profits. In these circumstances branding, well-designed packaging supported by advertising, is a familiar promotion strategy. In order to boost sales in the short term and, perhaps, gain or retain the brand loyalty of wavering customers special offers and money-off coupons might be employed.

Sales promotion and advertising are aimed at distributors as well as the final consumer. Wholesalers and retailers are more likely to stock a product if they are offered in-store display units or if there is the promise of a national advertising campaign. Unless the producer has control of his own retail outlets he needs to persuade people to stock his goods.

Advertising can be either very cheap or very expensive according to the medium chosen. Only goods with large markets will find national television advertising an economic proposition. Earlier in this chapter we spoke of the advertising elasticity of demand. Unless advertising increases demand it will add to the total cost of the product.

When a business has a 'family' brand name – that is, a brand which is common to a number of products – the cost of advertising can be spread over all the products. This may have unfortunate results if one product receives bad publicity.

The choice of advertising media will depend on the following factors:

1 *The market segment* Magazines and television companies analyse their readers according to interests, age, tastes and income in order to provide information on which they can sell advertising space. A brief glance through marketing magazines will provide examples of the media advertising their advertising potential. Feature articles in magazines can provide a vehicle for advertising.

2 *The amount of money which is available for advertising* Media which, in turn, spend money advertising themselves will charge more for advertisements.

3 *The size of the market* It is pointless for a small business to advertise nationally unless its product is both unique and expensive. Products of this type are often advertised in specialist magazines or, in the case of consumer goods, by word of mouth.

4 *The media chosen should also relate to the product* Different people read or watch different magazines or programmes. The efficiency of the media in

selling is recognised by attempts to restrict advertising of certain products when it is felt that the advertisers have an unfair advantage.

Distribution

Distribution is concerned with getting the product from the producer to the buyer. The method of distribution chosen can be viewed from two aspects, its physical means or its organisation:

- *The physical means of distribution* Different methods of transport may be more or less cost effective, depending on the cost of transport in relation to the price of the good, or the type of good being transported in relation to the speed with which it is required. Drugs may be sent by air; so too may fruit out of season, and flowers. Coal, which is cheap in relation to transport costs, is moved by sea, rail and road depending on the distance involved. Transport is also a service. Cost advantages may be outweighed by the efficiency of that service.

- *The organisation of distribution.*
  (a) Is the product to be sent direct to a retailer? If the product depends for its reputation on the quality of its after sales support, this might be the best route. Large retailers with market power will buy direct from the manufacturer. They might impose their own quality control, designs and branding on the manufacturer.
  (b) Is the product to be sent direct to the consumer? Specialist manufacturers may follow this route using mail order. Local markets may be inadequate for their needs but they do not wish to lose control over the product by selling to a wholesaler or a retailer. This is a traditional method of distribution for perishable goods. Farm shops and markets give farmers the opportunity of selling their produce fresh to the consumer. Trade exhibitions provide a point of contact between the manufacturers of industrial goods and the businesses which are their consumers.
  (c) Is the product to be sold on organised commodity markets? A world market for commodities like tin, pepper, sugar and wheat results in the growth of specialist businesses trading in these commodities.
  (d) Household consumer goods such as washing powders may be sold direct to the retailer but will also follow the traditional path of manufacturer to wholesaler to retailer to consumer.

The organisational pattern of distribution is frequently referred to as the **channel of distribution**, whereas the method of transport chosen might be referred to as the **physical channel of distribution**.

Constraints on marketing decisions

When considering the options available to a business in making marketing decisions it is important to remember that the choice is not unrestricted. Selecting a marketing mix is a planning process in which marketing objectives are set, resources are considered and external constraints are taken into account.

External constraints

1   *The government* Successive governments have contributed to a body of legislation which restricts the ingredients, construction and processing of goods for the purposes of health and safety. Other legislation is concerned

with the conditions under which services may be offered and limits the claims that can be made in advertising.

(a) The Sale of Goods Act 1979 consolidated previous legislation that had begun with the Sale of Goods Act 1893. Goods must be of 'merchantable' quality – that is, they must be able to perform the functions for which they were sold.

(b) The Consumer Protection Act 1961 laid down safety requirements for certain types of goods, such as, for example, electrical equipment and toys.

(c) The Consumer Safety Act 1971 extended the safety requirements to other types of goods.

(d) Unsolicited Goods and Services Act 1971 curbed inertia selling – the sending of goods to people and then demanding payment for them.

(e) The Consumer Credit Act 1974 regulated the behaviour of businesses which lend money to the consumer. They must have a licence from the Office of Fair Trading and disclose the true rate of interest at which the money is being lent.

The European Economic Community (EEC) is also becoming increasingly active in this field, and is developing a comprehensive approach to consumer protection which could have a major impact on the national legislation of member countries.

Legislation relating to market structure may also determine the marketing policy of a business.

2 *The activities of consumer and environmental groups* can affect the marketing policies of a business. Tobacco and alcohol advertising are among the continuing targets of a variety of groups. The Consumer's Association actively campaigns for changes in the law relating to consumer goods and services and, by testing products, provides an independent assessment of their comparative value for the subscribers to *Which?*, its monthly magazine. The results of these surveys are often summarised in the media.

3 *The behaviour of competitors*   The marketing mix selected must take into account the marketing strategies of businesses producing similar products. The number of other businesses producing the same or similar products, the degree of market power enjoyed by competitors, prices charged, advertising policies and sales promotion tactics will all be important. The attention given to the behaviour of competitors will vary according to the type of market in which the business is operating. A business operating in an oligopolistic market with little difference between the products is likely to concentrate its marketing effort on presenting its product as being intrinsically better than that of its competitors – provided it does not misrepresent its claim. The accent in the marketing mix will be on branding, advertising, sales promotion, the quality of the sales force, packaging and distribution. The objective of these activities is to have a better service than competitors and, at the same time, *differentiate* the product from those of its competitors in the minds of consumers.

4 *The buying behaviour of consumers*   The reasons for the choice of one product instead of another similar product and the way in which consumers make their decisions is the subject of considerable research. If, for example, there is evidence that consumers have no strong preference between competing products but make their final selection at the moment of purchase – that is, at the point of sale, the marketing mix might emphasise packaging and in-store promotions backed up by extensive advertising campaigns.

5 *The state of the economy*   A recession might place greater emphasis on the

importance of price; prosperity might increase the importance of persuasive advertising.

Conclusion

Marketing is an art rather than a science. There are no right answers, only the ones that work. The perfect product sold in the wrong place at the wrong time will fail where a less than perfect product might succeed. Advertising and promotion must be in tune with consumer preferences. There are so many subdivisions of the basic elements of the marketing mix that the scope for error is enormous.

The art of marketing is, or should be, based on the statistical analysis of data. To this extent, at least, marketing is a science.

A case study

The problems of football

When Fiona was fourteen she was an ardent supporter of the local first division football club. Her ambition in life was to go to a match. For some time her ambition was thwarted by her mother, who felt that football grounds with their reputation for violence were no place for her daughter. Fiona's father was not a great deal of help in the matter either. His support for the team was shown by listening to radio commentaries and watching televised matches. He was too old, he said, when his daughter pleaded with him, to spend Saturday afternoons standing on freezing cold terraces. Besides, he had far too much to do.

Fiona and her father personalise the major marketing problem facing British football clubs: a poor image and the development since 1945 of rival attractions. A number of football clubs face financial problems, and unless they get their marketing right could face closure.

The product and promotion

At first sight this is no more than a game of football, the winner of which will gain points to determine its place in the league table or will go into the next round of another competition. In fact this product has a number of components: the state of the ground, the conditions offered to spectators, the safety of the ground (in terms of health and safety and also the danger of crowd violence). The style of play offered by the team and the star quality of the leading players are also important. Most teams have a hard core of regular supporters the size of which is related to the degree of success a team is enjoying. A run of defeats will reduce the attendance at matches. A successful run in a European competition will result in higher gates. Not all teams can be successful, and the cost of players can be high. The most sought-after players operate in a continental market, and some European clubs can offer transfer fees of three and four times the maximum paid in the United Kingdom.

Most clubs augment their income by diversifying. The club shop will sell a range of items in the club colours and using its name and insignia. These will sell, not only to the match attenders but also to the army of television supporters. Lotteries can bring in useful income. Commercial sponsorship, too, can help offset the running costs of the club. It is important to remember that the success of all these ventures will depend on the success of the club in playing football. A club that reaches the Cup Final might double its takings from trading activities and find it easier to secure lucrative sponsorships. A bad playing season can see a slump in revenue.

For many clubs the ground itself is a valuable and under-utilised asset. It is open to the elements, and too heavy a use is not advisable. Installing artificial pitches enables the ground to be used all the year round and not only for football matches. Not all clubs approve of such pitches. Inevitably, they affect the play, and some would argue that the quality of the artificial turf leaves a great deal to be desired.

Part of the general product package are the facilities offered by the clubs. Cold, open terraces might be part of the tradition of football but are not likely to attract a family audience when rival amusements offer more comfort. Refreshment facilities are often minimal. Some clubs are already improving these areas.

The problems associated with crowd violence are matters for the football industry as a whole to solve, although individual clubs can make their contribution. The distribution of tickets for 'away' matches can control the type of supporter who represents the club. Ticket-only schemes have the dual advantage of providing some degree of control over supporters and giving the club a secured income. Violence at one match will reflect on the image of the industry and have repercussions for other clubs.

Price

Pricing reflects the desire of supporters to congregate together and contains a control element for 'away' supporters. Basic ticket prices – standing room only – vary little over the country as a whole. A price range between £2.50 and £3.50 appears to be the average (1986). This gives access to the part of the ground usually favoured by supporters of the home team. Supporters of the team playing away may be charged between £3.00 and £5.00.

The place

Inner-city football clubs would seem to be ideal candidates for a move to a green field site. The existing ground could be sold for development and the new land would be relatively cheap with ample car-parking provision. Supporters no longer live within walking distance from the ground, and travel to the outskirts of the city would be easier particularly if there was motorway access. Traffic congestion during home games would be a thing of the past. Against this is the fact that the place is often an important part of the product and promotion. Would supporters have the same feeling for the team if matches were played in an anonymous stadium? Would a change in location affect brand loyalty? Most fervent football supporters would predict disaster if it was suggested that the place should be changed. For a football club the problem lies in judging how long it would take its supporters to develop a new loyalty to place.

Professional marketing in football is a relatively new phenomenon. The captive audiences of the pre-1939 era, when the match was the standard Saturday afternoon occupation for whole communities are no longer in existence, and audiences have been falling steadily. There is still a great deal of support for some teams. Can the football clubs capitalise on this? More important, do they want to do so, or is the ruling ethic still that of a club rather than a profit-making business? To what extent do players, ground, success, image and prestige contribute to defining the product?

Review

1   Wainwrights is a small engineering business producing a single product. The total capacity of plant is 25 000 units per annum, but sales seldom exceed 80 per cent of this figure. The product is priced on a full cost basis with overheads of £60 000 allocated to sales. Direct costs are £7 per unit produced.

   (a) Assuming that Wainwrights' objective is a 20 per cent profit expressed as a percentage of turnover, at what price should it sell the product?
   (b) Wainwrights is offered an additional contract for 4 000 units at £10 per unit. Should it accept the order? Justify your answer, explaining the assumptions you have made.
   (c) As a result of an up-swing in the market Wainwrights' sales rise to 95 per cent capacity. Calculate the profit as a percentage of turnover, assuming the product was sold at the original price.
   (d) In view of the change in market conditions outlined in (c), should Wainwrights change its pricing policy? What additional information would be required to answer this question?

2   A business manufactures a household consumer product. Until recently its marketing drive has been based on the concept of the perfect housewife. Periodic promotional campaigns have been sufficient to maintain its market share, but this is now being eroded by its competitors. Market research suggests that women find the advertising approach condescending. The product itself is technically superior to that of its immediate competitors, and the advertising elasticity of demand for the market as a whole is greater than 1. Suggest ways in which the business might revitalise its product. What factors, other than those given above, might it need to take into account when deciding upon its tactics?

3   The retailing market for a range of products has five large companies with respective market shares of 12.0 per cent, 11.9 per cent, 11.3 per cent, 6.8 per cent and 4 per cent. The rest of the market is served by businesses with a more limited product range and serving geographically isolated markets.

   (a) Describe the possible effects of this product structure on the price, sales and promotion policies of the businesses concerned.
   (b) What additional information might you require before making a judgement on this?

4   Jason Designs manufactures clothes which it sells directly to quality, up-market retail outlets. The brand name is respected for quality and its imaginative but conservative interpretation of fashion trends. The business is also extremely successful in the export market, particularly to North America. This market accounts for 40 per cent of its sales.
   In 1986 Jason Designs invested in additional capacity with the objective of entering the high-fashion market, targeting the 16–25 age group. A range was designed, and the production department experienced no difficulty in operating within the cost and quality parameters set for it. These were lower than those of the original range but still high when related to that of the rest of the market. The problem lay in naming the new range. One faction within the business was in favour of keeping the original label with the possible addition of the word 'young'. The opposing group advocated inventing a totally new name, perhaps with a discreet press leak to the glossy magazines concerning its origin.
   Outline the arguments for and against the two approaches to marketing the new range given above, stating any additional information which would be necessary before a decision could be reached.

5   Study the graph and the table below.

Total sales of sports equipment by UK manufacturers for the period 1961–77:

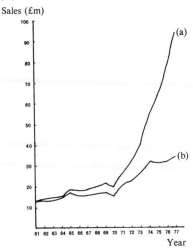

(a)   Sales at current prices.
(b)   Sales deflated by sports equipment price index.

Exports and imports of sports equipment

	Exports (£ thousand)	As proportion of total UK manufacturers sales	Imports (£ thousand)	As proportion of total UK manufacturers sales
1970	9 888	50.99	3 105	15.99
1971	13 562	48.47	4 285	15.31
1972	15 209	46.01	5 775	17.47
1973	20 393	48.76	8 981	21.47
1974	25 935	47.05	13 850	25.12
1975	32 184	50.42	18 168	28.46
1976	36 187	47.30	20 500	26.80

Source: Business Monitor PQ 494.3.

(a) Briefly explain why the two lines on the graph diverged between 1971 and 1977.   (2)
(b) On graph paper, construct a bar chart to compare Exports and Imports for the years 1971, 1973 and 1975.   (10)
(c) (i) Calculate the relative increase in both Exports and Imports between the two years 1970 and 1976.   (4)
     (ii) Identify *four* economic and social factors which might have led to these changes.   (4)   1986 (AEB)

6   Study the extract from the annual report of United Biscuits on page 159 and answer these questions:

(a) Define the terms 'Dividend per Share' and 'Earnings per Share' and explain the difference between them.   (6)
(b) Why has the increase in profits been quoted as 'Pre-Tax' instead of profits after tax?   (2)
(c) (i) In financial terms, explain why an increase in their market share is important to United Biscuits.   (2)
     (ii) From the text, identify *six* other *non-financial objectives*.   (6)

(d) Explain *three* ways in which United Biscuits maintains product quality. (6)
(e) Explain the term 'brand leadership'. (1)
(f) What are the advantages to the company of selling the complete range under the same brand name? (2) 1986 (AEB)

United Biscuits
1983: Another very successful year

Profits before tax increased by 21%, from £68.4 m to £83.2m.
Earnings per share increased by 24%.
Recommended dividend increase of 21%.
Investment reached record level at £95m.

Extracts from the Statement by
Sir Hector Laing, Chairman

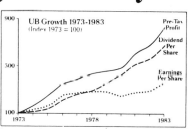

The UK Biscuit Market
During 1983 we increased our share of the market by 1.3%—to the highest level ever—with maintained margins. This is a remarkable demonstration of the substantial progress and continuing pre-eminence of our biscuit operations.

While maintaining the strength of established high volume lines, we see growth coming from trading up to higher added value lines, and we have a number of exciting new products in the pipeline.

The USA Biscuit Market
Keebler had yet another excellent year, with the successful launch of a number of high quality new products and encouraging progress on the West Coast.

However, a competitive development in the market has been the introduction of a new soft cookie which has been very successful in its test market area. Keebler has installed new plant and will shortly be launching what we consider to be a superior product. This widening of the market augurs well for the future and the long term rewards of winning this battle by means of product quality will be substantial.

The Frozen Foods Market
This is one of the most dynamic sectors of the UK food industry: the retail sector has grown by nearly 30% in volume in the last three years, and the cater-ing sector has also shown volume improvement.

U.B. Frozen Foods produces a wide range of products for the retail and catering sectors and provides distribution and supply services to caterers. During 1983 our retail product range was re-launched under the McVitie brand, resulting in a 40% sales increase and brand leadership in several categories. The recent formation of TFC-Sorge has created the largest supplier of frozen foods to the catering trade in this country.

The Fast Food and Restaurant Markets
Meals eaten outside the home are also increasing steadily and in 1983 the fast-food market increased by 15%.

The Wimpy image has been transformed with higher standards overall: at the end of 1983 there were 370 table-service restaurants and the number of counter-service outlets had increased to 53 with many more planned.

Our Restaurant Company is making good pro-gress—it now operates 190 units with plans to open a further 30 this year.

Outlook
Despite the costs of exploiting the new opportunities in the USA, present indications are that profits and earnings per share for 1984 will again be very satisfactory.

7 The Pirongs Company has hitherto produced just one product which seems to be at the end of its life cycle. The company has two projects to develop new products that are encouraging but, since capital is short, it feels that it could undertake no more than one of these projects. No immediate capital expenditure is required in either project. The financial details are given on page 160.

The financial details are given on page 160.

(a) Examine what is meant by the phrase 'product life cycle' and recommend to Pirongs how this may be extended in their company. (4)
(b) Define what is meant by the term 'depreciation' and comment on the depreciation policy of the Pirongs Company. (4)

	Year (End of year figures)				
	1	2	3	4	5
Project I					
Net cash inflow/ outflow	−10000	−5000	10000	15000	20000
Less depreciation	0	0	5000	5000	5000
Net profit	−10000	−5000	5000	10000	15000
Project II					
Net cash inflow/ outflow	0	0	10000	10000	10000
Less depreciation	0	0	2000	2000	2000
Net profit	0	0	8000	8000	8000

(c) Calculate the net present value of the two projects on the assumption that the cost of capital is 10 per cent. On the basis of this decide which, if either, of the projects should be undertaken.   (8)

(d) What other methods of capital investment appraisal could have been used? Compare the advantages of these to the net present value method.   (4)

(e) What other considerations would you take into account in choosing whether to prolong the present product life cycle or to undertake one of the new projects?

Present values of £1 in future are given below at various rates:

	10%	12%	14%	16%
One year hence	0.91	0.89	0.88	0.86
Two years hence	0.83	0.80	0.77	0.74
Three years hence	0.75	0.71	0.68	0.64
Four years hence	0.68	0.64	0.59	0.55
Five years hence	0.62	0.57	0.52	0.48

(5)   1985 (CLES)

Activities

1   Select a good or service you might be able to supply to the local community. Undertake a market research exercise on this product and use the statistical techniques outlined in chapter 5 to analyse the information. What problems did you encounter? What steps could you take to overcome them?

2   Analyse three issues of a popular magazine. You should attempt to identify the readership aimed at in terms of age, sex, occupational category, income, interests, why they read that magazine and what subjects they are interested in. Your analysis should cover both the advertisements and the editorial content. Would you use that magazine as a medium for advertising if you were trying to promote:
(a) detergent?
(b) high-fashion clothes?
(c) an expensive range of kitchen equipment?
(d) products based on micro-chip technology?
   Explain your answers and find magazines that would be ideal vehicles for the advertising of the products listed above.

3   Survey the market for a product, either good or service, that you intend to

offer. Analyse the results of your market research using the statistical techniques outlined in chapter 5. Draw up a projected balance sheet and profit and loss account for your business over the first three months of its life.

4 Select a locally produced good which is marketed nationally. Discover, through observation and interview with the marketing manager, the marketing mix used by the business in question. What are the reasons given for the policy? You may repeat this exercise for a variety of products, being careful to compare and explain the results of your investigations.

5 Select a range of advertisements and analyse them according to whether or not they can be considered informative and/or persuasive, the market segment they are aimed at, the wants they are designed to appeal to, the stage in the product life cycle. Pay particular attention to any advertisement that uses statistics to support its selling points. Are these in any way misleading? What additional information would you require to make an informed buying judgement?

6 Select a product that has been the subject of a recent *Which?* (the magazine of the Consumers Association) test report. Make a list of the features you, or somebody of your acquaintance, would find desirable when choosing that product. On the basis of this list select the model you would buy. Compare your selection with the *Which?* test report. Does your choice vary from the 'best buy'? If so, in what way? Would the information given in *Which?* influence your final decision? What insight has this activity given you into consumer buying behaviour?

Suggested projects

1 A critical comparative study of the distribution channels used by two businesses manufacturing the same product.

2 An evaluation of the promotional methods used by a small business operating in a local market.

3 An appreciation of the impact of market structure on the marketing strategy of a business.

4 A critical investigation into the extent to which a non-profit-making organisation operating in the public sector needs to promote its activities.

Essays

1 Discuss the impact of the findings of market research on the marketing and production strategies of a business.

2 A business manufactures a number of diverse products, some of which it subsidises. Comment on the view that such behaviour constitutes a waste of resources.

3 A business uses a single brand name to promote a range of products. Comment on the reasons why it might adopt such a strategy and discuss the problems associated with it.

4 Identify and discuss the information a business will require before deciding on the pricing strategy for a new product.

5 Discuss the view that costs are the most important determinant of price.

6 A business is aware that the demand for its products is relatively price elastic. How may this information influence its marketing strategy?

7   Comment on the factors a business will take into account when deciding on the distribution channel for its product.

8   To what extent can advertising be considered a waste of resources (a) for the individual business, (b) for the industry in which that business operates, and (c) for the economy as a whole?

9   A business is described as being 'market oriented'. What do you understand by this description? Discuss the implications for marketing and production policies.

10   An enterprise invests a large sum of money in promoting its corporate image, with particular emphasis on the contribution it makes to the community. Comment on the reasons for such a strategy.

11   A business is about to launch a new product. Identify and discuss the information it will require before deciding on a pricing strategy.   1985 (AEB)

12   A furniture manufacturer is concerned about a reduction in sales of its existing product range. What action should it take?   1986 (AEB)

13   (a) What is meant by full cost pricing?   (5)
     (b) In what circumstances would you advise the use of marginal cost pricing, and why?   (5)
     (c) Why is the profit earned on a product important?   (15)   1985 (CLES)

14   'The role of advertising is to awaken customers to wants that they never had.' Discuss.   (25)   1986 (CLES)

15   (a) What pricing strategies are available to a firm launching a new variety of non-stick frying pan on the market?   (8)
     (b) What might be the differences in pricing policy for the longer term, and what information and analysis is likely to be necessary?   (17)   1986 (CLES)

16   You are the marketing manager of a firm selling polyunsaturated margarine. In its annual budget, the government cuts direct taxation. Soon afterwards, a promotion campaign is launched by the Butter Information Council, and the government forbids advertising that suggests that margarine is healthier than butter. In the light of these events, what changes would you consider in your marketing strategy?   (25)   1986 (CLES)

Chapter 9   **Production**

It is almost a truism to say that the most fundamental activities a business engages in are those which result in the product, whether it is a good or a service, and those which make the product available to the customer: in other words, production and marketing. In chapter 8 we looked at the marketing function. Throughout that chapter it was necessary to refer to the product, the quality and the costs of production. Traditionally these are the province of the **production function**. In other words, the marketing activities of a business are dependent on the production activities.

In this chapter we will find that the markets in which a business operates place constraints on the production activities it undertakes. This is true not only of the market for the good or service which it is producing but also for the markets in which it buys its stocks of raw materials, components and finished goods. The interdependence of the marketing and production activities of a business cannot be over-emphasised. You will appreciate this more if you realise that in a small business they are usually the responsibility of one person. This person is then able to make decisions on the basis of knowledge of both areas. When production and marketing are separated into different departments, communication problems can arise. The organisation of a business is designed to minimise such problems and, by allowing production and marketing to work more closely together, result in a business that is truly market-oriented rather than one which considers the market in theory rather than in practice.

What is the production function? The **production operations** of a business can be defined as those activities which it is necessary for a business to undertake if it is to produce the goods and services required by the customer. In order to do this a business must answer the following questions:

- What is the product?
- What premises and equipment will be required?
- Where shall we produce?
- In what quantity shall we produce?
- What is the best way of organising the production processes?

The answers to these questions will depend upon such variables as the market, the technology employed and the rate of innovation, the labour available and its skill (including that of management), the availability of suitable sites, the availability of finance, decisions taken by other firms and the attitude of government and society to the industry in general.

In addition, the production decisions will be determined by the policy decisions of the senior management, which are designed to ensure that the long-term objectives of the business will be achieved.

The product

The product is the good or service the business sells in order to make a profit. This is a very simple definition. Reality is much more complex. There are very few products which fall neatly into one or other of those two categories. Most products contain both a physical element and a service element.

Consider the statement below. The man who made it works in the purchasing department of a large company.

> We seldom buy on price alone. For example, it is no use buying something at a saving of £10 per unit if the delivery is likely to be late. We have got to keep that production line going otherwise the extra cost will wipe out any savings in our purchasing.

He went on to explain the other factors which go into the mix of a purchasing decision. The goods he was buying were engineering components. He was the customer for another business in competition with other producers. Providing the quality was right, the service a business could offer him in terms of delivery dates and security of delivery were an important element in making the final decision.

Let us look at another example, this time in a consumer market:

> A woman wanted to buy a two-seater settee. She finally found the design she liked in the furnishing department of a large store. The salesman quoted a delivery time of three months. She asked if she could buy the display model, pointing out that there was a three-seater settee in the same design which could be used as a display model for both two- and three-seater settees. Her request was refused. The customer was annoyed at the poor service. The business lost a sale and the goodwill of the customer.

The product of a retail store is service, and in the opinion of this customer the service was poor. On the other hand, the store policy could have been based on the knowledge that customers liked to see what they were buying, and in satisfying one customer they might have lost three more. Perhaps the fault lay with the purchasing department, which had not made sure that there were sufficient stocks to meet demand – or with the manufacturer, who could not meet the demand. Whatever the truth of the situation, the good being sold did not overcome the reluctance of the customer to tolerate the level of service, and a sale was lost.

We saw in chapter 8 that the buying decisions of individual customers was a complex mix rather than a rational decision based only on price and quality. Goods are valued not only for what they do but also for the overall contribution they make to the needs and lifestyles of the customer. Service must, therefore, be an important element in the product, whether it is a consumer good or an industrial good.

SELF-ASSESSMENT

1 State two ways in which the efficiency, or otherwise, of a marketing department can affect the efficiency of the production department of the same business.
2 Explain how the satisfaction of a customer may be affected by the materials and service in the following products: car servicing, hire of a television set, purchase of a washing machine, purchase of a new car.

Design of the product

The design of any product is not simply a matter of an attractive appearance, although the importance of these qualities should not be under-estimated. An unpleasant job becomes less repellent if the tools to be used are attractive to look at. This can increase the productivity and job satisfaction of the workforce as they are made happier in their working environment. A good appearance can also help attract initial sales. However, to ensure a high level of repeat orders the equipment should also be easy, safe and economical in use.

The responsibility of the design team can, therefore, be defined as interpreting the needs of the customer, and translating these needs into a form suitable for use and which the production capacity of the business concerned can produce without incurring excessive costs.

The design team in the business can be the responsibility of the production manager. In a small business it will not exist as a separate entity and it is unlikely that any professional designers will be employed. In a small business producing goods such as fabrics, clothes and jewellery the designer might also be the entrepreneur. Design in these areas has a higher profile than design in the manufacture of industrial machinery. This does not mean that it is more important.

The design process

Every product has a design, whether it is consciously developed as such or not. The process of designing a good may be an integral part of the marketing/production decisions, or it may be a defined progression which is consciously evaluated by the business at each stage. Whichever is the case, the stages given below will be present.

The idea

This may come from the marketing department. Research has indicated that a product is required and that there are no competitors in that field. It may be the original idea of a person intending to start a business. Remember, a service has to be designed to meet the need of customers. At this stage an outline of the idea is laid down.

In a business manufacturing consumer durables this will take the form of a draft **specification** (a detailed description of the product, including the type of materials to be used, size, colour and so on). The draft specification for a washing machine would include the number of washing programs, the spin speed, the size, colour range and any other qualities that market research has suggested is needed for success. For fabric it would include the basic design, colours and material to be used. Even at this stage there will be close co-operation with production. The initial design process will use resources, and if it is developed in isolation the opportunity cost of failure will be high.

The original idea should contain specific data to act as a guide for the future stages in design. This information should include:

- the standards of reliability, performance and quality required (market research);

- the appearance that is most likely to be acceptable (market research);

- the maximum price at which it will sell (marketing and production);

- the maximum cost of design – you should remember that design costs are production costs;

- the maximum quantity that will be needed – in chapter 6 we saw that the cost per unit can be influenced by the scale of production;

- any special safety features or operating features that should be incorporated: for example, if a machine operator will need to use two controls at the same time or in a particular sequence it makes sense for them to be situated together and for the lay-out of the controls to reflect the sequence; on the other hand, if the use of two controls together is potentially dangerous then the design can incorporate safety measures. Some safety features are required by law – for example, roll-over bars on tractors and safety belts on cars.

Testing

At this stage the initial idea is tested for viability. The assessment of the concept takes place on a relatively small scale using mock-ups, scale models and mathematical calculations to test its viability. The methods used will vary according to the product. The increased availability of computer technology has made this task easier in complicated projects. The speed with which computers can process data has meant that a number of alternative solutions can be tested in a shorter period of time.

Prototype

The information gained from the second stage is used to make a full-scale model. This is to make sure that the increase in scale does not introduce more problems into production.

Specifications

These are laid down for the production of the good.

Production

For some products this may be a test production run and the products will be test-marketed to see if they are acceptable to the market. If the product is a failure the production will go no further. Large and expensive products cannot have a test run; it would make the product prohibitively expensive. For such goods the testing stage is likely to be extended.

The design process is one of problem solving and the minimisation of risk. Look at the stages closely. They are illustrated in Figure 9.1. You will see that they echo the planning pattern that has already been repeated several times in this book.

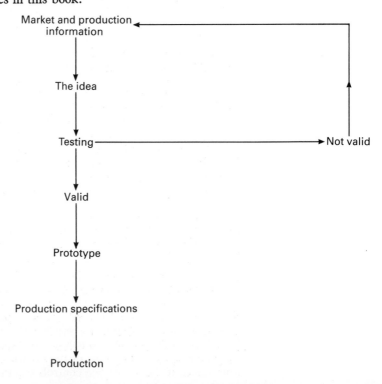

Figure 9.1   The product planning process

SELF-ASSESSMENT

1 State two ways in which each of the following departments in a company could influence the design of a new product: finance, marketing, personnel, production.
2 Using the flow chart illustrated in Figure 9.1 as a guide, draw up a flow chart for the design process of a simple good.
3 Most households own a plastic bucket. The shapes of all buckets are very similar. If a company decided to enter this market could it bypass the design stage? Explain your answer.

Location

Factors in the choice of location

The selection of a location for a factory, workshop or retail shop is essentially a problem of cost and availability of market. For the owner of a small retail shop the location problem may be confined geographically to one small town. The manufacturers of a consumer durable, on the other hand, may have the choice of a number of countries. The importance of any particular influence on the final location decision will depend on the type of business, the size of the business, the demands of the production processes and the importance of the market. The list of factors influencing the final choice of location is a long one but will not be applicable to all businesses:

1 *Labour* A business is interested in labour with specific skills. It may be attracted to an area because there is a high concentration of labour with those skills available. On the other hand, it may prefer an area with unskilled labour rather than compete with other businesses for skilled labour in short supply. Its final decision may depend upon the ease with which its production processes can be simplified and the quality of the further education provision. In some industries the availability of labour is not a major factor. The existence of valuable mineral deposits will encourage a mining company to move the labour to the job. The exploitation of the North Sea oilfields can be seen as an extreme example of this situation.

2 *Services* The major services required by a business are power (gas and electricity), water, drainage and waste disposal. In a modern industrialised economy this is unlikely to be an important element in the location decision in that they will be readily available in the quantities required. In more remote areas and in less industrialised parts of the world this could be more important. A business requiring a large amount of electricity could overload a limited local electrical supply. This in turn may require the provision of additional capacity in the supply of electricity, perhaps by the business itself.

3 *Transport* A good transport system can allow a business greater freedom in its choice of location. The decision is likely to be influenced by the cost of transporting the raw materials compared with the cost of transporting the finished goods to the market. Heavy transport costs for raw materials will predispose a business to move closer to its sources of supply. Where the costs of transporting the finished goods to the market is greater, then the business is more likely to be situated closer to the market. On the other hand, a business buying bulky raw materials, expensive to transport from a wide area, may find no advantage in being located close to one source of supply. It might be an advantage in this case to minimise the costs of transporting the finished product – that is, it would locate close to its market (see Figure 9.2).

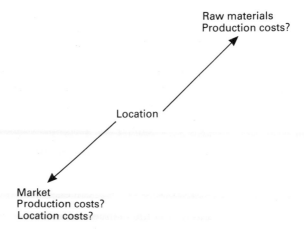

Figure 9.2   The relationship between market, location and source of supply

4   *Source of supply*   The importance of the source of supply of raw materials and components will depend upon the transport system available. In addition, managers responsible for the purchasing of supplies often prefer to be close to their suppliers.

5   *Local services and amenities*   We have already pointed out that the existence of a good system of technical education can be important if the business is faced with the need to train or re-train its workforce. The existence of a good primary and secondary system of education, a range of housing, shopping facilities and entertainment provision can also be a factor in a location or relocation decision. An entrepreneur whose business has no outstanding location requirements might choose to locate to satisfy his personal lifestyle rather than for strictly economic reasons and so, perhaps, contribute to the drift away from urban to rural areas.

6   *History*   Once an industry is established in an area it requires powerful economic reasons to force it to leave. A group of businesses producing the same type of goods can lead to the establishment of ancillary services which, if it moved to an entirely new location, it would have to provide for itself and at higher cost. It is likely that local colleges would provide suitable training courses which would not be economic without a concentration of industry, and there would be a pool of labour with the relevant skills. A business with several locations within a given area might want to locate new plant within that area to maintain communications and control. The unwillingness of businesses to move too far away from their existing location is generally referred to as **industrial inertia**.

7   *Central and local government grants*   These can be seen as an attempt on the part of central and local government to provide the powerful economic incentive required to overcome industrial inertia. The decline of older industries has left a number of areas of the United Kingdom with chronic

problems of high unemployment. The provision of low-interest loans, low rents and special grants for capital investment are designed to attract industries to these areas. Unfortunately, if the grants are seen as the major reason for moving and other location factors are not given due weighting, the end of the subsidy, particularly if accompanied by a general recession, can mean that these are the first factories to close.

8 *Geographical factors* The climate is obviously the deciding factor in businesses engaged in farming and horticulture. Although there are some marginal crops whose high value and demand can make them economic to grow under artificial conditions (for example, the growing of tomatoes in the United Kingdom), most crops are grown in areas in which the climate suits their demands. Manufacturing industry is less dependent on climate but can be influenced by the geological structure of a particular area both in terms of the topography of the region and whether or not the sub-soil will be able to bear the loads placed on it.

9 *Politics* Unstable governments, the threat of war and governments opposed to private enterprise might deter investment in a country. Equally, they may be ignored if the projected returns from that investment are sufficiently high.

Factors in the choice of a site

The nine factors influencing location given above are concerned with the general region, whether a county or country, within which a business decides to locate. The availability of a suitable site is a tenth factor. The choice of site is as complex as that of the general location:

- *Availability of transport* A site giving good access to the national motorway network will have advantages over a similar site 5 miles distant that involves a journey using busy roads. Transport can also affect the availability of labour.

- *Local by-laws and the reaction of local inhabitants* Local authorities may have regulations about the level of noise, smells and traffic that they are prepared to tolerate in a particular area. Even when these do not exist, or where there is some doubt as to whether or not the business is infringing upon them, local people might form pressure groups to prevent the building of a particular type of factory. Widespread publicity following industrial accidents which have affected the local community can have repercussions for other businesses in the same industry regardless of the level of their safety precautions.

- *The influence of national and international pressure groups* A threat to the wild life of a region can affect the siting of a particular enterprise, regardless of the attitudes of the local people.

- *The size, cost and physical qualities of the sites available* Where the production processes require heavy machinery, a large, flat site with a sub-soil capable of bearing the weight of the machinery will be a priority. Land will also be required for the storage of raw materials and finished products together with parking space for private cars. This type of land is more likely to be available at a reasonable cost away from city centres, and such sites on the outskirts of towns are described as **green field** sites and are growing in popularity.

- *Provision of services* This can often depend on the attitude of the local authority. The willingness to provide industrial estates and to provide, or help to provide, for the disposal of industrial waste and to lay on gas, electricity, water and sewage services to a green field site is not a statutory duty of a local authority and will depend upon local attitudes and needs.

For some businesses the major factor in the choice of site may be the proximity of similar businesses. In this case the design of the building to be used – whether a factory, an office block or a retail shop – will be dictated by the site available. Both single- and multiple-storey buildings have their advantages and disadvantages, and individual businesses will have their own priority in requirements.

1 *Costs*   A multi-storey building will have lower site costs. Single-storey buildings, particularly those using modern building technology, will have lower building costs.

2 *Organisation of departments*   A single-storey building may make the flow of goods from one department to another easier to organise and automate and so lower handling costs. A multi-storey building may have the same effect in a service industry – for example, retailing or insurance. Departments will have a well-defined area which will facilitate control.

3 *Ventilation and use of natural light*   Both are easier in a single-storey building and therefore reduce costs. On the other hand, heating costs are likely to be lower in a multi-storey building with a lower ratio of external surfaces to working space.

4 *Use of floor space*   The location of heavy machinery within a factory will be limited by the ability of certain parts of the building to bear the load. This is less of a constraint in a single-storey building.

The location decision, like most business decisions, is an exercise in comparative cost: in other words, which location will give the lowest cost of production and marketing? Transport costs can often be the deciding factor.

SELF-ASSESSMENT

1 A country develops an extremely efficient transport system over a period of twenty years. Would this have the effect of concentrating or dispersing business activity? Explain your answer.
2 What are likely to be the major factors in determining the site of a hairdressing salon?

Organisation of production

So far we have looked at two questions: what to produce, and where production will take place. The next important question is how production will be organised. The methods of organising production are generally referred to as **types of production** or **production methods**. There are three main types of production:

- job production;
- batch production; and
- flow production.

Job production

The term 'job production' describes a situation in which a single product is completed by one person or a group of people. Servicing a car, the making of a piece of furniture to the specification of an individual customer, the design of a computer system to meet the requirements of an individual customer can all be seen as examples of job production. The organisation of job production will be a fairly simple matter when the product is simple and demand is relatively small. When demand increases or the product is technically complicated, the demands on the organisational abilities of management increase. This can increase the costs of production to such a level that management will seek alternative methods. Whether or not they adopt them will depend upon the needs of the product, the willingness of the market to pay the necessary price to cover costs and the availability of sophisticated technology to help limit the increase in costs. Job production is the most common form of production in very small businesses.

Advantages of job production

1   The product can be tailored to meet the needs of the customer. This is not impossible using other types of production, but job production does give more flexibility in this matter.

2   When things go wrong it is easier to isolate the source of the problem – although it is not necessarily easy to analyse the problem! The owner of a garage, for example, faced with an irate customer complaining about the standard of servicing given to his car will know which of his mechanics was responsible for the servicing. It may be more difficult to find out why that particular job went wrong. The fault may lie in the skill of the mechanic, the degree of supervision, a fault in a piece of equipment or a failure on the part of the customer to provide sufficient information or permission to pursue the fault.

3   Greater involvement on the part of the workforce. The sight of a completed job gives a person greater satisfaction than contributing to a small part of a project. Either working alone or as part of a small work group individuals prefer to see what they have achieved and to know that their contribution was an important part of the final product.

Disadvantages of job production

1   When job production is used to tailor a complex technical product to the needs of customers, the sales force will be relatively large and a high degree of technical expertise will be required. Smaller firms may overcome this problem by using the services of an agent. The cost of selling will then be spread over all the firms employing him as a principal. Effectively, the agent is selling his knowledge of the market and his technical skills. The business employing him is reducing the overheads of maintaining a sales force.

2   The business is likely to need to own or lease a wider range of machinery. Machine A may be required to produce parts for jobs X, Y and Z. Depending on the importance of the time factor and the cost of resetting Machine A, the business may need the use of more than one machine to meet the delivery dates for its orders. Delivery dates are set by the market. A firm is less competitive if it offers a delivery date six months after a firm order is placed than one that can offer a delivery date two months after the order is placed. The truth of that statement will, of course, depend upon the uniqueness of the product concerned. A business with a virtual monopoly in a market is in a far stronger position than one competing with a number of firms offering close substitutes for its product.

3   Job production requires a flexible workforce. The technically simple product presents few problems. A more sophisticated product demands a highly skilled workforce able to perform a wide range of specialised tasks. This can be expensive in labour costs. Add to this the need for highly competent supervisors and a flexible management team able to undertake technical supervision, costing and labour management, and it becomes clear why more economic methods of production have been developed.

Standardisation, specialisation and simplification

Before we examine batch and flow types of production we should look at the qualities needed for job production. Using job production, there is the potential to produce a unique good or service – that is, one which is unlike any other on the market. This is not always necessary. A measuring jug used by a cook must be reasonably accurate in its measuring abilities, but that is all. A nut is a nut, provided it fits the bolt for which the customer intends it. It does not require a great leap in imagination to see that if you can design a simple item that can be used by a large number of people for a variety of purposes, then it will be easier to produce. Simplifying a product reduces the possibility of mistake in its manufacture. A simple product needs a less skilled labour force because people become highly skilled at a small range of tasks. A simple product needs a smaller range of machinery.

A product might be simple because of its nature, as in the example of a measuring bowl. It may be made simple by design. In the latter case we talk of **standardisation**. 'Standardisation' means that the goods produced conform to a standard. Dictionaries are not helpful in defining the word 'standard'; perhaps the most useful, but archaic, definition they give refers to the 'conspicuous flag or object used to determine the rallying point in a battle'. A standard, in this definition, is something people are trying – or should be trying – to reach! For the moment we will ignore the ambiguities in that statement. We will concentrate on the business which wants to make as many nuts as possible. To do this the business will have to make sure the nuts fit as many bolts as possible. This problem has been made easier for the business because over the last 170 years the users of bolts and nuts have realised that if they all use the same size range (*standardise* their requirements) there will be separate businesses that will provide these parts in large quantities and far more cheaply than they could do so themselves. The standards set are very precise. The internal diameter of a nut that varied more than 0.025 mm above or below the standard set would make that nut useless for the bolt on which it was used. Of course, the variation which will be tolerated will depend upon the physical size of the nut in question. A nut used in the manufacture of a car will have a more precise tolerance level than the nut used to hold on the propeller of a ship.

When a product has been simplified and standardised it becomes easier to make. The labour does not have to be so skilled, machinery can be devised to take over the more routine tasks. It becomes easier for people and machines to be given a specific job to do. Men and machines can be **specialised**.

These principles may seem common sense to you. If you live in an industrialised society you are used to the idea of buying spare parts when some household object goes wrong. You are familiar with the fact that people perform highly specialised jobs to help make a product. It will do you no harm to remember that the knowledge of these principles has been part of human knowledge for many thousands of years. Their deliberate exploitation has a much shorter history. Adam Smith wrote his *Inquiry into the Nature and Causes of the Wealth of Nations* in 1776. He isolated the division of labour (a sub-set of specialisation) as a major contribution to the wealth of nations. In that work Smith was simply summarising the experience of the economy of his contemporary England and its near Continental neighbours. Individual businesses, both in the United Kingdom and United States, began to appreciate the advantages of standardisation in technical goods. In ordinary household products the three principles have a longer history. Abraham Darby produced cast-iron cooking pots to a standard design and (for his time) in large quantities. He used superior technology to produce an old design economically. In the early eighteenth century the Lombe brothers had a factory producing silk that was considered ahead of its time. It was fifty years before the market for cotton goods persuaded manufacturers that they should follow his example.

Standardisation, simplification and specialisation can be part of job production. They become more important when a business uses batch or flow production methods.

Batch production

A batch of goods is simply a group of products which undergo production at the same time. The simplest example is a batch of loaves. These are the loaves that are put into the oven, by the baker, at the same time.

Batch production can be defined as a method of organising the work on any product so that it is divided into a number of operations and each operation is completed for a group of products (the batch) before it is moved on to the next operation. Under batch production all items in a particular batch move from one process to another simultaneously. This can lead to organisational problems. For example, if the batch is too large and one operation takes longer than another, then workers and machines can stand idle while they wait for the next batch to reach them. One solution to this problem is to have a 'buffer' stock of work-in-progress that can be drawn on. This ties up capital in stock and has an effect on the working capital of the business.

Advantages of batch production

1 Compared with job production it can lead to a saving in the amount of machinery used;

2 it enables a costing system to be employed which can allocate costs to each completed product; and

3 the system generates a large quantity of stock between different production processes. Although this ties up capital it can also act as a buffer. The existence of such stocks can give management greater flexibility in organisation.

Disadvantages of batch production

1 A large amount of capital is tied up in work in progress;

2 there is a long production time for making each part – any one item in a batch will not be completed significantly before any other item;

3 there is a need for a very efficient system of control in planning and production. This can be time-consuming for management.

Flow production

We have already seen that in batch production each item in the batch has to wait until all other items have completed that stage of the production process before it can move, with the rest of the batch, to the next stage of production. Flow production is a method of organising the work processes where each individual item being produced moves on to the next stage of production immediately. This eliminates the waiting time and the existence of large quantities of stock and work in progress. On the other hand, it requires the business to be very specific about the design of the product and demands a high degree of standardisation in terms of tools, methods and parts used. Machinery is arranged in lines according to the order of its function in the overall process, and the operators tend to have a more limited range of tasks to perform. For flow production to be viable in terms of the investment required there must be a comparatively large and steady market for the goods being produced. The product, therefore, must appeal to a wide range of customers. Flow production utilises the concepts of simplification, standardisation and specialisation to a far greater extent than either job or batch production.

Flow production has been accused of reducing the status of the workforce to that of mere cogs in a machine, taking from them their pride in their jobs and the satisfaction inherent in seeing a completed product. The amount of investment in machinery to keep the line flowing and the disruptive effects of a breakdown or bottleneck in any part of the line can impose constraints on other parts of the business. The purchasing department, faced with the costs of an idle production line, might find reliability the most important priority in its purchasing mix, and give price a far lower priority than it might have done under conditions of job or batch production. On the other hand, the use of flow production has brought the majority of consumer durables within the reach of a greater number of people than would otherwise have been the case.

The choice of production method is complex for a business. It can be said to depend on

- the stage of development a business has reached; and
- the nature of the product.

A start-up business making a standard good – for example, furniture or clothes – is likely to work on a job production method. The orders are unlikely to be large and will not justify the investment in labour/machinery demanded by batch or flow production. As the orders increase, they may move towards batch production. Several large orders for a range of garments for a specific line might make batch production viable. On the other hand, these orders may not be repeated.

Some businesses will never make the transition. The owner may be interested only in producing for a limited market and/or be unwilling to undertake the additional risk. The production of luxury goods with high status appeal is likely to be undertaken by job production methods.

An international company producing antibiotics does so under conditions of batch production, as do breweries. Both industries have the same basic task: to provide the ideal environment in terms of food and warmth for micro-organisms to flourish and give off their desired by-product. In the case of beer the by-product is alcohol; for the drug companies, antibiotics. The organisms are different; the temperature, food and end product are different; but the principles are the same. Essentially the process is the loading of a large vessel with the required food, the monitoring of the temperature and the production of a *batch* of the product. It has much in common with our earlier example of a batch of loaves.

In a large brewery the products of this type of batch production are likely to be processed using flow production methods. It will be the responsibility of the production manager to make sure that batches are ready to feed the bottling production line. This combination of production methods is common in industry.

A machine may have a variety of uses but needs to be re-tooled when moved from one use to another. 'Re-tooling' is the term used for re-setting a machine to do a different job. With some machines using, for example, computer and/or laser technology, this can be a relatively simple task. Other machines require the services of a skilled toolmaker to make the change. It therefore makes sense to make a batch of products which need the same tools before changing the machine to make another batch of products.

SELF-ASSESSMENT

1 State the production method used in each of the following types of business: a retail shop, a family-owned farm, a large-scale car factory, a company extracting oil.
2 'Job production must be better than flow production. After all, it gives the consumer precisely what he or she wants.' This statement may or may not be true. What other information would you need before making a final judgement?

Scale of production

Economists use the term '**economies of scale**' to describe a situation in which production costs fall as the scale of the organisation increases. We have already examined some of the factors that will cause this to happen – for example, fixed cost per unit will fall as output rises (average fixed costs). Discounts for bulk purchasing might also reduce material costs. Economies of scale can occur in all aspects of a business's activities. We will examine them in this chapter with the emphasis on production.

1 *Technical economies* Technical economies of scale are the true production economies. These arise where the costs of expanding capacity increase more slowly than the increase in output. The fixed cost per unit will fall. As a simple example let us assume that it costs £100 000 to buy a machine with the capacity to produce 100 000 items and £150 000 to buy a machine with a production capacity of 200 000. Assuming that all other costs stay the same, the first machine will produce units at a cost of £1 while the second will produce units at a cost of 75p.

A business may have a machine that is operating at 50 per cent capacity while the rest of the factory is operating at full capacity. If the business expands to the point where that machine can be operated at full capacity then production costs will fall.

2 *Buying economies* Buying economies do not come only from discounts. Purchasing is a specialised skill, and a man with a narrow range of goods to purchase for his company is more likely to develop expertise in the products available, the reliability of the firms with which he is dealing and an understanding of how often and in what quantities 'his' products will be needed. Such a division of labour is only possible in a large business.

3 *Marketing economies* The costs of advertising, distribution, sales promotion are high, and can be a large proportion of the total cost of a good produced by a small or medium-sized business. Large businesses can undertake advertising on a national scale secure in the knowledge that spread over their total output the addition to cost per unit will be minimal. Should advertising increase demand for a product over and above the cost of the advertising (advertising elasticity of demand greater than 1), there may be technical economies possible in addition to the marketing economies. In industries where the production unit is relatively small either by tradition or because the nature of the business or the technology employed dictates relatively small-scale production, there may be attempts to gain marketing economies by co-operation. Agricultural marketing boards are an example of such a type of co-operation.

4 *Financial economies* Large businesses have more assets, more products and greater reserves than smaller businesses. This reduces the risk of lending to them, and they can, as a result, often negotiate loans at a lower rate of interest

than smaller businesses. The risk associated with launching a new product is less traumatic for a large business with the resources to cushion the shock of failure.

5   *Administrative economies*   These include not only the ability to pay for and use efficiently the services of the best management ability available but also to employ sophisticated computer systems that would be beyond the financial resources of a small business.

The five economies of scale given above can be considered as *internal* to the business. Large industries and a concentration of an industry in one area can often benefit small firms as well as large. Administrative services such as the computer processing of payrolls are available to all firms. The provision of suitable educational courses by local colleges, maintenance services offered by independent companies and the existence of businesses specialising in the production of certain components can all reduce the costs of individual businesses and are known as *external* economies.

SELF-ASSESSMENT

1 Distinguish between internal and external economies of scale.
2 In what ways might a medium-sized business still benefit from internal economies of scale?

Inputs and outputs

A business buys raw materials, components and semi-finished goods and puts them through a variety of processes that make them more useful. The end result of this process may be sold to another business to become a component or semi-finished good at the start of its processes, or it may be sold direct to a consumer. Many businesses do both. A car battery is useful to the owner of a car, who sees it as part of his current expenditure. It is also essential to car manufacturers, who regard it as an item of stock. The input of one business is the output of another business. In this section we are concerned with the input to the business – that is, the purchasing function and the monitoring of stock levels within a business.

The purchasing function

The importance of purchasing varies according to the type of business. In service industries materials may be a very small part of the final cost of a product. In a manufacturing business the material cost may be a large proportion of the final cost. In the latter case it is essential that the right stocks are bought at the right price, in the right quantity and at the right time. The role of purchasing goes beyond this simple statement. The purchaser is a buyer in a market. This provides him with the opportunity to know what products are available in that market and to make this information available to the design department. He should also be able to advise on delivery times, which is essential information for stock control.

Stock control

Stock control is concerned with assessing the materials needed according to projected output, storing the materials in a suitable manner (that is, to keep them safe and in good condition) and issuing materials when required. The relationship between purchasing and the stock-control activities of a business will vary according to the size of the business and the organisational decisions.

The maintenance of the 'right' level of stocks is very important to the health of a business:

- In many industries the cost of materials used to make the product is a high proportion of final cost. Stocks can represent a considerable investment for a business.

- Stocks cost money to store. These costs can be seen as the opportunity cost of holding the stock. Stocks do not earn any money. If a business holds a stock valued at £10000, then it is sacrificing, at least, the interest on £10000 held in a bank at, say, 10 per cent. It is also sacrificing potential profit. The minimum cost of holding this stock can be seen as £1000 per annum. In addition, there are the costs of storage and the risk of stocks deteriorating in value.

- Stocks are frequently a major part of working capital, and this can have implications for the liquidity of the business.

The ideal situation in stock control is to hold stocks for the shortest possible period of time between ordering and the conversion of stocks into goods sold for a profit. In this way the cost of holding any one item of stock is minimised. This ideal cannot be realised by the work of the stock-control department. It will rely on production efficiency generally and the organisation of the factory to achieve a rapid throughput of work.

Stock levels

We have already established that it is desirable for a business to keep stocks as low as possible. On the other hand, if stocks are too low then there is a danger of production stopping because of short-fall in materials. A business will have a minimum stock level, sometimes called the **buffer, safety** or **insurance level**, below which it will not allow stocks to fall and a maximum stock level, above which the costs of holding the stock outweigh the advantages of holding it. The minimum and maximum of stock held are relative rather than absolute figures and will depend upon a combination of factors:

1 Storage space available and costs of storage. Space used to store materials can be seen as space that could be used for manufacturing. In some businesses there may be a physical shortage of space that puts a clear limit on the amount of stock they can hold safely and without risk of excessive spoilage.

2 The **lead time** is the interval of time between the identification of the need for an order and the availability of that order to the production department. It is *not* the same as delivery time. Lead time includes ordering, delivery and receiving time. The longer the lead time the higher the minimum level at which stocks will have to be held.

3 The amount of capital available will influence the stock level. This does not mean that a successful business will hold a higher level of stocks than a similar but less profitable business; in fact, the reverse might be true. Lack of available capital might force a business to hold a lower level of stock than it considers strictly desirable.

4 The type of stock. Perishable goods will be kept in smaller quantities than non-perishable stock in order to reduce the risk of loss. The 'life' of stock does not depend only on whether or not it is likely to deteriorate; it also

depends on the life span of the final product. If the product goes out of fashion, the stocks bought in to make it will be useless.

5   The economic ordering quantity will determine the amount of stock bought at any one time. Discounts available might offset the costs of storage and encourage a business to raise its minimum stock level.

6   External factors can influence the level of stocks held. A business might hold a high level of essential stocks if it can foresee a future shortage brought about by a possible crop failure or pressure on supplies as a result of war.

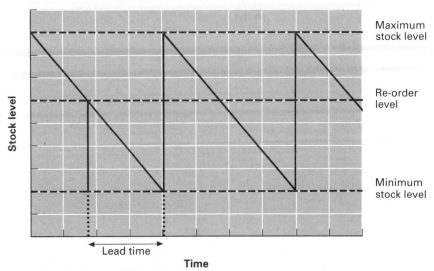

Figure 9.3   Simplified stock control graph

Figure 9.3 is a simplified stock control graph. Its value lies in its illustration of the main elements within stock control.

SELF-ASSESSMENT

1 A buyer has price and reliability as his two main concerns when selecting a supplier. What other considerations might be influential in his final purchasing decision?

2 Unusual weather conditions lead to reports that availability of an important raw material crop is likely to be below normal. What might be the reaction of a business which uses this raw material? What other factors would it take into account before reaching its final decision?

Value analysis

So far in this chapter we have been looking at the production function in general terms. **Value analysis** is an approach to evaluating the effectiveness of producing a component or product. It is an exercise designed to answer the question: Can we achieve the same result more efficiently and therefore at a lower cost? It is included because it emphasises the interdependence of the different functions of the business.

Stages in value analysis

1   *Definition of the function of the product*   If the product concerned is a component, then this stage should produce a precise statement of what it

must do if it is to perform its job correctly. A good definition may immediately suggest more cost-effective ways of achieving that function. The definition of a finished good should also take into account the market for which it is designed. A company producing wrist watches for the luxury market might destroy the market if they used a cheaper metal casing in an effort to control costs.

2 *Collection of data* At this stage the company may only *think* they know what the product is. They need detailed information if they are going to evaluate it. This information should include the following:

(a) Detailed technical specifications of the product.
(b) Marketing information (including the existence of similar products, the life expectancy of the product and the data from market research) will have a role to play in the final decision. A major design exercise will not be worthwhile if the product has a limited life span. On the other hand, value analysis might be used to identify strategies to extend the life span of the product.
(c) A detailed breakdown of costs in order to indicate the areas which it may be advantageous to investigate and also to define the constraints on any changes that might be suggested.
(d) The technology available to make the product. This should include details of new developments and their possible effects on production costs and quality control.
(e) The required quality of the product and details of the control procedures used to achieve this level. This relates to the quality required by the market but also to the production processes of the business.

3 *Evaluation* It is likely that a number of alternative solutions will be suggested to the same problem. Each solution will then be evaluated against the criteria established by the original product definition.

Value analysis is not limited to the existing products of a business. It can be used by a firm entering a market for the first time to decide the market segment for which it is aiming. Its importance lies in its integrated approach to the problem. An effective value analysis team would contain experts in each of the major business functions.

Production control

The production department, like all other departments in a business, will have targets set to contribute to the business plan. In addition, the production department will also have *quality* targets. The desired level of quality is not necessarily the best quality attainable for that product. The tennis racket made for a professional player will have to stand greater stresses than that used by an amateur. The professional will pay more for that quality. Quality control can be seen as minimising the rate of failure within limits set by costs and the market price. There may also be safety standards to which a product must conform.

Quality control is also important when applied to material stocks and work-in-progress. After all, the further a faulty part progresses in the production process the greater the cost of scrapping the product of which it is a part.

Where the output is high, quality control inspectors will work on a sample of goods and use the statistical techniques outlined in chapter 5 to analyse their findings. When results are unacceptable, changes in suppliers, working practices, selection and training techniques might be necessary. Poor quality is not necessarily the result of careless workers.

SELF-ASSESSMENT

1 A business decides that it is losing its market share because the price of its product is too high. State two problems it may encounter in trying to reduce the price assuming that profit margins will stay the same.
2 State three reasons for poor quality control.

Conclusion

It is important to remember that the production processes of a business do not exist in isolation. An inefficient production department which delivers faulty goods or fails to deliver on time can lose sales for the business. On the other hand, the production department is subject to constraints.

Production in extractive and manufacturing industries has the most physical presence of all business activity. It is difficult not to be aware of sheer size of plant in some industries. The plant owes its existence to the market for the goods it makes, and if that market should decline or the marketing department fail to exploit it then even the largest factory will close.

Review

1   A business buys in a component used in the assembly of its product. It uses the component at a steady rate of 50000 per month and prefers to keep a month's supply in stock. Lead time is two weeks. The maximum amount of stock the business prefers to hold is 200000.
   (a) Draw a graph to show the changes in the stock of components over a period of six months.
   (b) At what level of stockholding should the business re-order?
   (c) At the end of the third month the supplier is involved in an industrial dispute which lasts for a fortnight. Assuming that no other supplies are available, sketch the consequences for the business on your graph.
   (d) How might the business react to each of the following situations?
       (i) an increase in the price of the component;
       (ii) a shortage of working capital;
       (iii) stockpiling by governments of an essential raw material;
       (iv) an expected rise in the demand for the final product;
       (v) improvements in stock-control techniques.

2   A business has developed a new product of advanced technological design. It was expected that the demand for the product would be low at first, rising steadily over a period of six months to 20000 units per month. Production levels were set at 15000 units for the first twelve months of the product's life. In fact, actual orders rose steadily to 40000 units over a period of six months.
   (a) Draw a graph showing the relationship between output, projected orders and actual orders.
   (b) Outline the marketing problems the business may experience as a result of this situation.
   (c) Assuming that it is impossible to expand production capacity before the end of the twelve-month period, how might the business increase the supply of the product? What difficulties might it encounter given the nature of the product?

3   Examine Figure 9.4.

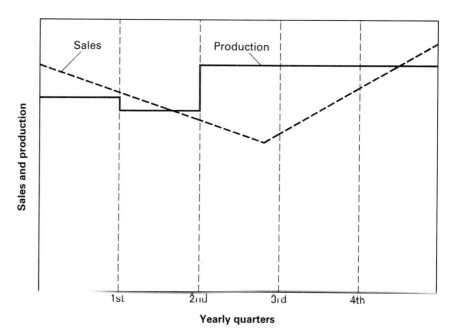

Figure 9.1 Sales and production figures over 16 months

(a) What problems might the business face as a result of this pattern of sales and production?

(b) How might (i) the production department and (ii) the marketing department attempt to solve these problems?

4 The following passage explains the advantages of using lasers to cut materials (for example, metals) in manufacturing industry. Read the passage carefully and answer the questions.

> Running on a fully automatic programme, a laser cutting tool can greatly improve precision, repeatability, flexibility and productivity. The combined effect of these improvements on the entire production schedule can make a manufacturing operation more productive by a factor that has been estimated to range from 8 to 20. Laser systems bring still other advantages: the absence of vibration, noise and dust, the reduction of fumes and the elimination of the need to buy, stock and maintain a variety of often expensive cutting heads.
>
> Together these reasons explain why laser tools can offer attractive cost benefits in spite of their high initial cost, which is estimated as being from 2 to 5 times that of conventional cutting systems. A short 'pay-back' time (a year or less) can be achieved with laser tools, which explains the rapid extension of such tools to a wide variety of cutting tasks.

(Adapted from 'Laser Applications in Manufacturing', Aldo V. Rocca, *Scientific American*, March 1982.)

(a) Explain how improved 'precision, repeatability and flexibility' can result in greater efficiency. (6)

(b) Give *three* ways in which 'the absence of vibration, noise and dust, the reduction of fumes' may be an advantage to a manufacturing company. (9)

(c) Given that laser tools are expensive, what justification might a business have for using them? (6)

(d) Explain the term 'pay-back' time. (4) 1984 (AEB)

5   Study the extract and answer the questions which follow:

Any company adviser who's done his homework can confidently recommend Hampshire, England, and its neighbouring Isle of Wight as, potentially, Western Europe's most profitable business location.

The reason is simple: in Hampshire doing business is truly cost-effective.

● Cost-effective premises. Modern buildings, ready to move into for a fraction of the cost of similar accommodation in, say, London. Town-centre locations, out-of-town business parks, sites for development.

● Cost-effective manpower. The skills you need backed by good training facilities – in information technology, integrated circuits, optical fibres, frontiers-of-knowledge projects, university research … Already, Hampshire's hi-tech industries employ more than twice the national proportion of the local work-force.

HAMPSHIRE ENGLAND

Where people like to work

HAMPSHIRE DEVELOPMENT ASSOCIATION

To Hampshire Development Association, Winchester, Hampshire SO22 5BS, England

Please contact me about relocation opportunities

Name_____

Position_____

Company_____

Address_____

_____

Type of Business_____   TE 13/4

● Cost-effective environment. The quality of life every family wants – villages, cities, downlands, forests, coast and sea, providing excellent recreation and top value living – including housing.

● Cost-effective communication. Excellent land, sea and air routes connect you economically with London, Europe and the world. Southampton is Britain's largest deep-sea container port and the site of one of its first freeports.

Among profit-conscious companies already located in this area are Cyanamid, IBM United Kingdom, Plessey, Pirelli General, Sun Life of Canada and Zurich Insurance. To discover how to join them, call Hampshire Development Association on Winchester (0962) 56060. From overseas, dial +44 962 56060. Or telex 477729. Ask for Peter Scruton. Or use the coupon.

Source: *The Economist*, 14 April 1984

(a) A major Japanese company is proposing to establish a UK manufacturing and distribution base for zip fasteners. Write a *brief* report, using a suitable format (5) to show the advantages (10) which the advertisement claims for Hampshire. (15)

(b) Identify *five* other items, not mentioned in the advertisement, which would need to be clarified before a decision on location could be made and show in each case why it would be important to the company. (10)   1986 (AEB)

6   A shop which holds 30 units of an item at the beginning of each week is concerned that this is too high a level of stock. It finds from an investigation that the weekly demand for this item in the past two years has been as follows (assume that the year has 50 working weeks):

No. of items sold	1–5	6–10	11–15	16–20	21–25	26–30
No. of weeks	4	10	50	15	20	1

(a) (i) Identify the modal group and calculate the arithmetic mean and median value of the above distribution. (7)

   (ii) Which measure of the central tendency is the most appropriate to use here and why? In what circumstances would it be preferable to use the other measures? (4)

(b) Each item makes a contribution of £50 before allowing for stock holding costs.

   (i) Stating clearly the assumptions you make, calculate the annual reduction in contribution if the shop decides to hold a stock level of 24 at the beginning of each week. (4)

   (ii) On arithmetical grounds, what stock level would you recommend if the weekly cost of holding an item was £2? Justify your answer. (3)

   (iii) What other factors should be considered in deciding upon the optimum stock level? (3)

(c) Over the past two years it has been found that the probability that an item will be returned because of a fault is 0.1.

   Write out expressions for the probability that, in a week when exactly five items have been sold:

(i) all items are faulty;

(ii) three items are faulty;

(iii) at least two items are not faulty.   (4)   1986 (CLES)

Activities

1 As a group select a simple craft product with which you are unfamiliar. Origami (the art of folding paper) might provide suitable examples. It should be possible to make the product using job, batch and flow techniques.

(a) Make a realistic assessment of direct labour and material costs.

(b) Divide into three groups, each using a different production method, and learn how to make the product. The learning process can be judged complete when products of an acceptable saleable standard are being produced. Calculate the cost of the learning process in terms of direct material and labour for each group.

(c) Continue to make the item for at least an hour.

(d) Comment on the following aspects of the exercise:

    (i) Assuming that you want to cover all costs, including development costs, and make a profit of 10 per cent on costs, what is the break-even point?

    (ii) Analyse the difficulties experienced by each group. This should include problems of materials and equipment, quality control and wastage rates, learning times, group attitudes to the exercise (did some members of the group think the exercise a waste of time? how did this affect their productivity and performance?), bottlenecks experienced and reasons for them.

There is no guarantee that your experience will reflect the conventional wisdom relating to different types of production. If there is a difference, can you explain it? You should remember that each individual has a unique set of skills and aptitudes and that the problems you have encountered reflect those of a production manager. Why might these problems be intensified in a period of relatively full employment?

2 Visit several business organisations and analyse the production function in each according to the outline given in this chapter. Your selection of businesses should include examples of job, batch and flow production organisation and, if possible, businesses operating in a variety of markets. Interview the production manager. What does he see as his main problems? Is it the market, people, finance or equipment that provide the biggest constraints on his decision making?

Suggested projects

1 Can Business X improve its stock control?

2 A critical evaluation of quality control within a business.

3 Can Business Y improve the use of its canteen facilities?

Essays

1 The concept of economies of scale suggests that large businesses are more efficient in their use of resources than small businesses. If this is so, why do small businesses survive and what justification can be offered for the investment of government money in the small business sector?

2 Discuss the constraints upon a business enterprise when deciding on a policy of quality control.

3   Outline and comment on the interrelationships which exist between the marketing and production functions.

4   The location decisions of a business are relatively independent of considerations of market and supplies. What are the implications of this position for (a) the business and (b) attempts by central and local government to control/influence location decisions in the private sector?

5   What factors contribute to making a business 'foot-loose' (that is, not tied to one place by things like raw materials, skilled labour, power sources)?

6   Discuss the factors a manufacturing organisation would consider before deciding to change its location.   1984 (AEB)

7   (a) What are the principal types of production system?   (3)
      (b) How would the management of a catering establishment choose between them?   (12)
      (c) What problems might arise in moving from one system of production to another?   (10)   1985 (CLES)

8   (a) What are the objectives of stock management?   (10)
      (b) How might each of these objectives be achieved   (15)   1985 (CLES)

Chapter 10 **People and business**

Businesses are the creations of people. They are organisations brought into existence in order to satisfy the needs and wants of society. They have an effect on the lives of people they employ by the way in which they are organised, by the wages they pay, the social opportunities they may or may not offer and the degree of job security they can ensure. In turn, people influence the growth and development of businesses: as customers with their buying decisions; as owners and employees by investment, purchasing, marketing and production decisions; as employees by their efficiency in their job.

People also influence business by the choices they make as citizens. The way in which individuals decide to vote will affect the political climate in which a business has to operate. Individuals with strong opinions on particular matters may join together in an organisation to publicise their concern and to try to persuade decision makers to take notice of their point of view (**pressure groups**). An environmental pressure group, for example, might influence the siting of a business.

We have already discussed the impact of consumer buying behaviour on a firm in chapter 8. In chapter 14, Business and Society, we will examine the way in which political, cultural and social attitudes can affect business generally. In this chapter, the main emphasis will be on the individual as a member of a business organisation. Figure 10.1 illustrates the interaction between people and the business community.

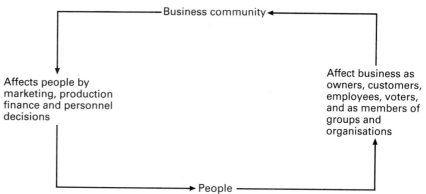

Figure 10.1 People and business

People as individuals

Each member of the human race is the unique product of heredity and environment. A person inherits physical characteristics from his or her parents, and their expectations of life are moulded by their unique experience. This is a very simple statement, and you should be aware that psychologists are still investigating the relative importance of hereditary and environmental influences on the development of personality. In this section we shall look at the way in which the needs, personalities and attitudes of individuals are important influences on the efficient running of a business enterprise.

The needs of the individual

What do people need to make them happy and contented? If you asked this question of any individual he or she could probably give you a long list of specific needs. It is also likely that at different times of life some of those needs would have greater importance than at others. In an attempt to provide a simple framework of needs Abraham Maslow (1970) drew up a hierarchy of needs. These are shown in Figure 10.2. Maslow argued that a person would seek to satisfy lower-level needs before moving on to the next level of needs. If it is not possible to satisfy needs, then the person experiences *frustration*, to which the response may be *apathy* (what is the use of trying? there is no chance of success) or *aggression*. Aggression may be expressed verbally – for example, by blaming other people for lack of success. In extreme cases it may result in physical violence either to people or to things. The nineteenth-century Luddites, faced with new technology that rendered their skills redundant and their livelihoods at risk, resorted to machine wrecking. Twentieth-century workers faced with the same problem might use the organised power of trade unions to express the same frustration.

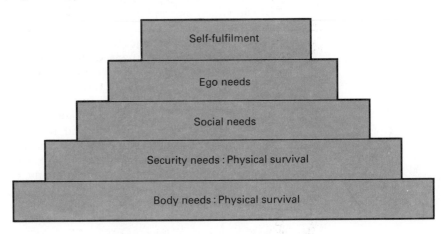

Figure 10.2　Maslow's hierarchy of needs

Maslow argued that in modern industrialised societies the lower-level needs were enjoyed by most people. The way to persuade people to work harder (that is, to **motivate** them) was to offer them the opportunity of satisfying higher-level needs – for example, control over their working arrangements, the achievement of independence. Maslow developed the idea of the *self-actualising* individual.

Frederick Taylor, writing at the beginning of this century, saw man as motivated by money. He saw man as *economic* in his needs. He argued that if jobs were designed to take maximum output possible, that if personnel were recruited for their ability, trained thoroughly and paid well according to output, they would work harder, achieve higher pay and the business would make more profit.

Taylor was an engineer by profession, and there is a strong element of technical efficiency in his ideas. When Taylor's ideas are put into practice it can lead to fear of loss of job security. As a result, unofficial limits may be put on the amount of work people might do in a day, the controlling force being the opinion of the people an individual works with rather than the management of the business.

In certain types of job money can be an important incentive. The place of work does not offer satisfaction for all needs. Some people do not want independence and control over their job. They would prefer a high money wage which they can use to purchase satisfaction of their other needs outside work.

In the 1920s Elton Mayo conducted important research that suggested that the most important influence on the way in which people behaved at work was the people they were in contact with during the day. When people felt they were appreciated for their efforts, when they enjoyed the company of the people they worked with they would work more productively. These experiments gave weight to the idea of man as a *social* animal.

The most publicised experiment in this area is known as the Hawthorne experiment. The Western Electric Company of Chicago had been experimenting to find the ideal light levels for maximum productivity in their company. They were surprised to find that wide variations in the level of lighting had little effect on output. Mayo led the research team from the Harvard University School of Business Administration that was invited to study this phenomenon. The published research resulted in an increased emphasis on the provision of sports and social facilities, a tendency to organise production so that people worked in small groups rather than on assembly lines and a management style that was consultative and supportive rather than authoritarian.

The study of human behaviour related to the working environment is continuing all the time. Taylor, Mayo and Maslow have been selected as people whose ideas have had a significant influence. Douglas McGregor developed Maslow's needs theory and suggested Theory X and Theory Y as typifying people's behaviour.

Theory X states that man is inherently lazy and uninterested in work. He needs constant direction and supervision by management if he is to be effective as a worker. Theory Y, McGregor's own theory, suggests that all people can be motivated to work hard and that it is the responsibility of management to provide the ideal circumstances to persuade them to do so.

Following Mayo, Herzberg defined the ideas of *maintenance* (sometimes called *hygiene*) factors and *motivators*. Maintenance factors are good heating, lighting, pay and social facilities. People do not work any harder because these are present, but if conditions deteriorate then their work output can decline. Poor maintenance factors can cause *job dissatisfaction*. Motivators – for example, a sense of achievement, the giving of responsibility, the prospect of promotion – lead to higher work output and *job satisfaction*. Herzberg described the building in of motivators into a work situation as *job enrichment*.

Recent research has moved away from the simple approach and has given weight to the idea of *complex* man. This can be summarised as follows:

1 People change throughout their lives. At one point their work may be the primary source of need satisfaction, defining them as people and providing them with a social life. Later, the more important satisfactions may come from their personal lives or from voluntary work. The importance of work, therefore, changes.

2 As individuals develop they are subject to a wider variety of influences, including the way in which the organisation in which they work affects them. Motives which they did not know they possessed or dismissed at the age of twenty might be dominant at the age of forty. The man who places a high value on money at twenty may be more influenced by promotion prospects and security twenty years later.

SELF-ASSESSMENT

1 The Hawthorne experiment suggested that people worked better if they felt valued. What evidence in the text supports this conclusion?
2 Give two reasons why the theory of 'complex man' might be more realistic than preceding theories.

Personality

Personality can be described as the total of an individual's behavioural and emotional tendencies which distinguish him or her from other individuals.

Over the years psychologists and psychoanalysts have attempted to describe and analyse broad patterns of personality in an attempt to classify people and so achieve a broader understanding of the ways in which they behave. A great deal of research has gone into this subject, but we shall only look at the classification of personality by *type* and the implications of this approach for a business.

Classification by type

1 *The extrovert* An extrovert is a person who is primarily interested in people or things outside his or her own self. Eysenck distinguished between stable extroverts and anxious extroverts. Stable extroverts are very good at making contact with people, and are often successful in jobs that require constant contact with people in order to persuade them into a course of action. Anxious extroverts, on the other hand, generate more tension. They can be found in high-pressure jobs, frequently those with a deadline to meet.

2 *The introvert* Introverts have a tendency to withdraw into themselves and seek their stimulus to action from their own resources. The stable introvert prefers quiet jobs with little human contact, whereas the anxious introvert takes this tendency to the extreme. The anxious introvert can be the truly creative person in business.

SELF-ASSESSMENT

1 Select five occupations in business, and state which personality type might be most suited to each.
2 Give three reasons why the personality of an applicant might be important in the selection of personnel.

Groups

If each person in the business enterprise is a unique product of heredity and environment with a complex and changing pattern of needs and a distinct personality pattern, what happens when they try to work together? The answer is that most people tend to modify their behaviour, to a greater or lesser extent, to suit the people with whom they come in contact and the needs of the job. In doing so the group gradually establishes an acceptable code of behaviour to which each person adheres which is known as the **group norm**.

Group norms can also be imposed upon the group by management. In many cases the standards of behaviour imposed by management are modified by the group when working. This can lead to problems. For example, a business may have a strict code of practice relating to the wearing of safety helmets. This code may cover the type of helmet that can be worn and the way in which it is worn. Employees may prefer to wear the helmet differently because they consider it is more attractive. This might leave hair exposed to moving machinery. People in that group who did not conform to the accepted pattern of behaviour might be subjected to pressure to do so. The pressure might take the form of comments designed to make the nonconforming individuals feel inferior. Whether or not the pressure would be successful would depend on the strength of character or stubbornness of the nonconformists as opposed to the leadership qualities of the people trying to make them conform. Look at the following example:

> A group of college lecturers arrived at work to confront an official union picket line belonging to another union. The lecturers were members of the staff of a college with 250 members of staff and 4000 students, many of whom they will only meet occasionally. They were also members of a union some of whose members they will never meet. It was the policy of their union to *recommend* that its members should not cross such picket lines. At first approximately two-thirds of the lecturers were prepared to cross the picket line. The one-third who refused to do so had a high proportion of the older members of staff whose length of service and seniority carried weight with their colleagues. In the end, considerably less than a third of the staff did cross the picket line.

This example illustrates the complexity of individual reactions to a situation.

1 The senior staff had no power over their colleagues in making this decision. However, the habit of the more junior members of staff of giving weight to the opinions of these people was carried over into a non-work situation.

2 As more people joined the senior staff in their decision so there was more pressure on the rest of the group to conform.

3 The group norms in this situation were partly defined by the recommendations of the trade union.

4 The designated leader of the group (the head of department) played a neutral role. He did not (and could not) use his authority in this situation.

5 The older members of staff had worked together for a number of years and had built up friendships outside the workplace. This gave their stand a cohesion that their opponents lacked.

6 The final result depended on the inter-personal relationships of the people concerned. Had the senior members of staff not been respected in their work roles, had there been resentment against them for the way in which they dealt with their colleagues, the group decision might well have gone the other way.

Read the example carefully. There are several different types of groups involved.

1 Groups to which people belong but where they do not have daily contact with all the members are known as **secondary groups**.

2 Both the college and the union exist for distinct purposes. So also does the department to which the lecturers belong. Groups which are formed as a result of the actions of an organisation are known as **formal** groups. They are part of the **structure** of the organisation.

3 When people meet one another at frequent and regular intervals we describe the group they belong to as **primary** groups.

4 When people form groups because of common interests and on a casual basis we refer to these groups as **informal** groups. Should they make rules for

joining the group and elect people to perform jobs related to the group it would then become a formal group.

Six men meet once a week in their local pub. Their common interest is in gardening. For an hour or so they discuss their plans for their different gardens and then part, only to meet again the following week. Sometimes one or other member of the group will volunteer to order a certain type of seed for the rest or somebody else will volunteer the loan of a piece of equipment. One day they decide to form a gardening society. They advertise in the local newspaper for people of similar interests to join them, book a hall, hold a meeting, draw up rules, declare an annual subscription and become affiliated to the national body. There is one person responsible for funds (the **treasurer**), another takes minutes of the meeting and sees to correspondence (the **secretary**), and someone else who presides over the meetings and makes sure they are run in an orderly fashion (the **president**).

The first group was informal. When it became a society it was formalised – that is, it had a structure and had to adhere to **agreed procedures**.

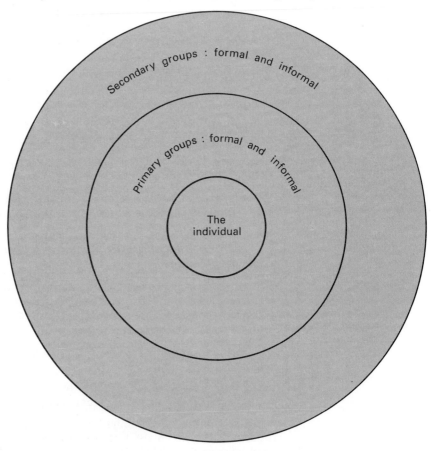

Figure 10.3   Formal and informal groups

SELF-ASSESSMENT

1 What is a group?
2 Distinguish between formal, informal, primary and secondary groups.

Leadership

In discussing groups it was implied that leadership affected the behaviour of groups. It is now time to examine this idea in more detail. We will look at the way in which leaders arise out of a group; the types of leadership that can be exercised; and the way in which the type of leadership is affected by the needs of the group.

The theory of leadership

Leaders are present in both formal and informal groups. A teacher/lecturer standing in front of a group of students, a supervisor in a factory, the managing director of a company are all exercising the power of leadership. They have, it is to be hoped, clearly stated *objectives* and they are *organising* the group in their control to achieve those objectives.

In any group of friends there is likely to be a leader. The person who says, 'Let's do this. I'll get the tickets, you find out the time of the buses.'

Both leaders, the first in a formal group, the second in an informal group, have the power to make people do what they want. The interesting question is: how does a leader emerge from the group? There is no single answer to this question. It is likely that the emergence of a leader depends on the interaction of a number of factors:

1   The character of the leader. People who accept and/or are given leadership tend to have certain characteristics in common. They are sociable and willing to make contributions to discussion. They are likely to be more intelligent than the rest of the group and have the ability to solve problems.

2   Leadership depends on the type of task being undertaken.

3   Leadership depends on the personalities of the rest of the people in the group.

4   Leadership may be imposed on the group, or the leader may be elected. The election of a leader does not have to be formal. It could be no more than a consensus among group members that one person has the ability to lead. Imposed leadership may come into conflict with the informal group leader. In circumstances where the informal leader is dominant, then the informal group norms will be followed rather than the norms imposed by the business. In extreme circumstances this can lead to low productivity, poor workmanship and failure, in the business as a whole, to achieve its objectives.

Leadership styles

There are two main types of leader: those who are autocratic and those who are democratic.

•   The autocratic leader sets his own objectives, allocates tasks and insists on obedience. As a result, the group becomes very dependent upon him. The members of the group do not have the necessary information to make their own decisions. Because they are dependent on the leader there is little cohesion among group members, and output, although high under supervision, may not be of good quality. Members of a group with autocratic leadership frequently appear dissatisfied with their leader.

On the other hand, autocratic leadership may be necessary in certain circumstances. The discipline imposed in the armed forces is based on the need to move large bodies of men from one part of a battlefield to another very quickly and to condition them to obey orders instantly.

- The democratic leader encourages participation in the decision-making process. He consults with members of the group and 'sells' the final decision to them, working on the assumption that people will work better if they know and believe in their objectives. This style of leadership requires good communication skills on the part of the leader. It results in greater satisfaction on the part of the group, the quality of output tends to be good and the members of the group make many suggestions. True democratic leadership increases the satisfaction within a group.

The type of leadership employed by any individual will depend on a number of factors:

1 *The task that is being undertaken*   We have already seen that military, authoritarian discipline was developed to meet the needs of the battlefield.

2 *The traditions of the organisation*   Organisations develop their own patterns of behaviour. An organisation with a tradition of autocratic management would put pressure on individual managers to conform. This is an instance of the development of group norms.

3 *The type of labour force*   Highly skilled people will have more to offer in a democratically led group than people lacking experience. With a group of unskilled workers autocratic leadership may be the only option open to the manager if the job is to be completed.

4 *The size of the group*   Autocratic leadership becomes more likely as the number of people a manager controls increases. The greater the number of people the greater the risk of a democratic style degenerating into confusion.

5 *The personality of the leader*   Some people are more suited to one leadership style compared to another. This might be the result of personality, previous experience (or lack of it) or a sense of insecurity.

6 *The personalities of the group members*   Some people may prefer to be directed in their work, either from lack of interest, from previous experience of autocratic leadership or because they believe that the manager is paid to take decisions and responsibility.

7 *The amount of time available to complete a task*   Persuasion and consultation take time, even if the result is a more efficient workforce.

It might appear that the style of leadership should change according to the situation: the democratic leader becoming autocratic when a rushed order has to be completed, with inexperienced staff or in an emergency. Research suggests that the majority of people prefer their leaders to have a definite leadership style.

SELF-ASSESSMENT

1 Identify two circumstances which affect leadership style.
2 From what you know of the needs of individuals explain briefly why people may prefer a definite leadership style.

Motivation

In the first part of this chapter we have looked at people in terms of their needs and personalities, the way in which they behave in groups and the leadership of those groups. In this section we will examine the way in which this knowledge of people might be used to **motivate** them – that is, to make each person *want* to work harder towards the objectives of the business. These techniques have been derived from the theories of researchers such as Maslow, Mayo and Herzberg outlined at the beginning of the chapter.

Individuals are unique, and group norms vary widely from business to business. What might motivate one group of employees could have the opposite effect on another group. Motivators may also vary for the same group of people over time.

Job enlargement

Job enlargement is concerned with widening the variety of tasks within a given job. It can also be described as the redesign of jobs. The tendency towards specialisation in the workforce, partly as the result of new technology and partly as a result of a drive for greater efficiency, has led to many jobs becoming smaller in scope. This has reduced the control of the worker over his or her day. Seemingly endless repetition of the same apparently meaningless task can lead to boredom and a lower standard of work. Given a variety of tasks, the worker can assign those which require less concentration to a time of day when their concentration levels are low.

Jobs may be rotated to produce the same effect. A worker may spend a certain amount of time on one task before being moved to another task or even another department. The following statement was made by a worker on a production line. He was talking about the effect on him of the economic recession which had led to the closing of a number of factories in his town and the closing down of all but one production line at his factory.

> I suppose I should be grateful I've still got a job but it's boring all the same. I never stayed in a job for more than a few years. When I got fed up with a place I would move on. Same sort of work but different people and a different place. It made life more interesting. Can't do that now. We used to swap around in here. Nothing formal but the supervisor turned a blind eye. A week or so on one line and then we would change to another. Now that there is only one line working that has gone too.

This is not an example of job rotation and job enlargement being deliberately used to motivate. It does, however, illustrate the needs these schemes are designed to satisfy.

The addition of tasks to a job can meet with resentment. Workers might see it as an attempt on the part of management to make them work harder for the same money.

Job enrichment

Job enrichment is the process of increasing the degree of responsibility that workers take for their own work and the formal recognition given to it. Job enrichment can also increase the promotion prospects of employees by adding to their range of experience. It might give employees more control over the way in which they organise their work, over the allocation of tasks to members of a group and over quality control. In order to be successful, job enrichment should be supported by a training programme so that workers can acquire the additional skills they will need.

Participation

When people take an active part in reaching a decision they are more likely to feel a sense of commitment to putting the decision into practice. There is a great deal of evidence to support the theory that worker participation in decision making is a highly effective motivator. Where participation is imposed on a workforce without adequate training or preparation, the sense of commitment lessens. In such cases workers may resent the calls on their time. Shop-floor representatives must be seen to have real influence in the decision-making processes and the information needed must be available to them, otherwise there is the danger that management might use its superior knowledge to initiate the course of action it wishes and worker representatives will be regarded as a rubber stamp.

Quality control circles

Quality control circles are a relatively new development in British industry. They can be viewed as a special development of worker participation. A small group of workers meet regularly to discuss problems they are experiencing in their jobs. They attempt to find the solutions to the problems. Management offers the resources to the workers to put their solutions into practice. A quality control circle works on the assumption that all workers have experience of the jobs they are doing which may be more relevant and immediate than the more theoretical knowledge of management.

The different motivational techniques have in common the idea that the greater the responsibility, recognition, respect and status accorded to individuals within a business, the greater the individuals' sense of involvement in that business and therefore the greater the degree of motivation. The solution to industrial problems is made to sound simple. In practice, of course, the success or failure of a scheme for improving motivation can depend on a number of factors:

1   *The state of industrial relations within a business*   We have already seen that people judge new events in the light of their experience. In an organisation with a history of poor industrial relations any scheme of management is likely to be viewed with suspicion. Even if there has been a complete change in management personnel the new men may inherit the reputations of the old.

2   *The attitude of trade unions*   A trade union might see a management scheme for worker participation as usurping their role in the organisation.

3   *The accuracy with which the original problems have been diagnosed*   Job enlargement, job enrichment, participation and quality control circles might seem an additional burden to a workforce whose apparent lack of motivation was due to overwork!

4   *The way in which a scheme has been introduced*   An imposed scheme will meet with more resistance than one in which prior consultation has taken place.

5   *The impact of management style* (allied to the last point)   A business with a tradition of autocratic management will find the workforce more apathetic and unwilling to co-operate than a business which has encouraged suggestions in the past. An autocratic manager may start out with good intentions, but his personality and, perhaps, a feeling of insecurity may cause him to retreat, thereby increasing the problems for future attempts.

Organisations

In chapter 2 we defined business in terms of organisations and systems. In chapter 9 we looked at specialisation, standardisation and simplification as aspects of organising production. In this chapter we are going to look more closely at the principles of organisation as they apply to the whole business.

A word of warning! There is no such thing as an ideal organisation. What works for one business may be potentially disastrous for another – even though they make the same product, are approximately the same size and use the same technology. The final organisational form of the business will depend on the following factors:

1 *The size of the business* The larger the business the more likely it is to have specialised departments. We saw in chapter 4 that the small businessman had to undertake most of the business functions himself. In the intervening chapters we have implied that these functions could be carried out by specialists.

2 *The traditions of the business* A family business might remain faithful to a certain type of organisational structure long after it should have changed to meet contemporary needs.

3 *The number of products* A business with a large number of products might organise so that each product was responsible for its own marketing, production and so on.

4 *The geographical spread of the business* A business whose factories are widely separated will have a different organisational structure from one with only one factory or whose factories are within easy reach of one another.

5 *The preferred style of leadership* Autocratic leaders will want to have control over decision making. This will affect the final structure of the organisation.

6 *The type of technology used* J. Woodward, writing in 1958 (in *Management and Technology*), came to the conclusion that businesses using similar technology or production processes, even if they were operating in different industries, tended to have very similar organisational structures.

Principles of organisation

In this section we are going to look at the decisions that any businessman, other than the very smallest, has to make about the way in which his organisation will work.

In a small business the owner will undertake all the activities of the business. He will:

- make decisions relating to the long-term objectives of the business;
- make sure the work in the business meets his long-term objectives;
- make the good or service that is the reason for the existence of the business;
- undertake to raise and manage finance, employ staff and solve – or try to solve – legal, financial and personnel problems that might arise;
- provide the services that keep the business going (for example, acting as a receptionist, cleaning).

As the business grows larger divisions of labour takes place and these roles are performed by different people. It is the relationship of these roles to one another that is determined by the principles of organisation.

> **SELF-ASSESSMENT**
>
> 1 From your study of production explain why the type of technology used by a business might influence its organisational structure.
> 2 Give one reason why there is no ideal form of business organisation.

Delegation

Delegation is the act of entrusting another person to carry out an act for which you retain responsibility. The person delegated must be given the power to perform the task (**authority**) and will have a responsibility to see that it is completed satisfactorily. The person who delegates will still be responsible for the task. An example from the field of education might help to clarify this distinction.

The headteacher of a school is responsible for the standard of education offered by the school and certain legally defined responsibilities relating to the welfare of the students. In a village school the job may be done by one person who is also the only teacher (**producer**). In a large secondary school it is impossible for one person to carry out all the work. Apart from other considerations he or she will not have the expertise to teach the range of subjects to the standard required. The heads of departments will, therefore, have responsibility for their own subject area. They must *account* for the way in which they exercise the responsibility to the headteacher.

If you place yourself in the position of the headteacher in this example you will see that before you were prepared to delegate authority you would want to be sure that you could *trust* the person concerned, and you would also want some form of *control* over his or her activities.

Centralisation – that is, a situation in which the majority of decisions remain the responsibility of relatively few people – can be seen as the opposite of delegation. Decentralisation is not the same as delegation but may often be accompanied by it. For example, a business which makes several products may decide to divide the organisation so that there is a management, production and service structure for each product. The major decisions concerning that product would be made by the senior management of that division. This can be explained by saying that control has shifted sideways (*horizontally*). Delegation implies a downward shift in control (*vertically*).

Even in decentralised organisations some functions might still remain centralised. Significant economies of scale in purchasing might mean that the buying function is controlled from the centre. The importance of investment could have the same effect on the financial function with divisions working to an agreed budget and requiring consent from head office for expenditure above an agreed maximum.

As usual in the study of business there is no one correct answer. Some arguments which support centralisation are shown below:

1 It facilitates rapid decision making. In a situation in which a business has to respond quickly to external pressures, such as changing market situations, centralised control reduces the amount of time spent in co-ordinating the activities of a number of different departments/divisions.

2 A business with a tradition of autocratic leadership might find decentralisation/delegation difficult to achieve. It can be a demotivator for people to have the theoretical power and authority to take certain decisions only to have these decisions overruled by more senior management.

3 Members of senior management have experience of decision making and, presumably, have achieved their present position by showing that they are successful decision makers. It is reasonable to expect that they will make better choices than people with less experience.

4 Centralised control provides senior management with an overall view of the position of the business and allows them to make decisions in terms of allocation of resources that contributes to the overall health of the business and the achievement of long-term objectives. Most people tend to regard the activities in which they are engaged as being of prime importance. This can

lead to marketing departments taking decisions without sufficient knowledge of production capability.

To summarise the above arguments, centralisation gives control to a comparatively small number of good decision makers who can use their power to achieve the most effective use of resources to promote the strategic objectives of the business. It can also lead to problems.

1 Centralisation can cause delay in decision making. If too many decisions have to be relayed through a number of people then there is greater likelihood of error. We shall look at this problem in more detail when we discuss communications.

2 There is a limit to the amount of work individuals can cope with. If senior management have too many decisions to make then the quality of their work will be affected and one of the chief advantages of centralisation will be lost.

3 Centralisation implies the existence of a comprehensive system of control. The operation of any system in business costs money. Centralisation can be judged as being more expensive than decentralisation/delegation.

4 Centralisation limits the opportunity for middle management to learn decision-making skills. If their job is simply to put into practice decisions which have already been made, they cannot develop experience in evaluating the evidence before making a choice.

5 Decentralised organisations might be more aware of individual problems than the senior management in centralised organisations. This may take the form of being aware of conditions in their own geographical area or the problems inherent in producing or marketing a particular product.

The final decision about the degree of centralisation in a business enterprise will depend on the skill of top management and their leadership style, including the amount of trust they have in the skill and experience of their subordinates. It will also be influenced by the size and geographical dispersion of the business units, the importance of the decisions to be made in relation to the overall objectives of the business and the degree of independence each part of the business possesses.

SELF-ASSESSMENT

1 Distinguish between authority and responsibility.
2 Distinguish between decentralisation and delegation.

Span of control

The span of control is the number of subordinates whose work is directed by a manager. The number will vary according to the situation in which control is being exercised – that is:

- the experience and personality of the manager concerned;
- the nature of the work (the simpler/more standardised the task the less need there is for managers to make decisions and therefore the greater the number of people they can control);
- the experience of those being controlled and their degree of commitment to the work.

The shape of organisations

To summarise, so far we have said that individuals bring into the business organisation their own personalities with their individual pattern of needs.

Within that organisation they will be members of a number of groups both formal and informal, and in each group they will have a role. In order to achieve its objectives, the business needs to direct the people working in it, co-ordinate the needs of the individual so that they are harnessed to the objectives of the business and operate control systems in order to check that the people working there are fulfilling the needs of the business. It is now time to look at the overall shape of the organisation.

The pyramid structure

Figure 10.4 is an example of an **organisation chart**. It is a statement of the major roles in an organisation and their relationship to one another in terms of authority and responsibility. It demonstrates the **hierarchy** of the business – that is, the rank and order of each role. The example given in Figure 10.4 is conventional. Each level in the hierarchy has a defined position, and orders flow down the levels and information flows upwards. We will examine the implications of this type of pyramid structure in terms of effective management when we discuss communications later in this chapter.

Figure 10.5 shows the variety of shapes the pyramid structure can take.

Although the pyramid structure is the most common organisational structure it can be supplemented or replaced by others.

The matrix structure

If you re-read the section on design in chapter 9 (see pages 164–166), you will see that the design team is drawn from a number of departments and, very probably, from different levels in the hierarchical structure of the business. The problem of design is one of many business problems that demands a range of skills and knowledge. Table 10.1 gives a simplified matrix showing the members of a design team and the roles they are expected to play in the design process.

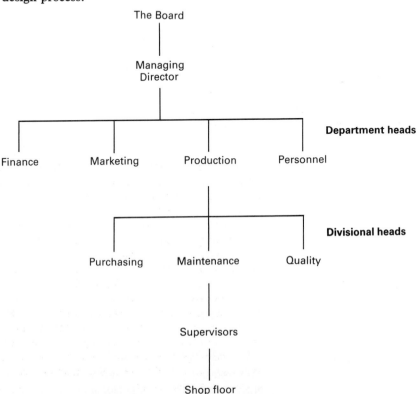

Figure 10.4   An organisation chart

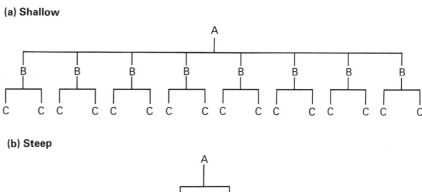

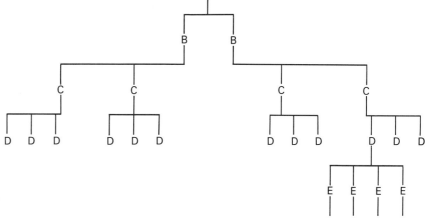

Figure 10.5 Some variations in organisational shapes

Design functions	Production	Marketing	Personnel	Finance
Information	✓	✓	✓	✓
The idea	✓	✓		
Testing	✓	✓		
Prototype	✓	✓	✓	✓
Specification	✓			
Production	✓			

Table 10.1 A simplified matrix of a design team

The matrix approach to organisation may be used in a business organised on hierarchical lines when complex problems need to be solved rapidly. By calling on a variety of expertise it saves time in communication and minimises the chance of impossible ideas being considered for too long.

Matrix organisations may be deliberately designed. Figure 10.6 illustrates the existing organisation of a college of further education. There is a clear **chain of command** from lecturers, through senior lecturers, principal lecturers, heads of department and vice-principal to the principal.

Now look at Figure 10.7, which shows the structure of the same college after reorganisation. The responsibility for organising subject teaching has been shifted *down* the hierarchy to principal/senior lecturer level depending on the degree of responsibility involved. Heads of department have *functional* responsibilities. They will be required to take their expertise in these areas to team meetings to solve problems relating to the college as a whole – for example, the overall pattern of courses offered by the college or the allocation of staff to subject areas.

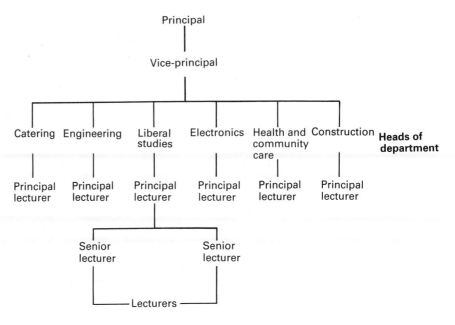

*Figure 10.6
Organisational structure of
a college of further
education*

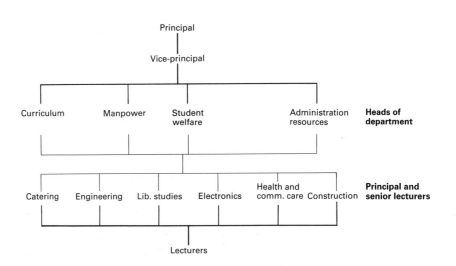

*Figure 10.7   Matrix
structure after
reorganisation*

Networks

A network can be defined as a system of criss-crossing lines or channels. We talk about a network of roads, railways and canals. To get from one point to another using these networks a person would select the route that was most suitable at the time. Figure 10.8 shows that to get from point A to point D there are two possible routes: one through B the other through C. The route through B is shorter but the road is blocked by snow. Route C is chosen.

To stretch this analogy a little further, let us suppose that D is a problem to be solved and B and C are people who can help A solve it. B would be preferred but is engaged on another problem. A and C therefore co-operate on the problem. When a similar problem arises in the future it might be A and B who co-operate on it. However, analogies are dangerous when they are taken too far. From this analogy you should take the following points about the network system of organisation.

- There are no levels of hierarchy.
- Membership of problem-solving groups is formed on an *ad hoc* basis according to the individuals available and the problem to be solved.
- Composition of the network can change without formality (for example, hiring and firing).
- It is likely that all members of the network will be considered equal in skill, although the skills may not be identical.
- Each member of the network is responsible for himself.
- The leadership of teams will vary according to the task in hand.

Networks can appear in a variety of business situations. A group of independent dress designers may co-operate in staging a fashion show. Systems analysts and programmers working on a freelance basis may co-operate on individual projects.

At its simplest level the appearance of a network may depend on personal contacts. In the case of the fashion designers they may have attended the same college. The systems analysts may have worked for the same company. Networks can also be sustained with a loose formal structure. A newsletter may be published or regular meetings held at which people can make new contacts who might be useful to them and reinforce old contacts.

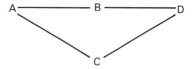

Figure 10.8   A simple network

SELF-ASSESSMENT

1 Name three factors which might influence the shape of organisations.
2 Distinguish between functional organisation and a network.

Communications

A discussion of networks as an organisational structure is a useful introduction to the subject of communications in business in that a network owes its existence to communications. You will be able to judge the importance of the connection at the end of this section.

Throughout this book we have made the reasonable assumption that people communicate with each other all the time. In this section we are going to examine the nature of communication, its problems and the relationship between communications and organisation.

What is communication?

Communications can be defined as the use of a common system of symbols, signs and behaviour for the exchange of information, ideas and emotions. To make the definition more precise we need to look at the phrases contained in it in more detail:

1 'A *common system of symbols, signs and behaviour*' The symbols can be words, either written or spoken, numbers, facial expression and the use of the body to convey a message. The use of words and numbers (whether written or spoken) is termed **verbal** communication. The use of facial expression and what is known as 'body language' is termed **non-verbal**

communication. The tone of voice in which a phrase is uttered can also influence its meaning. The phrase, 'He's a worker' could be spoken in a complimentary sense meaning, 'He works very hard'. It could have political connotations: 'He does the type of job which is defined as being part of the working class in my philosophy.' Or, from the other end of the political spectrum, it could be used derisively as in 'He is *only* a worker'. The same expression will be interpreted in different ways according to the tone of voice and the facial expressions of the person who uses it.

2   *'Exchange'*   This word implies that communication is a two-way process. One person communicates an idea, the second person responds to it. The response is known as **feedback**. Feedback may modify the first person's view of the situation. The extent to which it does so will depend on the strength of the evidence and his or her willingness to accept it.

Communication networks

Communication networks show the pattern of transmission and feedback of information within an organisation. The diagrams illustrated in Figure 10.9 are based on the work of Alex Bavelas in 1948. He drew a number of conclusions about the potential leadership, problem-solving abilities and group satisfaction based on these patterns of communication.

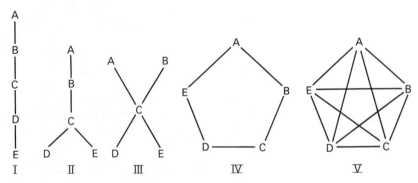

Figure 10.9
Communication networks

The leader of Group I is likely to be C in that he will have the most power in deciding which messages will be transmitted to the rest of the group. The lack of contact between members of the group and the lack of opportunity to exchange ideas means that originality and problem-solving ability of the group are likely to be low.

Contrast this with the interchange of messages in Group V. The volume of messages means that problem solving is likely to be slow. There will be a large number of ideas to be assimilated before a solution is reached. On the other hand, this profusion of ideas is more likely to lead to originality of solution. Any member of this group can be the leader. Groups I and V can be seen as the extremes. In Groups II and III the leaders are likely to be C.

Problems in communications

Problems in communications may arise in the circumstances outlined below:

1   *In some organisational structures*   When the chain of command is long messages can become distorted and blurred as they move from one level of the hierarchy to another.

2   *In certain attitudes among people concerned*   Individuals interpret messages they receive by verbal and non-verbal methods of communication according

to their previous experience. The message they think they are receiving may not be the one they were intended to receive. Their *perception* acts as a 'filter' to the meaning. An individual's understanding of the message may be affected by the language used, the personality of the person sending the message and by attitudes to race, religion and politics.

3   *In relation to the language used in the message*   If you look back at the definition of communication you will see that it uses the phrase 'a common system of symbols'. In order to be effective, all parties must understand the symbols used. The extreme case of this is when those attempting to communicate with one another have an imperfect command of the spoken language used. Technical terms used by a specialist to a non-specialist can have the same effect. Statistical and accounting data can be incomprehensible unless the reports that contain them make the important points clear at a level the recipients can understand.

4   *If the media used are inappropriate*   Oral communication is most useful for a rapid exchange of ideas. Written communication provides a clear record that can be referred to at a later date. The practice of taking minutes at meetings is a way of combining the advantages of oral and written communication. A complex series of instructions given orally with no written back-up is more open to genuine misinterpretation.

5   *In the selection of the information intended to be passed on*   Information that reflects badly on an individual's own work performance might be suppressed and too much emphasis placed on favourable information.

6   *If the information flow is too slow or if people at either end of the chain feel that their messages are being distorted*   Bypassing of the formal channels of communication in favour of the use of informal groups within a business can lead to feelings of insecurity in the people left out. Carried to extremes this can lead to the 'grapevine' – the rumours that exist in any organisation – being given more weight than official communications.

Communications and information technology

The rapid progress of innovation in information technology has led to a claim that communications and organisations are being revolutionised. It can be accepted that the potential for revolution exists. Whether or not it will be as great as some of the claims suggest will depend upon the interaction of a number of factors.

1   Technology can help to increase the speed with which information is transmitted, its clarity and its availability. However, the type of information transmitted, the words used and the willingness or ability of the receiver to make use of the information are still of vital importance.

2   Improved technology can lead to changes in the organisational structure. It can reduce the need for different levels in middle management and so reduce the number of levels in the hierarchy. This will reduce the chances of error in communication.

3   Improved technology can lead to greater centralisation. When this divorces decision makers, geographically, from the production processes this can mean that important information is lost. The nuances of a situation may be missed.

4   Technology relies on well-trained people to use it. Poorly trained operators and antagonistic users can sabotage the most advanced technology.

5   Improvements in technology can break down barriers between people by providing a 'common set of symbols'.

6   Information technology can only improve verbal communication. It may improve communications by distancing people and minimising the effects of prejudice.

SELF-ASSESSMENT

1 List three production and three marketing problems which might arise as the result of poor communication.
2 Describe two ways in which improved communication technology can lead to improved communications and two ways in which its effect may be neutral.

Conclusion

People are the building blocks of organisations. They can be organised into working groups and given structures within which to operate, but unless they have the motivation to work within those structures they will, either consciously or unconsciously, adapt them to their own needs. At the beginning of this chapter it was pointed out that business exists for, by and because of people. A person is more complex than the most sophisticated techniques and technology employed in the business world. This chapter can do no more than indicate the complexities of the problems implicit in managing them.

Review

1   Dorcas Training Centre is a management agency for the MSC (Manpower Services Commission) providing off-the-job training for the YTS (Youth Training Scheme). The centre offers training in upholstery, joinery, cabinet making, catering and the caring services. As the majority of trainees are classed as premium grade – that is, they require additional support in basic literacy, numeracy and life skills – an important part of the role of staff is to provide this education through the medium of their vocational training.

The staff of the centre consists of a manager, a deputy manager and eight supervisors. All are men in their mid-thirties to early fifties, and the majority have recent experience of redundancy. Their qualifications are good in their particular field, and all have taken or are taking City and Guilds courses to train them as technical teachers.

In October 1986 a new deputy manager was appointed from within the staff. This caused some grumbling. There was a faction in the rest of the staff which considered the man unsuitable for the job. The atmosphere in the staffroom was not pleasant. Partly for this reason, and partly because of the responsibilities of his job, the deputy manager ceased to spend his breaks in the staffroom and spent most of his time in his office.

By Christmas the situation was worsening. The deputy manager had begun to comment on the way in which the supervisors were conducting their training. The supervisors took the view that they were the experts in their field and that they knew what was necessary for the trainees to know and the best ways to convey this knowledge to them. The situation reached a climax when one of the supervisors was appointed to the Civil Service, and celebrated his departure by telling the manager that the reason he was leaving was the unwarranted interference and incompetence of the deputy manager.

The manager consulted with his deputy, who made the following points:

- The ill-feeling was not quite as widespread as the departing supervisor had suggested.
- The main instigator of the ill-feeling had been the departing supervisor, who had believed that his administrative experience made him more suited for the deputy manager's job than the man appointed.
- Some of the supervisors were not training in accordance with the philosophy of the YTS. Rather than devising ways of educating the trainees using their experience, they were relying on classroom lessons, imparting knowledge through instruction and typewritten handouts.

The deputy manager went on to point out that, although it was the stated policy of the centre that any handouts should be prepared by the trainees to give them experience in the use of office equipment, the supervisors had fallen into the practice of preparing these materials themselves and doing their own photocopying, their justification for this being the length of time it took to explain to the trainees what was required and the high error rate. It was his statement that all reprographic equipment in the centre was for the use of trainees that had caused the initial outburst of grumbling.

The manager was extremely concerned about the situation outlined to him. His own direct contact with the supervisors was relatively small. He decided to interview each one individually, in the presence of the deputy manager, and try to discover their point of view. Approximately 50 per cent of the staff interviewed declared themselves to be dissatisfied and cited the deputy manager's interference with their training methods as the principal reason.

(a) What reasons can you suggest for the existence of this situation? You should present your analysis in terms of communication problems, leadership and group behaviour.
(b) What steps might the manager take to resolve his problem?
(c) Outline the possible consequences for the quality of training offered by the centre if the problem is not resolved.

2   The growth of Marionette Enterprises had been a rather haphazard process. It had started in the mid-1970s in a workshop in a converted nineteenth-century factory building making marionettes. These had proved a success but, realising the need for diversification if the business was to survive, John Stephenson, the owner, had added high-quality toys, well-crafted in wood, to his product range. As each new product was introduced a new workshop was acquired. By 1980 Marionette Enterprises had eight separate workshops scattered about the same industrial complex and a small, rather poky office, in a different location entirely.

As far as production was concerned this slightly unorthodox system appeared to work very well. In financial and administrative terms it was less successful. Each workshop had its own complement of machinery, all rather old but still operating smoothly. The senior skilled man in each workshop accepted responsibility for organising the work, quality control and training. Stephenson believed that if he could rationalise his production processes he could buy additional machinery which could be shared by all sections of his business. Wood offcuts from the more expensive toys could be used to make a range of cheaper, mass-produced toys and his own task of management would be made easier. Accordingly, in 1985 he rented a purpose-built unit on a modern industrial estate designed for small and medium-sized businesses. He recruited a production manager with extensive experience and reserved for himself the role of marketing and financial manager.

Within a year it was obvious that something had gone badly wrong. The reputation for reliability that the business had built up was suffering from delayed orders. There was an increase in customer complaints concerning quality, and levels of absenteeism and lateness seemed unusually high. The production manager placed all the blame on the workforce. They did not, he claimed, understand the need for factory discipline.

Stephenson was naturally worried about the situation and, meeting Michael Carr, one of his original employees, outside the local supermarket when they were both waiting for their wives, he took the opportunity to sound him out about the situation in the factory. Carr looked embarrassed but after some persuasion offered the following reasons for the problems of Marionette Enterprises.

Well, I don't know if you are going to like this but we were doing nicely the way we were. The work had to be done and we knew exactly what we had to do. You would come in, give us an order and tell us the completion date. After that it was up to us. I suppose we did get into bad habits. For instance, if an order was going well and there was no other work outstanding we used to cover for each other if we wanted a half day off. The lads got used to that and it helped if there was a child ill. It added a bit of flexibility. At least two of the wives went back to work because they knew we would be able to cover most emergencies. We never bothered with this clocking on and off either. If somebody arrived ten minutes or so late they made up the time during the day. Young Joey thought he was on to a good thing when he first came but we soon sorted him out. We got hold of him one break and pointed out it was not a holiday camp. If the work did not get done and done properly we would all be out of a job. When machines broke down we would phone up one of the other shops and one of us would stick the wood into the van, drive over there, machine it and bring it back. That is how we used to get your rush jobs done. Now all this organisation is getting us down. Every time we try to get a job done we seem to be breaking some rule or other.

What can John Stephenson do?

Activities

1   Observe a meeting. You can simulate this by asking another group of students to solve a simple problem – for example, placing objects in ranking order. This activity works well as a group activity because the group interaction is complex and it can be difficult for one person to observe and record all the elements of behaviour.
   (a) Does one person dominate the group? If so, how? What mannerisms, gestures, tone of voice, verbal expressions did he/she use to gain dominance? For example, one student assisting in this exercise gained effective leadership by sitting in the seat normally used by the tutor and using the gestures and tone employed by the tutor. The other students in the group did not enjoy this; the tutor and the observers did!
   (b) Was any conflict generated during the discussion? Who disagreed with whom and what were their physical positions in relation to each other?
   (c) Were any members of the group not participating? Can you give possible reasons for this?
   (d) What was the pattern of communication around the table? Did the participants address the group leader or did they tend to speak to the people beside them or opposite to them?
   (e) Was the general attitude of the group supportive? You can get a rough estimation of this by classifying every remark said. Implied compliments, jokes, tension-relieving comments will tend to give a supportive group. Remarks that can be classified as aggressive and which denigrate the opinions of others can be classified as non-supportive. Be careful with

this observation. The words used are often the least important part of the evidence. Analysis of an extremely argumentative meeting with a number of departmental heads fighting for their fair share of resources produced evidence of an extremely supportive group.

When you have completed the analysis present your results in the form of diagrams and tables. What insights into group behaviour have you acquired?

2   Produce an organisation chart for an organisation with which you are familiar. What are the limitations of this chart? Does it reflect all the communication patterns in the organisation?

Suggested projects

1   A critical evaluation of working attitudes in Business X.

2   A study of the importance of promotion prospects in the motivation of student nurses.

Essays

1   Distinguish between informal and formal systems of communication. Discuss the symptoms of a breakdown in the system of formal communication within a business enterprise.

2   Outline the major classifications of leadership style, and comment on their appropriateness in a business organisation.

3   Distinguish between job enlargement and job enrichment, and discuss the effectiveness of both as methods of motivation.

4   The motivation of employees must be regarded as an art rather than an exact science. Discuss.

5   Outline the organisational problems that may be encountered as the result of a merger between two businesses. Comment briefly on the ways in which these problems might be overcome.

6   Comment on the view that the personality of a manager is as important as his skills and experience.

7   Discuss the factors a business should take into account when changing its organisational structure.

8   'The job of a manager is to make decisions rather than to motivate others.' Discuss this statement with relation to the production manager of a soft drink canning factory.   (25)   1986 (CLES)

9   (a) Suggest an organisational structure that might be appropriate for a domestic airline.   (10)
    (b) How might fluctuations in exchange rates affect the budgeting for operations, and the profitability, of an international airline?   (15)   1986 (CLES)

Chapter 11   **Managing people**

In chapter 10 we described the uniqueness of each individual in terms of needs and personality. We also looked at the theories concerning the ways in which they could be motivated and the theoretical structure of an organisation and the way it could contribute to motivation. In this chapter we will examine the practical aspects of managing people – that is, the personnel function.

The personnel function is practised by the prospective businessman when he examines his own skills, qualities and shortcomings before he starts a business. It is also practised by the man employing no more than one or two people, by the supervisor on an assembly line in a factory employing 7000, by the marketing, production and finance managers in organising and managing their departments and by the board of a multi-national company when appointing a managing director.

The personnel function can be divided into three main areas:

- the *use* of people;
- the *motivation* of people; and
- the *protection* of people.

There is some overlap between these areas. The use and protection of people can contribute towards motivation. Attempts to increase the motivation of individuals will influence the ways in which they are treated as employees and the degree of protection, over and above that required by law, which they are offered. As you work through the chapter you should be aware of this integration, although each element of the personnel function will be treated separately.

The use of people

Any business must be able to answer the following questions before it can use its staff effectively:

- What are the objectives of the business in the long and the short term? Changes in marketing, production and financial strategies will all influence the number and type of people employed. A business with an objective of growth may need to recruit a man skilled in the management of mergers. Or it may employ another business to provide that skill.

- What is the size of the existing workforce? What skills do they possess? What is their training potential? It may be cheaper to recruit somebody who already possesses the required skills than to re-train people already employed.

- What numbers of workers, skills and training will be required by any projects to be undertaken in the next few years?

- What finance is available to carry out the changes needed?

- To what extent are the existing staff utilised? For example, a business wishes to expand. If it has a number of staff who are already working short time there may be no need to recruit. If they are working overtime, then the only way to expand may be through recruitment unless changes in organisation and/or the introduction of more advanced technology could use the existing workforce more efficiently.

These are all *internal* constraints that a workforce imposes on a business which is attempting to achieve its objectives. A business is hiring labour and is, therefore, operating in a number of labour markets depending on the skills of the people it wishes to employ.

The labour markets and the economy generally impose additional *external* constraints on its decisions:

- What is the state of the economy? Even in a depressed economy some businesses are more prosperous than others. A business wishing to expand will find it easier to recruit the right type of labour at a lower price when the economy is depressed than when it is expanding. A prosperous economy with a shortage of the required type of labour might cause a business to re-train its staff rather than recruit or to simplify certain jobs so that they can be performed by people with less skill.

- A shortage of labour may be the result of technical change rather than an expanding economy. In depressed economies undergoing technical change, for example, it is likely that the skills associated with the new technology will be in short supply and therefore will command higher prices than other skills.

- What is the wage rate paid by other firms? A business may want this information so that it does not pay more than is necessary. It may also want it so that it can outbid its competitors in the labour market. A multi-national company moving into an area at a time of relatively full employment might use this information to set a wage level for certain skills 25 per cent higher than those of other businesses in the area.

- Have trade unions negotiated any national agreements with respect to working conditions with which a business will have to comply? Can the problem be avoided by a change in production technology so that members of less powerful unions can be employed?

Internal and external constraints imposed by a workforce are shown in Figure 11.1.

If the type of question asked above seems familiar, that is not surprising. The information such questions provide will form the basis of the **manpower plan**, a part of the overall business plan and subject to the same general constraints as the master business plan and the plans of all other departments within the organisation. A completed manpower plan will contain the following information:

1 jobs that will appear/disappear in the time period covered by the plan;

2 training needs, including any re-training;

3 the recruitment/retirement/redundancy programmes that will need to be implemented;

4 the implications for industrial relations; and

5 the control systems necessary to ensure that the manpower plan continues to serve the objectives of the business.

The manpower plan (see Figure 11.2) will also have implications for the decisions of the production and marketing departments. Its needs will contribute to the master budget.

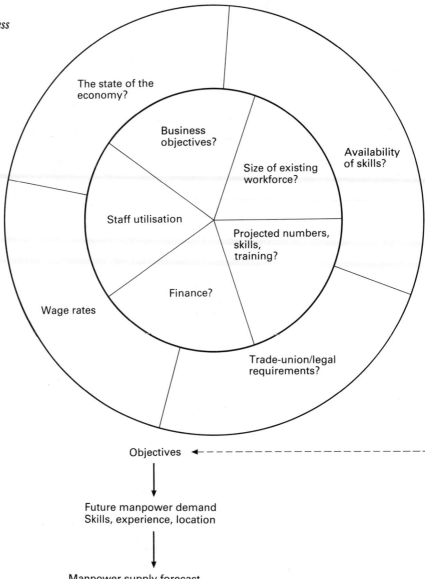

Figure 11.1   The use of people: internal and external constraints

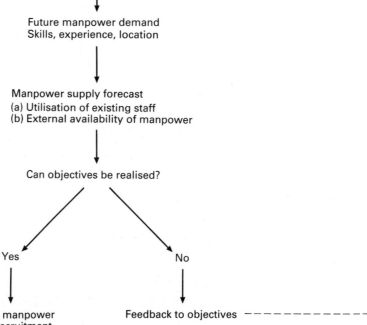

Figure 11.2   Outline of manpower planning process

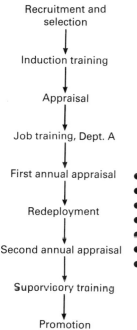

Recruitment and selection

↓

Induction training

↓

Appraisal

↓

Job training, Dept. A

↓

First annual appraisal

↓

Redeployment

↓

Second annual appraisal

↓

Supervisory training

↓

Promotion

Figure 11.3 Progress of a clerical worker over a period of three years

SELF-ASSESSMENT

1 Define the personnel function.
2 Identify two internal and two external constraints on the personnel policy of a business.
3 State three ways in which a manpower plan can help a business operate effectively.

Once the manpower plan has been drawn up the business can begin the process of organising its labour force to help achieve the business objectives. This will involve a number of activities:

- recruitment;
- selection;
- training;
- appraisal;
- redeployment;
- promotion;
- redundancy/retirement/dismissal.

The activities have been listed in this order so as to reflect the experience of a person employed by a business. They could also reflect the way in which a person running a one-man business might assess his own needs and skills in relation to his ambition. Figure 11.3 charts the progress of an imaginary clerical worker in the first three years of his employment by a business. You will notice that some of the activities listed above recur throughout the clerical worker's career.

Recruitment

Before you go out to buy something you usually take the trouble to decide what you need. A business purchases materials needed for its production processes according to the specifications laid down in the design of the goods it is making. It is the same process when it comes to hiring people.

In chapter 4 we said that a prospective businessman should examine the skills and personal qualities he possesses and match those skills against the ones needed to run a particular type of business. In the same way, when employing staff he should have a clear idea of the job which he expects them to do and the skills and personal qualities which will be needed to do that job successfully. This is also important in **motivating** people. A person engaged in work which is beyond his or her ability or which he or she considers boring is unlikely to work with enthusiasm.

The stages in defining a job and the skills needed to perform it efficiently are these:

- job analysis;
- job description;
- job specification; and
- job requisition or recruitment profile.

Job analysis

Job analysis is a detailed examination of a job, the tasks performed, the skills and personal qualities needed to perform them successfully and the circumstances in which they are performed. Job analysis is used in order to:

1 select personnel, either by employing people from outside the business or by redeploying or promoting existing staff ('redeployment' is the term used

when staff are moved from one part of a business organisation to another to perform a different task of the same status as their previous job);

2   establish the training needs for a particular job, which will also help to minimise training costs by a more careful matching of existing skills and aptitudes in the people employed with those required by the job;

3   help in the selection of suitable equipment and prevent waste on the purchase of unnecessary equipment;

4   identify the experience of people who have performed a job and assist in the process of staff development and promotion;

5   help in establishing rates of pay and in accounting for differences in payments made to different members of staff;

6   isolate the possible risks of accident and assist in the design of equipment and procedures to reduce the risks.

Job analysis, therefore, is not simply to help in recruitment: the activity can be seen as a fundamental part of the personnel function. It may be expanded into **job evaluation**, which attempts to put jobs in the order of their importance to the business. Job analysis is not an easy operation to carry out successfully.

- It is a very slow process. Observation of a job might give an outline of a task that needs to be performed, but it can be misleading in terms of the skill needed to perform that task. A skilled operator will make a job look easy. If you observe a plasterer at work he does not appear to take a great deal of effort to provide a smooth finish to a wall. An attempt to do the same job yourself will demonstrate the level of skill required. Watching the plasterer tells you nothing about the mental decisions he is making – for example, about the consistency of the plaster or the type of surface he is working on.

- Observation will produce very little useful information when much of the work is carried out in the mind. A manager attempting to solve an organisational problem may be simply sitting at his desk and staring into space.

- When questionnaires or interviews are used to analyse a job, the attitudes of people can influence the way in which they answer questions. A person seeking promotion might be tempted to exaggerate the complexity of his present job.

- People do not always remember all the tasks that comprise their job. Some tasks may be performed infrequently, perhaps only once a year, and are easily overlooked.

Good job analysis will use a variety of methods and also use information already existing about the job – for example, from work study reports. Observation and interviews with the person doing the job and with the manager responsible can be supplemented by analysis of the equipment and materials used. Together, this information will give a more accurate picture of the job.

Job description

A job description is a broad statement of the purpose, scope, duties and responsibilities of a particular job. It will normally contain:

- the title of the job;
- a broad statement of its duties;

- the title of the person to whom the worker is responsible; and
- the titles of those who will report to the person doing the job.

A job description places a job in the context of the organisation. It contains elements relating to *role*, *authority*, *responsibility*, *communications* and *span of control*. It also defines the degree of *specialisation* relating to a job.

Job specification

A job specification is a more detailed development of a job description. It states the physical and mental abilities required. This is usually expressed in terms of activities, requisite knowledge, and the type of judgement required, together with the factors affecting such judgements and the factors affected by such judgements.

Although job analysis, job description and job specification are described here as part of the recruitment procedure of a business, these methods also provide invaluable information for the following personnel functions:

- Selection of staff for promotion. A knowledge of acquired and practised skills can enable managers to identify people who have the necessary aptitudes for a more highly graded job.

- They can be used to identify training needs for the business as a whole and for individuals as part of staff development. In the latter case training needs can influence promotion decisions and act as a motivator.

- They can provide an objective statement of the job to establish targets which should be achieved by people performing the job (**performance standards**).

- They can provide an objective standard against which the efficiency of the staff engaged in a particular job can be judged (**staff appraisal**).

If you read the uses of job analysis, job description and job specification carefully you should become aware of the fact that they are likely to become a subject of dispute between the owners of a business and their employees.

A very precise job specification places a weapon in the hands of people who are dissatisfied with the way in which they are being treated. They can refuse to perform a task on the ground that it is 'not my job'. When that particular task has been widely performed on a goodwill basis prior to a dispute, there could be delays and organisational problems as a result of this response.

A job specification which is imprecise can contribute to **demarcation disputes** between trade unions. In such a case a union will claim that a task should be performed only by its members. It is usually a matter of concern when a union feels its members' jobs are threatened.

The use of detailed job specifications in the appraisal of staff can lead to disagreements between the person being appraised and the appraisor. When this involves people who have to work together this can have a detrimental effect on working relationships and the efficiency with which a job is performed. In open appraisal schemes, where the person being appraised has access to the report, a tick by the statement 'Not yet ready for promotion' can act as a de-motivator and a potential source of conflict between the two people concerned.

Job requisition or recruitment profile

This will exist formally in large organisations where the job of recruiting staff is given to a person who may have no direct knowledge of the job itself. It is designed to allow the person responsible for selecting staff to understand the requirements of the job and to know enough about it to be able to answer any questions the applicant might ask. A recruitment profile for a skilled operative would be drawn up in consultation with the production manager, but the interviewer might be a specialist in the personnel department. A job requisition will include details of the work involved, conditions of employment, qualifications necessary, amount of experience and personal qualities required.

The job requisition is the final link between the job and the person who will be employed to perform it. The person responsible for filling the post must now decide where he will find that employee.

Selection of personnel

When a vacancy exists a business may fill it either from its existing labour force (**internal recruitment**) or by employing another person (**external recruitment**).

Internal recruitment

When using internal sources, a business may promote or redeploy individuals. The use of internal sources can have the following advantages:

1 It is cheaper than other methods of recruitment. There is no need for extensive and expensive advertising and, because the personnel are already known in the organisation, there is less chance of having to re-advertise. It is also faster, and this in itself will save costs.

2 Labour is redeployed when it is no longer needed in its present activity. The alternative might be short-time working or even redundancy. Internal recruitment can be seen as a way of avoiding expensive redundancies and of giving workers a greater feeling of security. In some circumstances businesses may agree with the trade unions concerned that all vacancies will be filled from internal sources. This is likely to happen where unemployment in an area or a skill is high.

3 Promotion prospects can act as motivators to staff. They are more likely to take on additional responsibilities that show that they are suited to promotion.

4 Internal candidates know the way in which the organisation works. They do not have to learn the systems or the unspoken codes of practice that operate in any organisation. They will become more effective more quickly than external candidates.

5 Internal recruitment can be said to be more certain than appointing people from outside the organisation. Application forms, interviews and references can be no substitute for the in-depth knowledge of an individual's personality, strengths and weaknesses that day-to-day contact provides.

Internal recruitment does have its disadvantages. When it is the result of agreements with trade unions it can mean that available candidates are not suited to the job and will be less efficient in performing it than somebody recruited from outside the organisation. Jealousy is not unknown, and a newly promoted person can find former colleagues unco-operative.

External recruitment

When it is necessary and/or desirable to recruit from outside the organisation, a business has a number of methods to choose from.

1   *Recommendations from existing employees*   This can be seen as an extension of internal recruitment. The people recommended are likely to have some knowledge of the workings of the business, if only by hearsay. They are more likely to know people already working for the business and will be less likely to leave. The people making the recommendation will also have an interest in making sure that the person concerned is suitable for the job. The extent to which a business will consider personal recommendations will depend on known qualities of the person making the recommendation.

   Personal recommendation can operate on a variety of levels in a business. It may be a manager who has met and worked with somebody outside the organisation and sees in the skills offered a valuable contribution to his or her own business. It may be a production worker recommending his son or daughter or the child of a friend to the personnel department, when many of the advantages of internal recruitment would still apply.

2   *Direct contact with schools, colleges and universities*   Many businesses maintain links with educational establishments. This can provide them with an initial screening service in that many such places will only recommend people who will reflect credit to their organisation or will use their own knowledge of students to select those who have the required skills and personal qualities. A personnel manager wishing to recruit a school leaver might find it worthwhile to phone the careers teacher in four or five secondary schools, state their requirements in general terms, fix a time for interview and be sure of having a number of good applicants for the job. Over a period of years it is possible that good links are established, and this method can become an extension of personal recommendation.

3   *Job centres/Careers Office*   Both services are run by the Manpower Services Commission (MSC) to provide a centre for those looking for applicants and those seeking employment. Job centres are for all unemployed, while the Careers Service is designed for the school leaver.

4   *Advertising*   This method is likely to produce the largest number of applicants but it is expensive both in terms of the cost of the advertising and in the processing of a large number of applicants.

   Advertising also presents problems in terms of choosing the media to be used. Advertising for specialist staff might be more effective in technical journals. A mistake can be expensive.

5   *Trade unions may recommend people for specific jobs.*

6   *Private employment agencies may also be used*   Although they charge for their services they still have the advantage to the business using them of undertaking the preliminary survey of applicants, thus saving costs in the business itself.

7   *'Head hunting'*   This is a colloquial term used to describe the activities of specialised private agencies acting on behalf of their principals in seeking out highly qualified staff who may not be actively looking for a job. The person approached is likely to be offered an attractive package in terms of salary and other benefits as an inducement to change his or her job.

8   *Professional Bodies Appointments Services/Ex-service organisations*   These bodies offer a specialised service for groups of people with specific skills and experience. Public services such as the police force and the armed forces

whose members may retire earlier than the rest of the working population have an employment service as part of their own personnel policy.

Selection

By the time this stage has been reached the business will be aware of the job to be filled, should have sought applicants using the methods listed and must now match the information provided by the applicant against the recruitment profile. This process is known as **short-listing**. Applicants who are considered unsuitable or who have a lower level of skills than the rest of the group are discarded. Those who are left are called for interview.

Interviews are useful in that they provide the opportunity for applicants to ask questions about the job and the business and find out information which may not have been available to them before. A good interview will also allow a candidate to see the place in which he or she will be working. There is research evidence to suggest that a failure to do this can lead to early resignations. For example, some people might have very strong feelings about working in an open plan office – either for or against. Interviews also give the business the chance of assessing the personality of the candidate in the light of the people he or she is likely to be working with.

The process of selecting people will vary according to the business and the type of job involved. There may be two or even three short-listing exercises undertaken, each followed by an interview. At each stage the number of applicants will be reduced. This may take place over a period of six months.

Interviews can vary from a short, formal session to a period of several days, which might include a formal interview, informal sessions and the use of selection tests to judge aptitudes and attitudes. In general the more responsible and complex a job the more complex and extended the selection procedure is likely to be.

Job offers

The offer of a job may be oral in the first instance and then confirmed by letter. The Employment Protection (Consolidation) Act 1978 states that all employees must be given a written statement of their conditions of service within twelve weeks of the beginning of their employment. This statement may be separate from the job offer or it may be incorporated into it. The latter procedure has the advantage of informing the new employee of his exact conditions of service at an early stage and reducing the risk of expensive mistakes.

Selection of recruitment method

A large organisation is unlikely to use a single method of recruitment. The method selected will depend upon the circumstances in which the organisation finds itself and its experience of the effectiveness of different methods.

Methods of recruiting can be assessed as shown below:

- In chapter 6 we studied the use of ratios in management accounting, and stated that the technique could be used to judge the efficiency of other areas of business activity. Ratios can be used to estimate the value of different methods of recruiting staff:

Number of interviews: Number of offers made.

A high level of interviews compared with the number of offers made could suggest that the selection procedure is at fault:

Number of offers made: Numbers starting work.

If people are not accepting the offer made to them there is the possibility that the information they received from the literature published by the business was misleading.

Number starting work: Number considered satisfactory.

Again this suggests a mismatch between the skills required and the ones considered to be required by the recruiter. Perhaps a more careful job analysis or a more precise recruitment profile might be required.

Cost of exercise: Number starting work.

The aim of a good recruitment procedure is to get the best possible workforce at the lowest cost of recruitment.

- The state of the labour market will influence the recruitment method chosen. If the local market is buoyant, with a large number of job opportunities but a low number of unemployed, a business that has traditionally advertised locally may be forced to advertise nationally to fill its vacancies. In a situation of high unemployment, a business might find sufficient suitable applicants by the use of the different types of personal contact rather than undertake the expense of advertising.

- The type of staff being recruited can be an important factor in deciding the method of recruitment. People with high-level skills in short supply may be head-hunted. In extreme cases – for example, where the skill is in a new technology – the labour market may be international.

The importance of good selection procedures must be emphasised. In chapter 10 and throughout the first part of this chapter it has been stressed that a business should acquire a labour force which has the skills and personal qualities to suit its needs. However, it should not be forgotten that the activity of selecting employees will depend on a number of factors, some of which may be beyond the control of the business. A shortage of labour might require the re-design of jobs so that they can be performed by people with a lower level of skill. Good selection procedures will contribute to the efficient working of the production, marketing and financial functions of a business, but its ultimate success could well depend on the state of the economy, the type of market in which it is operating, the state of that market and, in some circumstances, the attitude of the government towards the type of business.

These external constraints can also affect the labour supply available to a business. Bad publicity concerning safety regulations in an industry can limit the supply of labour to a firm in that industry no matter how effective its own safety procedures might be. People concerned about job security are unlikely to take a job in a declining industry unless their choice of job is restricted. Moreover, a business operating in a declining industry is unlikely to be able to offer wages competitive with more prosperous firms.

SELF-ASSESSMENT

1 State briefly the stages in a selection procedure.
2 Explain the value of two methods of assessing recruitment procedures.

Training

'Training' is the term used to describe all the activities involved in bringing a person to a desired degree of proficiency in the skill or knowledge required for a job, or the attitude desired for it.

Like all other business activities training should follow a *plan* and is limited by the equipment, finance and personnel available in the business and also by the state of the economy, government intervention and the attitudes of society as a whole.

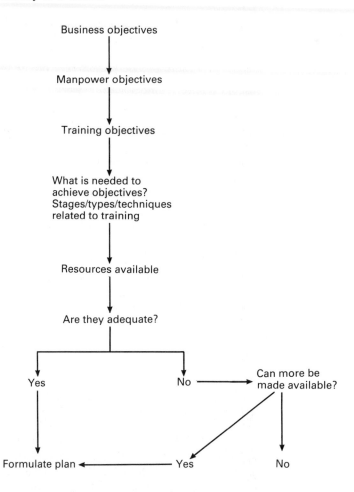

Figure 11.4   The training plan

Figure 11.4 illustrates the steps involved in organising training. In a small business it may outline the mental processes of the owner of a business when he has recruited a new member of staff. In large businesses it may be a formal process resulting in a written document that will contribute information for a training budget. The background to such steps will involve the following factors:

1   *Establishment of objectives*   The most important objectives will be those of the business. From these and the manpower plan derived from them, it will be possible to draw up priorities concerning the types of training most needed. Following this analysis of jobs, it will be necessary to know the standard of expertise required and the expertise of the existing workforce before the objectives of the training department can be formulated. A

business operating in a high-cost, high-quality market is likely to require highly skilled labour. If, in addition, it is operating in an environment of rapidly changing technology, the plan may need to make provision for a constant up-dating of skills.

2 *Steps necessary to reach the objectives* At this stage the business draws up an outline programme of training. This might include a statement of the stages in the training programme and the appropriate techniques that might be used.

3 *Resources* Having decided what it *should* do the business must then decide what it *can* do. It must see what resources it has to achieve the programme in terms of personnel, equipment and finance. It should also take into account external resources that might be available to it. In chapter 9 we saw that the local college of further education may be seen as an external economy of scale. It will charge for its courses, but the fees are likely to be lower to a business sending five students than it would be to employ somebody to educate those students and provide the equipment. The five students will be, perhaps, a third of the final class. Government grants can be used to finance training, and we will look at these in more detail when we consider MSC schemes such as the YTS and Open Tech.

4 *Modification* If the original plan cannot be funded by available resources, then it may have to be modified.

5 *Evaluation* Like all plans the training plan must contain monitoring systems – that is, methods of gathering statistical and financial information to check the success of the scheme.

Many employers consider training to be an expensive, time-consuming exercise with the prospect of well-trained employees resigning for better paid occupations. What are the advantages of training to the employer?

1 Well-trained workers give greater profits. A skilled craftsman is likely to be able to work faster, more accurately and with less waste than somebody with a lower level of skill. As a result, his productivity will be higher and production costs lower. A shop assistant who has been trained to present the right attitude to a customer, who knows the stock available and is prepared to discuss the customer's requirements is more likely to make a sale than an assistant with no interest in stock or customer.

2 A well-trained employee needs less supervision. This will reduce costs by widening the span of control possible and reducing the number of supervisors needed. It can also act as a motivator. In Chapter 10 and later in this chapter we discussed the role of job enlargement as a motivator. In order to make a contribution to job enlargement the person concerned will need extra training.

3 Training can also reduce the accident level in a business by drawing attention to the danger areas, and may, by improving skills, knowledge and attitudes, reduce the possibility of them occurring.

4 Well-trained staff are more versatile, and this can be important in times of rapidly developing technology when the skills required by the business are likely to change.

5 A good training programme will raise the prestige of the business and attract good applicants for its jobs. The products of a good management training programme are more versatile than people whose training has been designed for one industry.

Education and training

Education can be defined as a programme of activities designed to develop the mental, physical and social skills of individuals without reference to a specific job. Training is a programme of activities directed to the acquisition of skills for a specific job. It may also contain elements in the programme designed to improve the general level of physical, mental and social skills of the people concerned. This, it is hoped, will improve the ability of the individual to cope with change. In many cases it will do so, but education is a co-operative effort between student and teacher/lecturer. If either party approaches the exercise with attitudes antagonistic to education, the hope is unlikely to be realised.

Methods of training

- *On-job training* is the oldest type of training in human history. In its simplest form the person being trained learns the job by working alongside somebody who has already acquired the skills. It is cheap, because there is no need to set up special training facilities and the trainee will learn in the conditions in which the work will be performed. This can be important in jobs where the working conditions might be stressful and unpleasant. On the other hand, trainees are likely to spoil materials and make mistakes, which will take more experienced people time to rectify. They may learn bad working habits, which can be inefficient and unsafe. The trainer may be unsuitable, lacking the communication skills essential for good teaching. They may also be unwilling to slow their own work-pace – particularly if they are being paid according to the amount of work they produce.

  On-job training is an integral part of most training programmes. Even in situations where the skills and knowledge are taught separately there will come a time when the trainee needs to apply acquired knowledge in a working situation. The academic qualifications for most professions can be gained in institutes of higher education, whether universities, colleges or polytechnics. But before people can be accepted as professionally qualified they must be able to produce evidence of work experience in a professional environment. A deck officer in the Merchant Service must be able to produce evidence of a specified amount of sea time before he is allowed to take the professional examinations of the Department of Transport.

- *Off-job training* may take place in specialist training areas or establishments within the business or, where there is sufficient local demand from several businesses, at a college of further/higher education.

  Off-job training has the advantages of specialist instructors who usually have actual experience of the job concerned. The trainees do not undergo the pressures of a working environment and can therefore increase their speed and accuracy to a high level following a carefully planned programme. It is easier to estimate the costs of the exercise and also easier to monitor the progress of the trainee. When the business provides the facilities, off-job training can be expensive. It can also pose problems for the trainee when he is required to transfer learned skills to the working environment, particularly if the equipment used in training is different from that used on the shop floor. If off-job training is provided by colleges belonging to the state sector of education, the business may benefit from external economies of scale.

- *The Manpower Services Commission* (MSC) is a government body which is intended to implement training for a variety of needs according to the perceived needs of the United Kingdom in the medium term. The Youth Training Scheme (YTS) is intended to provide the young school leaver with an opportunity to 'taste' a variety of occupations and select the one to which he or she is most suited and also the chance to learn 'life skills' (how to apply for a job, interview well, live independently of parents), which they may lack. Open Tech gives individuals and people seconded by businesses the chance to update their existing skills under the guidance of a college tutor.

Types of training

1 *Induction training* Its purpose is to introduce the new recruit to the business and to the objectives, methods, organisation and the people he will be working with. The length of time devoted to an induction course can vary from a few hours to several months depending on the job. The first six months of training for a student nurse might be classified as induction training. This will involve experiencing different types of nursing in a variety of institutions. The induction course for a clerical worker may take no longer than an introduction to the supervisor and ensuring that somebody will take care of the newcomer in the first few days. In recent years the importance of induction training has become appreciated particularly for its effect on reducing labour turnover.

2 *Training in attitudes* is a long-term process and less easy to evaluate than other forms of training. In chapter 10 we saw that the attitudes of an individual are formed by their experience. Attitudes are difficult to change. Attitude training might be on-job, with the encouragement and example of a person judged to have the right attitudes, and off-job, using role play, case studies and other simulations, followed by group discussion. The purpose of the exercises is to extend the experience of the individual in a relatively controlled environment.

3 *Training for promotion* Depending upon the type of job and its demands, training for promotion will use a mix of the techniques given above. A person about to be promoted to supervisor might need knowledge of health and safety legislation (short courses or lectures) and will also need to develop skills in man management (simulated exercises and case studies).

4 *Training for change* Organisational and technological change will require training programmes. A change in technology may mean that all the skilled operatives employed in a business will need familiarisation with new equipment and techniques.

Evaluation of training

The effectiveness of training can be judged in terms of the following factors:

1 The number of accidents and their causes.

2 The rate of labour turnover. Induction training was given a more important place in the training programmes of business when it was realised that a high proportion of resignations occurred in the first few months of employment because people found a workplace strange and unwelcoming.

3 The number of suitable candidates for internal promotion.

4 The quality of the work produced, the number of rejections, the amount of waste and the level of productivity.

In each area a business will have acceptable levels. To aim at perfection would be expensive, and the effectiveness of training is judged against its cost.

Appraisal

The English language contains many words whose interpretation depends upon the attitude of the listener. Appraisal is one of them. According to the dictionary it infers the existence of an expert who reviews the progress, appearance or capability of a person or thing. A dealer appraises an antique for its provenance and value. A teacher appraises the progress of his/her pupils.

Appraisal of staff is necessary for the following reasons:

- to select the people who are suitable for promotion;
- to check the efficiency of recruitment, selection and training practices;
- to improve the way in which people are doing their job;
- to make individuals aware of the objectives of the business.

Appraisal takes place each time a manager checks on the work of a subordinate, discusses that work and indicates how it could be improved. Appraisal is part of the job of any person who is responsible for the work of other people. Some large organisations have introduced formal systems of appraisal. This usually involves a standardised appraisal form and an interview at regular intervals. This can lead to a number of problems:

- People become resentful if they feel their work is being criticised. This can result in less efficiency rather than greater efficiency as working relationships deteriorate.
- Badly designed forms can require subjective judgements on a person's ability.
- The existence of an appraisal form and a set time for an appraisal interview can tempt managers to leave the task of appraisal to the time designated. Appraisal should, of course, be on-going and directed towards improving performance. The formal interview should be no more than a summary of previous discussions.
- Some jobs are more difficult to appraise than others. The more complex the job the greater the difficulty in judging the efficiency with which it is done and the greater the difficulty of finding somebody capable of analysing problems and offering constructive support.

Redeployment and transfer

We have already stated that organisational and technological change can make it necessary for a business to transfer workers from one department to another. This may also be done as a deliberate move in staff development – that is, to widen the range of experience of staff and make them more suitable for promotion. It may be part of a job enrichment/enlargement scheme. Employees may also request transfer for personal reasons. They may believe that experience in a particular department will enhance their promotion prospects. They may dislike the people with whom they are working. In a large organisation, they may request a transfer to another part of the country because their spouse has taken a job there.

Employee-instigated transfers and those which are clearly seen by the staff to have personal advantages present few problems, inability or unwillingness on the part of the business to agree to the transfer being the major one in that it can lead to the dissatisfaction in the employee who has been refused. Transfers instigated by the business for organisational reasons are potentially more difficult in that the person concerned may feel threatened in job security and status. The majority of people do not enjoy the experience of a totally new environment. Job change is an acknowledged cause of stress.

Resignation, dismissal and redundancy

Resignation

The relationship between an employer and his employees is defined by law. In the section on recruitment (page 216) we saw that an employer was required to give an employee a written contract of employment within twelve weeks of the date when work started. Resignation is the decision on the part of the employee to terminate the contract of employment. The notice of his intention to do so may be included in the contract of employment or it may be based on the customary practice for that occupation.

It may be customary in certain occupations for the length of the notice required to coincide with the periods at which people are paid. A person paid weekly may give a week's notice. A monthly paid employee may need to give a month's notice. In the field of education, where employees are paid monthly and the organisation of schools and colleges is on a termly basis, dates may be specified by which a resignation must be given. These will be designed to coincide with the payment periods and to minimise disruption to the work of the school or college during a term.

The practice of making the period of notice correspond to the period of payment reduces the risk of dispute over the amount of money due to the employee, although holiday pay and bonuses due can still cause problems. The greater the degree of disruption an employee could cause by resignation the more likely it is that termination of contract will be included as a clause in the written contract of employment. Where a highly specialised employee is concerned, he or she may be required to complete specific tasks before employment can be terminated rather than be tied too rigidly to a time period. A scientific research worker whose contract requires three months' notice may be released after one month if he has finished a project rather than allow him to start on a further piece of work which another person would have to take up.

Dismissal

The ability of employers to dismiss staff was limited by the Industrial Relations Act and confirmed by the Trade Union and Labour Relations Act 1974. The grounds for fair dismissal are as follows:

1 *Inability to perform the work required*   The employer has a legal responsibility to ensure that adequate training is given and to warn the employee of the unsatisfactory nature of his work. If a business finds this a problem then it should revise its recruitment and training procedures.

2 *Misconduct*   The employer must be able to show that warnings suitable to the gravity of the offence have been given. Summary dismissal – that is, dismissal without notice – may be justified if an employee has endangered lives, perhaps by drunkenness. For other offences an established pattern might include:

- several informal warnings by the supervisor;

- if the offence persists, a formal oral warning by the manager with the supervisor and a trade-union representative present;

- a written warning which may be handed to the person with the same degree of formality.

The Advisory, Conciliation and Arbitration Service (ACAS) has drawn up a code of practice relating to dismissals. It states that employees should be aware of the disciplinary procedures of the business, that there should be a system of warnings similar to the one outlined above and that an appeals procedure should be in operation.

3   *Redundancy*   A dictionary defines the word 'redundant' as meaning superfluous or characterised by an excess. Under the terms of the Employment Protection (Consolidation) Act 1978 a person can be made redundant if the employer can show that the type of labour offered by the employee is no longer required (superfluous) or that the need for it has decreased (that some employees are in excess of requirements). (See also the next section.)

4   *There may be legal restrictions on employing a certain category of person*, for example, children.

The law relating to unfair dismissal is open to interpretation, and employees who believe themselves to have been dismissed unfairly on grounds such as their right to join a trade union, the right to strike, discrimination under the provisions of the 1976 Race Relations Act and/or the 1975 Sex Discrimination Act have the right of appeal. They should take their case to an Industrial Tribunal which, if it finds in the favour of the employee, can order reinstatement, re-engagement or compensation. The choice lies with the employee.

Redundancy

The definition of redundancy given in the previous section should be sufficient to make it clear that it is an unpleasant experience for the person concerned even when accepted voluntarily. It can attack the status and security of the individual concerned and, in extreme cases, undermine his or her lifestyle and that of his family. Because it can affect individuals dramatically it can also have serious problems for the business forced to make redundancies. Such implications are listed below:

1   It is expensive, and the better organised and more powerful the labour force the more expensive it is likely to be. If redundancy proposals are opposed by the trade unions concerned there could be industrial action which would further disrupt production with the resultant loss of output and possibly sales. When redundancy is not opposed, the trade union may be able to negotiate terms involving additional redundancy payments above the legal minimum. These costs may be considered short term by the business and can be offset against savings as the result of greater efficiency in the long term.

2   Rumour and fear of redundancy can affect the morale of existing employees. Assurances of no further plans to make people redundant may be disbelieved and the business may experience problems in maintaining output and quality. They may also lose valuable staff.

> I am getting out. They've got 1500 men to get rid of in the next two years. They tell me my job is safe but I can't take any chances. There is the mortgage to pay and the kids to keep.

The man speaking had no difficulty in finding another job with a firm he considered more stable. Given his qualifications and experience it was unlikely that he would have been made redundant but he felt too insecure in an atmosphere of threatening redundancy to take the risk.

3   The image of the business is likely to suffer. This in turn could affect recruitment, and a business might find it difficult to attract good employees even in areas where redundancy is unlikely. Redundancy, even as a result of re-equipping plant with advanced technology, carries with it the implication of failure.

4   When a business follows a policy of voluntary redundancy, it takes the risk of losing skilled and versatile staff who may see a generous redundancy payment as a way of financing their future plans.

5   Redundancy may be against the declared policy of the business. In this case the need for redundancies will reflect on its public image. It can also lead to conflict at managerial and Board levels.

In theory, redundancy should not be necessary if the business has a good manpower plan. In practice, the rate of technological change and changes in the market can make it difficult for a manpower plan to project very far into the future. To some extent the industry in which a business operates and the type of materials it uses will affect its ability to forecast its manpower requirements with any degree of accuracy.

Where a business can identify a future problem it may review its marketing policy. Can it increase sales by changing the advertising and pricing strategy? Is it targeting its efforts on the right market segment? Could a change in distribution methods help? Is the packaging right? Could sales promotion increase revenue?

This approach will be most helpful when redundancies are caused by declining sales. When redundancies are the result of a change in technology the marketing department may already be efficient. In this case a marketing drive will have only a marginal effect on redundancies.

Redundancies might also be avoided by cutting down on part-time work, subcontracting and overtime. Work-sharing could also be introduced, and, in occupations with a pension scheme, early retirement might be encouraged.

So far in this chapter we have looked at man management in terms of the natural life of an employee within the business from the time of employment, through training and job changes to the point at which the contract of employment is terminated by either the employer or the employee. In the next sections we shall be looking at the responsibility of management during the period of employment: the *need* to motivate and the *responsibility* to provide working conditions which take account of the health and safety of employees.

SELF-ASSESSMENT

1 A manager is preparing to dismiss an employee. State two reasons why he may be reluctant to do so.
2 Redundancy can lead to a feeling of insecurity in the remaining employees. What effects might this have on the production manager?

Motivation

A business needs to motivate its workforce if it is to make the best possible use of the financial and material resources at its disposal. In chapter 10 we examined the theory of human motivation. Here we shall look briefly at the practical ways in which a business might attempt to motivate its employees.

Remuneration

Most people have to work in order to survive. An attractive salary is likely to be one of the features that persuade people to apply for a job. In the market for labour it is reasonable to suppose that successful businesses can offer higher salaries than their competitors and so attract well-qualified workers. Logically, this should mean that these businesses will continue to be successful because the quality of their decisions in finance, marketing and production and the resulting product offered to the market will continue to be better than those of their competitors. In practice, there is some debate about the continuing importance of money as a motivating factor. People's perceptions of what constitutes a good salary change. The man who is employed at a salary 10 per cent higher than his previous salary might be pleased initially, but when he compares his earnings with those of his colleagues he may be less satisfied.

The way in which people are paid can also help determine whether or not money can act as a motivator.

Payment by results

This term covers schemes based on measurement of the work done, and the amount paid is related directly to the amount of work completed. It can include piece rates, commission and bonus incentive schemes. F. W. Taylor laid down the principles for a successful scheme of payment by results in terms of good job design, careful selection of the workforce and good training. It can be expensive for a business to operate in terms of the clerical work associated with records, and changes in technology or working practice might make it progressively easier for people to reach the targets set and achieve high bonuses. This erodes any advantage to the business of introducing new methods, and any attempt on the part of the business to redefine standards is likely to be met with considerable opposition from the workforce. In other words, the scheme is a potential source of conflict. This conflict is not necessarily between management and workforce. Payment by results can also lead to inter-group conflict where one group of workers perceives the targets set for it as being high compared with targets set for other groups in the organisation. The use of payment by results as an incentive to hard work can also be limited by the following three factors:

1 The complexity of the scheme. If it is unintelligible then there will be less incentive to work hard, as workers will not have a clear concept of the relationship between effort and payment.

2 The establishment by working groups of a group norm in relation to production standards. Pressure may be brought on people working hard to conform to the standards of the group.

3 Proposed changes in technology and/or working practices will be met with suspicion which workers will see as an attempt to erode their wages.

Participation

The involvement of employees in the decision-making processes of a business reduces the feeling of alienation which may be present and increases employee commitment to the achievement of objectives. Participation may be as simple as a suggestion box with financial rewards for cost-reducing suggestions. It may consist of an elaborate system of meetings of employee representatives, or it may be merely meetings between management and employee representatives to inform the employees of decisions already taken.

Participation can be time-consuming, and some employees will take the view that they are not paid to make decisions, that that is the job of management. The past history of the business will also influence the success of a participation scheme. A business with a tradition of autocratic management will find implementation more difficult. Employees will not be accustomed to making decisions, and there may be suspicion and resentment.

Employee shareholding is seen by some authorities as an extension of the idea of participation with advantages in motivating the workforce. The argument is simply that, if workers have a financial stake in a business, then they have a greater reason for working harder and making sure the business is a success. Privatisation of nationalised industries with priority in buying shares given to employees and management buy-outs with employee investment have led to an increase in shareholding among employees. Critics of this point of view argue that the shares will eventually be sold for a profit and in the long term the increase in employee shareholding will be negligible. At the time of publication tax advantages make it profitable for the shares to be held for five years. It is too early to say what will happen when the majority of schemes have existed for this length of time. Much of the discussion on the value of employee shareholding tends to be coloured by political thinking, which makes it more difficult to evaluate.

Job rotation, job enlargement, job enrichment, training and promotion prospects all have a place in determining the level of motivation within a workforce. So also does leadership style, the relationship both within and between groups and the environment within which a business is operating. In chapter 10 we discussed the complexity of human beings. If the workforce are to be motivated their needs must be met, but those needs are changing and vary according to the individual. To design motivation schemes to suit all workers at all times would seem an impossible task.

Poor motivation can lead to a high rate of labour turnover, high absenteeism, poor-quality products, low productivity and poor industrial relations.

Monitoring personnel policy

The effectiveness of a personnel policy can be judged by a number of measures:

- the safety record of the business;
- the level of absenteeism;
- recruitment records;
- the rate of labour turnover;
- the level of productivity;
- the quality of the work produced and the level of wastage.

Problems in any of the above areas will indicate a personnel problem. The degree of control the business has over the problem will vary according to the environment in which it is working and over time. Labour turnover is likely to be high for a boring job in a period of full employment. A business employing innovative technology might find it difficult to recruit people with experience in the technology and, for a time, have high levels of labour turnover together with low productivity and wastage.

Protection

Work is a dangerous activity and it is the responsibility of an organisation to ensure that the risk to its employers is minimised. The responsibility of a business to protect its employers can be divided into three areas:

1   protection from accidents;
2   protection from the effects of the industrial processes involved;
3   protection from fire.

The legal responsibilities of a business towards its employees were established by the Health and Safety at Work Act 1974. This did not replace the Factory Acts but rather emphasised the responsibilities of employer, self-employed and employee to ensure that working practices reached a high standard of safety. Employers are required:

- to prepare and distribute to their employees a written statement of safety policy;
- to educate and train their workforce in the need for safe working practices;
- to ensure that working practices are safe, that all products are safe and, if necessary, clear instructions are issued for safe use;
- to co-operate with and consult employees' representatives.

Failure to comply with the Act can lead to charges under criminal law with a range of penalties including fines and imprisonment.

Apart from legal and moral responsibilities the prevention of accidents and careful attention to the health of employees is good business practice. Accidents cost money. Working time is lost, there may be a need to re-train people, work may have to be re-scheduled. The accident may have damaged equipment and, of course, compensation may have to be paid.

Conclusion

The people involved in business can be seen as the most important resource of that business. Finance, production and marketing are, after all, only words given to a group of tasks performed by people. The success or failure of each will depend largely on the quality of the individuals undertaking the task, their motivation and commitment. It could be argued that chapters 10 and 11 are the most important chapters in this book, and the implications of the subject matter stretch far beyond the immediate concerns of the personnel department.

Review

1   Forsythe plc produces large-scale industrial equipment. The company has a history of poor industrial relations dating back to the mid-1960s, and the situation was not improved by the economic recession of the 1970s and 1980s. To make matters worse there was over-capacity in the world market, and the major foreign competitors – West Germany, Japan and Korea – were all more cost effective than Forsythe. In order to survive, Forsythe's management invested in new equipment and proposed changes in working practices. Rigid demarcations between jobs were to be abolished, and all employees including skilled workers were to take their turn in 'service' jobs (such as cleaning and painting). Working hours became more flexible. It was expected that these measures would be met with considerable opposition from the workforce and expressed through the trade unions.
   (a) What steps might the management of Forsythe's take to ensure the success of their proposals?
   (b) What external factors might contribute to the acceptance of these proposals by the workforce?

2   Peter Jackson has just been appointed production manager at a small clothing factory. Within a short time of taking up his job he is aware that morale in the factory is low and, judging by the number of complaints on file, that quality

control is poor. He decides to introduce a system of quality circles – that is, a small group of employees who meet regularly and voluntarily to discuss technical problems associated with their work and decide on ways in which these might be overcome. The scheme met opposition both from employees and from other members of the management team.

SHOP STEWARD: It is pointless, isn't it? Sitting round talking when we should be getting on with the job. My members are paid by results. Wasting time talking will just reduce their pay. Besides, it is the management's job to sort out problems – that is what they are paid for.

MANAGING DIRECTOR: A waste of time. Most of them are uninterested in working. If we paid them time rate they would just sit talking all day. Giving them time to meet to discuss problems will just be an extended tea break to them.

Peter Jackson persevered with his idea and won reluctant permission for his experiment from both management and the shop stewards. By the end of six months there was a perceptible improvement in quality, costs were down and the production flow had improved.
(a) From your knowledge of the advantages of participation, explain why the quality circles in this instance were successful.
(b) Outline the arguments used by Peter Jackson (i) to the managing director and (ii) to the shop steward to persuade them that the experiment was worth making.
(c) What conditions would have to be satisfied to ensure the success of quality circles?

3   A small manufacturing company is proposing to appoint a personnel manager for the first time.
(a) List the functions of a personnel manager.
(b) For each function state who is likely to be performing that function before the appointment of the personnel manager.
(c) What organisational advantages and disadvantages might arise from the appointment?

Activities

1   Interview someone who is employed in an area in which you have a special interest. Analyse the job from the results of the interview and draw up a checklist of personal characteristics, skills and experience that are needed.

2   Interview a number of people on their attitudes to work and working conditions. Analyse the results of these interviews. Do they suggest any problems in motivating workers?

Suggested projects

1   Should Business X employ a safety officer?

2   Make a critical evaluation of the payment system in Plant Y.

Essays

1   Define job evaluation and assess its utility to a business enterprise.

2   Outline and comment on the impact of current employment protection legislation on a business enterprise.

3   Discuss the ways in which a manager might attempt to improve the morale of the workforce.

4   The personnel function is fundamental to the success of a business enterprise. Discuss.

5   Analyse the essential principles of a good training programme.

6   The head of a school/college will be interviewing a short-list of three candidates for the post of A-level business studies teacher. Candidate A is professionally well qualified, has worked in industry but has no teaching experience. Candidate B is moderately qualified and has two years' successful teaching experience. Candidate C has just qualified as a teacher of business studies. Suggest factors which might influence the head's choice and consider:
   (a) how the head might brief himself for the interviews;
   (b) the questions he might ask each candidate;
   (c) the information he might seek before making his decision.   (25)   1986 (CLES)

Chapter 12   Business and decision making

An underlying theme throughout this book has been the need for a business to take decisions. This derives from the basic fact that all resources are scarce in relation to the number of available alternative uses for them. To recapitulate briefly: it is necessary for a business to take decisions in relation to the use of financial, manpower and technical resources which will in turn affect the financial, marketing and production activities of the business. In previous chapters some decision-making practices and techniques were introduced as an integral part of the chapter – for example, DCF, break-even charts and the need for planning to implement decisions. It is now time to look in more detail at the decision-making process and the types of decision a business needs to take.

Types of decision

The type of decision a business makes can be classified according to the number of unknown variables which may have an influence on the outcome of a particular course of action and the type of problem involved.

Decisions and constraints

The overall objectives of a business are long term and are therefore subject to constraints imposed by competitors, governments and society in general. The decision as to whether or not to pitch prices at a high level compared with those of potential competitors (**skimming**) or a low level (**penetration**) will depend on the judgement of management about the potential behaviour of competitors. Similarly, the decision to invest in North Sea oil, which involved relatively high production costs, depended on a reading of the future market for oil and its potential world market price. In general, these decisions relate to the *profitability* and, ultimately, the *survival* of the business in its present form. They have become known as **strategic** decisions.

Most decisions in business can be described as **tactical**: there are a limited number of options open to solve the problem concerned, and solutions tend towards the routine. When tactical decisions have to be taken on a day-to-day basis they become **recurrent** – that is, they recur over and over again. There is a danger in this. Many different problems can display the same symptoms. A high rate of absenteeism, for example, might have its origins in recruitment, training and remuneration policies. It could also be the result of a poor working environment which reflects on the organisation of the production function or may be out of the control of the business. A workforce unaccustomed to rigid working hours may not see the need for regular attendance. Using this example, the high level of absenteeism might become a routine problem, accepted as the norm, and therefore there would be no attempt to analyse the problem in spite of the fact that it could become a serious internal constraint upon the achievement of strategic objectives.

Making decisions

The process of making decisions is the same regardless of the type of decision being made. In routine decisions the process may be formalised with set procedures to be followed. In 'one-off' decisions the process may be more apparent and could take months or even years. A decision as to whether or not to go ahead with a major civil engineering project will be taken only after the results of a prolonged feasibility study are known and have been evaluated. The process can be summarised in the following stages:

1   *Statement of the objectives* to be achieved.

2   *Definition of the problem* to be solved. We have already suggested that this may not be as easy as it appears: a product which is not reaching the predicted level of sales might be over-priced, carry a bad reputation for quality or have the wrong distribution channel.

3   *Collection of available information*   This will determine the internal constraints (manpower, availability of finance, production capacity and so on) and external constraints (such as the economic environment, the market in which the business operates and any legal limitations on the course of action).

4   *Drafting of alternative solutions* to the problem. It is very rare for there to be only one solution available. At this point it is necessary for the business to reconsider its objectives. Some courses of action are more likely to achieve these objectives than others. This process involves the analysis and evaluation of the different courses of action. We have already seen some of the techniques that might be used to find and analyse information. However, decision making also involves risk, and mathematical techniques to evaluate risk – such as decision trees – might be used.

5   *Implementation* once a decision has been reached, using the planning procedures outlined in previous chapters. You should remember that this process involves the collection of information in order to evaluate the progress of the plan. The same information will contribute towards the evaluation of the effectiveness of the original decision.

Business problems

To each owner or manager of a business it might appear that his problems are unique. To a certain extent this is true. Each business is a unique organisation. It has evolved out of a set of circumstance that are unique to its experience. On the other hand, it is possible to group problems into major areas which have appropriate techniques to contribute to the solution of the problem.

Problems of resources

Accepting that all resources are scarce compared with the demand for them, the existence of competing uses for the available resources of a business leads to the necessity to decide how they shall be allocated. The business is faced with problems concerning the use of time, manpower and production capacity. To which product should the resources be devoted? What proportion of the resources of a business should be allocated among departments? Which is the most important at the present time – marketing, research and development? Information for the solution of these problems is derived from market research as well as from the internal records of the business. At this level deciding on the allocation of resources may involve the use of different costing techniques, contribution analysis, market research and manpower planning.

Resource allocation is not only concerned with the allocation of resources to different business functions. Given that the equipment available in any one department is limited, the problem arises how best to use that equipment.

A small factory produces a range of engineering components all of which have to be processed through Machine A. There is only one such machine in the factory, and the possibilities of sub-contracting are limited. Theoretically, Machine A has the capacity to process all the components in the time allowed. In practice, the machine has become a bottleneck. The business is finding difficulty in meeting orders for the fastest-moving components while stocks of other components are building up.

Machine A is a limited resource. The evidence suggests that it is not being used efficiently. It also suggests that priority should be given to the more popular components while less popular items could be processed at a more leisurely rate, which would have the advantage of reducing the stocks of high-value finished goods. In this example, because there is no evidence to support the installation of an additional machine there are no additional demands on the total resources of the business. The solution might lie in a coding system to give priority to the fast-moving components. This is likely to have implications for the use of manpower, such as changes in working practices and priority for Machine A by the maintenance departments. Taking this problem from the point of view of the components it can also be interpreted as a *queuing problem*.

Where a variety of resources are needed for several projects which need to be completed in sequence, or where a business has control over resources which can be used in a variety of projects, then a technique known as **critical path analysis** (CPA) can be usefully employed. This is a collection of techniques designed to find the cheapest method of completing an operation. If resources are kept idle because other stages of the project have not been completed, this will increase the costs of the project. A small builder will plan a job from experience. He will estimate the time that each activity will take and make arrangements to hire any additional equipment he might need to fit in with the time sequence of the job. A mistake in his estimations might cost him additional hiring fees. Where he needs to sub-contract he might make plans to do another, shorter job in the time available to him. The builder is using a rule-of-thumb CPA. In more complex jobs a network will be drawn up before the work begins indicating the sequential order of activities, their dependence on each other and the degree of flexibility in the use of scarce resources (*float*).

Replacement problems

Unfortunately, equipment has a limited life and at some stage a business has to decide whether or not to replace obsolescent or worn-out machinery. This decision will be made on the basis of the estimated market for the final product – for example, the expected life cycle of the product, the cost of the machine and alternative uses for the resources.

Maintenance also generates replacement problems. The failure of a machine might cause delays in the work process. On the other hand, the activity involved in repairing or replacement of that machine might cause greater delays. This is a costing problem. Which alternative involves the least cost to the business concerned? A business employing outside contractors to service its office equipment at a fixed service charge per call plus an hourly rate for the work itself might find it cheaper to leave the repair of routine equipment until it has several tasks to be done. Alternatively, the same business might be prepared to call in the contractor if the equipment to be repaired is essential for the operation of the whole system.

Location problems

In chapter 9 we outlined the factors a business would take into account when deciding where to locate a factory. It was also indicated that each factor would have a different degree of importance in each decision, and this can be translated into costs. For example, if a factory serves five customers over a given area, which site would reduce transport costs by the greatest amount? The same basic problem is involved in the setting up of service departments within a business to supply several factories. One solution involves the use of a transportation matrix which can be solved by the use of linear programming.

Inventory problems

We discussed the importance of stock control in chapter 9. The techniques which might prove useful for a business in this area include costing, statistical analysis of the problem and the results of market research.

Queuing problems

Parts queue to be processed by machines, customers queue to take their turn at the check-out counter of a supermarket. It makes sense in terms of low costs and customer satisfaction to reduce the waiting time as much as possible with the minimum use of additional resources. In a small shop the problem will be solved by observation. Tuesday morning and Thursday morning might be busy times for a sub-post office with a large number of pensioners registered with it. It will also attract custom for the general shop next door. Common sense will tell the owners of both whether or not they will need additional staff on those mornings.

Where trade is less certain it becomes more difficult to assess the requirements. When trade is random the business will be interested in how often an event occurs in a given unit of time: in other words, how many customers are likely to need service between 9 a.m. and 12 noon on a Tuesday? The Poisson distribution, which is derived from the binomial distribution (see page 88), can provide a useful approximation for these purposes. If the average rate of arrivals at a check-out counter is ten per hour, it would be possible to calculate the probability of an unacceptable number of customers arriving – unacceptable, that is, in terms of the length of time they would have to wait and the damage this might do to the future trading prospects of the business.

Monte Carlo simulation

The decision must be made whether or not to buy more machinery and/or employ more people in order to eliminate a queue. One way to collect information on which to reach a decision is by observation. Collecting information by observation is time-consuming, expensive and boring. The real-life pattern of behaviour can be simulated by using random numbers.

A random number table is generated by a computer. All numbers have an equal probability of occurring provided the table is used in a constant manner, for example, provided you take every fifth number and not the fifth, the ninth, the thirtieth and so on. By selecting numbers at random it is possible to build up an imaginary picture of what might happen in a queueing problem. This will not make the decision.

Marketing problems

Marketing problems must also include production problems. The product mix, quality control, distribution channels and pricing are likely, in larger businesses at least, to be based on the analysis of historical data using statistical techniques outlined in chapter 5. Linear programming can also be used to determine the optimum product mix.

When marketing their products businesses will also be concerned with the reactions of their competitors. This relates to the question of market power we discussed in chapter 3. When a major oil company reduces the price of petrol it is likely that its competitors will follow suit in order to retain their share of the market.

Revision

This section is no more than a summary of the different ways in which a businessman can collect and use information for decision making. We have already said that the planning and decision-making processes are inseparable. This was underlined by the sub-titles of chapters 5 and 6, 'an aid to decision making and control'. If you look at the chart given below (Figure 12.1) you can see the major types of decision and the techniques associated with them. Statistical and accounting information appear in each section.

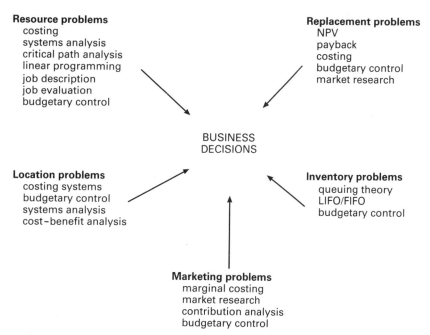

Figure 12.1 The major types of decision and their associated techniques

People, decisions and risk

Risk occurs when there is more than one possible outcome from a decision, and some risks are less desirable than others. The way in which people react to risk taking has been the subject of study by psychologists. What makes one man willing to make a particular decision when his colleagues are urging caution? Why does a person take an apparently irrational decision – one which, on the surface at least, is unreasonable given the available evidence?

In chapter 10 we developed the idea that each individual has his or her own unique 'bundle' of objectives and personality traits which influence the behaviour of that individual in any given situation. Freud suggested that some of the motives which influence the way in which people act are in fact subconscious. His argument was that, if we knew what these subconscious motives were, then irrational decisions would appear rational in the light of additional information.

During the 1940s and 1950s psychologists continued to study this question. Their main interest was whether or not individuals tried to maximise their satisfaction from any decision they made. This personal satisfaction might include monetary reward but only as one of their motives. (We discussed this in chapter 10 when we looked at the role of money as a motivator.) The *utility* of a decision to an individual – that is, the extent to which it satisfies the desires of the individual – is *subjective*. In other words, it is the perceived utility that is important to people.

Any event has an actual (*objective*) possibility of occurring. If you toss a coin there is a one-in-two chance it will come down heads, assuming that the way in which it tossed each time does not vary and it does not land on its edge. In decision making, therefore, the logical thing to do is to select the decision that will lead to the outcome with the highest probability of occurrence and will give the maximum utility. There is some evidence to suggest that people use subjective probability when making decisions even when the actual probabilities are known: the coin-tossing example is a case in point. No matter how often the coin is tossed, the probability that it will show heads as a result of the next toss remains one in two. If you toss the coin ten times and each time it shows heads, many people would argue that there was a greater chance of it showing tails on the next toss. This is not true. A subjective rather than an actual probability is being applied, and may be justified in terms of 'Well, it's the law of averages'. A subjective judgement of the situation is not based on numbers but on an intuitive understanding of the probability.

To summarise the argument so far, we are saying that people tend to make decisions on the *subjective expected value* of its outcome – a long phrase to describe decision making based on subjective estimates of probability combined with the subjective utility of the perceived outcome.

Subjective probability is not only a matter of intuition. It will also depend on the level of knowledge and experience of the decision makers concerned. A man who follows horse racing and studies the form of horses closely will still make his final selection of the horses on which to bet by his subjective judgement of their chances of winning, but his choice is more likely to be accurate than a man who selects his horses because he likes their names.

Unfortunately for good decision making, there is a considerable body of research which suggests that people do not use all the evidence at their disposal. Given a limited amount of information most people make a good, reasoned decision. When the data are too extensive there is a danger that much of it will be ignored. Individuals will select the information that, in their subjective judgement, is the most important.

Given the fact that in many business decisions information is incomplete either because the cost of collecting it is too high or because the information is not available, it is not surprising that the record of a management team for making good decisions is taken into account by investment analysts when attempting to forecast the future potential of a company.

Techniques of decision making

By its very nature decision making implies the taking of risks. The person taking the decision is attempting to forecast the pattern of future events on the basis of historical data. This cannot be seen as a satisfactory state of affairs, and, not surprisingly, a number of techniques have been developed to help decision makers in estimating the extent of the risk they are taking and to minimise it where possible.

So far the decision-making techniques we have discussed have been concerned with specific decisions. Here we will examine some decision-making models which have been developed in order to provide some estimate of the element of risk present in each possible outcome. The models, however, have to be constructed by people, and this can lead to the following problems:

1   The data on which the model is constructed may be inaccurate. At best this situation increases uncertainty; at worst it can lead to the wrong 'certainties'.

2   It is difficult to know how variables within the model will react to changes in the situation. A decision-making model is an attempt to simulate part of a system, and changing one part of the system will change the rest of that system with potentially unpredictable results.

3   External variables can also be changed by business decisions, and again it is difficult to predict the way in which they will change to accommodate the new situation.

Cost–benefit analysis

Businesses are part of the community, and some commercial decisions made by a business will affect the general well-being of a community. The most obvious example is, perhaps, pollution as the result of industrial processes carried out by a business. Many of these decisions will be internal to the business and implemented within a known legislative framework, such as the Clean Air Act 1956.

In other cases, the consequences of business decisions are less clear cut. A business applying for planning permission to build a factory on a particular site might argue that it is bringing employment into the area, boosting the revenue of the local authority by paying rates and improving the appearance of the area by building a modern factory with landscaped grounds on what was, previously, a derelict area. Weighed against this might be the arguments of the local residents concerned about congested roads, pollution and noise.

Local authorities and the central government face a similar conflict of interest when undertaking projects concerning the provision of services and the improvement of the infrastructure of an area. Will a bypass designed to take traffic from the centre of a market town assist the development of the town by reducing congestion and noise, or will it contribute to the decline of the town by taking away passing trade and making it easier for local residents to travel to a better shopping centre some miles distant? Will closing an uneconomic branch line of the railway system or axing a loss-making bus service destroy local community life – and what other hidden costs will be incurred by the decision and who will bear them?

A distinction can be made between the *private costs* of any decision – that is, the cost to the individual or organisation responsible for the decision, which is usually reflected in the production cost of the business and therefore in the price of the product – and the *social costs*, which are borne by the community as the result of that decision. This implies a conflict of interest in many decisions between financial criteria and social/political criteria. Cost–benefit analysis is a collection of techniques which attempts to find an objective measure of the utility of a proposal based on the range of people's values in a community, and to measure these values on a common monetary scale. The diagram below gives an imaginary cost–benefit analysis used in the selection of a site for the dumping of industrial waste.

Costs:
   New roads
   Heavier traffic
   Loss of amenity land
   Environmental considerations

Benefits:
   Increased employment
   Landfill and reclamation
   Revenue from dumping

Decision trees

Decision trees take their name from the branching form of the diagrams associated with them. A decision tree is an attempt to trace through all known outcomes of a decision in order to clarify the possible consequences. These can then be evaluated as part of the decision-making process. Figure 12.2 is a simple tree diagram showing the possible outcomes of the decision whether or not to resign from a job.

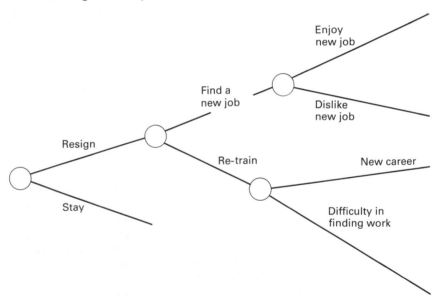

Figure 12.2   Tree diagram

Decision trees go further than this by attempting to allocate probabilities to each event. By multiplying the probabilities of the occurrence of each possible outcome by the expected profit or loss of that outcome they arrive at an **expected value** (EV).

We have already discussed the nature of subjective probability, and it is important to realise that the probabilities assigned to each outcome will depend on the information available.

Let us look at a situation in which a manager is considering entering a new market. The first step is straightforward: to enter or not to enter? If the business enters that market, initial costs will be £250 000. If it does not enter, then costs will be nil. It is impossible to make this decision without examining the outcomes. Assuming that there is an estimated 0.6 chance of a level of demand that would generate an income of £950 000 at the end of one year (£700 000 net of initial costs) and a 0.4 chance of a level of demand that will generate £200000 at the end of one year (−£50000 net of production costs), the decision tree will now look like this:

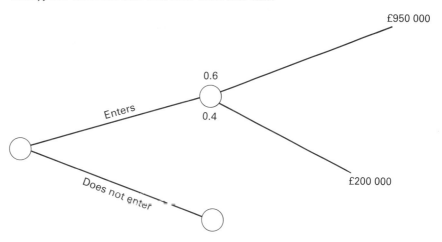

£950 000

0.6

Enters

0.4

£200 000

Figure 12.3   The decision tree

Does not enter

The expected value of his decision to enter the market is the *sum* of the two possible outcomes:

$$(0.6 \times £700000) + (0.4 \times -£50000) = [(£420000) + (-£20000)]$$
$$= £400000$$

The initial investment of £250000 has an expected value of £400000 after one year. This is, of course, predicted cash flow, and calculation of net present value (NPV) (see page 134) might still suggest that the investment is uneconomic. The example can be continued, but at each stage the decision will be taken in the light of the results of the previous stage.

Game theory

Game theory is the mathematical study of the strategies used by individuals and organisations to achieve their objectives in situations of conflict. It began in 1928 when the mathematician John von Neuman published a paper entitled 'Towards the theory of party games'.

If you consider the rules of some of the games with which you are familiar – games based on strategy rather than chance – you can see the analogy that exists between the choices facing individual players and the businessman contemplating a price rise in an oligopolistic market. The question in both cases is the same: if I do this, how will my competitors react? Game theory is an attempt to predict the probable reactions of external variables to a particular decision.

It is generally accepted that game theory requires further development before it can be confidently used to analyse complex situations. It has been included in this section to illustrate the way in which mathematical theory can contribute towards the decision-making processes.

The minimax criteria

The minimax criteria may be seen less as a decision-making technique than as a strategy to help decision makers cope with uncertainty. When faced with a problem a manager may have a number of alternative courses of action – for example, the size of a factory or its potential location. He will have estimates of the cost of each project and the potential revenue. Using the minimax criteria he will select the option that will give the worst result that could happen.

There are variations on this approach, including the concept of **minimax regret**. This can be seen as a calculation of the opportunity cost inherent in a decision. Let us assume that a medium-sized factory is built in preference to a large one on the basis of projected sales figures. The market for the product turns out to be greater than expected and the business could have sold the output of a larger factory. As a result, the business has missed the opportunity of greater revenue. This missed revenue is the *regret*, or the cost of making one decision rather than another. Projections based on different sales levels would give the business the level of regret associated with each decision. The manager might therefore decide on a course of action which would minimise this regret.

Both the minimax and the regret approach to decision making are inherently conservative and, applied throughout a business enterprise, would reduce the opportunities for maximising profit. They can be useful in minimising risk when information is scarce and other decision-making techniques are invalid. Both can be applied over a wide range of decisions as the final criteria when all possible research has been undertaken.

Network analysis

In chapter 10 we discussed the concept of networks in communication and organisation. The same concept can be applied to any collection of jobs which are needed to complete a given task. Some jobs may be done at the same time as others – that is, *simultaneously*. Other jobs must precede or follow each other; that is, they are *sequential*.

Simple networks can be analysed intuitively, and the analysis is often passed on as part of the learning process. The instructions included in a recipe are a form of network analysis:

1   pre-heat oven;
2   separate egg yolks from egg whites;
3   beat egg yolks;
4   whip egg whites until they are stiff;
5   combine egg yolks with egg whites;
6   incorporate flour into the mixture;
7   pour batter into cake tin;
8   bake for forty minutes.

A traditional oven could take a quarter of an hour to reach the required temperature, and an experienced cook would interpret the first instruction as 'Switch on the oven'. The oven would then be heating up while stages 2–7 were taking place – that is, simultaneously. We can illustrate this by an **arrow diagram** (Figure 12.4).

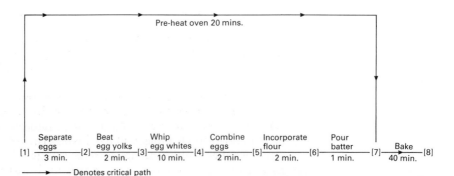

Figure 12.4   The arrow diagram

The arrows in the diagram represent *activities*. Each activity has a *start*, represented by the tail of the arrow, and a *finish*, represented by the head of the arrow. The circles, or nodes, indicate the stages.

This domestic example has been used to introduce network analysis. There are a number of different techniques used in network analysis including **critical path analysis** (CPA) and the **program evaluation and review technique** (PERT) developed by the United States Navy. France and the Soviet Union have also developed methods of network analysis.

The final decision

Whatever techniques are used in decision making, whatever criteria are judged as important, the quality of the final decision will be affected by the following factors:

1 The quality of the information on which the decision is made. We have already seen that acquiring information costs money. The more detailed the information required the more difficult it is to acquire, then the greater will be the cost. The more information a manager has at his disposal, then the greater the probability of his reaching a good decision, but this in turn will depend on the resources the business can afford to devote to decision making.

2 The importance of the decision. Decisions which involve large sums of money are more likely to have manpower resources devoted to them than those which involve comparatively small sums of money and are seen as routine. Yet poor routine decisions can have a cumulative adverse effect on the efficiency of a business.

3 The structure of the organisation can also affect the quality of decisions. We discussed this in some depth in chapter 10 when we looked at the relationship between types of organisational structure which were suited to different problems.

4 The context in which a decision is made is also important. Research has been done into the extent to which pilot error contributes to plane crashes. Pilots operating under conditions of stress and danger might be more open to error than under normal operating conditions. The same criteria apply to businessmen making decisions under conditions of stress.

5 The personality of the decision maker will undoubtedly influence the decision. Some people are happier with the idea of risk than others. Where one man might be prepared to accept the risks associated with a course of action leading to high profits, another man, given the same information, might use a minimax approach to the problem.

Conclusion

People must make decisions because the resources and, therefore, the courses of action open to them in a situation are limited. Every decision made implies a change in the environment, and this will need the making of further decisions.

The uncertainty inherent in any situation can be reduced by information. However, information is by no means certain. Its validity will depend on the care with which it is assembled (which implies cost) and the perceptions people bring to its interpretation. Techniques for decision making can only be as good as the information they process and the people who apply them.

In Part III we will look more closely at the external constraints upon the decision-making process – that is, the interaction between the business system and the systems within which it operates.

Review

1 (a) Identify the main features of the operational research approach to problem solving.   (5)
   (b) The network in the figure below shows the sequence of activities within a project. (The numbers represent the number of days needed to complete each activity.)

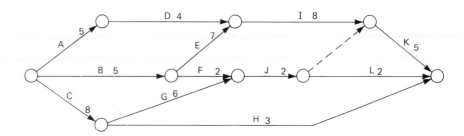

Identify the critical path and calculate the total duration of the project.   (4)
   (c) Distinguish between total float and free float and calculate them for each activity.   (9)
   (d) As work on the project was about to begin, it was found that before activity E could be undertaken, activity C and two new activities, X and Y, would have to be completed. Sketch the new networks diagram, given that X must be preceded by A, and Y must be preceded by B.   (4)
   (e) Why is project management sometimes seen as an important control mechanism in production processes?   (3)   1986 (CLES)

2 (a) Discuss the main advantages and disadvantages of using decision trees in decision making.   (4)
   (b) What is the purpose of using the concept of expected value in decision trees?   (4)
   (c) An investor is deciding whether to buy £10000 worth of unit trusts or an investment bond. Unit trusts have been quite volatile in price lately, investment bonds less so. Whatever he buys he contemplates selling either six months ahead or a year ahead. His objective is to maximise the expected cash value of the deal on the basis of capital gain alone. His subjective evaluations of the likely price movements are as follows:

Unit Trusts
After six months: 50 per cent probability of £1200 and 50 per cent probability of £1000.
After one year:
   (i) if price after six months was £1200, 50 per cent probability of £1500 and 50 per cent probability of £1000;
   (ii) if price after six months was £1000, 50 per cent probability of £1200 and 50 per cent probability of £900.

Investment Bond
After six months: 50 per cent probability of £1500 and 50 per cent probability of £700.

After one year:
(i) if the price after six months was £1500, 50 per cent probability of £2500 and 50 per cent probability of £1200;
(ii) if the price after six months was £700, 50 per cent probability of £800 and 50 per cent probability of £500.

Draw a decision tree to show the features of this problem.   (8)

(d) Calculate the expected values and on the basis of these decide which is the better investment.   (6)

(e) What practical difficulties would you be likely to encounter in applying this concept and how might they affect your decision?   (3)   1985 (CLES)

Part III   Business in society

Chapter 13   Business and the economy

In chapter 2 we examined the business community as part of the economic system of the United Kingdom. Now we will explore this idea further by concentrating on the impact on business of a change in the behaviour of the economic system and the possible effects of governmental attempts to control the system.

To simplify a very complex pattern of relationships we will divide the first part of this chapter into the following subjects:

- the level of economic activity;
- changes in the value of the currency both within the country and in the world;
- the competitive trading position of the country in relation to the rest of the world; and
- improvement in the material standard of living within the country and the rest of the world (economic growth).

These aspects of an economy are interdependent. Rapid inflation can change the overall competitiveness of British goods compared with those of their international competitors and so make it more difficult for British business to export. This in turn can lead to higher levels of unemployment. This situation is likely to be made worse if inflation causes cash-flow difficulties for business leading to an increase in the number of bankruptcies and company liquidations.

It is important to remember that this is an overall view of the way in which the economy can affect business. The theory on which it is based is still a matter of debate among economists. The emphasis therefore will be on what *might* happen in certain circumstances rather than what *will* happen. A great deal will depend on how the rest of the system reacts, and, as that will depend on the decisions people make, it is likely that the response to the situation will change over time. These decisions will have ideological, social and political dimensions as well as reasons that could be considered purely economic. Some of these influences have been considered in chapter 10 and will be further developed in chapter 14.

The level of economic activity

At any given instant a community will possess a finite number of resources with which to produce the goods and services it needs. If the people in that community are to enjoy the best possible standard of living that the resources can produce, then *all* the resources must be used as *efficiently* as possible; that is, the highest possible output must be obtained from the lowest possible input.

When some of the resources in an economy are not active (that is, not employed), **unemployment** is said to exist. When resources are employed, but not as fully as possible, we speak of **under-employment**. When all resources are fully and efficiently employed, the economy is said to be enjoying **full employment**.

None of the terms defined in the previous paragraph is an absolute. They are all open to debate and, on occasions, acrimonious political argument. In a market economy employment statistics will always show some people as unemployed. Employment statistics are based on the number of people registering for work. Even in a booming economy there will be people registering as unemployed while they change jobs and other people who have a limited choice of the work they can do through mental or physical handicap.

Full employment in statistical terms can disguise under-employment. Businesses might continue to employ people they see as key workers when demand for their products drops, in order to avoid the costs involved in recruitment. This will be a short-term measure but will lead to a time lag between the onset of a **recession** (a general decline in the demand for goods, in profits and in investment) and the resulting unemployment. This time lag can be lengthened by employment protection legislation and trade-union activity.

Some economists (and those politicians who agree with their theories) argue that it is impossible for an economy to work efficiently if there are vacancies for everybody who wants to work. To them full employment is that level of employment at which the economy works most efficiently – with, perhaps, 5 per cent unemployed compared with the levels of 1 per cent and 1.5 per cent that were achieved in the late 1950s and 1960s. In contrast to this view, other politicians argue that people have a right to work and that jobs should be created in sufficient numbers for everybody who wants one.

At any particular instant, there will not be complete agreement on either the level of economic activity that is being achieved – there may be criticism of the statistical methods of the government – nor on the precise level that is considered desirable. There may, however, be a consensus that the level of activity is generally too high or too low. It is with the causes and consequences of this general situation that we will be concerned for the rest of this section.

A simple model of the economy

There are many small, rural communities in the world that are virtually self-sufficient. People grow the crops and gather the wild produce of the surrounding countryside to provide themselves with the basic necessities of food, clothing and shelter. We can classify these activities into the *producers* of goods and services (*business*) and the users of goods and services (*households*), although the activities themselves may be carried on by the same people in the same building. A father and son working as glovemakers in a medieval town would have a workshop within the family home. As members of that household they would use the goods and services provided by their own business and other businesses, for which they would pay. Also, as members of the household they would sell their services as glovemakers to the business, for which they would receive payment. This relationship is presented more generally in Figure 13.1.

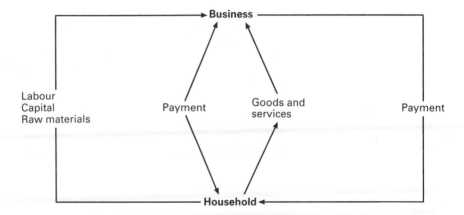

Figure 13.1   The relationship between business and household

Provided that all the goods and services produced are bought and all the money received by households is spent, then the level of activity in this economy will stay the same over time. We say that it is in **equilibrium**. Of course, not everybody might be involved in this economy. Equilibrium does not necessarily mean that there is full employment, only that the level of economic activity remains the same. If the level of activity in this simple economy is to change, then there must either be an increase in the resources available to it (that is, an **injection** into the econmy) or a decrease in the resources available to it (that is, a **withdrawal** from the economy).

The simple economy has served its purpose in establishing the basic relationship between households and business. In examining injections and withdrawals we will be concerned with more complex economic systems.

SELF-ASSESSMENT

1 Distinguish between unemployment and under-employment.
2 Explain simply how one person can be a producer, a consumer and contribute towards government policy.

Injections

'Injection' is an economic term used to describe a flow of resources into an economic system. All injections fall into one of the following categories: government expenditure; investment; or exports.

Government expenditure

Central and local government spend money on the provision of the goods and services to which they have a political commitment. Some of this money is spent directly. The maintenance of a civil and local government service requires the purchase of paper and office equipment as well as the purchase or lease of buildings. In this area the government is also a major employer of labour with a wide variety of skills. Central and local government both have responsibilities for the provision of health and education services as well as the maintenance of the infrastructure of the community: roads, water and sewage services. Because the influence of government spending is so widespread, the following examples can only indicate the possible effects of expansion or contraction on different sections of the business community.

- The construction industry is dependent on government spending. Most major civil-engineering enterprises need some financial support from government – for example, a projected river barrage on a tidal estuary to generate electricity using hydro-electric power. It has been estimated that the market for privately owned housing is nearing saturation point and therefore any further expansion in housebuilding will be in the public sector. Expansions in education and health services will also affect the construction industry.

- Increased spending on social security is likely to benefit those businesses which provide low-cost goods and services for low-income groups. Businesses providing goods and services that might be classified as luxuries could also benefit. The rental of a colour television set and a video recorder provides cheap entertainment for a family that people enjoying a higher income (and therefore a wider range of options) might forgo.

- Spending on scientific research creates jobs for scientists and demand for equipment. Indirectly, it lowers the production costs of businesses and makes them more competitive by providing them with the expensive research which is essential if they are to develop new products.

- All government spending results in additional demand for businesses that service the main industries involved. Publishers, paper makers and the manufacturers of computers, cars, steel, electrical equipment, radars, aeroplanes, furniture and food will experience an increase or decrease in demand depending upon the level of government spending. The importance for an individual business will depend on its own degree of competitiveness in its own market.

Indirectly, and subject to the same market constraints, the suppliers of consumer goods will experience a change in demand. The market constraints are important, and you should remember them. Later in this section we will be discussing imports. When imported goods are more competitive than domestically produced goods or when the home market cannot supply the goods and services people want to buy, any benefits from an increase in government spending will be withdrawn from the domestic economy by spending on imports and become an injection into another economy as payment for an export.

In general, government spending tends to be labour-intensive (think of activities such as teaching, nursing, maintenance, cleaning and construction). Wages per individual tend to be low, but the total wage bill is high and is quickly converted into spending power. This is useful in a stagnant economy with a low level of costs and little international trade because any increase will fuel the domestic economy comparatively rapidly. In an economy with a high level of foreign trade, a level of inflation greater than that of its major international competitors and an aggressive international market, government spending may not be a valid option to boost the level of activity in an economy. The reason will become clearer in this chapter.

Exports

Exports act as injections because home-produced goods and services are sold abroad for their costs plus profit and provide an increase in the wealth of the economy. When a country exports, it can benefit from specialisation. The United Kingdom can only grow oranges at an enormous cost compared with countries with a more favourable climate. In the eighteenth and nineteenth centuries superb (and enormously expensive) hothouses provided the rich with semi-tropical fruits. The expansion of trade has made a much wider range of fruit and vegetables available to a greater proportion of the population. On the simplest level, foreign trade is a matter of exchanging what you have for what you want. Without foreign trade the potential standard of living would be lower than necessary.

The West German economy expanded rapidly in the years following the Second World War in part because of the favourable conditions which existed in international markets for its exports. This **export lead** growth encouraged investment in exporting industries and fuelled demand in the domestic market, thus encouraging further investment.

The import and export of goods (**visibles**) and services (**invisibles**) depends, in a free market economy, on the buying decisions of individuals and organisations. In order to export a business must be able to compete with foreign businesses in terms of cost, quality and service. The overall exports of a country will depend on the general level of competitiveness of individual businesses. Governments attempt to help in this by providing **subsidies** to exporting firms. A subsidy is a payment made to a business to prevent an increase in price (an example of government expenditure) or to help businesses lower prices which are seen as uncompetitive. Subsidies may be made to businesses operating in the domestic as well as in foreign markets. Subsidies to exporting businesses can cause friction between governments. Claims that goods are being sold abroad at less than cost price (**dumping**) may lead to the imposition of trading restrictions on imported goods by another country and the loss to the exporting country of that foreign market.

Exporting businesses bring more money into the economy, which generates further income and demand in the home market for other goods and services. For the moment this statement is satisfactory, but when we look at international trade and the balance of payments in more detail the complexities of the situation will become more apparent.

Investment

Investment is the organisation of resources saved from a previous time period to produce **capital goods**. These are goods which will be used for the production of other goods and services for sale. Some of this investment will be to replace worn-out or obsolete equipment. Other investment will be to extend the range of activity of a business. Replacement investment alone will maintain the existing level of economic activity. Investment in addition to this (**net investment**) will raise the level of economic activity in a country by creating additional demand for capital equipment and labour.

Businessmen, as you should by now be aware, are not inclined to invest unless they can see the possibility of profit. The level of net investment in a country will depend upon the way in which the majority of owners and managers are confident that there will be a sustained and effective demand for the goods and services they produce. The total level of net investment will therefore depend on the investment decisions made by individual businesses, using the criteria discussed in chapter 7.

SELF-ASSESSMENT

1 Classify each of the following under the main groups of injections:
   (a) The Ministry of Defence pays for a new submarine built by a British shipyard.
   (b) A private company builds a new plant.
   (c) A West German business buys a consignment of components from a British firm.
2 What effect does an increase in injections have on the level of economic activity in a country, assuming all other things stay equal?

Withdrawals

Withdrawals are the opposite of injections, and the terms used in association with the word reflect this: 'taxation', 'imports' and 'saving'.

Taxation

Taxes are payments made to central and local government in order to finance the activities of government on behalf of the community. Money is therefore withdrawn from the circular flow of income by this activity.

It is necessary to understand the different ways in which taxes are levied in order to appreciate their potential impact on business. It is also important to remember that this is an area of some controversy.

1　*Direct taxes* are paid directly to government by individuals or organisations. These include income tax and corporation tax.

2　*Indirect taxes*, such as Value Added Tax (VAT), import duties and excise duties on alcohol, tobacco and oil are paid on the quantity or value of the goods and services being taxed.

3　*Progressive taxation* is a tax system designed to take a greater *proportion* of the income of the rich compared with the income of the poor. Income tax is designed as a progressive tax.

4　*Regressive taxation* takes the same amount of tax from everybody, irrespective of ability to pay. Regressive taxes are usually levied on goods and services, to that people can choose whether or not to pay the tax. If the tax payable on a washing machine is £100, the man with an income of £8000 per year will pay the same tax as the man with an income of £40000 per year, though the sacrifice of the man on the lower income will be greater.

Some of the effects of taxation on business are listed below:

1　It has been argued that a high rate of progressive taxation on income may act as a disincentive to work and risk taking. People on a high income with a wide range of leisure activities open to them may opt for leisure rather than work when taxation rates are high. For example, a person whose union has negotiated a productivity agreement might find that he can earn enough money to satisfy his needs by working a four-day week. By working a fifth day he could earn an extra £100 but 50 per cent of this would disappear in tax. He makes a personal decision that the extra £50 is not worth the sacrifice of leisure. This type of absenteeism could cause problems in production organisation for a business, reduce production levels and increase costs.

The argument against this is the fact that money can act as a motivator. People will tend to work to a given 'take-home' pay. When increased taxation reduces the amount of money they have to spend, they will look for opportunities to increase their income. High taxation may be seen as an incentive to work, particularly by lower income groups.

A business will take corporation tax into account when estimating the profitability of an investment project. High taxation will reduce the NPV of cash flows. The greater the perceived risk of the investment the greater the disincentive effect of high taxation.

2　High levels of direct taxation may also affect the demand for the products of some businesses. Luxury goods with a high income elasticity of demand will suffer from a sharp increase in the level of income tax and benefit from a fall.

3　A tax on a good or service can be seen as an increase in the production costs of the business. It therefore has the effect of shifting the supply curve of the industry to the left.

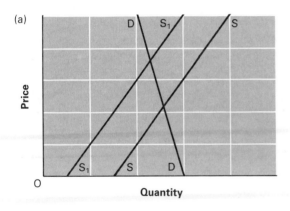

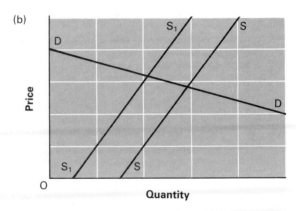

Figure 13.2 The effect of tax on an industry, with different demand curves

Figure 13.2 shows the effect of the same tax on an industry but with different demand curves. In Figure 13.2A the demand curve is relatively inelastic. Most of the tax is passed on to the consumer in terms of higher prices. In Figure 13.2B the relatively elastic demand curve forces the industry to absorb most of the tax itself. A firm operating in the situation illustrated in Figure 13.2B might be forced out of business by the tax if its profit margins were already low. In both cases business will have to absorb some of the tax, which will lower profit margins and, possibly, be taken into account when considering future investment plans.

Imports and savings

Imports take money out of the economy. They compete with domestically produced goods and services. Saving is the result of a decision made by a person or an organisation not to consume or invest.

In defining injections and withdrawals there are two things you should remember:

1   A flow of money into and out of the economy is defined as an injection or withdrawal depending on its immediate effect. Thus taxation is defined as a withdrawal. The money does not become an injection until the government makes a decision to spend it. Saving is a withdrawal, although businesses may decide to use their savings for purposes of investment. It is possible for a government to decide *not* to use all its tax revenue, in which case the level of activity in the country will fall *unless* there is a corresponding increase in the amount of private investment undertaken and/or in the level of exports.

2   Government expenditure and taxation have been given more attention in this section than the other injections and withdrawals. This does not mean they are more important. The decision to save is implicit in all purchasing and investment decisions made by individuals and organisations. Chapters 7 and 8 indicated the factors which affect the consumption, saving and investment decisions of individuals. Chapter 7 also described the way in which savings can be made available for investment through the workings of the money and capital markets.

Exports and imports will be analysed in more detail later in this chapter. The emphasis on government spending and taxation in this section is a matter of convenience rather than principle.

Summary of the circular flow of income

●   When injections and withdrawals are exactly the same over a period of time, the level of activity in an economy will not change.

- An increase in the level of injections and/or a decrease in the level of withdrawals will lead to an increase in the level of activity in the economy.

- A decrease in the level of injections and/or an increase in the level of withdrawals will lead to a decrease in the level of activity in the economy.

Changes in the value of money

The value of a currency can change internally by inflation/deflation and externally by appreciation/depreciation. The internal and external values of a currency are interrelated.

Inflation

Inflation is a *general* rise in the price level of a country and a fall in the purchasing power of the unit of currency. A rise in the prices of one industry does not constitute inflation although it may contribute to it, particularly if the industry is an important one in the economy of the country.

The precise causes of inflation are a matter for debate. The list that follows states the potential causes of inflation without attempting to give any weight to their significance. To a businessman the most important thing about inflation is that it exists.

1 Cost push inflation is the result of a general rise in the costs of production. A general increase in wage levels in excess of increases in productivity, an increase in commodity prices on the world market and an increase in the cost of capital as a result of high interest rates in the international money markets could fuel inflationary pressures in an economy.

2 Demand pull inflation is the result of an excess of demand over production.

The **inflationary spiral** is the term used to describe the relationship between cost push and demand pull inflation. Let us assume that in a particular year a number of powerful trade unions in key industries are successful in gaining wage increases for their members in excess of increases in productivity. The increase in production costs resulting from this are passed on to the customer, at least to some degree. Individuals begin to find their income inadequate to purchase the goods and services they see as essential to their lifestyle. This in turn leads other unions to press for wage claims to keep up with the increase in the cost of living. If these wage claims are not linked to productivity agreements, this results in a further increase in costs. Competitiveness between groups of workers makes the situation worse. The desire to preserve wage differentials between craftsmen and unskilled workers and the attitude 'If they can get it why can't we?' between workers in different industries add to the inflationary effect. At the same time, the increase in purchasing power – which is not accompanied by an increase in the quantity of goods available – leads to the situation where too much money is chasing too few goods. Businesses find that even if their costs have increased so also has the price people are prepared to pay for the goods they produce. Soon the gains from the original round of pay bargaining are lost and the process begins again.

It is unfair to place all the blame for inflation on trade unions and the bargaining process they engage in with employers. In 1960 the Organisation of Petroleum Exporting Countries (OPEC) was established by the major oil-producing and -exporting countries, accounting for approximately 90 per cent of the world's oil exports – a situation which gave OPEC considerable market power. Oil was cheap during the 1950s and 1960s and is an important industrial commodity, not only as a source of fuel (electricity generation and smelting) and power (petrol) but also as a raw material in industries as diverse as plastics and man-made fibres. In 1973 the member countries of OPEC agreed on a massive increase in oil prices supported by agreements to limit output. The reliance of industry upon oil meant that the effects were immediate, dramatic and inflationary in the industrialised economies of the world.

Governments can also cause inflation. A government has the ability to create money. An increase in the money supply of an economy will increase the overall level of demand but will not necessarily lead to an increase in levels of production – a classic case of too much money chasing too few goods.

Inflation and business

Some factors in this relationship are examined below:

1 Temporary demand inflation can persuade businesses to invest. Prices rise and money profits rise with them. Investment increases productivity and sustains demand so the inflationary spiral is wiped out. This is possible after a period of stable prices. Economists argue that once inflation is accepted as part of the economic system, individuals and organisations budget for sustained inflation. Wage claims are made, not on the present level of inflation but what it is expected to be. If inflation has been rising at 1 per cent per annum for five years, then wage claims will be made on a minimum of the existing rate of inflation plus 1 per cent.

2 Inflation can cause problems in the accounting procedures of a business. When assets are valued at historic cost and profits at present cost, the profits, and therefore the taxation position of a business, can be overstated.

3 When inflation is constantly eroding the value of incomes and when a significant proportion of taxation is based on income, the purchasing power of consumers can be eroded in spite of major income rises. A wage increase of 20 per cent might compensate for inflation, but if it takes people into a higher tax bracket it could still reduce their purchasing power. For those on low incomes this is further complicated by the loss of government transfer payments. A married man with a family but on a low income, who then receives a substantial rise in pay, might still find it inadequate to support his previous purchasing pattern if it takes him into the tax-paying category and he loses state benefits. This **poverty trap** will also have implications for businesses selling to this section of the population. The importance will depend on the number of people involved and the total value of the purchases.

4 Inflation increases the importance of the management of working capital. Borrowing becomes more expensive, credit extended to customers loses money value, so it is in the interest of customers to delay payment, and stocks valued at purchase price have to be replaced at a higher price.

5 Persistent inflation can erode business confidence. When faced with an investment decision a businessman might decide not to re-invest, particularly if money markets are offering a high rate of interest. The temptation might be to invest in capital-intensive technology. A widespread trend in this direction can lead to unemployment, a decline in demand and decrease in the level of economic activity within the economy.

Deflation

Deflation is a reduction in the general level of prices. The effect on business will depend upon whether or not costs fall more rapidly than the price of the products. A rapid reduction in essential commodity prices can lead to higher profits if market prices for finished goods are maintained.

Deflation may also come about as a result in the decline of the general level of economic activity in the country. Higher levels of unemployment will lead to a reduction in the demand for goods and services and therefore for the factors of production used to make the goods and provide the services. This may be the result of deliberate policies on the part of a government in order to counteract inflation.

Inflation and foreign trade

Inflation within an economy will change the pattern of competition, as some sectors of the economy will be affected more than others and some businesses will be more efficient in responding to the problems caused by inflation than others. If the inflation rate within a country is high compared with that of its major foreign competitors, this can have serious consequences for the economy, making the goods and services it produces more expensive than foreign goods and services both in the domestic economy and in world markets.

The exchange rate

The exchange rate is the value of a currency measured in terms of other currencies. On one particular date in 1986 the value of the £ sterling expressed in terms of foreign currencies was:

France   10.06 francs
Germany   3.11 Deutschmarks
United States   1.485 dollars

A good produced in England for £1 and assuming no other costs (for example, transport or import duties) would sell in France for 10.06 francs, in Germany for DM3.11 and so on. The reverse would also be true. West German products produced at a cost of DM3.11 would sell in this country for £1.

The exchange rate of a currency can be seen as its price, and this is determined by the interaction of the supply and demand for that currency. When the value of sterling rises, the value of other currencies in relation to it will fall. £1 sterling might then be exchanged for DM5. You need more of other currencies to 'buy' £1. When the value of sterling falls, fewer units of another currency will be needed to buy £1.

A rise in the value of sterling will make British goods less competitive in West Germany and any other country whose currency has fallen in value compared with sterling. Goods which had been sold in West Germany for DM3.11 will now cost DM5. On the other hand, West German goods sold in the United Kingdom will be cheaper and more competitive with home-produced goods.

Inflation can have the same effect of making British goods more expensive abroad. If we assume that the price of British goods doubles as the result of inflation, the exchange rate stays the same and West Germany experiences no inflation, then the real price of British goods being sold on the West German market will double. The prices of West German producers will be more competitive.

In theory, the fact that British goods are less competitive in international markets should shift the demand curve for sterling to the left and lead to a fall in the value of sterling until the effects of inflation have been wiped out. In practice, other variables come into play that stop this happening.

Inflation and movements in international currency markets are not the only things that make British-produced goods uncompetitive on world markets. Design, efficiency and service will play their part. Inflation and currency movements will always remain important.

Changes in the exchange rate and the effects of inflation will not have a uniform impact on all sectors of the British economy. When the pound is weak exporting firms may have a competitive advantage, but businesses which rely on imports for raw materials/components will find their costs rising. This may make them less competitive in both domestic and foreign markets. The final impact on an individual business may well depend upon the flexibility of its response in terms of production and marketing.

Foreign trade

In the previous section we looked at the way in which changes in the value of the exchange rate and inflation could affect the competitiveness of British business. In this section we will look at the way in which the overall trading position of a country can affect its general level of prosperity. We will also examine some of the organisations which exist to facilitate and regulate trade between countries.

The balance of payments

The balance of payments is a summary of all transactions between individuals and organisations in the United Kingdom and the rest of the world. It is compiled from information provided by participating organisations. Like the accounts of a business, the information needs to be compared over time and interpreted, in order to be of value.

The balance of payments is divided into the following sections:

1 *The balance of trade*, which is concerned with the import and export of goods (**visibles**).

2 *The balance of trade on current account*, which includes the balance of trade and invisibles – that is, income received from or paid for the selling of services (for example, tourism, banking, insurance, shipping and royalties from books, films and patents).

3 *The capital account*, which is concerned with the movement of private and government investment capital into and out of the United Kingdom.

A surplus on the balance of payments is an injection of income into the economy. When the level of economic activity is low this can lead to an increase in employment. This is known as export lead growth. If the economy is already at or approaching full employment, a surplus on foreign trade, by adding more income, can lead to demand pull inflation.

A surplus on the balance of payments also means that the demand for sterling is high in relation to available supply, and the value of the pound will rise.

An overall deficit on the balance of payments means that income has been withdrawn from the economy, which can lower the level of economic activity and weaken the pound.

The International Monetary Fund (IMF)

Trade between nations is essential in the modern world economy. It allows specialisation and larger markets with the advantages of economies of scale, and increases the range of goods and services available to the consumer. As in all free economies, not all countries are equally competitive, and a pattern has emerged in which some countries are more likely to have a surplus or a deficit on the balance of payments than others.

Faced with a consistent pattern of deficits, it is tempting for a government to try to export the unemployment thus caused by imposing duties and quotas on imported goods. This will have varying effects on the business community. Consumers might still prefer to buy imported goods regardless of the increase in price (inelastic demand) and so the benefit to home producers might be negligible. On the other hand, efficient exporters might find their overseas markets blocked by retaliatory measures of foreign governments. Unemployment might be shifted from one sector of the economy to another and, if the trend towards protectionism becomes world-wide, the world economy is likely to move into recession – that is, the overall level of world economic activity would fall and the less competitive nations would be the worst affected.

This pattern of protectionism did emerge during the 1930s and contributed to the economic problems of the time. To prevent the same thing happening after the Second World War the Bretton Woods Agreement in 1944 established the International Monetary Fund (IMF). Member countries contribute money to the fund, the precise amount depending on the importance of foreign trade to the economy of the country. Countries with a temporary balance of payments problem can draw on the fund to cover their debts and are thus enabled to go on trading. Conditions of the loan vary but usually include a requirement for the country to deflate its economy. A lowering of the level of injections or a rise in the level of withdrawals will reduce the level of economic activity and so reduce the demand for imports of both raw materials/components and finished goods. It is rather like a bank manager telling an overdrawn client to cut down his spending.

John Maynard Keynes, a British economist involved in the conference that led to the Bretton Woods Agreement, wanted a complementary system of penalties to apply to countries which were consistently in surplus, arguing that they, too, contributed to international payments problems, but this was not adopted.

The General Agreement on Tariffs and Trade (GATT)

This was established in 1947 with the aim of promoting world trade by reducing tariffs and, through negotiation, removing non-tariff barriers to trade such as quotas and subsidies.

There are a large number of organisations that co-ordinate the movement of funds between countries and contribute to research into the behaviour of international markets. The IMF and GATT have been included here because they are most likely to have a direct impact on business. Organisations such as the World Bank and the Organisation for Economic Co-operation and Development (OECD) can help expand world markets by investing in countries and, by raising the standard of living, increase the total demand for goods in the world.

The European Economic Community (EEC)

The EEC was established by the Treaty of Rome in 1957. At that time there were only six members – France, West Germany, Italy, the Netherlands, Belgium and Luxembourg – but since then the number has expanded to include the United Kingdom, Eire, Denmark, Greece, Spain and Portugal.

Political union between member states is a long-term objective of the EEC but the greatest part of its activity is commercial.

The objectives of the EEC can be stated as follows:

1   To provide a large common market by removing restrictions on trade including tariffs, quotas, subsidies and restrictions on the movement of labour and capital. The existence of this market would provide the incentive for specialisation and the growth of large-scale businesses and the benefits of economies of scale.

2   To co-ordinate national policies in agriculture, transport and industry.

3   To standardise commercial legislation regulating such things as monopoly.

By far the greatest proportion of the funds available to the EEC are absorbed by the Common Agricultural Policy (CAP), and for this reason we shall use it as an example of the way in which the EEC can affect British business.

The Common Agricultural Policy (CAP)
The CAP works to support agriculture in two main areas:

- by supporting the income of farmers through intervention in the market; and
- by improving agricultural productivity by the availability of improvement grants.

Target prices are set for a range of products including cereals, milk and beef. Should the market price start to fall below these target prices CAP buys up the surplus and stores it against future scarcity. At the same time European prices are protected against the effect of low world prices by the imposition of import levies which raise the price of imported foods to slightly above the target price.

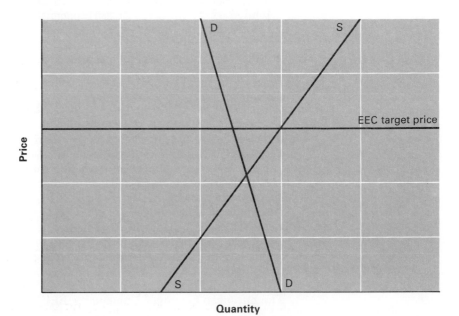

Figure 13.3 Maintenance of price levels in the EEC

If you study Figure 13.3 you can see that CAP imposes a minimum price on agricultural products. This leads to an excess of supply over demand. It is this excess which is bought up by the Community at the target price.

The stocks accumulated by CAP have given rise to 'milk lakes' and 'butter mountains', and this in turn has led to considerable criticism of the CAP for waste of resources.

The potential impact on business varies according to the type of business and the geographical area in which it operates.

1 Guaranteed prices above the level of the world market mean that farmers receive higher incomes, and this improves the general prosperity of rural areas and the businesses which serve them.

2 Improvement grants generate demand for farming equipment and so benefits businesses supplying farmers.

3 Changes in the CAP support system – for example, reducing the quotas that milk farmers are allowed to produce – can lead to changes in the product mix of farming. When this happens suddenly it can cause investment problems, particularly for the small farmer.

4 It is argued that the prices set by the CAP discourage efficiency in the farming industry. Farmers produce the crops that will give them a maximum income rather than the crops to which the land and climate are most suited.

5 CAP policy results in higher food prices. This means that people have less money to spend on other goods and services. This is particularly true of lower income groups who spend a higher proportion of their income on food than other people.

SELF-ASSESSMENT

1 Name three international organisations whose policies could have an effect on British industry.
2 State three ways in which membership of the EEC affects British business.

Economic growth

The term 'economic growth' describes a situation in which the standard of living in a society improves over time. Net investment has an important part to play in this, but there are other factors which are less easy to quantify. Trade unions, bad management, inflexible institutions, inadequate education and training have all, at one time or another, been set up as scapegoats for Britain's relatively low rate of growth compared with its international competitors. As usual, there is no easy answer.

The multiplier effect

So far we have treated the relationship between an increase in the level of injections/a decrease in the level of withdrawals as having a once-and-for-all effect on the general level of economic activity. An injection into the economy is likely to encourage further injections. Take as an example a small town with a limited range of shops designed to appeal to and serve the local community. The local economy has an unemployment level of 15 per cent. A factory is built on the edge of the town employing local labour and external capital. There is an injection into the economy. Incomes rise, business improves and local shopkeepers are persuaded to expand using hitherto unused capital. They, in turn, employ more people. Other inhabitants in the area begin to see business opportunities. A restaurant is opened, new houses are built and people offering professional services such as accountancy and law begin to move in bringing their own injections of capital with them. That initial injection might lead to double or treble its amount in terms of increased income. The ratio between the initial capital injection and the final level of income is known as the **multiplier**. So, if £1m leads to £2m increased income, the multiplier is said to be 2.

Of course, it is not as simple as that. If a man earns an extra £30 a week as a result of the expansion in the local economy, not all of that money will go back into the economy. He will save some, spend some on imported goods and some will be withdrawn by taxation. The proportion of any increase in income which will be withdrawn from the economy is known as the **marginal propensity to withdraw**. It does not take much thought to see that if everybody saved all their additional income the level of economic activity would stay the same. The final multiplier effect will therefore depend on the marginal propensity to withdraw in the economy. The multiplier can be calculated as follows:

$$\frac{1}{1-w}$$

where w = the marginal propensity to withdraw.

In a situation where a country is not competitive internationally, an increase in government spending might be siphoned out of the economy by a high marginal propensity to import.

SELF-ASSESSMENT

1 Define the multiplier effect.
2 Of every £1 in income 40p is spent on imported goods, 20p is saved and 25p is taxed. Assuming all other things remained equal, what would be the effect on national income if the government increased its expenditure by £100m?

Managing the economy

Since 1945 it has generally been accepted that the major economic objectives of government are

- the maintenance of full employment,
- the maintenance of a stable currency,
- a sound balance of payments, and
- economic growth.

Employment

Although these are the main objectives of any government the priority given to any one of them will depend on the economic environment in which the government is operating, the political philosophy of the government and the relative importance given to the achievement of an objective. The methods used to achieve these objectives will also vary according to the economic environment and economic analysis of the way in which the economy behaves.

It has already been pointed out that the term 'full employment' can be interpreted in a variety of ways, and the official level of unemployment depends on the number of people who register for work. Many people may be actively looking for work but fail to register because they may not be eligible for unemployment benefit. On the other hand, there are people registered for work who have only a limited number of jobs available to them. Whatever the level of employment for which the government is aiming, the methods used to achieve it must relate to the causes of unemployment. At any one time the number of people unemployed will be caused by a combination of the following factors.

Frictional unemployment

This describes the period of unemployment that occurs in the interval between leaving one job and finding another. Frictional unemployment can be made worse by geographical immobility. There may be an excess of vacancies over applicants in one part of the country and a reverse situation in another part of the country. Lack of information can also worsen the problem. Governments can help reduce frictional unemployment by improving information about job vacancies through the Careers Service and Job Centres, by giving people financial incentives to move from one part of the country to another and by re-training schemes. Successful government policies to combat frictional unemployment can reduce recruitment costs of business, reduce training costs and limit loss of production through recruitment problems.

Structural unemployment

This describes unemployment which arises out of a change in the industrial structure of the country – the decline in importance of an industry, for example. Steel, shipbuilding and textiles have all declined in importance over the past thirty years in the British economy. When the decline is relatively slow the unemployment caused may be described as frictional. Rapid decline and a lack of other job opportunities can contribute to **regional unemployment**, a situation in which one part of the country has consistently higher levels of unemployment than the national average. Regional and structural unemployment are not synonymous – there may be political and geographical considerations contributing to regional unemployment in addition to the decline of industries – but there is a high level of correlation between the two.

Government (including local government) may attempt to combat structural unemployment by giving grants, low interest loans, and exemption from rates to businesses establishing themselves in areas with a high level of structural unemployment and by making regulations to discourage or forbid industries from establishing themselves in areas with an excess of vacancies over applicants. Such policy measures can reduce the costs of the businesses concerned but also increase their costs if the desired locations are too far from the market and the transport system is inadequate. An important part of policy, then, is to improve the infrastructure of the region concerned.

For example, a multi-national company supplying the car industry with equipment was refused permission to open a factory in the Midlands in the early 1960s. Instead, it was offered an attractive financial package to locate in the North-east, Merseyside, Scotland or Northern Ireland. Merseyside at that time had the largest concentration of car factories in the country outside the Midlands. The closure of another factory had released for employment people with similar skills to those required by the new firm, which in turn reduced training costs. The existence of the port and rapid access to the national motorway network decided the matter as far as the company was concerned.

Some people argue that incentive packages to industry to locate or relocate in depressed areas are exploited by 'foot-loose' industries.

When the decline of an industry is attributed to foreign competition a government may respond by imposing import duties or quotas, but this may lead to retaliation, which is likely to be aimed at strong exporting industries of the country rather than the declining industry. Further international complications come from membership of GATT.

Technological unemployment

This can be the result of a switch on the part of a company to capital-intensive methods of production. This may be done to avoid high labour costs, improve quality or avoid industrial disputes, or it may be the result of a radical change in the type of technology used by a society. The remedies for technological unemployment centre on re-training schemes, particularly in the latter case, where businesses may be short of the required skills. It may also involve changes in educational policy, with implications for businesses that supply this sector of the economy. It is unlikely that a major change in technology would be on a national level only; it may be taking place in response to international trends, and the need to remain competitive can be a driving force in government support in this matter.

Cyclical unemployment

This derives its name from an observed tendency in industrialised economies to experience successive booms and slumps in the level of economic activity, which is known as the **trade cycle**. Theories to explain this phenomenon are still being developed. They can be summarised as those theories which emphasise the importance of the total demand for goods and services in an economy – **demand-deficient** unemployment – and those which emphasise the importance of *supply*.

Keynes, in his *General Theory of Employment, Interest, and Money*, published in 1936, gave added impetus to the demand-deficient theories. He summarised, synthesised and added to the work of previous economists to suggest that unemployment was the result of a low level of demand and, in a situation where private enterprise was unable or unwilling to make good this gap, it was the responsibility of governments to do so. After the Second World War Keynesian economic theory was applied by governments, and a number of standard economic policies were developed:

- Increased government expenditure on labour-intensive industries and occupations, such as civil engineering, which would have the added advantage of improving the infrastructure of the economy to support business activity.

- Incentives, information and support for exporting businesses to improve the level of injections.

- Incentives to investment for all industries in the form of tax exemptions, grants and so on.

- Reduction in the level of taxation to increase the level of disposable income in households and generate demand for consumer goods and consumer durables.

Keynes was writing in the 1930s, which was a period of sustained deflation. The policies worked well immediately after the Second World War and led to a period of sustained growth in the Western economy. Towards the end of the 1950s economists were becoming concerned about the possible results of stop–go policies. Spending to maintain the level of employment led to inflation and balance of payments problems as the level of imports rose, and was followed within the space of a few years with deflationary policies to correct these problems.

This could not be seen as an ideal climate for sustained business growth. The period of boom saw an increase in orders, but there was little incentive for businesses to invest in new plant and equipment when they expected a government-inspired recession within a few years. Instead, it was argued, the tendency was for businesses to allow their order books to lengthen, the resulting backlog helping them to ride the expected recession. This did not do a great deal for the reputation and competitiveness of British industry on international and domestic markets.

Other economists, notably Milton Friedman of the University of Chicago, expressed increasing concern about the long-term effects of these policies. **Deficit budgeting** – a situation in which government expenditure exceeded revenue from taxation – meant that the gap between government spending and revenue from taxation had to be financed by borrowing. When this borrowing drew on the unused savings of the private sector the problem was relatively small. Inflation would result, but it would be minor and would tend to be wiped out as production increased. On the other hand, when government spending was financed by the creation of new money through the banking system, it had an immediate effect on the economy but the inflation generated was longer term with the problems for business that we have already discussed.

The **stagflation** – a stagnant economy in terms of growth and a rising level of unemployment combined with inflation – of the late 1970s should not have happened, according to the original Keynesian model. Inflation should only occur when the economy is reaching the level of full employment and there is competition for resources. Economic opinion swung towards monetarism, which advocated:

- the control of the money supply: ideally the supply of money in the economy should increase at the same rate as the supply of goods and services;

- increased emphasis on promoting the supply of goods and services rather than the demand for them.

This is a more sophisticated version of **Say's law** – supply creates its own demand. In the United Kingdom there was greater reliance on the working of a free market economy to promote efficiency through competitiveness and an attempt to reduce the role of government in the management of the economy.

It is too early to draw firm conclusions concerning the success or failures of these changes in economic and political attitudes. Some consequences and implications for the business community can be observed, but whether or not they will be long- or short-term trends it is impossible to say:

1 The attempts on the part of the government to control the Public Sector Borrowing Requirement (PSBR) resulted in an immediate decline in demand for those businesses which supplied the public sector.

2 An unemployment level of over 3 per cent, which some economists would argue is necessary to keep the rate of inflation low, means an inevitable reduction in the level of actual demand for goods and services compared with the potential demand.

3 The fall in the rate of inflation from 10 per cent in 1982 to less than 5 per cent in 1986 stabilised the position of businesses in management of cash flow provided the rate can be maintained. Major international competitors such as Japan and West Germany are experiencing lower rates of inflation with the consequences for British international competitiveness outlined in the section on inflation and exchange rates.

4 It is claimed that an increase in unemployment combined with legislation that limits the power of trade unions has resulted in decreased militancy and an improvement in industrial relations.

5   **Privatisation** – the transfer of ownership and control of nationalised industry from the public to the private sector and the opening to private tender of services formerly supplied by central or local government – has been pursued by the government in a belief that the introduction of market forces will improve efficiency. Critics argue that the transfer of ownership of state monopolies to the private sector will simply create private monopolies which will be less accountable for their actions. This could have important effects on businesses who use their services by reducing their power.

The general thrust of government policy between 1979 and 1986 has been the freeing of the economic system combined with policies to reduce the level of inflation as the prerequisites for economic growth and, therefore, long-term and stable growth in the level of employment. In the discussion of games theory in chapter 12 we pointed out the problems inherent in predicting the behaviour of competing groups – problems that become more difficult to control the greater the variables involved. The one thing that can be predicted with certainty about government economic policies is that they will lead to change in the business environment, the general problems of which for the individual businessman are dealt with in the next chapter.

> **SELF-ASSESSMENT**
> 1 Define 'stagflation'.
> 2 Give one example from your own knowledge of each of the types of unemployment listed above.

Inflation

Standard policies to reduce the level of inflation in an economy are directed towards the control of the money supply, a reduction in the level of injection/ a rise in the level of withdrawals and a decrease in demand. High interest rates to encourage saving also discourage investment. Increases in taxation will also reduce demand, although some people argue that it is more likely to reduce savings as consumers maintain their lifestyle at the expense of savings. As a result the overall level of withdrawals may not rise by the increased rate of taxation. Controls on hire purchase and the availability of credit may be imposed to the detriment of industries the purchase of whose goods are financed in this way.

The balance of payments

Policies designed to improve a deficit balance of payments will concentrate on improving exports by subsidies, loans and services offered by the government to private business. High interest rates will also help with this by attracting foreign capital into the country and increasing the earnings of the banking and financial services sector of the economy. When import controls can bring retaliation the reduction of the level of imports can only be achieved by reducing the general level of demand in the country – so increasing unemployment.

Conclusion

The economy is a complex system and, like all such systems, attempts to alter the way in which it works can have unforeseen consequences. This chapter has done no more than outline the way in which the economy works.

- The balance between injections and withdrawals determines the level of economic activity.

- The working of the British economy is affected by foreign economies and international organisations of which the United Kingdom is a member.

- Government policy will determine priorities of economic objectives, and this will influence the level of economic activity.

- The importance of the general state of the economy as a constraint upon the decision-making processes of individual businesses has been stressed.

Review

1 A government wishes to raise the level of activity within the economy. The following suggestions have been made by a political adviser:
   (i) a reduction in income tax;
   (ii) a reduction in the general level of taxation balanced by a reduction in public spending and an increase in borrowing;
   (iii) an increase in the level of import duties together with quotas on imported foreign goods;
   (iv) tax allowances against all investment projects in industry;
   (v) the abolition of national insurance contributions;
   (vi) an increase in training schemes such as YTS combined with generous allowances to persuade people to start their own businesses.
   (a) For each of the above options state what additional information you would require before you could judge whether or not it was valid.
   (b) For each of the above options state the potential effects on British industry.

2 Outline the possible effects of each of the following on a business producing consumer goods and a business producing goods for an industrial market:
   (i) a fall in the value of sterling;
   (ii) an increase in interest rates;
   (iii) rapid fluctuations in the level of interest rates;
   (iv) a rapid change in the technology used by industry;
   (v) a rise in the general level of unemployment;
   (vi) an increase in the average wage rate of 3 per cent combined with an inflation rate of 5 per cent.

3 Agricultural support policies are increasingly coming under attack. Developed countries are using a variety of measures to protect domestic agriculture:
   (i) the imposition of a minimum price and a guarantee that the government will buy surplus produce at this price;
   (ii) quota systems under which farmers are granted permission to produce a limited quantity of a crop;
   (iii) payments made to farmers to make up the difference between the market price and the guaranteed price for the crops; and
   (iv) controls on the resources that can be used in farming – for example, limiting the amount of land that can be cultivated.
   These domestic policies usually result in higher food prices for the consumer. In order to limit competition from developing countries which often have cost advantages in production, they are accompanied by trade policies which impose tariffs and quotas on imported produce and, when support policies result in a surplus, subsidised exports.
   The economic effects of these policies can be divided into four separate areas:

(i)   income is redistributed from urban, industrial consumers to the rural economy;

(ii) high food prices encourage farmers to produce more and so use a greater proportion of national resources than they would otherwise have done;

(iii) high food prices are in competition with other consumer goods; and

(iv) developing countries face a falling demand for their agricultural products.

The following extract is adapted from the article 'Agricultural Protection in Industrialised Countries' published in the *Economic Progress Report* (September–October 1986).

A study carried out by the World Bank constructed a model of supply and demand for grains, livestock products and sugar (which accounted for about three-quarters of world agricultural trade in 1980–82) across all major countries or country groups. The model was used to quantify the effects of agricultural protection (both domestic and trade policies) by comparing the current system of protection with more liberal regimes.

As with any results based on a model of this kind, the exact estimates of the effects of protection should not be regarded as precise. Also the consequences for the agricultural sectors, which account for a significant proportion of economic activity and employment in industrialised countries, and the consequent dynamic effects, are not spelled out in detail. Nevertheless the results are striking. They indicate that the liberalisation of agricultural protection would generate a marked shift in agricultural output away from industrialised countries and towards developing countries, as well as causing a net increase in world food prices. There would be a marked transfer of income away from farmers in industrialised countries, but this would be more than offset by gains to consumers and taxpayers as a result of overall gains in economic efficiency. . . . If developing countries liberalised their agricultural sectors at the same time as industrialised countries, both groups of countries would be better off. Only the centrally planned economies, who are the main beneficiaries from current policies, would lose. Overall, the world economy would gain in terms of economic efficiency to the tune of over $40 billion.

(a) Explain, using diagrams where appropriate, the effects of agricultural support policies on market price and quantities produced.

(b) Outline the arguments a government of an industrialised country might use to justify agricultural subsidies.

(c) Explain how the liberalisation of agricultural trade might help producers in the secondary and tertiary sectors of the economy. Are there any subgroups in these sectors who might suffer as a result of liberalisation?

(d) You are a livestock hill farmer (both conditions qualify for subsidy). Discuss the marketing and production strategies you might consider in the event of liberalisation. The discussion should be in general terms of marketing and production principles.

4   The following passage is adapted from 'Business Brief' (*The Economist*, 29 October 1983). Read the passage carefully and answer the questions which follow.

The recent decision of Nissan's chairman to drop his opposition to building cars in Britain means that a formal announcement of the controversial investment is only weeks away. Arriving at that decision took three years of indecision. This was caused by anxieties over:

1. The duration of the recession in the United Kingdom economy.

2. The amount of UK manufactured components to be used in Nissan's cars.

3. Whether or not Britain would continue to be a member of the Common Market.

4. The number of unions Nissan would have to deal with. It would prefer to work with only one negotiating body.

N.B. Nissan is a multi-national company.
(a) Define the term 'multi-national company'.   (2)
(b) State and explain
    (i) *two* reasons why a multi-national might be welcomed by the host country;
    (ii) *two* reasons why a country might be suspicious of a multi-national's wish to invest in it.   (8)
(c) Explain why the four anxieties of Nissan listed in the passage made the company reluctant to invest in the UK.   (15)   1985 (AEB)

Activities

1   Interview two farmers. One produces subsidised/controlled goods. The other is in an unregulated sector of the agricultural economy. From the results of the interview comment on the effects of agricultural support policies on business planning.

2   Investigate the impact of a rising/falling level of unemployment on the recruitment procedures of a business.

3   Select a trend in the national economy which is widely reported in the press. Collect as much evidence as possible concerning the effect of this trend on the business community. Your evidence may be from primary sources – for example, by interview with local businessmen/consumers – or from secondary sources. Analyse the information, paying particular attention to the diversity of response. In what ways and why does your analysis differ from that of an economist?

Suggested projects

1   A study of the impact of rising local unemployment on the business community of a small town.

2   The effects of government regional policy on local small business opportunities.

Essays

1   Comment on the impact of rising unemployment and inflation on a manufacturer of consumer goods.

2   Outline and discuss the effects of changes in the value of sterling on manufacturing industry.

3   A government has the control of inflation as a priority in its economic policy. Comment on the effect on the business community of the measures it might take in order to achieve this objective.

4   Representatives of an industry have been successful in persuading the government that the industry is in need of protection from foreign competition. What measures might the government employ to provide the protection? What possible effects could these have on an individual business within the industry (a) in the short term and (b) in the long term?

5 'We will reduce the level of direct taxation and so increase the incentive to work.' (Prime Minister: the General Election, 1983) Do you think such a policy would achieve its objectives?   (25)   1985 (CLES)

6 (a) 'Marketing managers need to know about elasticity.' Why?   (10)
   (b) If the Bank of England introduced a tighter monetary policy, what, in your opinion, would be the consequences of this for a firm producing video machines?   (15)   1985 (CLES)

7 What would be the consequences, for industry, of the Chancellor of the Exchequer increasing the rates of expenditure taxes?   (25)   1985 (CLES)

8 The Government is proposing to introduce further credit restrictions.
   (a) How might this policy be implemented?   (5)
   (b) What effect would you expect these measures to have on:
       (i) the motor car industry;   (5)
       (ii) builders' merchants supplying the do-it-yourself trade;   (5)
       (iii) the overall level of economic activity?   (10)   1986 (CLES)

Chapter 14 **Business and society**

The social system of each country is unique. At any one time it is the result of the interaction over the years of ideas and ideals and their translation into actions by people and by organisations and institutions. The social system also interacts with the ecological system of a country. In a developed economy with the greater proportion of its population living in urban areas this may not be so obvious. Societies which depend on hunting or agriculture have a social organisation that can be seen to relate to the needs generated by the land, the type of crops they can grow or the animals they can rear. A nomadic tribe following the herds of a particular animal is probably the most obvious example of this. In urban areas lifestyles, attitudes and group relationships might be affected by the way in which the working day is organised. It can also affect and be affected by patterns of authority and responsibility, the evidence of conflict and the strength of existing institutions.

It is not the purpose of a book on business studies to look too closely at the sociological aspects of a society. Yet business is a part of that society, and the general trends which can be observed in the business world at any time will influence the behaviour of society as a whole and will, in turn, be influenced by it. In this chapter we will examine some themes that are often considered the province of sociologists, together with some institutions that have an effect on the behaviour of businesses. These are

- conflict in society;
- trade unions;
- pressure groups;
- business and change; and
- ethics and business.

Conflict in society

A system is an assembly of interrelated parts that are connected together in such a way as to achieve a stated objective. A society consists of a multiplicity of sub-systems each with their own objectives. Every person within that society will have a personal hierarchy of goals that they hope, with varying degrees of intensity, to achieve. When the objectives of individuals are different from those of the systems in which they operate we say there is conflict. The same is true of the relationship between systems.

The most dramatic result of inter-system conflict is war. Between individuals it is murder. Most conflict does not go to these extremes. It can lie hidden, show itself in anger or be ritualised through the existence of organisations. It is the existence and impact of inter-group conflict in the business environment that concerns us most.

Sources of conflict in business

Varying objectives

1 *The owner of the business* This person or group of people may have a number of objectives relating to the business itself. We listed profitability, survival,

prestige among them in chapter 2. The owner will also have personal objectives which may or may not conflict with those of the business. In a one-man business there is more likely to be a greater identification between personal and business objectives. In large organisations where shareholder numbers run into the thousands it is inevitable that the objectives of some shareholders will be at odds with those of the business.

2 *Management* Professional managers should have a primary responsibility to the profitability and survival of the business. This may bring them into conflict with shareholders, who may want larger dividends rather than the allocation of profit to the reserves. Managers are also people. Private objectives of power and prestige might lead them to advocate policies that are commercially unwise. Departmental managers can lose the overview and argue for departmental objectives even when these are at odds with those of the business.

   Where there has been insufficient emphasis on the overall objectives of the business and insufficient integration between departments, then the different departments may be working at cross purposes. In simple terms, the marketing department might launch a major advertising campaign without checking that there is sufficient production capacity to meet the expected increase in demand. Planning and budgetary systems are designed to minimise this type of conflict.

3 *The employees* Most conflict in business is seen as a difference in objectives between those who are employed and want more money or better working conditions and the managers and/or the people who employ them. In fact, this conflict reflects the conflict between managers and owners and inter-departmental conflict.

4 *Customers* Where a business wants to maximise its profits customers want to maximise their satisfaction and, if they are also other businesses, reduce their costs so that they can increase their own profitability: a conflict of interests exist.

Bad organisation
Conflict might arise out of bad organisation. A failure to create the necessary lines of communication or the framework in which teams of people with varying expertise can operate (for example, design) can mean that people are making decisions on insufficient information. This can lead to misunderstandings and overt conflict – such as attempts to allocate blame when things go wrong.

Organisational structure
Conflict may also be generated by the organisational structure. Clearly defined hierarchical structures give individuals a clear chain of command and, usually, an established pattern of career progression. A change to matrix structure, for example, could give an individual several superiors who may not agree on priorities or resource allocation. This problem may be intensified if one or several of the superiors see the ability to command obedience from the subordinate as a matter of prestige. In this situation conflict can be generated at two levels: between departments and also between the organisation's objectives and personal goals of security and promotion.

External factors
The level of conflict generated will also depend on external factors. Employer/employee conflict is likely to be more marked when the employees

are members of a powerful trade union, when there is a tradition of labour militancy in the industry as a whole, where demand for the product is declining and management responds with rationalisation of plant and manpower.

Problems of organisational conflict

Persistent conflict can lead to low productivity, low morale, poor industrial relations, excessive bureaucracy and the involvement of top management in relatively trivial decisions in order to resolve it. Conflict implies that there has been a failure to integrate the objectives of individuals with those of the business – in other words, a failure to motivate. This can lead to poor-quality goods with the expected result on the demand for the products of the firm. Inter-group conflict between management – for resources or prestige – and between shop-floor workers in demarcation disputes, is also likely to lead to lower productivity and, in the latter case, disruptive industrial action.

In Western culture there is a tendency to see all groups and individuals as being in conflict with one another. Thus conflict is seen as healthy and desirable competition; that by pursuing their own objectives individuals and groups will automatically contribute to the common good. Conflict, in this belief, leads to growth. The extreme form of this argument was put forward by Adam Smith as the *laissez-faire* system of economic organisation: a free market economy in which there is minimal government intervention.

This approach does not take into account the varying degrees of power possessed by individuals and organisations. One person may be better equipped to dominate in a system of conflict by reason of brute strength, intelligence, acquired skills or personality. There is no reason to believe that his personal objectives will contribute more to the greater good of humanity than a person with less competitive skills. In chapter 3 we examined the way in which market power might be used by a business to further its own objectives – not necessarily to the benefit of its customers.

The process of developing group cohesion may generate conflict between the group and other groups. The adoption of group identity symbols creates stereotypes that may attract hostility and aggression. This may reduce conflict levels within the group at the expense of external relations with other groups. When people have a close identity with the organisation they work for, internal sources of conflict may be ignored in order to increase the business's competitive position. Over the centuries rulers have used aggressive foreign policies to distract the attention of their subjects from problems at home. While their armies are winning battles abroad citizens are more prepared to tolerate bad domestic conditions!

> **SELF-ASSESSMENT**
>
> 1 State *two* sources of conflict within a business enterprise and indicate how they might be avoided.
> 2 For each of the sources of conflict given above state *one* problem a business might experience as a consequence.

Trade unions

Trade unions are inseparable from the business community, but they are separate organisations with distinct objectives and should therefore be seen as part of the external environment in which a business operates.

Trade unions developed as a response to the changing economic and social conditions in eighteenth- and nineteenth-century England. The increasing urbanisation of the working population, the growth in factory size and the improvements in communication provided by the railways and cheap postage created the conditions in which combinations of large numbers of workers with common objectives could be organised.

Combinations of workers in a particular trade for the purpose of protecting pay and working conditions were known as early as 1715. They were met with hostility from employers, and it was not until 1826 that combinations in protection of labour were made legal. Even after this date other laws were used against them. In 1834 a group of farm workers in Tolpuddle, Dorset, attempted to organise a union and were prosecuted for taking illegal oaths. They were sentenced to seven years' transportation to Australia, and the Tolpuddle Martyrs still provide a rallying cry for the trade-union movement and a focus for group identity.

The haphazard growth of the trade-union movement to meet changing circumstances has led to the development of several distinct types of trade union:

- *Craft unions* represent skilled and semi-skilled workers in an industrial trade. They are the oldest form of union, for it was skilled workers in the eighteenth and nineteenth centuries who had the economic power, the education and the organisational experience.

- *General unions* represent a wide range of workers, often unskilled, whose interests are not represented elsewhere – for example, the Transport and General Workers' Union. General unions developed at the end of the nineteenth century. Their use of the strike, virtually the only weapon open to them in an overcrowded labour market for unskilled labour, led to a period of opposition to the trade-union movement that showed itself in restrictive legislation and the increased use of police and the army to combat strikes.

- *Industrial unions* are restricted to the workers of one industry, although they do not necessarily represent all the workers in that industry.

- *White-collar unions* are the most recent development in the trade-union movement and reflect the increased proportion of the working population engaged in administrative and technical services. The Manufacturing, Scientific and Finance (MSF) reflects their sphere of influence in its title. Other specialised white-collar unions in the public sector are the National and Local Government Officers' Association (NALGO) and the Confederation of Health Service Employees (COHSE).

The objectives of trade unions

The general objectives of trade unions may be defined as follows:

1 the protection of terms and conditions of employment relating to wages, health and safety;

2 the protection of job security; and

3 the protection of conditions of entry – for example, formal qualifications required, the training provided, apprenticeship conditions.

The ability of a trade union to achieve these objectives depends to some extent on the number of members it possesses. Union membership provides the trade union with funds and power to fight disputes. To protect that strength it may find itself in conflict with other unions recruiting among sections of the working population that it has come to regard as its own preserve.

Employers' associations perform the same protective function for employers that trade unions do for employees. An employers' association will represent the businesses engaged in a particular range of activities, although not all employers will be members and not all industries have such an association. Professional associations – for example, the British Medical Association (BMA) – fulfil very much the same function as trade unions but it is extended to cover professional behaviour. Both in their objectives and in some of the tactics they use to achieve those objectives the professional associations have much in common with trade unions.

The existence of organisations with protective functions encourages the development of group stereotyping and the habit of hostility towards the opposing group. According to the attitudes/prejudices of any given individual, trade unions may be seen to be destructive organisations working for the good of their own members to the detriment of society at large, or employers can be seen as oppressors and exploiters of the poor. Both attitudes are extremes, but their existence to any degree is likely to lead to mistrust and work against the resolution of conflict.

The conflict of interest between employers and employees has the potential to cause considerable disruption in the workplace. In order to minimise this the relationship between the two groups is conducted within a framework of rules – that is, it is **institutionalised**. The rules will vary between industry and industry although some will be laid down by law. The process is known as **collective bargaining** and, when legal constraints are non-existent or low, as **free collective bargaining**.

In addition to being used to settle disputes covered by main union objectives, collective bargaining is also used to establish procedural systems designed to prevent the escalation of relatively minor disputes. It takes place on three levels:

1 *National advisory level* This is concerned with setting guidelines within which collective bargaining can take place. The National Advisory Council (NAC) will include representatives of the Trade Union Congress (TUC), the Confederation of British Industry (CBI) and the government. This is a consultative process, and its success or failure can depend on political factors as well as those of the business world. In a time of rapid inflation the TUC might back a voluntary incomes policy and recommend that all wage claims are kept within a given limit. How this is translated into practice will depend on the way in which the negotiators in industries conduct their negotiations and the circumstances of that industry.

2 *National participative level* It is this level of bargaining that produces the most dramatic clashes between unions and employers. Participants are national paid officials of the trade union concerned and employers/representatives of employers or the employers' association. Bargaining at national level is concerned with basic wage rates, conditions of service and employment.

3 *Local participative level* This deals with all the minor disputes including alleged infringement of procedures, unfair dismissal and matters relating to the individual members of trade unions. Productivity deals may be negotiated at local level, although whether or not they are validated is likely to be a matter for national negotiation.

Collective bargaining has the advantage of allowing employers and employees to reach agreements that are suitable to their situation rather than suffering an imposed agreement. This can be useful at local level where people are likely to have some insight into the causes of disputes and the way in which they could be avoided. It can also be argued that the fewer people involved in a bargaining process the greater the potential for effective communication and the greater the chance of resolving the dispute.

However, the conflict still exists and it can be argued that the existence of two clearly defined groups encourages rather than dissipates it. Again, the success of one or other group does not depend on the justice of their cause but more on the relative power of each group. In the next section we will take constraints on the power of trade unions as an example of this, but you should remember that the employer involved in collective bargaining will have a similar set of constraints to take into account.

Constraints on trade union power

Constraints on the power of trade unions are listed below:

1   *The market demand for labour*   When a particular skill is in short supply relative to the demand for it, then the union is in a strong bargaining position. In extreme cases workers with the skill may not feel the need for union protection because they are offered satisfactory terms without it. When demand for labour is low the power of the trade union to gain high wages is more limited.

2   *The available technology*   Technological developments have superseded a number of traditional skills and reduced the demand for others. Where the technology can offer a high level of consistent accuracy combined, possibly, with low wastage and a short payback period, it will be preferred to labour – particularly if the industry has a history of bad labour relations.

3   *The market for the finished product*   Labour as a factor of production has a demand derived from that of the finished product. Aggressive competition from abroad, product obsolescence or a poor record in quality and service can make a business/industry less competitive and reduce the demand for labour.

4   *The attitude of members*   Not all trade unions enjoy the same reputation for militancy and cohesiveness. A union whose members have shown a reluctance to engage in industrial action may be thought to be at a disadvantage when it comes to negotiations. On the other hand, if such a union were to threaten industrial action it may be thought that they must have a case.

5   *The structure of the labour market*   **Monopsony** (that is, where there is only one employer of a given type of labour) restricts union power, particularly if there are several trade unions involved in the negotiations.

6   *The skill of the leadership of both employers and employees relative to each other*   There are varying levels of skill in negotiation including the handling of public relations, the media and the projection of personality.

7   *The attitude of government*   Governments provide the framework of laws in which collective bargaining is conducted and can have considerable influence on the outcome of negotiations in nationalised industries.

8   *The cost of labour relative to other business costs*   If labour is important in the cost structure of the business, a relatively small increase in wages could lead to a large increase in costs that will have to be passed on in higher prices. If the market will bear this – that is, demand for the final product is inelastic – then the union will have greater power than if the market for the final product is elastic.

Need trade unions and business conflict?

Trade unions, the owners and the managers of a business have a common interest in ensuring the survival of the firm. The conflict is rooted in the allocation of the resources of the firm. While trade unions argue for a share for the employees, owners are arguing for higher dividends and managers may be more interested in building up the reserves to increase profits. Profit sharing and share participation schemes have been suggested as ways of tying the interests of employees more closely to those of the firm.

> **SELF-ASSESSMENT**
>
> 1 The workforce in an industry may be represented by a number of trade unions. On the other hand, a single trade union (an industrial union) might dominate the industry. Give *two* problems management might experience in each of these situations, illustrating your answer with examples.
> 2 Using the list of constraints on trade union power as a guide, outline the constraints upon management/owner power when negotiating with a trade union.

Pressure groups

A pressure group is an organisation with objectives that lie within the sphere of politics but which lacks the political power to achieve them directly. The activities of a pressure group may be solely concerned with persuading central and local government to give weight to its views in the decision-making process by direct approach to politicians, or it may combine this function with practical activities to achieve at least some of its objectives in the short term.

Trade unions, the National Society for the Prevention of Cruelty to Children (NSPCC) and the Royal Society for the Prevention of Cruelty to Animals (RSPCA) fall into the latter category. Organisations such as the Campaign for Nuclear Disarmament (CND) by the nature of their objectives tend to fall into the first category. All pressure groups devote time and resources to collecting evidence to support their case and, by influencing public opinion, attempt to put pressure on politicians through the electorate. When they are successful their aims may be adopted as policy by a political party.

Pressure groups vary in size, power and organisation. Large national or international pressure groups will have paid employees for administration and research together with acknowledged links with members of Parliament who will present their case in Parliament. At the other end of the spectrum, a group of mothers meeting informally and complaining about the difficulties of crossing a busy main road when they take their children to school might put pressure on the local authority to provide a crossing and warning signs by writing letters and staging demonstrations. In this case none of the members of the pressure group will be paid and it will cease to exist when they have achieved the limited objective. They might, of course, discover other things in their environment they object to and, encouraged by success, go on to further campaigning.

The business community can be affected by the activities of pressure groups in three ways:

- Generally, when the pressure group changes the climate of public opinion and there are changes in the law.

- Specifically, when the activities of a pressure group are directed towards a particular industry or firm. This might affect decisions such as siting or could lead to the closure of plants (for example, the opposition of ecological pressure groups to nuclear power).

- Incidentally and on a relatively small scale, when the activities of a pressure group directed against other organisations interfere with the normal running of a business. The mothers in the example given above may picket the road, causing employees to be late.

Where a business is directly affected by the activities of a pressure group it may experience the following problems:

1 The public image of the business will be affected. This may lead to difficulties in recruitment and possibly reduce the demand for products. A sustained publicity campaign about the dangers to health and safety of an industry's production processes can result in more able candidates for jobs failing to apply, which can lead to problems in selection and training. A sustained campaign against the political policies of a foreign country, combined with an appeal to boycott the products of that country, can lower the sales of retailers selling those products and force them to look for alternative suppliers. The effects may be marginal, but there is still the potential for an increase in costs. The business will also incur additional costs in improving its own public relations. Advertising to emphasise its value to the community, educational material and improved access for the public in terms of visits may have to be undertaken.

2 When the activities of a pressure group are directed against a specific business and the tactics of the group include the use of legal procedures this will involve the business in legal costs in the employment of solicitors and barristers.

3 In confrontations arising out of production processes (for example, pollution complaints), the business may have to rethink its production methods and purchase new equipment in order to minimise the harm done, with a resultant increase in costs.

4 The activities of a pressure group may also lead to industrial unrest within a business. The trade unions concerned may begin to question working practices, health and safety procedures and compensation for industrial injury or disease.

We have already seen that the degree of success achieved by a trade union or business enterprise engaged in an industrial dispute will depend upon the relative power of the parties concerned. The success or failure of a pressure group also depends on the internal and external constraints on its situation.

- The size, organisation and expertise of the pressure group will affect the outcome. A multi-national company with extensive resources would be a formidable opponent for a small group of ratepayers attempting to protect the amenities of their town from a bad siting decision.

- The general economic environment of the area can also influence the success or failure of a pressure group. In an area of high unemployment the maintenance of a wild-life environment is likely to be seen as less important than the jobs that a factory built on that site would create.

- The existing public image of the pressure group will also influence the outcome. Where the pressure group is perceived as being extremist, public sympathy for the campaign is likely to be low and the impact reduced. When a pressure group has a reputation for exposing dangerous or undesirable practices public opinion is more likely to be sympathetic.

Trade unions and pressure groups have been selected as examples of organisations whose objectives can appear to be in direct conflict with those of business. Other organisations can also be in conflict with business, but their impact is less obvious and less sustained. In chapters 10 and 11 we saw the ways in which a business can attempt to integrate the personal goals of its employees with those of the business through a variety of motivational techniques. When this strategy is successful it is likely that the business is satisfying many of the objectives of the trade-union movement, and conflict with trade unions will be reduced, if not eliminated, for long periods of time. Collective bargaining and negotiation between dissenting parties in society cannot resolve all conflicts. When both parties are convinced that they are right or one party refuses to concede to the rights of others, then a system for resolving conflicts must be established.

SELF-ASSESSMENT

1 Define a pressure group and give *five* examples of pressure groups with different interests which might affect a business enterprise.
2 Outline, with examples, three constraints upon the ability of pressure groups to achieve their objective and the corresponding ability of owners/managers to resist them.

The resolution of conflict

The oldest method of resolving conflict in society is by drawing up a set of rules governing the relationships between individuals, organisations and the state by which all citizens must abide. These rules constitute the law of the country. Not all infringements of the law are clear-cut and not all are admitted to. The administration of the law is concerned with deciding who carries the responsibility for a particular action or set of actions. This is done through a system of courts, each of which has limitations on its authority, and the decision of each can be appealed against in a higher court – that is, one which carries more authority. The final Court of Appeal is the House of Lords in all matters of dispute.

The body of law in the United Kingdom is divided into **civil law** and **criminal law**. Civil law is concerned with the **law of contracts and torts** (that is, **wrongs,** such as negligence). Civil law courts settle disputes and award compensation in financial terms for the offence. Criminal law concerns offences which are considered so detrimental to society that the rules are enforced by the state and a code of punishment drawn up for proven offenders. Adulterated food might be a matter for civil law if the adulteration was the result of negligence, but it might be a matter for criminal law if it occurred as the result of deliberate activities on the part of the business.

Every area of business activity is governed to some extent by the law. The law of contracts is implicit in all buying and selling, including the hiring of labour.

The use of the law courts to settle disputes can be a long and expensive process. To overcome these problems and still enjoy the advantages of impartial, objective decisions, a system of arbitration and tribunals has developed.

Arbitration

Provision for arbitration can be the result of a written agreement between the parties concerned (such as in a deed of partnership). Such cases are governed by the Arbitration Acts of 1950 and 1975. On the other hand, provision may be established by Act of Parliament – for example, by the Advisory, Conciliation and Arbitration Service (ACAS), which was established by the Employment Protection Act 1975. Where arbitration agreements exist they must be adhered to before the parties concerned can use the courts to settle the dispute.

Arbitration has the following advantages:

1   It is relatively cheap and quick compared with the use of the courts. The speed with which arbitration takes place can also save money, apart from legal costs, because normal trading can be resumed sooner.

2   The arbitrator is selected with the consent of both parties and can be somebody with experience and understanding of the problems of that branch of business.

3   Arbitration hearings can take place in private rather than in an open court.

Once an agreement has been reached under arbitration it is considered valid and binding on the parties who agreed to arbitration, provided that it is reasonable, within the scope of the original arbitration agreement and has taken into account every matter referred to it. When a party is dissatisfied with an arbitration agreement it can appeal to the High Court on points of law. Failure of one or other party to comply with an arbitration award can lead to legal action for breach of contract.

The structure of ACAS is as follows. Its chairman is assisted by a board of nine members to which the Secretary of State for Employment, the CBI and the TUC each nominate three people. It has a staff of civil servants with experience in industrial relations who operate eight regional offices offering conciliation and arbitration services throughout the country.

The services of ACAS include:

• conciliation in industrial disputes when invited;

• conciliation between employers and trade unions or individual employees concerning alleged infringements of legislation (such as unfair dismissal);

• advice on procedures and practices relating to personnel and collective bargaining in the form of Codes of Practice;

• the reference of an industrial dispute, with the consent of all the parties concerned, to the Central Arbitration Committee.

• nomination of members to the Central Arbitration Committee.

The Central Arbitration Committee can also be specified as the final stage in a voluntary agreement between trade unions and employers concerning the procedures for conducting an industrial dispute.

Industrial tribunals

Industrial tribunals consisting of a chairman who is a qualified lawyer and two members sit in most parts of the country and have permanent offices in cities. The tribunals are appointed by the government – the chairman by the Lord Chancellor and the other two members by the Department of Employment. They are concerned with alleged infringements of the law under such Acts as the Equal Pay Act 1970. Any legal queries arising out of their judgement can be referred to the Employment Appeals Tribunal.

SELF-ASSESSMENT

1 You have suffered a prolonged illness as the result of eating contaminated food. There is evidence to suggest that the contamination was the consequence of poor quality control in the business concerned. Assuming the business refused compensation should you seek redress through criminal or civil law.
2 Arbitration and conciliation are technical terms used in the field of industrial relations. From your experience give *one* non-business example of each of the terms.

Business and change

Change from external causes

The social system is not static but is constantly changing. The time scale of the change will vary from society to society and will depend on the following factors:

1 The nature of society and the receptiveness of its members to change will depend on a large number of interconnecting factors, some of which are extremely difficult to prove. A population weighted towards the younger age groups will, it is sometimes argued, be more receptive to change than a society with an ageing population. If change is seen as disturbing a comfortable way of life or carrying with it too great a risk of failure, then it will not be accepted.

2 The institutions of a society may also discourage change. Institutions develop to meet a set of circumstances. When society begins to change the patterns of behaviour of institutions may slow down the change.

3 Rapid change in society will accelerate change. The rapid growth of population in the eighteenth and early nineteenth centuries meant that the social institutions of the United Kingdom were totally inadequate to cope with the new circumstances. The period saw the rise of 'self-help' organisations such as trade unions and building societies, and a radical change in political institutions.

4 The speed and efficiency of communications will affect ideas and make people more receptive to change.

5 The attitude of governments will affect the rate of change. If social organisation suits the governing class then they have a vested interest in preserving the status quo by law or by force. The converse of this is revolutionary change when a government takes power that sees the status quo as positively harmful.

Business as part of society must change with society, otherwise it runs the risk of becoming irrelevant and dying. This can be seen as *voluntary* change. The business perceives change in society as a problem and meets it with its normal decision-making process. Businesses may also instigate change in order to achieve their own objectives.

There is also an involuntary element in business change. A business is run by people, with people and for people. As the attitudes and ethics of people change so also will the nature of the business. Although the process might be almost imperceptible, nevertheless it will be there.

To summarise, a business will experience change in the following ways:

- *Personnel*   As employees leave a business and others are recruited, there will be changes in experience, attitudes and objectives of the remaining employees, which in turn will be reflected in the working groups of which they are members. The more senior the individuals concerned and the greater the authority and responsibility they carry the greater the potential for change.

- *Technology*   A change in technology may lead to changes in production methods, products and the organisation of the business. This will have implications for the recruitment, selection and training policies of the business as well as for marketing and production policies.

- *Demand*   A change in tastes and preferences can affect the production department but may also require the business to re-examine its marketing methods and distribution policies.

- *Government*   A change in government policies may have far-reaching effects on a business. The introduction of the YTS has changed recruitment and training policies. Government economic policy may have consequences for the financial and investment policies of the business.

- *The economic environment*   We have already seen the ways in which persistent inflation can affect a business. Recession can lead to changes in debt management and internal reorganisation. The business will react to changes in interest rates and demand with changes in production and marketing strategies.

Internal change

So far we have considered change as something which is forced on a business as the result of changes in the environment in which it operates. These changes have come about because of a large number of individual choices made by people and organisations. The implication was that the business faced with these changes must adapt to them. In doing so the business will need to make decisions. This internal reorganisation can be hindered by an unwillingness on the part of top management to follow through a course of action because of what they see as undesirable side effects. Delegation, for example, might be seen as giving too much potential power to the shop floor and opening management decisions to more informed criticism. The same objection might be made against an improved system of communications. Large organisations which have become too bureaucratised might be particularly resistant to change, as might the trade unions and the workforce concerned.

The need for change

The need for reorganisation can be identified in the following circumstances:

1 *Failure to respond to external change*   A decline in market share and profitability can indicate a failure in the organisation to respond to changes in the environment. The research and development of the business may not be as innovative as those of its competitors. It may be the recruitment, selection and remuneration policy which is at fault, or it could be the result of overloading research workers with administration. To quote a cynical lecturer whose administrative work had been interrupted by the need to take a class: 'If it was not for all this teaching we could get on with the job.'

2 *Conflict*   The existence of conflict within the organisation might suggest the need for new organisational structures. This is likely to indicate the need for new management structures, improved communication systems and possibly

a re-grouping of activities when two departments which need to work together are structured separately.

3 *People are working too hard* There is nothing wrong with hard work, but if a person or group of people have so much work to do that jobs are skimped or decisions made without sufficient thought then it can be a sign of poor organisation.

Successful change

Any deliberate change in the way in which people work which is seen to take place will meet with some degree of opposition. In times of high unemployment it is likely that any change will be seen as a threat to job security irrespective of management reassurance. To work with new people and in new organisational situations requires a re-learning process that may induce stress and lower efficiency. This can reduce job satisfaction as people see their efficiency falling while they are working harder as the result of imposed change. For change to be successfully undertaken with the minimum of disruption, the following conditions are necessary:

1 the full support and commitment of top management;

2 careful diagnosis of the existing problems;

3 communication of the reasons for change and a willingness to listen to the ideas and opinions of people who will experience the change, though this may bring up further problems;

4 a clear programme and timetable for change which is communicated to all personnel concerned; this programme should also include contingency plans for problems that might arise at each stage of the process of change;

5 completion of all necessary re-training before the process of change begins, in order to increase the confidence of the people concerned in a situation that invariably attacks security; and

6 establishment of systems of control and evaluation so that the process of change can respond to new problems rapidly and with minimum disruption.

SELF-ASSESSMENT

1 Give *two* instances in which change in business might be (a) voluntary and (b) involuntary.
2 Assuming a business experiences a change in technology, give *two* ways in which this will stimulate change in (a) personnel, (b) demand and (c) the social and economic environment.

Ethics and business

Ethics are a set of moral principles and values which govern the conduct of individuals and groups within a society. For the majority of people the ethics by which they conduct their life is a set of unwritten and unquestioned rules which they have acquired through the process of socialisation. They are expressed in their attitudes to a situation and in their behavioural response to situations.

It is easy to dismiss ideas as unimportant, but the pattern of ethical beliefs that the majority of people in a society subscribe to will colour their attitudes to what they see as fair and unfair behaviour and have an important influence on the political, social and economic institutions of society.

Attitudes to work

The work ethic goes further than the simple need to have a job in order to earn enough money to live. A job is seen as conferring status on an individual, providing both structure and purpose to life. Redundancy or enforced retirement can have disastrous psychological consequences for the people concerned and their families. This attitude to work has caused demarcation disputes between trade unions and organised opposition to the introduction of new technology where it is feared that this will lead to redundancies. It can also lead to overtime bans, work to rule, go slow and, in extreme cases, the sabotage of new machinery. The word 'Luddite' is often used to describe these activities after the semi-mythical Ned Ludd who was thought to lead a band of machine wreckers fighting against the introduction of power looms into the textile industry in the early nineteenth century.

How far people's attitudes to work are coloured by the status it is seen to confer and how far by the need for economic security is difficult to determine, and probably varies from individual to individual. Access to work without discrimination – for example, by women and ethnic minority groups – have a firm foundation in the need to acquire economic power and a standard of living comparable with the rest of society. It also carries with it the belief that without integration into the economic system the political and social status of these groups also suffers.

Values

The values by which people order their lives form a complex structure and hierarchy that will govern all their actions, whether they are operating in the economic, social or political sphere. These values may cover what is seen as acceptable behaviour in terms of honesty, inter-personal relationships and sexual morality, and judgements on the relative value of goods and services compared with education.

The values a society holds in general will affect such matters as the responsibility that a business is perceived to have towards its customers, shareholders, employees and the environment in which it operates. This can place external constraints on the business in its decision-making processes and thus in its allocation of resources. Pressure groups such as the Consumers' Association and Friends of the Earth can have a strong influence on the production and marketing decisions of a business subject to the limitations we have already discussed. The responsibility of a business to its shareholders may conflict directly with its responsibility to its employees. A recent suggestion that above a minimum level pay should be linked with the profits of the employing business illustrates this conflict of interest. If implemented, this would align the interests of employees more closely with those of the owners of the business. It has been suggested that carried to extremes this system would encourage existing employees to resist the expansion of employment because it would reduce their own potential earning power. For the same reason they might be against the ploughing back of profits as this would reduce present earnings for the potential benefit of future employees.

The concept of responsibility is inherent in any decision-making process. A decision to follow one course of action carries with it the sacrifice of another course of action (opportunity cost) and this in turn implies that a course of action which is of benefit to one section of the community may injure another section of the community.

Responsibility carries with it the idea of accountability. In chapter 6 we gave a rigid definition of this idea in providing a true and fair account of the way in which a business had used the funds entrusted to it in a given time period. Throughout the book we have implied that a business is accountable under law for a wide range of activities which affect the individuals and groups to which it may be held responsible. There is also the additional dimension of ethical and moral responsibility for those activities which are not subject to law. In the short term a business may refuse to accept these responsibilities and refuse to see itself as accountable. However, a long-term change in the ethics and values of a society is likely to be reflected in a change in the ethics and values of the personnel. Commercial considerations might also force them to conform and changes in the law might formalise their accountability.

SELF-ASSESSMENT

1 Give *two* instances in which social values might influence (a) the marketing decisions of a business and (b) the production decisions.
2 Give *two* instances in which the values of an individual will colour their response to (a) a marketing problem and (b) a change in production technology.

Conclusion

This chapter is entitled 'Business and society', and there is a certain arrogance in that title because it is impossible in a few thousand words to explore the intricacies of the relationship between the business community and society as a whole. The chapter has argued that:

1 Conflict exists in society at all levels, and this is reflected in the experience of business. Conflict arises out of differing objectives, and the integration of objectives is important in the elimination of internal conflict.

2 Organisations such as trade unions and pressure groups form part of the environment of conflict in which a business operates, and the relative power of both is limited by internal and external constraints.

3 The framework of law provides an external system for the resolution of conflict that cannot be resolved by other methods.

4 The whole is influenced by the abstract concepts of ethics and values which are so much part of an individual's personality that it is difficult to form objective conclusions at any moment in time. A failure to appreciate what society or his peer group accepts as reasonable behaviour has ruined the career of many a man.

Review

1 In the case studies at the end of chapter 4 we met Joseph Baines and his wife, who were planning to start a nursery. Their plans collapsed when the Highways Department of the local authority recommended that the Planning Sub-committee of the council should reject the submission for change of use of the building. The reason given was the possible increase in traffic on a side road giving access to a main road. Joseph Baines submitted his own evidence that the road on which the nursery was to be situated was not, in itself, busy in the mornings and evenings, mainly because access for cars to the main road was so difficult. This evidence was not judged to be adequate.

With planning permission turned down the Baineses began to look for alternative accommodation. This was not easy. Buildings that were suitable carried with them the same disadvantages as the existing site, and many had the possible additional disadvantage that there might be objections from neighbours to the change of use. A standard form was issued to all ratepayers by the local authority asking if they had any objection to the change of use of the building. Eventually the Baineses found an under-used squash court. It was a relatively modern building, but the owner was about to close it because the revenue it generated did not cover the cost of upkeep. There was ample parking space, but unfortunately access was to the same road that had caused the original planning submission to be rejected. The Baineses negotiated a price for the building and for the conversion work subject to planning permission. In the meantime they had discovered a further complication and were not sure whether or not it would work to their advantage. The buildings were in the jurisdiction of one local authority but the road was in the jurisdiction of another. Which one would have the right of veto?

The latest information on the Baines nursery is a recommendation from the Local Authority Planning Committee that they should be given permission for their squash court project.

(a) In this chapter it was pointed out that a code of laws could prevent conflict arising and might help in the resolution of existing conflict. On the basis of this, justify the existence of planning regulations (i) in relation to the Baines nursery, and (ii) in relation to other business activities.

(b) In the role of adviser to the Baineses prepare a statement for the Planning Sub-committee outlining the advantages of the enterprise to the community.

(c) Consider the possible costs to the Baineses of the rejection of their planning application. What were the costs to the community?

2   A company has acquired a number of acres of land in a rural area. They have reason to believe the land has a quantity of a mineral which they intend to mine, using open-cast methods. The area is not part of a national park nor has it been designated as an area of outstanding natural beauty. The company does not expect to experience any difficulty in obtaining permission for its mining operations and has given a firm promise to the local authority that, apart from key technical personnel, all recruitment would be done in the area.

The scheme ran into opposition from two distinct groups: naturalists who claimed that the area in question was an important wild-life habitat supporting several rare species of birds and mammals; and residents who had settled in the villages of the region, many of whom commuted to a large industrial town 30 miles distant and had elected to live in the country in order to improve the quality of life.

(a) Outline the conflict of interests inherent in the above situation.

(b) State some of the ways in which the decisions of the business concerned might affect the community in which it is located.

(c) As a representative of the business, prepare a list of the arguments you might use in an attempt to reconcile the opposing groups to the mining operation.

(d) As a leader of one of the opposition groups, outline a plan of action to prevent the business from starting mining operations.

(e) What other factors might affect the eventual outcome?

3   Mrs Johnson had been employed by a large company for a period of ten years. An active trade unionist, Mrs Johnson was aware that she was regarded by certain members of the management as a trouble-maker: she had successfully led an equal-pay-for-equal-work campaign within the factory. As part of a reorganisation exercise the company decided to reduce its

workforce. Mrs Johnson was informed verbally that her employment would be terminated at the end of the following week. She was the only worker in her section to have her employment terminated at that time.

(a) Mrs Johnson considered she had been unfairly dismissed. What grounds had she for this belief and what procedures should she follow?

(b) In what ways might Mrs Johnson's union help her in this matter?

(c) Apart from legal considerations, what other factors might determine the outcome of Mrs Johnson's case?

Activities

1 Follow the progress of an industrial dispute. In addition to the causes of the dispute you should also take note of the way in which it is conducted, the tactics used, the interplay of personalities among the negotiators, the political considerations, the morale of the workforce, effects on the community and short- and long-term results. At the time of writing the 1984–85 miners' strike and the teachers' industrial action are suitable cases for study.

2 Study the impact of a large company on the community life of a town.

3 Select a business activity which would require planning permission – for example, the construction of a factory on a given site. Do not choose an industrial estate. Investigate the procedures you would have to go through in order to receive permission. Interview local government officials and residents to discover their views on the matter. Analyse the results of your survey and prepare a report on the likely success or failure of the project, giving reasons for your conclusions.

Suggested projects

1 An evaluation of employee attitudes to technical change in Company X.

2 What are the effects of legislation on the operations of Enterprise Y? (A small business would be suitable for this project.)

Essays

1 A merger is proposed between two businesses of approximately the same size and producing complementary products. What conflicts may emerge from this situation and how might they be resolved?

2 To what extent can the legal constraints on business activity be seen as counter-productive to the economy as a whole?

3 'The activities of a pressure group are a valid expression of concern by the community in which a business operates.'

'Pressure groups represent minority interests. Their activities increase costs and place unreasonable constraints on the wealth-creating sectors of society.'

Reconcile and discuss the above statements with reference to business activity.

4 Consider the statement that all business activity should be made accountable to the society in which it operates.

5 Change and conflict are inevitable accompaniments to life. Comment on the implications of this statement for business organisation.

6 To what extent should a government legislate to control business activity? 1984 (AEB)

7 The manner in which businesses develop is determined by a complex interaction of a variety of forces, both internal and external. Identify these forces and examine the ways in which they interact in the conduct of a business. 1985 (AEB)

8 Outline the obligations a business has to its employees and show how they may conflict with its obligations to other groups. 1985 (AEB)

9 Discuss all the implications arising from the introduction of computer technology throughout the administration of a long-established and traditional family business.

10 Argue the case for the reform of British trade unions. (25) 1985 (CLES)

11 You are the managing director of a firm producing telephones. The government has decided to privatise the British telecommunications industry.
(a) How might the employees of your firm view the decision? (5)
(b) How might you view the decision, and in what way might your perception of the government's action be (i) similar to, and (ii) different from, that of your employees? (8)
(c) What short- and long-term financial and organisational issues might the government's decision present? (12) June 1985 (CLES)

12 As leader of a union negotiating team, which has just had an initial pay claim for an 8 per cent increase in wages (3 per cent more than the current inflation rate) rejected by the Board of Directors of a cross channel ferry line, prepare a discussion document for other members of your team outlining alternative dispute procedures and their likely effectiveness. (25) 1986 (CLES)

Chapter 15   Conclusion

No body of knowledge is ever complete. It would be satisfying to claim that if you had worked your way through this book you know about business. Unfortunately, to make such a claim would not only be untrue but – worse – the less perceptive among you might believe it.

So what have you achieved? Where do you go from here?

The answer to both questions depends on how you have used the book. For people who know, or think they know, the information and techniques contained in it the answer is to get out into the world of business, talk to people who do the jobs and begin to appreciate the wide range of interpretations that can be placed on these principles. A textbook can do no more than guide you. Those of you who have already tried some of the activities suggested at the end of each chapter will already be aware of the numerous ways in which each principle can be translated into valid practice.

In business there is no right answer to a problem: the answer will depend upon the internal and external environment of that business. You should also remember that today's decisions create tomorrow's environment.

In 1984 a local authority created two middle management posts in two separate organisations. The job description was vague and the job specification was non-existent. Both posts were given the same title, the same salary structure and the same job description/specification. Three years later the two post holders met and compared notes. They agreed on the major constraints on their decision making. They gave each other ideas for solving similar problems and commented when the solutions would not be ideal for their situation and also why. The organisational structures of their jobs were very different. Faced with similar problems in differing circumstances they had found different but valid solutions!

The same principle holds true of social institutions such as marriage and the family. One of the major conflicts in life is that of a person moving away from the family circle for the first time and discovering that the values and habits of his or her family are not universally honoured.

If all businesses are unique, how do we make sense of their experiences? At the beginning of this book we attempted to do this in a formal way by looking at the experiences all businesses had in common and by classifying them according to their differences. We can extend this unification by looking at a number of themes that have recurred throughout the main body of the text. Sometimes these themes have been referred to explicitly; sometimes their importance is implicit in the text.

Planning

To plan is to establish future objectives based on present knowledge. We have discussed the business plan in chapter 4 and the plans that are drawn up within the separate business functions in Part II. Planning, whether formal or informal, is a basic human activity. Individuals make plans all the time. They draw up career plans and plans for improving their social lives. They submit plans – that is, outlines of their objectives and the way in which they intend to achieve them – to the planning department of a local authority when they want to build or alter their homes.

All human activity can be seen as the process of making plans. Very few people live entirely in the present and, as soon as a person begins to set goals, he or she is planning.

If individuals and organisations establish objectives then they must make decisions as to the way in which they intend to attain those objectives. A course of action must be chosen, and this implies that other courses of action are rejected. A sacrifice must be made to which we give the name 'opportunity cost'.

If people and organisations are planning in order to achieve their own objectives then it is more than likely that the course of action they select will conflict with the plans of others. We explored this theme in chapters 10 and 14. It is inherent in all business decisions.

Another important aspect of planning is its on-going nature. Short-term planning objectives may be realised in a matter of minutes, hours or days. When objectives are not expected to be achieved for a longer period of time, it is necessary to check to see that the plan is on course. This checking process is known as 'control'. The information gained might be used simply to correct decisions so that the original objectives will be reached. Where the information suggests that the original objectives are no longer feasible the information may be used to set new objectives.

The scale of business enterprise

The size of a business may be dictated by the market in which it operates, the technology used, the finance available to it, the age of the business and the objectives of its owners and/or managers. A small business may compete successfully in a market dominated by large organisations if it can find a niche in that market to exploit. This, in turn, may limit its capacity for growth. Tolerated while it restricts its activities to one sector of the market, it may find the market power of the dominant firms too great to challenge in other sectors.

Praise of small businesses is fashionable at the moment. Compared with larger businesses they require a relatively small amount of start-up capital, they are more amenable to change, communications and human relations can be improved more easily and there is less chance of destructive conflict building up. On the other hand, they can often find it more difficult to raise finance, the managers may lack specific areas of expertise and, more important, may not appreciate this deficiency and fail to employ specialist firms to supply it. Unless the optimum size of that type of business happens to be small they will not benefit from economies of scale.

Of course, this is theory. If you have been observing businesses as part of your course and analysing the response of owners and managers to situations, you will know that the individual response to the matter of size will vary greatly according to the individual circumstances of the business.

Business *accountability* is another recurring theme. Individuals are held accountable for their actions. Friends and family can bring social pressures to bear upon them. In extreme cases they have to answer in law. Businesses are also accountable in law. The greater their potential impact on society the greater the number of legal constraints within which they have to operate. Pressure groups formalise social opinion and force a business to conform. Accountability will influence or constrain all business decisions.

Chapters 5 and 6 introduced the theme of *control*. All business decisions must be checked to ensure that support the objectives of the business, their effects must be tested and the information on which they are made should be verified. These activities are undertaken within the organisational framework of the business so that its activities are regulated. Control systems are essential if a business is to be accountable.

The way in which a business develops depends upon the interaction of a wide range of influences and circumstances it encounters from the moment of its launch. Like individuals, businesses develop characters of their own. The personality of the original founder may establish behaviour patterns in such things as leadership style, industrial relations and the long-term objectives of the business which may affect the long-term plans of the business years after the founder has moved out of active management. Managers will be selected on their 'fit' to this unspoken ethos of the business.

External influences are also likely to mould the character of a business. Some businesses will react cautiously to changes in the market, the economy and the law. Others will be more adventurous. Different businesses will react in different ways to changes in society and the political environment in which they operate. Some will survive, some will not. All will change, subtly or radically, to meet the changing circumstances. It is this very diversity of business activity which makes business studies so fascinating.

The question posed at the beginning of this chapter might be answered as follows: You have acquired a very basic body of knowledge that will enable you to analyse the business environment. In addition you are aware of the complexity of the subject and the important role business plays in society.

Review

The following case study and questions formed Paper 3 of the Business Studies examination set by University of Cambridge Local Examination Syndicate, June 1986.

WOOD LTD

Wood Ltd is a company run by Mr Wood, supplying garden products and plants to the trade. Originally, the company sold a limited range of plants and fertilisers. Recently, it has expanded these areas and entered the garden furniture market. The company's products are now split into three departments: garden furniture, plants and fertilisers. They are fairly labour intensive and some of their products are imported, particularly bulbs and pot plants from Holland. During the early 1980s, as income rose with inflation, more people turned to gardening as a hobby. The company succeeded in increasing sales volume by raising prices at just below the inflation rate. Economies of scale enabled them to improve their *return on assets*. However, their fortunes have become more varied. They face stiff competition from overseas, particularly in the pot plant market where cheap imports from the continent are cutting into their traditional markets. The situation has not been helped by the recession and high interest rates which have affected both consumers' *disposable income* and the company's *interest cover*, both of which have fallen. At the same time, imports have become more competitive and this has had a considerable impact on sales. Wood Ltd also faces growing competition from the large garden centre chains and specialist nurseries. Profit margins are falling and this is reducing the funds that the business can generate for expansion and further investment.

There has been pressure for higher wages from the staff who are paid less than comparable employees in the same geographical area. There has been a considerable turnover of staff, and recruiting sufficiently skilled people is proving both time-consuming and costly. The garden furniture department faces a particular problem, since frequent design changes in response to changing tastes have meant that production problems often occur. In addition, too much time is taken in recruiting and training new people and in training the existing staff in new methods. Mr Wood has been aware for some time that there are only limited opportunities for further mechanisation and that it would not be possible to reduce staff significantly. However, he needed to improve the efficiency of his staff by increasing sales turnover without taking on more people. Mr Wood thought that there was sufficient under-employment in the labour force for greater output, if he could buy more land or alter the product mix and improve productivity.

The current system of distribution used by the company is through wholesalers, garden centres and buying offices for multiples with gardening departments. Small retailers buy from the wholesalers but the company now deals directly with some of the local garden centres. Margins vary according to the type of buyer. Usually, wholesalers add a 50 per cent mark-up on the prices charged by Wood Ltd, while retailers add another 30 per cent to that figure. Buying offices for multiples and direct sales to garden centres add a 60 per cent mark-up to Wood Ltd's ex-works price lists.

Departments are organised on a product basis, each responsible for making profits. Some of the functions such as selling and administration are handled centrally and these costs are allocated to each of the departments on a percentage of sales basis. The cost figures for 1985 are shown in Appendix 1. For ease of interpretation, the company has calculated unit prices and costs at an average for each department. Profitability was down in 1985 and Mr Wood is considering what he can do to improve it. He has decided to discuss the figures with each department and see what options are open to him. He was wondering how to balance the risks of further diversification against concentrating on the areas where the company had a distinctive competence.

PLANT DEPARTMENT: Mr Andrews has run the plant department for many years and is reasonably satisfied with its performance during 1985. He is aware that there have been some shortages of particular plants, but client contact is good and the quality of the plants and bulbs he is selling is appreciated by the buyers. He has managed to build up considerable loyalty amongst the buyers because of the prompt and efficient service and the quality of the plants sold. Inevitably, business is seasonal, with major deliveries taking place in the spring and summer. The seasonal nature of demand means that the workforce has to be flexible. When not involved in getting the plants ready for delivery they are preparing the ground and planting. In this way the workload is spread fairly evenly throughout the year. At Christmas, they have diversified into the sale of pot plants, largely imported, although some were grown under glass by the company, and Christmas trees. The experience of the last few years has shown this to be successful since the margins are high and the plants and trees do not remain in stock for long. Mr Andrews is aware that one of the reasons for the success of the plant department is that many of his customers appreciate the advantage of purchasing fertilisers and garden accessories at the same time. In this way they can deal with all their requirements together.

GARDEN FURNITURE DEPARTMENT: Recently, Mr Wood had employed Mr Turner to expand sales of garden furniture. Some of the furniture is manufactured by Wood Ltd whilst other lines are bought in from overseas suppliers. Products in this department have the advantage of large margins and are thus considered particularly valuable to the company. Mr Turner was especially happy about the year's sales and profits which were higher than forecast (see Appendix 2). 1985 had been a good year and sales increased significantly, although this was partly explained by a fire in another supplier's factory which led to several large and unexpected orders from some of the multiples and garden centres. The competitor's factory is likely to be back in production in the second half of 1986 and will be using some of the latest manufacturing equipment. Mr Turner is confident that he can keep the new custom and he sees improved sales as a clear result of his success in expanding the department.

Turning to production problems in the furniture department, Mr Wood said, 'You know that our highest margins come from the most up-to-date designs – that's not surprising because they carry the most risk – but it seems to me that it is creating tremendous problems in scheduling. It is never clear far in advance what this segment of the market wants, and it is always looking for new designs each year. Sometimes we don't back the winners and then we have to sell off old stock cheaply, and this segment accounts for 25 per cent of our market. Then the overtime costs connected with production are getting very high as we approach the seasonal peak. Last year we had some quality problems following the last-minute introduction of a new line. Can't we alter our system so that the production level is more constant throughout the year?'

FERTILISER DEPARTMENT: The department buys raw materials and packs them into bags, selling the fertiliser under the Wood brand name. In the light of the sales figures for 1985, Mr Wood is concerned at the poor performance of the fertiliser department and is considering closing it. Mr Johnson who runs the department was depressed by his recent meeting with Mr Wood. They had been looking at the figures and Mr Wood had said, 'We are losing money with every bag of fertiliser we sell – 60 pence per bag in 1985 – and although you predict an increase in sales, that will clearly only reduce profit further. In any case, we are running at near capacity in our bagging operation and unless we expand further we will not have the room to hold all the stocks we will need. It seems to me that it would be better to expand our garden furniture activity where we are making better profits.' Mr Johnson was not happy with this analysis. He felt that the allocation of overheads was unfairly weighted against his department since the market for fertiliser was price-sensitive and the margins were slim. In terms of space, selling and administrative time it was the smallest of the three departments. He was sceptical about the effects of cutting out his own department since he did not believe that the company profits would increase. Indeed, he felt that the fertiliser side could do better if the volume expanded, taking advantage of bulk buying which would reduce unit costs and lead to increased sales. His supplier had indicated that a guaranteed order of 25 000 bags would lead to a new raw material price discounted by 50 pence per bag. He was convinced that there was sufficient capacity for this increase in order size, and even if he did not achieve the sales he expected, any stocks could be held over to the following year.

There is a shortage of space and land for cultivation. Mr Wood is considering a five-year lease of a neighbouring site costing £40 000. There will also be an option to purchase the land after the lease expires. The company is already *highly geared* but Mr Wood is reasonably confident that he can obtain the necessary funds. The leasehold will have to be purchased and paid for in 1986. The expected net cash flows for this project are set out in Appendix 3. The cash flows are affected by the product mix between the three departments. Mix **A** allows for the expansion of the garden furniture department and includes the extra promotional expense Mr Wood considers necessary to achieve higher sales. Mix **B** gives greater emphasis to the plant and fertiliser departments where estimates of future sales are more certain.

Both assume there are no increases in foreign competition and volumes are calculated by extrapolating past trends. The company's cost of capital is 15 per cent.

Appendix 1

Profit Statement for Wood Ltd for 1985

	Plant Department	Garden Furniture Department	Fertiliser Department
Sales volume (units)	27000	9000	15000
Sales Revenue (£000)	135	90	45
Direct Costs (£000)	81	45	37.5
Overheads (£000)	49.5	33	16.5
Profit (£000)	4.5	12	(−9)

Appendix 2

Forecast and actual figures for the Garden Furniture Department for 1985

	Forecast	Actual
Sales volume (units)	7000	9000
Sales Revenue (£000)	70	90
Direct Costs (£000)	32.48	45
Overheads (£000)	27.72	33
Profit (£000)	9.8	12

Appendix 3

Projected net cash flows for product Mix **A** and Mix **B** (£000)

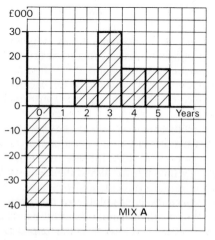
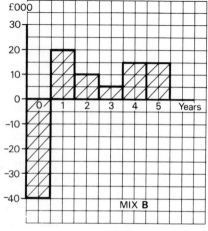

Discount factors @ 15%:

Year 0: 1.000,   Year 1: 0.870,   Year 2: 0.756,   Year 3: 0.658,   Year 4: 0.572,   Year 5: 0.497.

Answer **all** *questions.*

1   Define and explain the following terms italicised in the text.
(a) *return on assets*
(b) *disposable income*
(c) *interest cover*
(d) *highly geared*   (12)

2   (a) Using the figures available in the case, produce a contribution statement for the three departments for 1985.   (5)
(b) Calculate the change in the company's profits if the fertiliser department had been closed at the start of 1985, assuming no change in total overhead.   (5)
(c) Is Mr Johnson right to argue that an increase in fertiliser sales will increase profits, given that Mr Wood has pointed out a loss of 60 pence per bag at the moment? Illustrate your argument with suitable figures.   (8)

3   (a) From the information contained in the case, analyse the variance between the budget and actual figures for the garden furniture department.   (10)
(b) Do you think that Mr Turner should be satisfied with his department's performance in 1985?   (10)

4   What are the merits of the different distribution channels?   (10)

5   How might a substantial change in the rate of interest affect Wood Ltd?   (15)

6   Using numerical and non-numerical arguments, advise Mr Wood on whether to adopt product Mix **A** or **B** in his future expansion plans.   (15)

7   What problems do you think will have to be faced by the company in the garden furniture department? How would you suggest Mr Wood sets about solving them?   (10)

The following case study and questions formed Paper 3 of the Business Studies examination set by University of Cambridge Local Examination Syndicate, June 1985.

GETLO LTD

Getlo Ltd is a small company in the engineering components industry, employing 40 people in June 1985. Mr Edwards has been managing director for more than four years, having been appointed early in 1981. Getlo manufactures and assembles some components itself, but much of its output consists of products that are assembled from bought-in parts, including an increasing number of electronic components made from parts imported from the Far East, which are then largely re-exported. Getlo had diversified into the latter group as the sales in their traditional markets declined. Mr Edwards felt that the company owed its survival during the seventies and early eighties to these high-technology products. The industry had weathered some rough storms during the seventies as it came under concerted competition from imports that were both cheaper and of better quality than domestically produced items. In addition, the industry had seen considerable rationalisation in the seventies, and it had become more *concentrated*.

Getlo itself had rationalised its operations by altering its production procedures and reducing its staff – at the end of 1981 it had laid off 35 people. The performance of the company had improved and in 1984 it had shown a small profit for the first time in several years. It was now able to beat off competition from both imports and the larger domestic companies which had the advantage of considerable *economies of scale* in both production and marketing.

The employees of the firm who had remained following the 1981 reorganisation were unhappy with the current situation and uncertain about job prospects and security. The managing director suspected that morale in the factory was low, but as there had not been any special delegations to see him, he thought that the problem was not too serious. He had introduced a system of monthly salary payments for all employees, which he knew was in their interest. Towards the end of 1984, the firm's chief accountant had suddenly left the company, claiming that it was impossible to work in the conditions Mr Edwards gave him. He said that there was too much information required by Mr Edwards and he did not have enough expert help to enable him to provide it. His parting comment had been, 'You've added these new people in the Accounts department who do not know how our system works, and moving us upstairs to a new office has made life much more difficult because we are no longer in the thick of it any more.' It was true that Mr Edwards had asked for more information, but that was because he was not receiving the financial information he felt he needed to run the company. At the time, Mr Edwards had wondered about the chief accountant's comments, although he knew that they were biased since the move to which he had referred had been undertaken to assist the accountant's office by separating it from the noise of the shop floor and packing rooms. Initially, there had been some trouble when the accounts department came in and found that they had been moved, but that had quietened down. Mr Edwards believed that it was best to let things sort themselves out and he avoided wasting too much time explaining the changes he had made. He felt that the staff would quickly see that he had actually improved their working conditions and he knew that this would lead to a better working performance. The changes were quite clearly an advantage and Mr Edwards felt that the chief accountant's complaint was unjustified.

Mr Edwards had just returned from an overseas sales trip that had been more time-consuming that he had expected. Six weeks away from the office had been too long. On his return he had been faced with a mass of paperwork and decisions. Mr Edwards knew that this was the consequence of the organisational changes he had introduced on his arrival at the company. In his previous job he had worked with a company that he felt was ruled by committee, and that never reached any rapid decisions. He had altered the structure at Getlo so that all information was reported directly to him, enabling him to see the whole picture and make his mind up quickly. He then told the *functional directors* of the decisions and left them to carry them out. As usual, he wondered whether he should let Bob Jones, the Sales Manager, go on these trips, but they were important to the firm and he had brought back some sizeable orders which he had given to Bob on his return. Bob hadn't been too happy when he saw them but that was probably because he had had a bad day. He had complained again about the company's policy of not giving salesmen commissions in line with their competitors, and had said that he was finding it increasingly difficult to keep his sales staff.

Sixty per cent of Getlo's sales were overseas (as opposed to 40 per cent two years previously) in highly competitive markets where price seemed to be the major factor in determining sales. In spite of changes in the *value of the pound*, the company's market share was rising abroad. Mr Edwards ascribed this to the constant addition of new products and the maintenance of a balanced development programme that enabled the company to have products in all stages of the product life cycle. Recently, in order to maintain and increase market share, margins had been cut, especially for the foreign market.

Mr Edwards had just received a letter from the bank manager expressing concern over the level of the company's bank overdraft. This surprised Mr Edwards because the company had always been on good terms with the bank, and he believed the company was now profitable and had been growing. He was shocked to discover that the overdraft was already at £299 000, well above the ceiling of £250 000 authorised by the bank, and it was only the end of May with seven months of the year still to go. He knew that the company had paid its tax liability for the previous year, as it always did in May, but that did not account for the huge overdraft.

He called in John Baxter who had been left in charge of the accounts office following the departure of the chief accountant. 'Can you let me have the projected accounts of the firm's operations for 1985, using the forecast sales figures (see Appendix 1), and bearing in mind that the cost of raw materials and bought-in parts represents 50 per cent of sales value?' he asked. He was not prepared for John's reply. 'Since the chief accountant's departure, and while you have been away, I have been trying to get to the bottom of the system we were using on the accounts, and so far I have only managed to finalise last year's balance sheet (see Appendix 2) and a projected profit and loss account for 1985 (see Appendix 3). I am only just getting the information on our payments schedule. Bob is adamant that we cannot reduce our average credit terms to our customers below two months' sales, and it seems that from the rate we have been paying our suppliers, they will give us three months' credit on purchases. Then we have to pay the interest on the loan and overdraft which I have assumed will be £20 000 per quarter, paid at the beginning of each quarter. The various overheads are paid at the end of each quarter. Depreciation is calculated at £20 000 per quarter. It will take me a bit of time to sort out the position from that.' Mr Edwards was not very happy with this response but there was nothing he could do about it, so he told John to prepare the necessary cash figures, saying he would check them when he received them.

Mr Edwards was also faced with a stock problem following the increase in sales. As a result of the *batch production* system used in the factory there had always been a high level of stocks, with an average stock turn equivalent to six months' supply of raw materials and bought-in parts.

This meant that the overall stock levels were rising and he was worried about the effects of this on the company. The production manager said that they were essential, as did Bob Jones, who claimed that new orders had been won as a result of the company's ability to deliver quickly. However, John Baxter had expressed concern. Mr Edwards was wondering how to resolve the various conflicts.

APPENDIX 1

Projected sales value (all on credit) for 1985 for Getlo Ltd.

Total Sales Value (£000's)

January–May	332
June	80
July	150
August	70
September	180
October	180
November	100
December	60

APPENDIX 2

Balance sheet for Getlo Ltd as at 31 December 1984

	£000's	£000's	£000's
Fixed Assets			
Land and Buildings		820	
Machinery at cost	800		
Less Accumulated depreciation	320	480	1300
Net Current Assets			
Current Assets			
Stocks	150		
Debtors	100	250	
Less Current Liabilities			
Creditors	90		
Bank Overdraft	200		
Provision for tax (1984)	20	310	(60)
Net Assets Employed			1240
Financed by:			
Shareholders' Funds			
Issued Share Capital		700	
Reserves		40	740
Long term Liabilities			500
			1240

APPENDIX 3

Projected profit and loss account for Getlo Ltd for the year ending 31 December 1985

	£000's	£000's	% of sales value
Sales		1152	100
Less Raw Materials and bought-in parts	576		50
Wages	288		25
Selling and Administrative expenses	100		9
Depreciation	80	1044	7
		108	
Less Interest		80	7
Profit before tax		28	
Tax @ 50%		14	1
Profit after tax (retained)		14	1
			100

*Answer **all** questions.*

1   Explain the following terms *italicised* in the text:
concentrated
economies of scale
functional directors
value of the pound
batch production   (15)

2   Explain how Getlo can be making profits and yet be faced with cash-flow problems requiring an increasing overdraft. (15)

3   (a) What evidence is there for low morale in the company? (10)
    (b) How do you think Mr Edwards might improve morale at Getlo? (10)

4   Using the arguments that might be advanced by each of John Baxter, Bob Jones and the production manager, how would you suggest Mr Edwards resolves the problem over stock levels? (15)

5   (a) Using the assumptions contained in the text, show that the overdraft will rise by £30 000 between 31 December 1984 and 31 December 1985.
    (b) Construct a projected balance sheet for Getlo Ltd as at 31 December 1985. (20)

6   How might a substantial change in exchange rates affect Getlo Ltd? (15)

Book list

Chapter 1   What is business studies?
J. M. Baddeley, *Understanding industry*. Butterworth with The Industrial Society.
Jim Clifford, *Decision making in organisations*. Longman.
David Dyer and Ian Chambers, *Business studies: an introduction*. Longman.
Tony Hocking and Richard A. Powell, *Investigating economics*. Longman.

Chapter 2   Business and the economic system
Peter Donaldson, *A guide to the British economy*. Pelican.
Geoffrey Hurd, *Human societies: an introduction to sociology*. Routledge and Kegan Paul.

Chapter 3   Markets
Alan Griffiths and Stuart Wall, *Applied economics: an introductory course*. Longman.
E. T. Martin, *Marketing*. Mitchell Beazley.
Peter Tinniswood, *Marketing decisions*. Longman.

Chapter 4   Starting and running your own business
Colin Barrow, *Financial management for the small business*. Kogan Page.
The mini co kit. Longman.
M. Mogano, *How to start and run your own business*. Graham and Trotman.
Starting a small business. Business Guidebooks: Self-help Guides for Small Businessmen.

Chapter 5   Statistics: an aid to decision making and control
D. A. Bryars, *Advanced level statistics*. University Tutorial Press.
A. Green, *A first course in statistics*. Stanley Thornes.
D. Gregory and H. Ward, *Statistics for business studies*. McGraw-Hill.
Russell Langley, *Practical statistics*. David and Charles.
Harold Lucas, *Statistical methods*. Butterworth.

Chapter 6   Accounting: an aid to decision making and control
Peter Corbett, *Accounting and decision making*. Longman.
Tony Hines, *Accounting questions and answers*. Checkmate/Arnold.
G. Holmes and A. Sugden, *Interpreting company reports and accounts*. Woodhead-Faulkner.
G. Taylor and C. Hawkins, *Accounting for business organisations: a practical approach*. Macmillan.
J. Townsley and R. Jones, *Numeracy and accounting*. Longman.

Chapter 7   Finance
C. J. Higson, *Business finance*. Butterworth.
David Myddleton, *Financial decisions*. Longman.
Ray Proctor, *Finance for the perplexed executive*. Fontana.
Leon Simmons, *The basic arts of financial management*. Business Books.

Chapter 8   Marketing

Tom Cannon, *Basic marketing – principles and practice*. Holt, Rinehart and Winston.
E. T. Martin, *Marketing*. Mitchell Beazley.
Robert G. I. Maxwell, *Breakthrough marketing*. Pan.
Gordon Oliver, *Marketing today*. Prentice-Hall International.
Nigel Piercy, *Marketing organisations: an analysis of information processing, power and politics*. George Allen and Unwin.
Peter Tinniswood, *Marketing decisions*. Longman.

Chapter 9   Production

H. A. Harding, *Production management*. Pitman, M&E Handbooks.
R. Hunter, *Production*. Mitchell Beazley.
Keith Lockyer, *Production management*. Pitman.
John Powell, *Production decisions*. Longman.

Chapter 10   People and business

Huw Benyon, *Working for Ford*. Pelican.
P. Bryans and T. P. Cronin, *Organisation theory: the study of human relations within the business organisation*. Mitchell Beazley.
Alan Bryman, *Leadership and organisations*. Routledge and Kegan Paul.
John Child, *Organisations: a guide to problems and practice*. Harper and Row.
Sandra Dawson, *Analysing organisations*. Macmillan.
Pierre Dubois, *Sabotage in industry*. Pelican.
Desmond W. Evans, *People, communications and organisations*. Pitman.

Chapter 11   Managing people

M. W. Cuming, *Personnel management*. Heinemann.
H. T. Graham, *Human resources management*. Pitman, M&E Handbooks.
M. P. Jackson, *Industrial relations*. Croom Helm.
K. J. Pratt and S. G. Bennett, *Elements of personnel management*. Van Nostrand Reinhold (UK).

Chapter 12   Business and decision making

Bryan Carsberg, *Economics of business decisions*. Penguin.
J. Curwin and R. Slater, *Quantitative methods for business decisions*. Van Nostrand Reinhold (UK).
V. A. Fatseas and T. R. Vag, *Quantitative techniques for managerial decision making*. Prentice-Hall.
S. C. Littlechild (ed.), *Operational research for managers*. Philip Allen Publishers.
John Powell and John Harris, *Quantitative decision making*. Longman.

Chapter 13   Business and the economy

A. G. Anderton, *Economics: a new approach*. Hyman and Bell.
Peter Corbett, *The economy and decision making*. Longman.
Tony Hocking and Richard A. Powell, *Investigating economics*. Longman.
Frank Livesey, *Economics*. Polytech Publishers Ltd.
Terry Price, *Basic economics*. Pan (Breakthrough).

Chapter 14   Business and society

John Child, *Organization: a guide to problems and practice*. Harper and Row
D. W. Fairhurst, *Business resources: an economic and social perspective*. Heinemann.
Gill Palmer, *British industrial relations*. George Allen and Unwin.
Norman Worrall, *People and decisions*. Longman.

Index